SOFTWARE FOR NUMERICAL MATHEMATICS

SOFTWARE FOR NUMERICAL MATHEMATICS

Proceedings of the Loughborough University of Technology Conference of the Institute of Mathematics and Its Applications held in April 1973

Edited by

D. J. EVANS

Department of Mathematics
Loughborough University of Technology
Loughborough, Leicestershire, England

1974

ACADEMIC PRESS · LONDON AND NEW YORK

A Subsidiary of Harcourt Brace Jovanovich, publishers

ACADEMIC PRESS INC. (LONDON) LTD.
24/28 Oval Road,
London NW1

United States Edition published by
ACADEMIC PRESS INC.
111 Fifth Avenue
New York, New York 10003

Library of Congress Catalog Card Number: 73–18998
ISBN: 0–12–243750–0

Printed in Great Britain by
ROYSTAN PRINTERS LIMITED
Spencer Court, 7 Chalcot Road
London NW1

Contributors

J. M. BOYLE; *Applied Mathematics Division, Argonne National Laboratory, 9700 South Cass Avenue, Argonne, Illinois 60439, U.S.A.*

C. W. CLENSHAW; *Department of Mathematics, Cartmel College, Bailrigg, Lancaster LA1 4YR, Lancashire, England.*

W. J. CODY; *Applied Mathematics Division, Argonne National Laboratory, 9700 South Cass Avenue, Argonne, Illinois 60439, U.S.A.*

M. G. COX; *Division of Numerical Analysis and Computing, National Physical Laboratory, Teddington, Middlesex, TW11 0LW, England.*

L. C. W. DIXON; *Numerical Optimisation Centre, The Hatfield Polytechnic, 19 St. Albans Road, Hatfield, Hertfordshire, England.*

VALERIE A. DIXON; *Oxford University Computing Laboratory, 19 Parks Road, Oxford, OX1 3PL and Division of Numerical Analysis and Computing, National Physical Laboratory, Teddington, Middlesex, TW11 0LW, England.*

B. EINARSSON; *Försvarets Forskningsanstalt, The Research Institute of National Defence, Box 98, S–14700 Tumba, Sweden.*

D. J. EVANS; *Department of Mathematics, Loughborough University of Technology, Loughborough, Leicestershire, LE11 3TU, England.*

R. FLETCHER; *Theoretical Physics Division, U.K.A.E.A. Research Group, Atomic Energy Research Establishment, Harwell, Didcot, Berkshire, OX11 ORA, England.*

B. FORD; *Numerical Algorithms Group, Oxford University Computing Laboratory, 19 Parks Road, Oxford, OX1 3PL, England.*

A. C. GENZ; *Mathematical Institute, Cornwallis Building, The University of Kent at Canterbury, Kent, England.*

S. J. HAGUE; *Numerical Algorithms Group, Oxford University Computing Laboratory, 19 Parks Road, Oxford, OX1 3PL, England.*

J. G. HAYES; *Division of Numerical Analysis and Computing, National Physical Laboratory, Teddington, Middlesex, TW11 0LW, England.*

M. D. HEBDEN; *Theoretical Physics Division, U.K.A.E.A. Research Group, Atomic Energy Research Establishment, Harwell, Didcot, Berkshire, OX11 ORA, England.*

D. HUTCHINSON; *Centre for Computer Studies, University of Leeds, Leeds, LS2 9JT, England.*

P. JESTY; *Department of Management Studies, Leeds Polytechnic, Leeds, England.*

SHIRLEY A. LILL; *Computer Laboratory, The University of Liverpool, Brownlow Hill and Crown Street, Liverpool, L69 3BX, England.*

G. F. MILLER; *Division of Numerical Analysis and Computing, National Physical Laboratory, Teddington, Middlesex, TW11 0LW, England.*

G. MITRA; *Department of Statistics and Operational Research, Brunel University, Kingston Lane, Uxbridge, UB8 3PH, Middlesex, England.*

M. J. D. POWELL; *Theoretical Physics Division, U.K.A.E.A. Research Group, Atomic Energy Research Establishment, Harwell, Didcot, Berkshire, OX11 0RA, England.*

J. A. PRENTICE; *Computing Centre, Loughborough University of Technology, Loughborough, Leicestershire, LE11 3TU, England.*

J. K. REID; *Theoretical Physics Division, U.K.A.E.A. Research Group, Atomic Energy Research Establishment, Harwell, Didcot, Berkshire, OX11 0RA, England.*

J. L. SCHONFELDER; *Computer Centre, The University of Birmingham, P.O. Box 363, Birmingham, B15 2TT, England.*

B. T. SMITH; *Applied Mathematics Division, Argonne National Laboratory, 9700 South Cass Avenue, Argonne, Illinois 60439, U.S.A.*

A. SYKES; *Theory Division, Culham Laboratory, U.K.A.E.A. Research Group, Abingdon, Berkshire, OX14 3DB, England.*

D. B. TAYLOR; *Edinburgh Regional Computing Centre, Edinburgh University, Edinburgh, EH8 9YL, Scotland.*

C. LL. THOMAS; *Theory Division, Culham Laboratory, U.K.A.E.A. Research Group, Abingdon, Berkshire, OX14 3DB, England.*

J. F. TRAUB; *Department of Computer Science, Carnegie-Mellon University, Schenley Park, Pittsburgh, Pennsylvania 15213, U.S.A.*

JOAN E. WALSH; *Department of Mathematics, University of Manchester, Manchester, M13 9PL, England.*

J. H. WILKINSON; *Division of Numerical Analysis and Computing, National Physical Laboratory, Teddington, Middlesex, TW11 0LW, England.*

Preface

The contents of this book are based on lectures and discussions given at the 'Software for Numerical Mathematics' conference held at Loughborough University of Technology in April 1973 under the sponsorship of the Institute of Mathematics and Its Applications. The conference was attended by some 220 participants drawn from fifteen different countries representing both academic and industrial interests.

The aims of the conference were to provide a forum for the exchange of ideas and information on the analysis, development, construction, evaluation, communication and usage of numerical algorithms—a rapidly expanding discipline intended to support the many areas of computer applications in mathematics, science and engineering. It was thought that the most effective way of emphasising attention to this important area was by bringing together in a meeting such as this, people of relevant experience currently making everyday contributions to the field.

In the conference organisation, I was ably assisted by a committee which consisted of J. R. A. Cooper, B. Ford, A. R. Gourlay and M. J. D. Powell who discharged their duties by arranging a conference programme divided into sessions in which eminent speakers were invited to give survey lectures to cover the basic issues of the topic, whilst a smaller number of research papers of a specialist nature was selected from people wishing to participate in the conference. After each presentation the floor was open for informal discussions in order to achieve as much cross fertilisation of ideas as possible.

These proceedings could not have been published so quickly without the co-operation of the lecturers who presented their papers lucidly and made them available for publication on time. Essentially, the content of each paper is the responsibility of the author concerned although I have made slight changes where necessary to aid clarity and presentation. The discussions, with some editing, have also been included to complete the proceedings.

I should like to conclude by acknowledging the support given by the Institute of Mathematics and Its Applications for the skilful arrangement of the many financial and domestic details in the administration and organisation of the conference, the Conference Committee, the Session Chairmen and to Dr. J. Wilkinson, F.R.S. and Professor L. Fox who provided wise counsel throughout the planning of the conference.

D. J. EVANS
Loughborough, December 1973.

Contents

1. Theory of Optimal Algorithms†

J. F. TRAUB

Department of Computer Science
Carnegie-Mellon University
Pittsburgh, Pa., U.S.A.

1. Introduction

Recent progress in the theory of optimal algorithms has led to new algorithms as well as theoretical bounds on the efficiency of any possible algorithm.

Historically there have been three major stages in the development of algorithmic analysis. They are:

1. Synthesis of *an* algorithm
2. Analysis of *an* algorithm
3. Analysis of *a class* of algorithms.

Initially the emphasis was on the synthesis of an algorithm. The second stage commenced around 1947 with the very careful analysis of particular algorithms. Within the last 10–15 years people have been looking at classes of algorithms and trying to find the best. This trend has recently accelerated and there is now tremendous interest in analyzing classes of algorithms in terms of computational complexity.

There are many reasons for studying computational complexity of which the most important are:

1. Constructing "good" new algorithms.
2. Filtering out "bad" algorithms.
3. Creating a theory of algorithms which will establish theoretical limits on computation.

To discuss optimal algorithms we need a measure of *cost*. The measure used throughout this paper is the total number of arithmetic operations, $+, -, \times, \div$. Gentleman (1973) and Reddy (1973) have discussed some of the

† This research was supported in part by the National Science Foundation under Grant GJ32111 and the Office of Naval Research under Contract N0014-67-A-0314-0010, NR 044-422.

other components of the cost which might be included. Other properties of a numerical algorithm, such as stability and domain of convergence, are critical. Measures of cost deserve more refinement.

2. Algebraic and Analytic Computational Complexity

We want to distinguish between two types of algorithms. The dichotomy depends on the nature of the underlying mathematical problem. A mathematical problem can be finite or infinite. Examples of finite problems are matrix multiplication and polynomial evaluation. Examples of infinite problems are the solution of an elliptic partial differential equation and the calculation of a polynomial zero.

Optimality theory for finite problems will be referred to as *algebraic computational complexity*, optimality theory for infinite problems as *analytic computational complexity*. Some examples will be given of work from each domain.

3. Recent Results in Algebraic Computational Complexity

Borodin (1973) gives a survey of the enormous recent activity in algebraic complexity. We will confine ourselves to some very recent results which deal with one set of related problems.

The problems are:

1. *Polynomial multiplication.* Given two polynomials of degree n, to find the product polynomial.

2. *Polynomial division.* Given two polynomials of degree n and $\frac{1}{2}n$, to find their quotient and remainder. More generally we divide a polynomial of degree n by a polynomial of degree m. The choice of $m = \frac{1}{2}n$ makes the "size" of the problem depend on just one parameter.

3. *Polynomial interpolation.* Given (x_i, y_i), $i = 0, 1, \ldots, n$. Find $P(t)$ such that $P(x_i) = y_i$.

4. *Evaluation of a polynomial at many points.* Evaluate an nth degree polynomial at $n + 1$ points given simultaneously.

5. *Evaluation of a polynomial and all its derivatives.* Evaluate an nth degree polynomial and all its derivatives at one point.

These problems take $O(n^2)$ operations classically. Using "fast" algorithms the first two problems can be done in $O(n \log n)$ operations while the next three problems can be done in $O(n \log^2 n)$ operations. Fast polynomial multiplication is done with the Fast Fourier Transform. Other fast algorithms are due to Moenck and Borodin (1972), Strassen (1973), and Kung (1973). Borodin (1973) summarizes the state of the art in fast algorithms.

The results above are asymptotic. They are only significant for rather large values of n. For example n^2 is smaller than $n \log^2 n$ until n is somewhat greater than 30. (All logarithms are to base 2.) Furthermore, analyses ignore asymptotic constants which can prove significant if n is not too large (Borodin, 1973).

The following is an example of a new algorithm which is better than the best previously known algorithm, not just asymptotically, but for all n. Given

$$P(t) = \sum_{j=0}^{n} a_{n-j} t^j,$$

and a number x, the problem is to calculate the normalized derivatives $P^{(j)}(x)/j!$, $j = 0, \ldots, n$. The standard algorithm is some 150 years old and appears in most numerical methods texts. It is known as the iterated Horner rule or a synthetic division. This algorithm can be written as

$$T_i^{-1} = a_{i+1}, \qquad i = 0, 1, \ldots, n-1,$$
$$T_j^{j} = a_0, \qquad j = 0, 1, \ldots, n,$$
$$T_i^{j} = T_{i-1}^{j-1} + xT_{i-1}^{j}, \qquad j = 0, 1, \ldots, n-1, i = j+1, \ldots, n.$$

It is not difficult to verify that

$$\frac{P^{(j)}(x)}{j!} = T_n^{j}, \qquad j = 0, 1, \ldots, n.$$

Observe that the first two lines of the algorithm define initial conditions. All the work is done in the recursion of the last line. The recursion is done $\frac{1}{2}n(n+1)$ times and there is one addition and one multiplication per step. Thus the iterated Horner algorithm requires $\frac{1}{2}n(n+1)$ multiplications and $\frac{1}{2}n(n+1)$ additions.

Consider now the following algorithm.

$$T_i^{-1} = a_{i+1}x^{n-i-1}, \qquad i = 0, 1, \ldots, n-1,$$
$$T_j^{j} = a_0 x^n, \qquad j = 0, 1, \ldots, n, \tag{3.1}$$
$$T_i^{j} = T_{i-1}^{j-1} + T_{i-1}^{j}, \qquad j = 0, 1, \ldots, n-1, i = j+1, \ldots, n.$$

It may be shown (Shaw and Traub, 1974a) that

$$\frac{P^{(j)}(x)}{j!} = x^{-j}T_n^{j}, \qquad j = 0, 1, \ldots, n-1.$$

In this algorithm all the multiplications are done as part of the initial conditions. The recursion involves additions only. The normalized derivatives are obtained by division using the x^j calculated as part of the initialisation.

Thus this algorithm, which is just as simple as the iterated Horner rule, yields the normalized derivatives in $3n - 2$ multiplications and divisions and $\frac{1}{2}n(n + 1)$ additions. The algorithm is of practical utility. It is also of theoretical interest since it demonstrates that only a *linear* number of multiplications and divisions are needed.

The problem posed here is a special case of the problem of calculating m derivatives of an nth degree polynomial. The algorithm presented above is a member of a one-parameter family of algorithms (Shaw and Traub, 1974a). The optimal choice of the parameter as a function of m and n is discussed by Shaw and Traub (1974b). Stability of these algorithms is established by Wozniakowski (1973).

4. An Efficiency Measure

The remainder of this paper deals with analytic computational complexity. Recent research includes the complexity of elliptic partial differential equations (Eisenstat and Schultz, 1973) and the complexity of systems of non-linear equations (Brent, 1973). A more extensive bibliography may be found in Traub (1972).

We confine ourselves here to the problem of calculating a real simple zero α of a real function f. This zero-finding problem may seem rather specialised, but it is equivalent to the fixed-point problem, a ubiquitous problem in mathematics and applied mathematics. It may be formulated in an abstract setting and covers partial differential equations, integral equations, and many other important problems, Traub (1972) and Kung and Traub (1973a, 1973b) may be consulted for the results reported in the rest of this paper and for proofs of the theorems.

Consider iteration algorithms for approximating α. Let the x_i be generated by an iteration function ϕ,

$$x_{i+1} = \phi(x_i)$$

To define an efficiency measure for ϕ we need measures of *goodness* and *cost*. As the measure of goodness we use the order p defined as follows. If

$$\lim_{x_i \to a} \frac{\phi(x_i) - \alpha}{(x_i - \alpha)^p} = S \neq 0$$

then $p = p(\phi)$ is the *order of convergence*.

The cost consists of two parts: the *evaluation cost* and the *combinatory cost*. Let ϕ use v_i evaluations of $f^{(i)}$. If $f^{(i)}$. If $f^{(i)}$ is rational, let $c(f^{(i)})$ denote the number of arithmetic operations for one evaluation of $f^{(i)}$;

otherwise let $c(f^{(i)})$ denote the number of arithmetic operations used in the rational subroutine which approximates $f^{(i)}$. Then

$$\text{Evaluation cost} = \sum_{i \geqslant 0} v_i \, c(f^{(i)}).$$

Let $a(\phi)$ be the minimum number of arithmetic operations to combine the $f^{(i)}$ to form ϕ by any procedure λ. Then

$$\text{Combinatory cost} = a(\phi).$$

Finally, the cost of performing one iteration step is

$$\sum_{i \geqslant 0} v_i \, c(f^{(i)}) + a(\phi).$$

We define the efficiency $e(\phi, f)$ of the iteration ϕ with respect to the problem f by

$$e(\phi, f) = \sum_{i \geqslant 0} \frac{\log p(\phi)}{v_i \, c(f^{(i)}) + a(\phi)}. \tag{4.1}$$

A discussion of this efficiency measure, including its relation to other efficiency measures, is given by Kung and Traub (1973b). Here I will only point out that earlier measures (Traub, 1972) did not include the combinatory cost $a(\phi)$) and that inclusion of combinatory cost is crucial.

The efficiency measure has the following two properties:

1. It is invariant under composition.

2. It is inversely proportional to total cost.

The first property can be written as

$$e(\phi \cdot \phi, f) = e(\phi, f),$$

where $\phi \cdot \phi$ denotes performing the iteration ϕ twice. This says that a sequence and a subsequence have the same efficiency. The second property is stated more precisely as follows. Let ϕ_1, ϕ_2 be two iterations used to approximate α to within a certain accuracy. Let the total cost of ϕ_j be W_j. Then

$$\frac{e(\phi_1, f)}{e(\phi_2, f)} \sim \frac{W_2}{W_1}.$$

Let

$$c_f = \min_{i \geqslant 0} c(f^{(i)}).$$

In this paper, we refer to c_f as the *problem complexity*. Let

$$v(\phi) = \sum_{i \geqslant 0} v_i \, (\phi).$$

Clearly, $v(\phi)$ is the total number of evaluations used in ϕ. Then by (4.1),

$$e(\phi, f) \leqslant \frac{\log p(\phi)}{v(\phi)\, c_f + a(\phi)} \,. \qquad (4.2)$$

This will be useful for obtaining upper bounds for $e(\phi, f)$.

The optimal efficiency depends on the family Φ to which ϕ belongs. Our classification for ϕ depends on the information required by ϕ. We can distinguish between iterations with or without *memory*. We restrict ourselves here to iterations without memory. That is, the new iterate x_{i+1} is computed using information only at the current iterate x_i. For iterations without memory we distinguish between *one-point iteration* and *multipoint iteration*. Roughly speaking, if f or its derivaties require evaluation at k points in order to generate a new iterate by the iteration ϕ, then ϕ is a k-point iteration. In particular, if $k = 1$ we call ϕ a one-point iteration and if $k > 1$ and the value of k is not important we call ϕ a multipoint iteration. This terminology was introduced by Traub (1964). Precise definitions are given by Kung and Traub (1973a).

The following two examples illustrate the definitions.

Example 4.1.   (Newton–Raphson Iteration)

$$\phi(f)\,(x) = x - \frac{f(x)}{f'(x)}\,.$$

This is a one-point iteration with $p(\phi) = 2$, $v_0(\phi) = v_1(\phi) = 1$, and $a(\phi) = 2$. Hence

$$e(\phi, f) = \frac{1}{c(f) + c(f') + 2}\,,$$

$$e(\phi, f) \leqslant \frac{1}{2c_f + 2}\,.$$

Example 4.2

$$z_0 = x,$$

$$z_1 = z_0 - \frac{f(z_0)}{f'(z_0)}\,,$$

$$\phi(f)\,(x) = z_1 - \frac{f(z_1)f(z_0)}{[f(z_1) - f(z_0)]^2}\,\frac{f(z_0)}{f'(z_0)}\,.$$

This is a two-point iteration with

$$p(\phi) = 4, v_0(\phi) = 2, \qquad v_1(\phi) = 1 \quad \text{and} \quad a(\phi) = 8.$$

Hence

$$e(\phi, f) = \frac{2}{2c(f) + c(f') + 8},$$

$$e(\phi, f) \leqslant \frac{2}{3c_f + 8}.$$

Given an algorithm ϕ and a problem f, we can use $e(\phi, f)$ as defined by (4.1) to calculate efficiency. We are also interested in the optimal efficiency of a class of algorithms. This motivates the following definitions.

It is natural to ask for a given problem f what is the optimal value of $e(\phi, f)$ for all ϕ belonging to some family Φ. Define

$$E_n(\Phi, f) = \sup_{\phi \in \Phi} \{e(\phi, f) \mid v(\phi) = n\}.$$

Thus $E_n(\Phi, f)$ is the optimal efficiency over all $\phi \in \Phi$ which use n evaluations. Define

$$E(\Phi, f) = \sup\{E_n(\Phi, f) \mid n = 1, 2, \ldots\}.$$

Thus $E(\Phi, f)$ is the optimal efficiency for all $\phi \in \Phi$. We will establish lower and upper bounds for $E_n(\Phi, f)$ and $E(\Phi, f)$ with respect to different families of iterations. When there is no ambiguity, we write $E_n(\Phi, f)$ and $E(\Phi, f)$ as $E_n(f)$ and $E(f)$, respectively. Since in practice we are more concerned with efficiency for problems f with higher complexity, we are particularly interested in the asymptotic behavior of these bounds as $c_f \to \infty$.

5. Efficiency of One-Point Iteration

The iterations most used in practice are one-point iterations. We derive lower and upper bounds on the efficiency of any one-point iteration.

We consider a particular family of one-point iterations $\{\gamma_n\}$. The first three members of this family are given by

$$\gamma_1 = x$$

$$\gamma_2 = \gamma_1 - \frac{f(x)}{f'(x)}$$

$$\gamma_3 = \gamma_2 - \frac{f''(x)}{2f'(x)} \left[\frac{f(x)}{f'(x)} \right]^2.$$

The family γ_n has been thoroughly studied (Traub, 1964, Section 5.1). Its important properties from our point of view are summarized in the following

THEOREM 5.1

1. $v_i(\gamma_n) = 1, \quad i = 0, 1, \ldots, n - 1, v_i(\gamma_n) = 0, i > n - 1.$
   Hence $v(\gamma_n) = n.$

2. $p(\gamma_n) = n.$

It can be shown (Kung and Traub (1973b)) that

$$a(\gamma_n) \leqslant \rho\, n^2 \log n \tag{5.1}$$

for some positive constant ρ. By (5.1) and Theorem 5.1,

$$e(\gamma_n, f) \geqslant \frac{\log n}{\sum\limits_{i \geqslant 0}^{n-1} c(f^{(i)}) + \rho n^2 \log n}. \tag{5.2}$$

For n small, $a(\gamma_n)$ can be calculated by inspection. Thus $a(\gamma_3) = 7$ and

$$e(\gamma_3, f) = \frac{\log 3}{c(f) + c(f') + c(f'') + 7}.$$

We now turn to general one-point iterations. Let ϕ be any one-point iteration, with $v(\phi) = n$, which satisfies a mild smoothness condition. Then by Traub (1964, Section 5.4), Kung and Traub (1973b, Theorem 6.1), $v_i(\phi) \geqslant 1$, $i = 0, \ldots, p(\phi) - 1$ and hence $p(\Phi) \leqslant n$. Since at least $n - 1$ arithmetic operations are needed to combine n evaluations of f and its derivatives, $a(\gamma_n) \geqslant n - 1$.

Hence, from (4.2),

$$e(\phi, f) \leqslant \frac{\log n}{nc_f + n - 1} = h(n). \tag{5.4}$$

It may be verified that

$$h(n) \leqslant h(3) = \frac{\log 3}{3c_f + 2}, \quad \text{for all } n, \text{ for } c_f > 4. \tag{5.5}$$

Since it is important to solve "difficult" problems efficiently, the condition $c_f > 4$ is not restrictive. Since

$$h(2) = \frac{\log 2}{2c + 1} = \frac{1}{2c + 1}$$

and $\frac{1}{3} \log 3 \doteq 0\cdot 52$, there is little difference between the bounds on the second and third order iteration.

One of the pieces of folk wisdom of numerical mathematics is that for most problems it is better to use a fairly low order method more often than to use a higher order method less often. The above result gives a theoretical justification in the case of one-point iterations. We shall see this does not hold for multipoint iterations.

From (5.2), (5.3), (5.4), (5.5) we obtain the theorem giving lower and upper bounds on the efficiency of one-point iterations.

THEOREM 5.2

For the family Φ of one-point iterations,

$$\frac{\log n}{\sum\limits_{=0}^{n-1} c(f^{(1)}) + \rho n^2 \log n} \leqslant E_n(f) \leqslant \frac{\log n}{nc_f + n - 1},$$

$$\text{for a constant } \rho > 0, \quad \forall n, \qquad (5.6)$$

$$\frac{\log 3}{c(f) + c(f') + c(f'') + 7} \leqslant E(f) \leqslant \frac{\log 3}{3c_f + 2}, \quad \text{for } c_f > 4. \qquad (5.7)$$

6. Efficiency of Multipoint Iteration

In the previous section it was shown that the order of a one-point iteration is at most linear in the number of evaluations it requires. This restriction does not apply for multipoint iterations. Furthermore, a one-point iteration of order p requires the evaluation of at least the first $p - 1$ derivatives of f. This restriction also does not apply to multipoint iterations. A high order multipoint iteration can be constructed that requires no derivative evaluations at all.

To illustrate these points we consider the family of iterations $\{\Psi_n\}$ defined by Kung and Traub (1973a, Section 4). The important properties of $\{\Psi_n\}$ from our point of view are summarized in

THEOREM 6.1

1. $v_0(\Psi_n) = n, v_i(\Psi_n) = 0, i > 0.$

   Hence $v(\Psi_n) = n$.

2. $p(\Psi_n) = 2^{n-1}.$

Thus Ψ_n requires just n evaluations of f, and no derivative evaluations, and is of order 2^{n-1}. In particular

$$v(\Psi_4) = 4, \ p(\Psi_4) = 8.$$

The best previously known result for four evaluations was order five.

Kung and Traub (1973a, Appendix I) give a procedure for computing $\Psi_n(x)$ in $\frac{3}{2}n^2 + \frac{3}{2}n - 7$ arithmetic operations. Hence

$$a(\Psi_n) \leqslant \tfrac{3}{2}n^2 + \tfrac{3}{2}n - 7.$$

More generally, we assume that

$$a(\Psi_n) \leqslant r(n), \tag{6.1}$$

where $r(n) = r_2 n^2 + r_1 n + r_0, r_2 > 0$.

Then by (6.1) and Theorem 6.1,

$$e(\Psi_n, f) \geqslant \frac{n-1}{nc(f) + r(n)}. \tag{6.2}$$

We choose n so as to maximize the right-hand side of (6.2). The maximum is achieved when $n = t$ where

$$t = 1 + \sqrt{\frac{c(f)}{r_2} + \delta}, \delta = \frac{r_0 + r_1 + r_2}{r_2}.$$

Let

$$M = \text{round}\ (t). \tag{6.3}$$

Then from (6.2) we can easily prove

THEOREM 6.2. *There exists a constant $\zeta < 0$ such that if $M = M(f)$ is chosen by (6.3) then*

$$e(\Psi_M, f) \geqslant \frac{1}{c(f)}\left(1 + \frac{\zeta}{\sqrt{c(f)}}\right), \textit{ for } c(f) \textit{ large.}$$

From (6.2) and Theorem 6.2, we have

COROLLARY 6.1. *For the family Φ of one-point or multipoint iterations,*

$$E_n(f) \geqslant \frac{n-1}{nc(f) + r(n)},$$

where $r(n) = r_2 n^2 + r_1 n + r_0, r_2 > 0$; and

$$E(f) \geqslant \frac{1}{c(f)}\left(1 + \frac{\zeta}{\sqrt{c(f)}}\right),$$

for a constant $\zeta < 0$, for $c(f)$ large.

Can still higher order be achieved with n evaluations of f? An upper bound is provided by the following theorem proved by Kung and Traub (1973a, Theorem 7.2).

THEOREM 6.3. *Let ϕ be a multipoint iteration with $v_0(\phi) = n$, $v_i(\phi) = 0$, $i > 0$. Then $p(\phi) \leqslant 2^n$.*

As the conjecture at the end of this paper shows, we do not believe that the bound of 2^n can be achieved. Since $a(\phi) \geqslant n - 1$,

$$e(\phi, f) \leqslant \frac{n}{nc(f) + n - 1} \leqslant \frac{1}{c(f)}. \tag{6.4}$$

Since Ψ_n is a multipoint iteration which uses evaluations of f only, from (6.4) and Corollary 6.1, we have

THEOREM 6.4. *For the family of Φ of multipoint iterations using values of f only,*

$$\frac{n-1}{nc(f) + r(n)} \leqslant E_n(f) \leqslant \frac{n}{nc(f) + n - 1}, \forall n,$$

$$\frac{1}{c(f)}\left(1 + \frac{\zeta}{\sqrt{c(f)}}\right) \leqslant E(f) \leqslant \frac{1}{c(f)},$$

for $c(f)$ large, where $r(n) = r_2 n^2 + r_1 n + r_0$, $r_2 > 0$, and $\zeta < 0$.

We can now give a lower bound on the ratio of the optimal efficiency of multipoint iteration to the optimal efficiency of one-point iteration.

For a given problem f let $E'(f)$, $E''(f)$ be the optimal efficiency achievable by one-point iteration and multipoint iteration, respectively. By Theorem 5.2 and Corollary 6.1,

$$E'(f) \leqslant \frac{\log 3}{3c_f + 2}$$

$$E''(f) \geqslant \frac{1}{c(f)}\left[1 + \frac{\zeta}{\sqrt{c(f)}}\right], \zeta < 0, \text{ for } c(f) \text{ large.}$$

Hence

$$\frac{E''(f)}{E'(f)} \geqslant \frac{3c_f + 2}{(\log 3)c(f)}\left[1 + \frac{\zeta}{\sqrt{c(f)}}\right] \sim \frac{3}{\log 3}\frac{c_f}{c(f)}, \text{ for } c(f) \text{ large.}$$

In particular, if f is a problem such that $c_f = c(f)$ and c_f is large, then the ratio between optimal efficiencies achievable by multipoint iteration and one-point iteration is at least $3/\log 3 \sim 1 \cdot 89$.

7. Two Conjectures

Section 6 showed that an iteration of order 2^{n-1} can be constructed using n evaluations of f. Kung and Traub (1973a) conjecture that this order is optimal for any iteration (without memory) using n evaluations of f and its derivatives.

CONJECTURE 7.1. *For any one-point or multipoint iteration ϕ with $v(\phi) = n$, $p(\phi) \leqslant 2^{n-1}$.*

The conjecture is very general. ϕ may use *any n* values of f or its derivatives evaluated at *any* points. This conjecture is one of the major open questions in analytic complexity.

If Conjecture 7.1 is true, it implies the truth of the following conjecture (Kung and Traub, 1973b).

CONJECTURE 7.2. *For the family Φ of one-point of multipoint iterations.*

$$E_n(f) \leqslant \frac{n-1}{nc_f + n - 1},$$

$$E(f) \leqslant \frac{1}{c_f + 1}.$$

This conjecture states, essentially, that the optimal efficiency for solving the problem f with respect to all one-point or multipoint iterations is bounded by the reciprocal of the problem complexity.

Acknowledgements

I would like to thank H. T. Kung, Pamela McCorduck, and Mary Shaw for their comments on this paper.

References

Borodin, A. (1973). On the number of arithmetics required to compute certain functions—circa May 1973.*In* "Complexity of Sequential and Parallel Numerical Algorithms" (J. F. Traub, Ed.). Academic Press, New York and London.

Brent, R. (1973). Some efficient algorithms for solving systems of nonlinear equations. *SIAM J. Numer. Anal.* **10**, no. 2, 327–344.

Eisenstat, S. C. and Schultz, M. H. (1973). The complexity of partial differential equations. *In* "Complexity of Sequential and Parallel Numerical Algorithms" (J. F. Traub, Ed.). Academic Press, New York and London.

Gentleman, W. M. (1973). On the relevance of various cost models of complexity. *In* "Complexity of Sequential and Parallel Numerical Algorithms" (J. F. Traub, Ed.). Academic Press, New York and London.

Kung, H. T. (1973). "Fast Evaluation and Interpolation". Report, Department of Computer Science, Carnegie-Mellon University.

Kung, H. T. and Traub, J. F. (1973a). "Optimal Order of One-point and Multipoint Iteration". Report, Department of Computer Science, Carnegie-Mellon University. (and *JACM*. To appear).

Kung, H. T. and Traub, J. F. (1973b). Computational complexity of one-point and multipoint iteration. To appear in "Complexity of Real Computation". (R. Karp, Ed.). American Mathematical Society.

Moenck. R. and Borodin, A. (1972) Fast modular transformations via division. *In* "Proceedings IEEE SWAT Conference".

Reddy, D. R. (1973). Some numerical problems in artificial intelligence. *In* "Complexity of Sequential and Parallel Algorithms" (J. F. Traub, Ed.). Academic Press, New York and London.

Shaw, M. and Traub, J. F. (1974a). On the Number of Multiplications for the Evaluation of a Polynomial and some of its derivatives. *JACM* **21**, 161–167. Also available as a Carnegie-Mellon Computer Science Department Report.

Shaw, M. and Traub, J. F. (1974b). "The Analysis of a Family of Algorithms for the Evaluation of a Polynomial and its Derivatives". To appear.

Strassen, V. (1973). Die Berechnungskomplexität von Elementarsymmetrischen. *Num. Math.* **20**, 238–251.

Traub, J. F. (1964). "Iterative Methods for the Solution of Equations". Prentice-Hall, Englewood Cliffs, N. J.

Traub, J. F. (1972). Computational complexity of iterative processes. *SIAM J. Comp.* **1**, 167–179.

Traub, J. F. (1973). "Complexity of Sequential and Parallel Numerical Algorithms". Academic Press, New York and London.

Wozniakowski, H. (1973). "Rounding Error Analysis for the Evaluation of a Polynomial and Some of its Derivatives". *SIAM J. Numer. Anal.* (To appear).

Discussion: Optimal Algorithms

MR. POWELL. Please comment on the relationship between the theory for multipoint iteration methods and the theory for iteration with memory. Also please offer an opinion on which may be better in practice.

PROF. TRAUB. The new efficiency measure has been applied to multipoint iterations and the results are reported here with additional material in Kung and Traub (1973). I looked at iterations with memory (in Traub, 1964) rather thoroughly. However, the new efficiency measure has not yet been applied to iterations with memory. We plan to do this soon.

Multipoint and memory are two techniques for increasing the efficiency of iteration. At this point I'm not prepared to say which will prove better in practice.

DR. WILKINSON. The expression given by Professor Traub gives the "efficiency" of an algorithm only in a restricted sense, since it is concerned only with its asymptotic behaviour. In practice, the convergence in the large and global convergence properties are often of paramount importance. Thus, the QR algorithm for symmetric matrices is far more effective than its cubic convergence implies. To a lesser extent, this is also true of Laguerre's method.

PROF. TRAUB. Dr. Wilkinson is, of course, absolutely correct. If an algorithm enjoys global convergence as well as being reasonably efficient, that is the best of all worlds. There are, however, few problem areas where we know globally convergent algorithms.

Analyzing an algorithm is a complicated matter. Efficiency, stability, convergence in the large, and robustness are some of the issues to be considered. I view a formal efficiency measure as another tool in the analyst's kit.

2. Linear Algebra Algorithms

J. H. WILKINSON

*Division of Numerical Analysis and Computing,
National Physical Laboratory
Teddington, Middlesex, England.*

1. Introduction

In this talk I shall restrict myself almost entirely to those algorithms which have been published in the Linear Algebra volume of the "Handbook for Automatic Computation". The Handbook project was initiated in 1961. The object was to provide well-tested algorithms in ALGOL in each of the main areas of numerical analysis. They were to receive pre-publication as papers in *Numerische Mathematik* and after they had been subjected to extensive field trials, the modified algorithms in each area were to be assembled in book form.

The first such collection to be published was that on Linear Algebra; this collection forms Vol. II of the Handbook Series, Vol. Ia being concerned with details of the restricted version of ALGOL to be used throughout the series and Vol. Ib with a description of its implementation on a computer.

In spite of the self-contained nature of the linear algebra field the preparation of a fully tested set of algorithms proved to be a far greater task than had been anticipated. Although it was realised that algorithms in Linear Algebra are the most widely used in numerical analysis and indeed provide the basic tools in most areas, the total number of really useful algorithms turned out to be surprisingly high. It soon became obvious that it would be impractical, even if desirable, to aim at completeness. Quite early in the history of the project we decided to restrict ourselves to those algorithms which, at least in some limited area, provide an optimum solution; this may be either from the point of view of generality, elegance, speed or economy of storage. Even so the decision was taken to go ahead with publication of Vol. II before this limited objective had been attained and the resulting book was already of some 440 pages. The omission of an algorithm should not therefore be taken as indicating that it has been found wanting;

17

in some cases it merely means that we were not fully satisfied with current implementations.

Some twenty people contributed directly to algorithms in this volume but indirectly more than half of those working in numerical analysis have played a part. Some algorithms have a very long history of development during which many have made decisive contributions to their effectiveness.

The publication of an algorithm in a high-level language presents difficulties of a kind which scarcely arise with normal research papers. It is essential that each algorithm should be rigorously tested during the refereeing stage and if this is done conscientiously it invariably throws up important suggestions for improving its performance. This in turn calls for a further detailed checking and if this is not done carefully an error may be introduced into an algorithm which previously enjoyed a long period of successful use. This process of improvement continued right up to the printing stage. That the final versions appearing in the volume seem to be relatively free from errors is mainly due to the vigilance of Christian Reinsch.

All algorithms in the volume are presented in a standard format in which there are seven sections:

(i) *Theoretical background* in which a brief resumé is given of the mathematical basis of the algorithm.

(ii) *Applicability.* Generally several related algorithms are given together and indication is given of the main range of application of each.

(iii) *Formal parameter list.* All input and output parameters are listed and, where necessary, explained.

(iv) *The ALGOL procedure* itself, presented in standard ALGOL 60.

(v) *Organisational and Notational details.* This explains any unusual features of storage etc.

(vi) *Numerical Properties.* The results of a rigorous error analysis are summarised. Where they do not exist, an indication is given of the expected performance.

(vii) *Test Results.* The performance of the algorithm on specific numerical examples is presented. Usually a simple example possessing no numerical difficulties is given first so that the formal working of the algorithm may be tested. Where it is relevant such an example is followed by more subtle tests designed to illustrate special features of the algorithm.

The book is divided into two main sections. The first deals with linear systems, linear least squares and linear programming; the second covers the algebraic eigenvalue problem. It was decided to include only direct methods of solving linear systems on the grounds that iterative methods are mainly intimately bound up with the problem area for which they are designed (e.g. partial differential equations). General sparse matrices were also generally excluded since techniques for dealing with them usually involve the use of two-level storage in a non-trivial manner; at the time the project was started, research on sparse matrices had not assumed its current importance. Each of the two main sections is preceded by a preliminary assessment of the relative merits of the algorithms and an indication of the range of problem each is intended to cover. A brief resumé of the algorithms in the Handbook is given in the next few sections.

2. Positive Definite Symmetric Linear Systems

Most of the algorithms for positive definite symmetric matrices are based on the LL^T and the related LDL^T factorizations. For full matrices there are two main sets of algorithms associated with the LL^T decomposition. They are *choldet 1, cholsol 1, cholinversion 1* and *choldet 2, cholsol 2* and *cholinversion 2*. The second set achieves economy of storage by working with the lower triangle only of the relevant matrix, stored as a linear array of $\frac{1}{2}n(n + 1)$ elements. The second set is marginally slower than the first.

In each case *choldet* produces the LL^T-factorization and also the value of the determinant. The latter should be suppressed if not required since it takes a disproportionately long time. This is because determinants vary so widely in order of magnitude that it is necessary to store a separate exponent. After using *choldet* systems of equations having that matrix of coefficients can be solved using *cholsol*. Note that there is no need to have the inverse matrix. *cholsol* may be used any number of times after *choldet*. If the explicit inverse is required for some reason this can be obtained by using *cholinversion*.

These algorithms give almost the optimum accuracy that can be expected for the precision of computation. However further algorithms *acc solve* and *acc inverse* are provided and these give iterative refinement of the solutions. They can continue the refinements until, for example, $||x - \bar{x}||_\infty/||x||_\infty$ is less than the machine precision, provided A is not too ill-conditioned, in which case an indication is given. These algorithms are important not merely for giving accurate solutions but for providing information on the significance of the solutions when A is not known exactly.

A single set of algorithms *symdet, symsol* and *syminversion* is given based on the LDL^T factorization. It would have been possible to have produced the two sets of the type given for the LL^T factorization and to have provided iterative refinement but this has not been done. There is little to choose in accuracy. Note however that the LDL^T factorization usually exists even *when A is not positive definite* and this set of algorithms can often be used in this case. *There is then no guarantee of numerical stability.*

Two algorithms *gjdef1* and *gjdef2* are given, based on Gauss–Jordan, for inverting a positive definite matrix *in situ*. They should not be used for solving equations but they provide elegant and accurate algorithms for matrix inversion.

For positive definite band matrices there are procedures *chobanddet* and *chobandsol* based on the LL^T-factorization. Naturally there is no inversion procedure in this set.

There is one algorithm *cg* based on the conjugate gradient algorithm for positive definite matrices. It has the advantage that it can be used on a sparse matrix since one need only provide a procedure for calculating Ax given A and x. Although the conjugate gradient algorithm is often thought of as iterative, it is not truly so, for with exact computation it gives the exact answer in n steps. The *cg* algorithm is less accurate than those given above but storage considerations may dictate its use.

A striking omission from the Handbook is an algorithm for solving general non-positive definite symmetric systems, though they can be solved of course using the methods of the next section.

3. Non-Symmetric Linear Systems

The procedures are based on the LU-factorization of A where U is unit upper-triangular and partial pivoting is used. The procedure *unsymdet* gives the LU-factorization of a real matrix and produces its determinant as a by-product. The procedure *unsymsol* may subsequently be used any number of times to solve systems having A as the matrix. The procedure *compdet* and *compsol* perform the analogous operations for a complex matrix.

Iterative refinements of the solutions are provided by *unsym acc solve* and *cx acc solve* respectively and behave as in the positive definite case.

The procedures *bandet 1* and *bansol 1* are designed to deal with unsymmetric band matrices. They can be used for non-positive definite symmetric bands but they destroy symmetry. *bandet 2* and *bansol 2* can also be used but are less efficient, they were designed primarily for use with symmetric band matrices for which they can be used to find the number of positive eigenvalues of $A - pI$, i.e. the number of eigenvalues greater than p.

4. Least Squares and Related Problems

There are two main procedures associated with least squares when the associated matrix is $m \times n$, with $m \geqslant n$ and rank $(A) = n$. Both are based on the factorization $A = QR$ where R is an $m \times n$ upper triangular matrix and Q is orthogonal.

In *least squares solution*, a Q is determined such that $QA = R$ as the product of Householder matrices of the form $I - 2ww^T$. The procedure incorporates iterative refinement analogous to that for linear systems but its performance depends on the relative size of the residual.

The procedures *ortholin 1* and *ortholin 2* use the modified Gram–Schmidt orthogonalization of A and give only the first n columns of Q which are all that are required. *ortholin 2* is to be used when there is only one right-hand side and *ortholin 1* otherwise.

When the $m \times n$ matrix is of rank less than n the least squares solution is not unique and one is usually interested in the solution of minimum l_2 norm. This is provided by the procedures *svd* and *minfit*; these give the solutions of minimum norm corresponding to any number of right-hand sides. The procedures may be used to find the pseudo-inverse.

5. The Linear Programming Problem

The LP problem has not until recently received a great deal of attention from numerical analysts. Standard implementations of the simplex method pay little attention to numerical stability. In the algorithm *lp* a stable variant is given based on a triangular factorization of the current basis A_J of the form $LA_J = R$. Since its publication, research on stable variants of the simplex algorithm has been very active and superior versions are currently becoming available.

6. The General Real Symmetric Eigenvalue Problem

There are a number of algorithms for dealing with the real symmetric eigenvalue problem. The most compact is the procedure *jacobi* which is based on the method of Jacobi. It may be used to find all the eigenvalues with or without the eigenvectors. The eigenvectors are always accurately orthogonal even when the eigenvalues are pathologically close. This algorithm is not so fast as some given below but the procedure is very simple and it is particularly valuable when used as a subprocedure to find the eigensystem of a small matrix as part of a much larger problem.

Several of the faster algorithms are based on a preliminary orthogonal reduction to symmetric tridiagonal form by Householder transformations. The relevant algorithms are *tred 1*, *tred 2*, *tred 3*. *tred 2* is used when all eigenvalue and vectors are required. *tred 1* and *tred 3* are used when no eigenvectors or some of them are required. *tred 3* economises on storage by working with the lower triangle stored as a linear array of $\frac{1}{2}n(n + 1)$ elements.

Having reduced the matrix to tridiagonal form there are several ways of proceeding. The QR algorithm (in the QL form) is used in *imtql 1*, *imtql 2*, *tql 1* and *tql 2*. The *imtql* use the implicit version and the *tql* the explicit version. They are more or less equally efficient. *imtql 2* and *tql 2* are used after *tred 2* and find all the eigenvalues and vectors, the latter being accurately orthogonal. *tql 1* and *imtql 1* find only the eigenvalues, and the eigenvectors must be found by a separate program.

An entirely independent program for finding eigenvalues of the tri-diagonal form is *bisect* which is based on the Sturm sequence property of the principal minors of $A - \lambda I$. It is designed to find eigenvalues numbered $m1$ to $m2$ where they are ordered so that $\lambda_1 \leqslant \lambda_2 \leqslant \ldots \leqslant \lambda_n$. Minor modifications could be made to find the eigenvalues in a given range; in fact the virtue of *bisect* is its extreme flexibility. It could be further speeded up by abandoning bisection when a root is isolated and moving over to a technique giving superlinear convergence. *bisect* is actually faster on multiple roots than on well separated roots.

The procedure *tristurm* is designed to find selected roots and corresponding vectors of a symmetric tridiagonal matrix. Like *bisect* the roots are found by the Sturm sequence property and bisection, and the corresponding vectors by inverse iteration. The speed of inverse iteration is such that on most computers this is actually faster than *tql 2* and *imtql 2* even when all vectors are wanted but it is less aesthetically pleasing.

Procedures corresponding to *tred 1*, *tred 2*, *tql 1*, *tql 2*, *imtql 1*, *imtql 2* for complex Hermitian matrices were not included in the Handbook but are now available. They are extremely efficient.

7. Symmetric Band Matrices

Symmetric band matrices are very common in practice and there are several relevant procedures in the Handbook.

bqr uses the QR algorithm directly on the band matrix, the band form being invariant with respect to QR. It finds the eigenvalue nearest to an assigned value t and repeated calls enable one to find m eigenvalues nearest to t in an efficient manner.

In *bandrd* the band is reduced to symmetric tridiagonal form and this can then be treated in any of the ways discussed above.

When eigenvalues have been found the eigenvectors may be found using *symray*.

8. Dominant Eigenvalues and Eigenvectors of a Symmetric Sparse Matrix

A prescribed number of the dominant eigenvalues and corresponding eigenvectors of a symmetric sparse matrix A may be found using *ritzit*.

This uses the method of simultaneous iteration. It requires a subprocedure to form Ax from A and x and this may be designed to take advantage of any sparseness in A.

9. The Generalised Symmetric Eigenvalue Problem $Ax = \lambda Bx$ and $ABx = \lambda x$

When A and B are full matrices and B is positive definite procedures *reduc 1* and *reduc 2* may be used to reduce the generalised problem to the standard symmetric problem. Thus if $B = LL^T$ and $Ax = \lambda Bx$ then $L^{-1}AL^{-T}(L^Tx) = \lambda(L^Tx)$ and one may work with the symmetric matrix $L^{-1}AL^T$. Similarly if $ABx = \lambda x$ then $(L^TAL)L^Tx = \lambda L^Tx$ and one may work with L^TAL.

When A and B are band symmetric matrices then the computation of $L^{-1}AL^{-T}$ is inefficient since it destroys the band form. *ritzit* may be used however since given x we may compute $L^{-1}AL^{-T}x$ without forming $L^{-1}AL^{-T}$ explicitly.

Algorithms to deal with the case when B is merely semi-definite were not in a satisfactory form when the Handbook was published.

10. Non-Hermitian Matrices

The most widely used algorithms for finding the eigenvalues of a real non-symmetric matrix are based on the use of the QR algorithm. The matrix is first reduced to upper-Hessenberg form using one of the procedures *elmhes* or *elmtrans*, *dirhes* or *dirtrans*, *orthes* or *ortrans*. The *hes* procedures are used in connexion with *hqr* and the *trans* procedures with *hqr2*. *elmhes* and *dirhes* (*elmtrans* and *dirtrans*) use stabilized non-orthogonal transformations the only difference being that in *dirhes* (*dirtrans*) inner-products are accumulated in double precision thereby reducing the effect of rounding errors; *orthes* and *ortrans* use orthogonal transformations and have a guaranteed stability, but in practice *elmhes* and *dirhes* are usually just as stable.

The eigenvalues of the Hessenberg matrix may be found using *hqr* which uses the double-Francis QR algorithm. After finding all the eigenvalues selected vectors may be found using the procedure *invit* which is based on inverse iteration.

All the eigenvalues and all the eigenvectors may be found using *hqr 2* which is again based on the double-Francis QR algorithm and accumulates all the transformations to give the eigenvectors. *hqr* plus *invit* is much faster when only a few of the vectors are wanted but is heavy on storage since the Hessenberg matrix must be retained. Even when all the vectors are wanted this combination is faster than *hqr 2* on most computers though it is less aesthetically satisfying.

For complex matrices the stabilised LR algorithm has been preferred to the QR algorithm. The matrix is first reduced to Hessenberg form using *comhes*. If all the eigenvalues and vectors are required this is followed by *comlr 2*; if only selected eigenvectors are required the combination *comlr* and *cxinvit* (based on inverse iteration) is used. Similar comments to those made in the real case apply.

Alternative methods for dealing with non-Hermitian matrices are based on the generalization of Jacobi's method. For real matrices one uses *eigen* and for complex matrices one uses *comeig*. These algorithms are very compact but on the whole for speed and accuracy those based on QR and LR are to be preferred.

11. Badly Balanced Matrices

Matrices often arise in practice which are in some sense 'badly scaled'. More accurate results will usually be obtained if such a matrix A is subjected to a diagonal similarity transformation $D^{-1}AD$ where D is chosen so that corresponding rows and columns have roughly equal norms. This has been done in the procedure *balance*; the matrix D has elements which are powers of the computer base so that no rounding errors are involved. The time taken by *balance* is only a small percentage of the total time for computing an eigensystem and for this reason there is little to be lost by including *balance* as a matter of course. *Its use is essential if A is badly scaled. balance* also determines whether by row and column interchanges the matrix can be put in such a form that some eigenvalues can be found without computation. Thus for example if A is a triangular matrix with its rows and columns similarly permuted then all eigenvalues are found without any computation.

12. General Comments

The main omissions in the Handbook are:

(i) Algorithms for the symmetric problem $Ax = \lambda Bx$ when B is semi definite.

(ii) Algorithms for the generalised problem $(\lambda^r A_r + \lambda^{r-1}A_{r-1} + \ldots + \lambda A_1 + A_0)x = 0$ including the case when A_r and A_0 are singular.

(iii) Algorithms for $Ax = \lambda Bx$ where A and B are of band symmetric form.

(iv) Algorithms for finding invariant subspaces rather than eigenvectors when the eigensystem is ill-conditioned.

Good algorithms in these areas exist at NPL and elsewhere and will be published in future series.

The algorithms in the Handbook are included in the Linear Algebra Section of the NAG Library in both ALGOL and FORTRAN. The algorithms dealing with the algebraic eigenvalue problem exist in FORTRAN in the NATS Library which is maintained by Argonne National Laboratory and its collaborators. The NATS Library includes a master routine EISPACK which selects the appropriate algorithm for the user. The NATS versions are to be published in the Springer series of lecture notes and will make the Handbook routines much more widely available.

One question of importance that remains unanswered is whether the standard Journals are the right places to publish algorithms. Algorithms are very voluminous and, with the general pressure on space, they are naturally a source of embarrassment to editors. Some feel that the amount of material that was published in *Numerische Mathematik* should be drastically pruned but it is my impression that users found it very valuable. Certainly it is a bare minimum for those contemplating modifying the algorithms! Opinions on such matters by users will be very welcome.

References

Wilkinson, J. H. and Reinsch, C. (1971). "Handbook for Automatic Computation, Vol. II, Linear Algebra". Springer-Verlag, Berlin, Heidelberg, New York.

Wilkinson, J. H. (1965). "The Algebraic Eigenvalue Problem". Oxford University Press, London.

Discussion: Linear Algebra

Mr. Beasley. (*Rothamsted Exp. St.*). I would like to support the policy of putting the mathematical background and error analyses with the published algorithms. When explaining an algorithm to somebody, it gives all the necessary information in one place instead of in many places.

Dr. Wilkinson. Thank you. That is my own opinion too.

Mr. E. L. Albasiny (*National Physical Laboratory*). Could you comment on the availability of the algorithms in FORTRAN.

Dr. Wilkinson. The algorithms are available in FORTRAN from NAG and from the Argonne National Laboratory.

Dr. Tingleff. (*Tech. Univ. Lyngby, Denmark*). Your package includes both the Choleskyian and the LDL^T decomposition. Which is the fastest and which is the most accurate? What are your opinions on using the special Choleskyian with the "flags" for symmetric, non-definite matrices?

Dr. Wilkinson. There is little to choose as regards speed. We use the LDL^T sometimes when A is not positive definite and we expect the factorization to be stable. We have used Cholesky with flags but it is more straightforward to use LDL^T.

Mrs. Linda Hayes (*Oxford University Computing Laboratory*). Are your routines able to cope with the following classes of matrices: (1) Skew symmetric, (2) Derogatory and defective?

Dr. Wilkinson. (1) A very fast and accurate program exists at NPL for skew symmetric matrices. It has not been distributed because we felt that there was no demand for it. (2) We have programs which give orthogonal bases for invariant subspaces in the case when a non-Hermitian A is derogatory or defective. We expect to publish them in due course but they will need very detailed documentation if they are to be used intelligently.

Mr. Cox. I should like to sound out your current views on elimination methods versus orthogonalisation methods for solving linear systems. In the past, the time for a multiplication was comparable to, or even slower than, the time to access an array variable. In a high level language, such as ALGOL, the array access time may far exceed the multiplication time. This effect reduces the advantages in speed of elimination methods over orthogonalisation methods.

Dr. Wilkinson. I should like to see more use being made of the QR decomposition in solving linear systems, particularly as such a decomposition is numerically more stable than the LU decomposition. Also, I feel that further tests are needed on the comparative merits of various methods.

MR. POWELL. In optimization calculations, a common problem is given an LDL^T factorization of a positive definite matrix, to revise the factorization when a change of small rank is made to the main matrix. Would you agree that algorithms for this and similar calculations should be provided in the linear algebra routines of subroutine libraries?

DR. WILKINSON. My answer is an emphatic "Yes". I regard them as being among the most important algorithms in linear algebra, though it is only comparatively recently that their importance has been fully realised.

3. Direct Methods for Sparse Matrices

J. K. REID

Theoretical Physics Division,
U.K.A.E.A., Research Group,
Atomic Energy Research Establishment,
Harwell, England.

1. Introduction

In this paper direct processes used in linear algebra in cases where the matrix is sparse will be considered. Most of our attention will be concentrated on Gaussian elimination for the solution of linear equations, but we will also mention the least squares problem and the reduction of the eigenvalue problem to a simple form such as tridiagonal.

This subject is still in its infancy and techniques are still under development. The principle aim here is to survey those techniques that seem most promising. Sections 2 to 6 are devoted to Gaussian elimination and include consideration of pivotal strategies, storage schemes and application in one area, the solution of elliptic partial differential equations. In Sections 7 and 8 we consider the least squares problem and the eigenvalue problem in a similar vein. Finally in Section 9 we say a little about computer subroutines that are available from those sources known to the author.

2. Gaussian Elimination

To solve a general sparse set of n linear equations

$$Ax = b \tag{2.1}$$

we decompose the matrix A into a product

$$A = PLUQ \tag{2.2}$$

where P and Q are permutation matrices, L is a lower-triangular matrix with units on its main diagonal and U is an upper triangular matrix. Given this decomposition the system (2.1) may be written in the equivalent form

$$
\left.
\begin{aligned}
P x^{(1)} &= b \\
L x^{(2)} &= x^{(1)} \\
U x^{(3)} &= x^{(2)} \\
Q x \;\;\; &= x^{(3)},
\end{aligned}
\right\}
\tag{2.3}
$$

readily verified by eliminating the subsidiary vectors $x^{(1)}$, $x^{(2)}$ and $x^{(3)}$. Each of the subsystems of (2.3) is easy to solve.

The decomposition (2.2) is obtained by $n-1$ stages of elimination. At the first such stage we choose a "pivot", say a_{pq}, and interchange row 1 with row p and column 1 with column q so that the pivotal element is brought to the (1, 1) position. Next multiples l_{i1}, $i = 2, 3, \ldots n$, of the first row are subtracted from subsequent rows, these multiples being chosen so that the resulting matrix has zeros in its first column, apart from the first row. At the second stage exactly the same operations are applied to the matrix of the last $(n-1)$ rows and columns, with the exception that the row permutation is applied to the vector of multipliers l_{i1}, $i = 2, \ldots n$, so that these are as if the second row permutation had been applied before these numbers were calculated. Similarly, at the mth stage multipliers l_{im}, $i = m + 1, \ldots, n$ are found and the row permutation used is applied to all the previous vectors of multipliers. It is straightforward to show that the upper triangular matrix eventually obtained is the required matrix U, that the multipliers l_{ij} make up the subdiagonal elements of L and that products of the row and column permutations used make up the matrices P and Q.

Since A is sparse we aim to choose the permutations in such a way that L and U are sparse too, and to save storage we normally keep only the non-zero matrix elements and corresponding indexing integers. We consider suitable storage patterns in Section 5, and pivotal strategies (i.e. choice of P and Q) in section 4. Once P and Q have been chosen the triangular factors L and U are normally unique, but there are situations in which they do not exist even though the system (2.1) is well-conditioned, or where they exist but the decomposition is unstable and in the presence of round-off errors the factorization differs substantially from the original matrix. This possibility of instability is sometimes overlooked in practical codes, perhaps because it cannot happen for certain classes of matrices. We examine this problem in the next section.

Choosing the pivotal sequence is, in general, a far more costly operation than decomposing A once the pivotal sequence is known or solving the equation (2.3). Examples of timings may be seen in Table 2 in Section 6. Furthermore it often happens that several matrices with the same sparsity pattern require factorization and also that several systems of eqns (2.1) with the same matrix A require solution. For these reasons it is usual, while choosing pivots, to store information to allow the subsequent tasks to be performed rapidly. This storage may be in the form of integer arrays indexing the non-zeros, stored in a convenient order, or it may be in the form of a long string of uninterrupted floating-point instructions referring to fixed addresses for the non-zeros (Gustavson *et al.*, 1970). The latter procedure cannot be implemented entirely in a high-level language and the code is bulky to store, but the advantage in speed is substantial if the code can be held in main store, typical gains being by a factor of $2\frac{1}{2}$ to 3. As an example of the bulk of the code, we estimate that the last example of Table 2 (of Section 6) would require about a million bytes of code to factorize a further matrix and about a third of a million bytes to solve a set of equations (given the factorization). In such a case the code would presumably be held on backing-store, but the cost of bringing it down before execution would probably exceed the cost saving of the intrinsically higher execution speed. A variant of the Gustavson procedure, proposed by Erisman (1972), mitigates these disadvantages. Erisman replaces in-line floating-point code by the use of integer arrays to control jumps to subroutines which perform such jobs as calculating the inner product between two vectors of which one has elements stored consecutively. In this way he reduces the length of code by a factor of about ten for his problems. A further advantage of Erisman's technique is that departure from a high-level language is no longer necessary.

A final remark we wish to make in this section is that given a decomposition (2.2) for A we can at once write down a similar decomposition

$$A^T = Q^T U^T L^T P^T \tag{2.4}$$

for A^T. We therefore see that solution of the equation

$$A^T y = c \tag{2.5}$$

is available to us, given the decomposition (2.2). At various points in this paper we discuss storage schemes and algorithms which are definitely biased towards rows or columns. Since, however, we could have worked equally with A^T there is always a dual in which the roles of rows and columns are interchanged. For simplicity we describe just one of such a pair and make no reference to the other, although both are important.

3. Numerical Stability

In addition to ensuring that the decomposition of A obtained by Gaussian elimination is sparse, it is important to check the stability of the process which is quite straightforward with the help of Wilkinson's backward error analysis. Suppose that the permutations P and Q of eqn (2.2) are fixed, but that the arithmetic is carried out in floating-point with a fixed word-length. Wilkinson's work (see for example Wilkinson (1961) or (1965)) consists of bounding not the errors in L and U but the difference

$$F = PLUQ - A \tag{3.1}$$

between the exact product of the factors actually obtained and the original matrix. A minor extension, Reid (1971b), of Wilkinson's work gives the bounds

$$|f_{ij}| \leqslant (3.01)\, \varepsilon\, ng_{ij} \tag{3.2}$$

where $\varepsilon\,(< 10^{-3})$ is the relative accuracy of the computation,

$$g_{ij} = \max_k |a_{ij}^{(k)}|$$

and $a_{ij}^{(k)}$ is the element corresponding to a_{ij} in the kth reduced matrix. This is a powerful result provided the elements do not grow drastically in size during the reduction. That such growth is likely to be disastrous is easy to see for the elements change by having numbers subtracted from them and can grow only by such a computation as (in 4 decimal arithmetic)

$$1 \cdot 234 - (- 123 \cdot 2) = 124 \cdot 4 \tag{3.3}$$

and in such a case it is clear that information (0·034) has been lost; such information may be vital to the solution. For these reasons we refer to an elimination in which severe growth in the size of matrix elements takes place as unstable.

Because it is not practicable to monitor the growth of all matrix elements it is usual to try to control

$$\max_{i,j} |a_{ij}^{(k)}|.$$

For example, it is easily seen that if all pivots are chosen to have maximum modulus in their row or column then the inequality

$$\max_{i,j} |a_{ij}^{(k+1)}| \leqslant 2 \max_{i,j} |a_{ij}^{(k)}| \tag{3.4}$$

holds. Such control does not constitute a sensible strategy, however, unless the matrix is well-scaled. Fortunately, it often happens that matrices are well-scaled naturally but particular care should be exercised where mixed units (e.g. neutron fluxes and feet) are in use. No really satisfactory algorithm for automatic scaling is known at present. For example studies made with

A. R. Curtis (Curtis and Reid, 1972) indicate that straightforward equilibration of row and column norms (e.g. scale all rows to have maximal element unity, then do the same by columns) can give very bad results for sparse matrices. Curtis and Reid (1972), following Hamming (1971), suggested choosing ρ_i, c_j to minimize

$$\Sigma(\log_\beta |a_{ij}| - \rho_i - c_j)^2 \qquad (3.5)$$

where β is the base of the floating-point computation in use and where the sum is over all i,j such that $a_{ij} \neq 0$; they then work with $\{\beta^{-R_i} a_{ij}\beta^{-C_j}\}$ where R_i and C_j are the nearest integers to ρ_i and c_j respectively. On test sparse matrices they were able to calculate ρ_i and c_j in the equivalent of 7–10 sweeps through the matrix and satisfactory scalings were obtained.

There are two important classes of matrices for which Gaussian elimination is bound to be stable for any choice of pivots from the leading diagonal ($P = Q^{-1}$). The first class is of those matrices that are diagonally dominant either by rows, where the relation

$$|a_{ii}| \geqslant \sum_{j \neq i} |a_{ij}|, \qquad i = 1, \ldots, n \qquad (3.6)$$

holds or by columns, when the relation

$$|a_{ii}| \geqslant \sum_{j \neq i} |a_{ji}|, \qquad i = 1, \ldots, n \qquad (3.7)$$

holds. In this case the maximal element of any reduced matrix is no greater than twice the maximal element of A. This result is proved by Wilkinson (1961, Section 8) for diagonal dominance by columns (relation (3.7)) and the corresponding result by rows may be proved similarly.

The second, and more important, class af matrices for which diagonal pivoting is always stable is composed of those matrices that are symmetric and positive–definite ($z^T A z > 0$ unless $z = 0$). These matrices frequently arise after discretization of elliptic partial differential equations (see Section 6). Wilkinson (1961, Section 6) has shown that for such a matrix A, if pivots are chosen from the diagonal, no element of any of the reduced matrices is greater than the greatest element of A. Also it is readily verified that symmetry is preserved in the remaining uneliminated matrix so that both the work and storage may be halved; if D is the diagonal matrix with diagonal elements equal to those of U then the relation

$$DL^T = U \qquad (3.8)$$

is easily proved so that the decomposition may be written

$$A = PLDL^T P^T \qquad (3.9)$$

and there is no need to store the off-diagonal elements of U.

4. Pivotal Strategies in Gaussian Elimination

At each stage of the elimination process a choice of pivot has to be made and this is usually based on a compromise between a good choice on stability grounds and a good choice on sparsity grounds. A zero pivot would give infinite growth, the limiting case of instability, and codes have always avoided such a choice. Some codes do no more than this, although small pivots are likely to cause large growth. It is usual therefore to restrict pivots either to those greater than a certain tolerance or to those which result in multipliers (elements of L) no greater than a certain limit. Curtis and Reid (1971) use the latter criterion on the ground that if all the multipliers are less than w then the largest matrix element cannot grow by a factor greater than $(1 + w)$ at each elimination, although of course they hope that overall growth at this rate will not be maintained for long. They found the choice of w not very critical but recommended $w = 4$ on the basis of a limited set of tests. Tomlin (1972) recommends the use of $w = 100$ in linear programming applications but includes the safeguard of checking the size of the residual vector

$$b - A\bar{x} \qquad\qquad (4.1)$$

where $\bar{x}$ is the computed solution. He repeats the decomposition with $w = 10$ if the vector (4.1) is unsatisfactorily large. Because the sets of equations (2.3) are solved accurately in the sense that the solution obtained is the exact solution of a slightly perturbed system (Wilkinson, 1965, for example), it follows that large residuals can only be caused by an unstable computation of L and U. We note in passing that small residuals do not necessarily imply an accurate solution for if the matrix is ill-conditioned then quite large errors in $\bar{x}$ may make little difference to $A\bar{x}$ and so leave the residuals small.

Next we consider sparsity criteria for the choice of pivot. Perhaps the most commonly used criterion (Markowitz, 1957) is to minimise the multiplication count, that is the product of the number of non-zero elements in the pivotal row and the number of non-zero elements in the pivotal column, excluding the pivot itself in each case. This is an upper bound for the number of non-zeros that may be created during this elimination. Alternatively we may minimize the number of non-zeros actually created. This latter strategy is more laborious and in practice usually gives similar fill-in (see for example Tables 1 and 3 of Section 6). The following example of Rose (1971) illustrates that it can give very much less fill-in, but here the initial matrix is about three-quarters full, which is hardly sparse. Note that minimizing the fill-in at each stage does not necessarily minimize the overall fill-in (Duff and Reid, 1973).

```
X |X X X X X X X X X X |  _____
 X |X                  | X X X X X X X X X X |
 X |  X                | X X X X X X X X X X |
 X |    X              | X X X X X X X X X X |
 X |      X            | X X X X X X X X X X |
 X |        X          | X X X X X X X X X X |
 X |          X        | X X X X X X X X X X |
 X |            X      | X X X X X X X X X X |
 X |              X    | X X X X X X X X X X |
 X |                X  | X X X X X X X X X X |
 X |                  X| X X X X X X X X X X |
   |X X X X X X X X X X|X X X X X X X X X X |
   |X X X X X X X X X X|X X X X X X X X X X |
   |X X X X X X X X X X|X X X X X X X X X X |
   |X X X X X X X X X X|X X X X X X X X X X |
   |X X X X X X X X X X|X X X X X X X X X X |
   |X X X X X X X X X X|X X X X X X X X X X |
   |X X X X X X X X X X|X X X X X X X X X X |
   |X X X X X X X X X X|X X X X X X X X X X |
   |X X X X X X X X X X|X X X X X X X X X X |
   |X X X X X X X X X X|X X X X X X X X X X |
   |X X X X X X X X X X|X X X X X X X X X X |
```

An organisational disadvantage of these criteria is that they require the sparsity pattern of the whole matrix at each stage, whereas it is convenient to delay operations on each column until it is pivotal and then perform them all together. This is convenient if a two-level store is in use and the matrix is stored by columns for the column is only modified once and so needs writing to backing store only once. It is also convenient in a one-level-store program because new non-zeros are created only within a column and the need to store the whole matrix as a linked list is avoided (see also Section 5). For these reasons it is quite common to choose the pivotal column order *a priori*. A merit number is attached to each column and the columns are ordered in increasing merit number; four common choices for this merit number are (i) the number of non-zeros in the column, (ii) the total number of non-zeros in those rows that have a non-zero in the column, (iii) the average Markowitz cost for the non-zeros of the column and (iv) the minimal Markowitz cost for the non-zeros of the column (where by the "Markowitz cost" of a non-zero we mean the product of the number of other non-zeros in its row and the number of other non-zeros in its column).

Experiments by Duff (1972) and Duff and Reid (1973) indicate that there is little to choose between the first three criteria but that the fourth is sometimes significantly inferior; they recommend (i) because it is the easiest to apply. Within the pivotal column the pivot is usually chosen as

J. K. REID

the non-zero whose row in the original matrix has fewest other non-zeros, subject to whatever stability criterion is in use. Duff (1972) and Duff and Reid (1973) experimented with two further techniques for choosing the pivotal element. One is to revise the row counts to allow for eliminated elements and the other is to revise the row counts to allow not only for eliminated elements but also for filled-in elements by using a probabilistic estimate due to Tewarson (1966). They found that the first method often gives extremely poor results, presumably because the original number of non-zeros in the eliminated part of the row is better than zero as an estimate of the number of non-zeros filled-in. They found little to choose however between use of the original row count and Tewarson's probabilitic estimate and prefer the former on grounds of simplicity. However these strategies not requiring the sparsity pattern to be kept and updated often result in significantly more fill-in than when the Markowitz criterion, requiring the sparsity pattern, is used (see Duff and Reid, 1973).

```
× ×    ×
  × ×    ×
× × ×    ×
      ×  ×
      × ×   ×
× × × × × × × ×
        × × ×
      × × × × × ×
          × × ×
        × × × ×    ×
          × × × ×
            × × × ×
          × × × × ×   ×
            × × × × ×
                × × ×   ×   ×
                × × × × × ×   ×
                    × × ×   ×
                  × × × × × ×
                      × × ×
                  × × × × × ×
```

We conclude this section by remarking that there is an important class of matrices for which a good pivotal strategy is to take pivots in sequence from the diagonal, namely when the matrix is variable-band, symmetric and positive-definite (Jennings, 1966), because if $P = I$ in the decomposition (3.9) then the first non-zero of each row of L occurs no earlier than the first non-zero of the corresponding row of A. Thus the above sparsity pattern, for example, is preserved without fill-in. If A maximal semi-band-width m, that is if $a_{ij} = 0$ when $|i - j| \geqslant m$ ($m = 6$ in the above example) then to calculate a particular row of L involves the corresponding row of A and at most the previous $(m - 1)$ rows of L. Therefore the earlier rows of L can conveniently be placed on backing store. A Harwell report (Reid, 1972) contains a Fortran subroutine implementing this algorithm. A more complicated procedure, allowing the algorithm to be implemented when very little main store is available or when m is very large, is described by Jennings and Tuff (1971).

5. Storage Considerations

There are two strong reasons for using sparse matrix techniques, namely, to save computational effort and to save storage. We save storage by holding only the non-zero elements but, of course, need additional integer indexing arrays to indicate where each non-zero belongs in the matrix. We discuss here some of the more commonly used storage patterns, viz:—

(1) The matrix is stored by columns, e.g. a_{11}, a_{21}, a_{51}, a_{22}, a_{42}, a_{33}, a_{43}, a_{14}, a_{24}, a_{44}, with row numbers held in correspondence with each non-zero; also held are pointers to the beginnings of the columns (including an imaginary $(n + 1)$st column), i.e. 1, 4, 6, 8, 11 in the above example.

(2) As (1), but instead of storing all row numbers, store just the first and last of each column and the bit patterns of the intermediate ones. For example the column a_{11}, a_{31}, a_{51}, a_{61}, a_{91} would involve the bit pattern (0101100).

(3) The matrix elements are not stored in any particular physical order but rather as a linked list. Associated with each non-zero is some combination of the following: pointers to the next and to the previous element in its row and in its column; row and column numbers. In addition there are pointers to the first elements of the rows and columns. The last forward pointer and the first backward pointer in a row or column is available for other purposes such as a pointer to the other end of the row or column or to hold the row or column number.

Structure (2) is very economical in storage if the non-zeros are close together within each column but the "bit-picking" necessary to work with this structure makes it rather clumsy, and it is generally rather out of favour, although Gentleman (private communication) has remarked that it has advantages on parallel processing machines with suitable instruction codes. Structure (1) is easier to use and yet is almost as economical in storage,

requiring only one integer to be associated with each non-zero. Its principal
disadvantage is that if it is used with a pivotal strategy that requires the sparsity
pattern to be kept updated then it is very clumsy because extensive shuffling
is necessary after each creation of a new non-zero. Curtis and Reid, (1971,
algorithm X) use this structure with the *a priori* pivotal column ordering
strategy described in Section 4, keeping the columns in (known) pivotal
order; non-zeros are created within one column at a time so that shuffling
is confined to this one column; essentially separate structures of type (1)
are kept for the columns that have been pivotal and the rest, the first
structure expanding as the second contracts and storage released by the
second may later be used by the first.

The linked list structure (3) allows each elimination with associated creation
of new non-zeros to be performed in a number of computer operations that
is only a small multiple of the number of multiplications involved. The
new non-zeros are placed physically at the end of the structure and the links
are adjusted, thus avoiding any shuffling or reordering. Similarly, interchanges
may be performed by adjusting links, avoiding any actual physical movement
of the non-zeros. The reason for avoiding such shuffling is principally
because the number of computer operations involved in a single shuffle is
likely to be about half the total number of non-zeros. It is, of course,
equally important to avoid doing a similarly large number of operations in
some other part of the calculation. Having all six integers (links and row/
column numbers) associated with each non-zero is convenient since it is then
straightforward to insert new non-zeros into the structure, to interchange a
pair of rows or a pair of columns and to identify the row and column of a
non-zero, but six integers per non-zero is usually considered to be too
wasteful of storage. The number of integers may be reduced at a little expense
in extra computation. For example, Curtis and Reid (1971), in algorithm Y,
do not use backward pointers but instead scan the row or column forwards
until the element for which the backward pointer is needed is encountered
and in algorithm Z do not use row and column numbers either but instead
scan the row or column to its end and arrange that the last pointer contains
the row or column number. Such scans are not unduly expensive since we
do not expect the average row or column to contain more than five or six
non-zeros, but of course it is important to arrange to do as few of them as
possible.

If the pivotal strategy and the final sparsity pattern is known then the
linked-list structure (3) shows no advantage over structure (1) which is the
more economical of storage. We work with the final sparsity structure, which
includes all the intermediate structures and so no fill-in takes place. Thus
when factorising a matrix whose sparsity structure is identical with one that
has already been factorized Curtis and Reid (1971, algorithm Z) use structure

(1) although structure (3) was used when choosing the pivotal sequence for the original matrix. Unless the pivotal sequence is known to give a stable decomposition (e.g. in the positive–definite case) some check should be made on stability, such as recording the largest number encountered or checking the size of the residuals when using the decomposition to solve a system of equations.

If stability considerations can be ignored while choosing the pivotal sequence (e.g. in the positive–definite case, again) then the non-zeros themselves need not be stored at all during this phase of the computation, making substantial savings in storage for all structures.

We conclude this section with some remarks on the use of backing store (e.g. disk). There is a good reason for avoiding backing store altogether for the general sparse matrix if at all possible. This is because during the elimination stage access is required to scattered portions of the matrix. It is usual to hold the matrix on backing store by columns and to use *a priori* column ordering so that all the operations on one column can be delayed until the column is pivotal, thus reducing the number of records needing to be written to backing store. However, several earlier columns, in general scattered, will be required in order to operate on that column. An exceptional case where a backing store may be used without excessive degradation of performance is when the Jennings variable band-width algorithm is in use (see end of Section 4).

6. Solution of Elliptic Partial Differential Equations

In this section we consider some sparse systems of linear equations that arise from the solution by finite differences or by finite elements of elliptic partial differential equations in two and three dimensions. We will not distinguish between finite differences and finite elements for our concern will be with the solution of the resulting system of algebraic equations rather than with their derivation. A mesh (e.g. triangular or rectangular) is placed over the region to give a number of nodes at which parameters determining the solution are required. We use as one of our test examples the problem of the determination of the solution of Laplace's equation

$$\frac{\partial^2 \phi}{\partial x^2} + \frac{\partial^2 \phi}{\partial y^2} = 0 \qquad (6.1)$$

over a rectangle with known values for ϕ at its edge. Taking a regular rectangular mesh with $l \times m$ internal modes and using the standard 5-point finite difference approximation yields a matrix of the form

$$
\begin{bmatrix}
T & D \\
D & T & D \\
 & D & T & D \\
 & & \cdot & \cdot & \cdot \\
 & & & \cdot & \cdot & \cdot \\
 & & & & \cdot & \cdot & \cdot \\
 & & & & & \cdot & \cdot & D \\
 & & & & & & D & T
\end{bmatrix}
\tag{6.2}
$$

where there are m blocks T, each of which is a tridiagonal matrix of order l, and $2m - 2$ diagonal matrices D of order l. We solve a corresponding matrix equation to obtain function values at each node. In a more general case there are several parameters associated with each node, perhaps because we are solving a coupled system of elliptic equations or perhaps because more than one parameter is associated with each node (e.g. function values and derivatives) in a finite-element approximation. With care it is possible to arrange that the matrix is symmetric and positive–definite, a property that is obtained automatically if the variational formulation of the elliptic equation is approximated by finite elements. It is highly desirable to do this because (see Section 3) then the pivots may be chosen from the diagonal without fear of instability, so preserving symmetry and allowing both the storage and the computational work to be approximately halved; also it allows the possibility of the use of Jennings variable band-width algorithm (end of Section 4).

To obtain the satisfactory band matrix form of (6.2) the points were numbered "pagewise". Such an ordering allows the use of the Jennings variable band-width algorithm (see Section 4) in a reasonably efficient way. A satisfactory way of numbering the variables in the general case is to number all the variables associated with each single node consecutively, and to use the following method (Cuthill and McKee, 1969) to order the nodes. We choose node 1 (for instance it is sensible to take a point on the edge of a thin side of the region) and we label its neighbours 2, 3, ... Then we add to the end of the list all unlabelled neighbours of point 2 then of point 3 and so on. A simple example is the following:

Two nodes are considered neighbours if they are both involved in a finite-difference expression or if they both belong to the same finite element. George (1971) reports particularly favourably of the use of the reverse ordering, calling this "reverse Cuthill–McKee". If either forward or reverse Cuthill–McKee ordering is applied to the 5-point approximation to the Laplacian (6.1) in a rectangle and if the first node is taken to be at a corner,

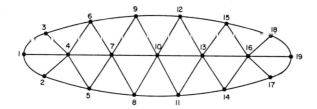

then ordering along diagonals results, which is more satisfactory than the pagewise ordering of the matrix (6.2) because, although the maximal bandwidth is the same, the average bandwidth is approximately halved. This ordering is used for the variable bandwidth results in Tables 1 to 3, below.

The use of a sparse matrix code obviates the need for a good ordering of the nodes, but as we remarked at the end of the last section it is undesirable if it cannot be performed in the main store. The actual gains in storage are not as substantial as might perhaps have been hoped. Some examples are shown in Table 1; the pivotal strategies used for the sparse codes were to minimize the multiplication count (unbracketed figures) and the fill-in bracketed figures) at each elimination, choosing pivots from the diagonal. In Table 2 we show some results obtained on the IBM 370/165 when experimenting (Reid, 1972) with subroutines for Jennings' algorithm (MA15), and sparsity coding using a minimal multiplication count pivotal strategy (MA17). In interpreting the storage requirements allowance should be made for the fact that the compiled code for MA15 was about 3500 bytes shorter than that for MA17. It will be seen that the two algorithms use comparable amounts of storage on small problems, but the Jennings' algorithm (MA15) can use more on large problems, although not all of this need be in core. In fact using disk backing store on the double-length version of the largest problem shown reduced the core storage required to 43·7 thousand bytes

TABLE 1. Non-zeros stored for Laplacian in $m \times m$ square

m	3	4	5	6	7	8	9	10
Non-zeros (Jennings)	28	62	115	191	294	428	597	805
Non-zeros (Sparse)	26 (26)	58 (58)	102 (102)	166	248 (248)	355	469 (472)	631

J. K. REID

TABLE 2. Laplace's equation in a rectangle.

l	m	Sub-routine	No. of non-zeros D, L	Time (secs) in double length to			Core storage (thousands of bytes)	
				Choose pivots	Factorize matrix	Solve equation	Single length	Double length
5	6	MA15	145	—	0·007	0·0017	0·8	1·6
		MA17	131	0·025	0·0026	0·0013	1·4	1·9
10	11	MA15	915	—	0·040	0·008	4·5	9·1
		MA17	728	0·21	0·018	0·007	7·1	10·1
15	16	MA15	2810	—	0·13	0·022	13	26
		MA17	1987	0·89	0·06	0·019	19	27
30	31	MA15	20245	—	1·3	0·16	88	177
		MA17	11328	12·2	0·6	0·12	102	147

and increased the factorization time to 1·4 secs and the solution time to 0·25 secs.

In three dimensions the picture is far less encouraging for elimination because the matrices have far wider bands with far more zeros within their profile. In Table 3 we show figures for the Laplacian in a cube in the same format as those of Table 1. It will be seen that the storage required is substantial. The amount of compution is also large. In fact it is usually advantageous to use iterative methods for three-dimensional problems.

It is interesting to note also from Tables 1 and 3 that the two sparse matrix strategies give comparable results and in fact there is one example in each table of the minimum fill-in strategy giving an inferior result.

George (1972) makes some very useful comments on ordering for matrices arising from finite-element discretizations. An obvious and very worthwhile saving can be made by eliminating first all those variables corresponding to

TABLE 3. Non-zeros stored for Laplacian in $m \times m \times m$ cube.

m	3	4	5	6
Non-zeros (Jennings)	183	696	2009	4830
Non-zeros (Sparse)	147 (146)	531 (551)	1377 (1350)	3281

points internal to the elements (sometimes known as "static condensation"). Next, if variables corresponding to all the nodes on an edge between two elements are eliminated then the effects are confined to those two elements and it is as if they had been combined into one element, parameterized by the remaining variables. It may be convenient to stop this procedure early and go over to straightforward band-matrix elimination or we can continue it, obtaining successively larger "elements" until the whole region is one "element". George applies this procedure to the finite element solution of a problem over the unit square obtained by placing over it a square grid of side $1/q$, each square of which is divided into two triangular elements and taking α variables at each node and β variables on each edge between elements. In this way he reduces the number of multiplications from

$$\tfrac{1}{2}(\alpha + \beta)^2(\alpha + 2\beta)q^4 + O(q^3) \tag{6.3}$$

to less than

$$22(\alpha + \beta)^3 q^3 + 8(\alpha + \beta)^2 q^2 (\log_2 q - 4\alpha - 4\beta). \tag{6.4}$$

Qualitatively this appears to be a large gain, from $O(q^4)$ to $O(q^3)$, but the leading terms in (6.3) and (6.4) are equal at some value of q between 22 and 44, so the gains in practice are unlikely to be large. Actually George's procedure can be improved by taking lines of nodes to be eliminated right on to the boundary whenever the "elements" under combination are at the boundary but it remains true that for grids likely to be used in practice there will be a gain smaller than one might expect from the reduction of the number of operations from $O(q^4)$ to $O(q^3)$. The procedure generalizes to uneven grids and to higher dimensions without difficulty.

7. Least Square Problems

In this section we consider the least squares solution of an over-determined set of linear equations

$$Ax = b \tag{7.1}$$

where A is an $m \times n$ ($m \geqslant n$) sparse matrix of rank n. The most straightforward method is the direct formation of the system

$$A^T Ax = A^T b \tag{7.2}$$

of normal equations followed by its solution via the symmetric decomposition (3.9), for it is straightforward to show that $A^T A$ is symmetric and positive–

definite. This method has the substantial disadvantage that the system (7.2), with the matrix $A^T A$ and the vector $A^T b$ calculated explicitly, is far more ill-conditioned than the original problem. This disadvantage is particularly marked when the elements of some of the rows of A are much larger than those in other rows since row scaling cannot be applied without changing the least squares objective function. The method's advantages lie in its economy in storage and arithmetic.

In order to overcome this ill-conditioning problem Golub (1965) suggested using the decomposition

$$A = QU \qquad (7.3)$$

where Q is an $m \times n$ orthogonal matrix (i.e. one whose columns form an orthonormal set) and U is the $n \times n$ upper triangular matrix. The normal equations (7.2) reduce to the form

$$Ux = Q^T b \qquad (7.4)$$

and may therefore be solved by a simple back substitution. Q is built up as a product of Givens or Housholder matrices. The procedure is very satisfactory in respect of numerical stability, but less so in respect of fill-in since a Givens reduction results in both the rows involved taking the sparsity pattern of their union and a Housholder reduction results in all the rows with non-zeros in the pivotal column taking the sparsity pattern of their union.

Wilkinson and Peters (1970) have suggested an alternative procedure for avoiding the ill-conditioning of the direct formation of the normal equations. They use the decomposition

$$A = LU \qquad (7.5)$$

where L is a unit lower trapezoidal $m \times n$ matrix and U is an upper triangular $n \times n$ matrix. The normal equations now reduce to the form

$$L^T L \, Ux = L^T b, \qquad (7.6)$$

which may be solved by forming the matrix $L^T L$ and using the symmetric decomposition (3.9). This algorithm is not quite so satisfactory from a numerical point of view as Golub's for it relies on the pivotal strategy used in the decomposition (7.5) ensuring that $L^T L$ is well-conditioned but Wilkinson reports good results in practice.

It seems unlikely that it will be possible to use theoretical arguments to compare the three methods from the point of view of fill-in for Duff (1972) has examples showing that the matrices $A^T A$ of equation (7.2) and $L^T L$

of equation (7.6) may each be arbitrarily denser than the other. His numerical experiments indicate that the normal equations method is usually the most economical in storage and arithmetic but that the algorithm of Wilkinson–Peters is quite computive whereas that of Golub is not. In view of the poor conditioning of the normal equations we therefore recommend the Wilkinson–Peters algorithm for general-purpose use.

8. The Eigenvalue Problem

There are well-established good methods for finding similarity transformations to reduce matrices to the simple forms of tridiagonal (symmetric case) and Hessenberg (general case) and it is natural to seek versions of these for the sparse case. Unfortunately the experiments of Duff (1972) indicate that this is unlikely to be a fruitful approach. He found that when orthogonal transformations were used the fill-in was so great on most of his problems that regarding them as full would have been more sensible; his only exceptions were artificially constructed and very sparse. Using stabilised elementary similarity transformations (analogous with Gaussian elimination) on the unsymmetric problem was a little more hopeful but even here the gain over treating the matrix as full was slight, in stark contrast with the massive gains one often gets in the case of linear equations.

There is, however, one important case where a direct reduction can be used to advantage. This is the algorithm of Schwartz (1968) for reducing a symmetric band matrix to tridiagonal form. This involves essentially no fill-in and the number of multiplications required if the order is n and the band-width is $2m + 1$ is not more than $n^2(m - 1)(4 + 6\cdot5/m)$ so that if $m \ll n$ there is a great saving over treating the matrix as full. An Algol program is included in Schwartz' paper which is also part of the Handbook of Wilkinson and Reinsch (1971).

9. Available Subroutines

The purpose of this section is to mention briefly those sources for subroutines that are known to the author. It should be appreciated that libraries continually evolve and the information may be out of date even by the time this appears in print.

Most of the Harwell subroutines have been documented in reports and all are available in machine-readable form for a nominal service charge. There are subroutines for solving unsymmetric band systems of equations; solving variable-band symmetric and positive–definite systems, with facilities for using disk storage if necessary; scaling matrices; solving general sparse and symmetric sparse sets of equations, each containing entries for choosing pivots, factorizing a matrix with given choice of pivots and solving a system when the decomposition is known.

The Handbook of Wilkinson and Reinsch (1971) contains ALGOL programs for symmetric decomposition of band symmetric matrices and solving corresponding sets of linear equations; and for reducing a symmetric band matrix to tridiagonal form.

The Nottingham Algorithm Group (NAG) library contains FORTRAN and ALGOL versions of the two Handbook subroutines mentioned in the last paragraph and of the Harwell subroutines for scaling and for solving general sparse systems of linear equations. They plan shortly to include the symmetric version of this too.

The IBM program product SL-MATH includes facilities for factorizing and solving band matrices both in the general case and in the symmetric and positive definite case. It also has facilities for general sparse matrices and here uses the Markowitz criterion. Again there are separate facilities for general matrices and symmetric positive–definite ones, pivots being chosen with a stability tolerance in the first case and from the diagonal in the second. Further matrices with the same sparsity pattern may be factorized using a given pivotal sequence and further systems with the same matrix may be solved.

Both the Harwell and the IBM subroutines use integer arrays to index the factorized forms of general sparse matrices. We do not know of a readily-available subroutine for generating loop-free code.

Acknowledgement

I would like to express my thanks to M. J. D. Powell for reading a draft of this paper and suggesting a number of improvements to the presentation.

References

Curtis, A. R. and Reid, J. K. (1971). The solution of large sparse unsymmetric systems of linear equations. *J. Inst. Maths Applics* **8**, 344.

Curtis, A. R. and Reid, J. K. (1972). On the automatic scaling of matrices for Gaussian elimination. *J. Inst. Maths Applics* **10**, 118.

Cuthill, E. and McKee, J. (1969). Reducing the bandwidth of sparse symmetric matrices. Proc. 24th National Conference, ACM, New York, p. 157.

Duff, I. S. (1972). "Analysis of Sparse Systems". D.Phil. Thesis, Oxford.

Duff, I. S. and Reid, J. K. (1973). A Comparison of Sparsity Orderings for Obtaining a Pivotal Sequence in Gaussian Elimination. To appear in *J. Inst. Maths Applics*.

Erisman, A. M. (1972). Sparse matrix approach to the frequency domain analysis of linear passive electrical networks. *In* Rose and Willoughby (1972), p. 31.

George, J. A. (1971). "Computer Implementation of the Finite Element Method." Ph.D. Thesis. Stanford University report STAN-CS-71-208.

George, J. A. (1972). Block elimination on finite element systems of equations. *In* Rose and Willoughby (1972), p. 101.

Golub, G. H. (1965). Numerical methods for solving linear least squares problems. *Num. Math.* **7**, 206–216.

Gustavson, F. G., Liniger, W. M. and Willoughby, R. A. (1970). Symbolic generation of an optimal Crout algorithm for sparse systems of linear equations. *J. Assoc. Comput. Mach.* **17**, 87.

Hamming, R. W. (1971). "Introduction to Applied Numerical Analysis". McGraw Hill.

Jennings, A. (1966). A compact storage scheme for the solution of symmetric linear simultaneous equations. *Comput. J.* **9**, 281.

Jennings, A. and Tuff, A. B. (1971). A direct method for the solution of large sparse symmetric simultaneous equations. *In* Reid (1971a), p. 97.

Markowitz, H. M. (1957). The elimination form of the inverse and its application to linear programming. *Management Sci.* **3**, 255.

Read, R. (1971). "Graph Theory and Computing". Academic Press, London and New York.

Reid, J. K. (1971a). "Large Sparse Sets of Linear Equations". Academic Press, London and New York.

Reid, J. K. (1971b). A note on the stability of Gaussian elimination. *J. Inst. Maths Applics* **8**, 374.

Reid, J. K. (1972). "Two Fortran Subroutines for Direct Solution of Linear Equations Whose Matrix is Sparse, Symmetric and Positive–Definite". A.E.R.E. report R.7119. HMSO.

Rose, D. J. (1971). A graph-theoretic study of the numerical solution of sparse positive definite systems of linear equations. *In* Read (1971).

Rose, D. J. and Willoughby, R. A. (1972). "Sparse Matrices and Their Applications." Plenum Press.

Schwartz, H. R. (1968). Tridiagonalization of a symmetric band matrix. *Num. Math.* **12**, 231–241.

Tewarson, R. P. (1966). On the product form of inverse of sparse matrices. *SIAM Rev.* **8**, 336–342.

Tomlin, J. A. (1972). Pivoting for size and sparsity in linear programming inversion routines. *J. Inst. Maths Applics* **10**, 289–295.

Wilkinson, J. H. (1961). Error analysis of direct methods of matrix inversion. *J. ACM* **8**, 281.

Wilkinson, J. H. (1965). "The Algebraic Eigenvalue Problem." Oxford University Press.

Wilkinson, J. H. and Peters, G. (1970). The least squares problem and pseudo-inverses. *Comput. J.* **13**, 309–316.

Wilkinson, J. H. and Reinsch, C. (1971). "Handbook for Automatic Computation, Vol. II, Linear Algebra." Springer-Verlag, Berlin.

4. Iterative Sparse Matrix Algorithms

D. J. EVANS

Department of Mathematics,
Loughborough University of Technology
Loughborough, Leicestershire, England

1. Introduction

In this lecture we shall be concerned with algorithms and techniques suitable for the arithmetic manipulation of sparse matrices of very large order on a medium sized computer with limited core memory. Such matrices are derived from problems involving electrical networks, structural analyses, power distribution systems, nuclear reactors and operational research.

Such matrices are usually much too large to be stored directly into the computer memory and consequently careful consideration as to the most suitable solution algorithm must be given.

Generally, an algorithm is a detailed list of instructions requiring no human intuitive or reasoning ability for producing the result. Thus, it would be interesting to explore what effect considerations such as minimum storage requirements, computing time and accuracy have on the chosen algorithms and investigate the efficiency achieved.

The main types of sparse matrices that occur in this range of problems (Evans, 1973a) are

(a) Constant or stepped bandwidth matrices, and

(b) Generally sparse or ordered sparse (striped) matrices.

For the banded matrices, where a fairly regular pattern of non-zero terms occur, programming techniques, to handle the regular sparsity, can be planned ahead and built into the algorithm to take advantage of the situation for both efficient store utilisation and computational purposes.

Zero matrix coefficients within the bandwidth are generally ignored and only a little efficiency is lost if these are few in number. The matrix is always stored in compact form and for a matrix with semi-band width p and order N, only Np vector space storage is required.

For the stepped bandwidth matrix, it is generally more convenient to associate each row with markers or flags indicating the first and last non-zero coefficients in coded form and to handle the computation by incorporating simple test and branch instructions in the inner loop to avoid unnecessary arithmetic work involving zero coefficients.

For the generally sparse and striped matrices, the matrix is always invariably stored in coded form using bit maps, index lists or directed graphs. These techniques certainly reduce the storage requirements to a minimum, but it is also important for the algorithm to handle the matrix elements efficiently within the calculation, and so efficient software techniques to unravel the coded form are essential within the inner loop to exclude all arithmetic operations on the zero matrix coefficients.

Invariably, direct methods of solution are used on the banded matrices and a robust general purpose program code is able to cope adequately with most cases. Reid (1974) has discussed some of these methods earlier in this volume. Iterative methods are mostly used on the generally sparse and striped matrices and for the remainder of this chapter discussion will be focused on some recent ideas on methods which (a) retain the original sparsity of the co-efficient matrix, and (b) those which attempt to keep the fill in terms introduced by the solution algorithm to a minimum level.

2. Basic Iterative Methods

These methods consist basically of relatively simple algorithms i.e., matrix–vector multiplications which convert an initial approximation to the solution into a closer approximation depending only on the given information which is usually the matrix A and the right-hand side vector $\mathbf{b}$. In most cases of practical interest, the methods converge too slowly so acceleration parameters are incorporated to speed up the process in order that satisfactory convregence rates are achieved.

Thus, for the linear system of N equations,

$$A\mathbf{x} = \mathbf{b}, \qquad (2.1)$$

where A is an $(N \times N)$ non singular sparse matrix, $\mathbf{b}$ is an $(N \times 1)$ vector of right-hand sides and $\mathbf{x}$ is the unknown vector solution, we now let

$$A \equiv D - L - U, \qquad (2.2)$$

where

$$D \equiv \begin{bmatrix} d_1 & & & \\ & d_2 & & \mathbf{0} \\ & & \ddots & \\ & & & \\ \mathbf{0} & & & \\ & & & d_n \end{bmatrix},$$

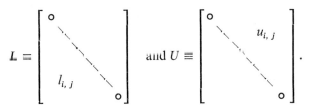

Thus, the D, L and U matrices are composed of the original entries of the matrix A, and the sparseness property of A is retained throughout. The fundamental equation for the basic stationary iterative method (due to Gauss) is obtained by using (2.2) and writing (2.1) in the form,

$$Dx^{(k+1)} = (L + U)x^{(k)} + b, \qquad (2.3)$$

where $x^{(k)}$ denotes the kth iterate to the solution vector x and with the proviso that the process converges. Using simple basic matrix convergence properties (Varga, 1963), we can show that convergence is obtained if and only if the spectral radius of $D^{-1}(L + U)$ is less than 1.

It can be readily confirmed that only the non-zero coefficients are used in the iterative process and thus any structure possessed by the matrix is relatively unimportant in this class of methods although certain types of partitioning can be used to advantage in block iterative methods as will be shown shortly.

Generally, the Gauss method as given by (2.3) converges too slowly for it to be applicable in most practical applications and so some form of acceleration or extrapolation technique is combined with it. Two forms of this idea are in common use i.e., where a constant factor α or a sequence of different factors α_k for each iteration is multiplied by each component of the residual vector $r^{(k)} = b - Ax^{(k)}$ and then added to each component of the present iterate $x^{(k)}$ to give a new value of $x^{(k+1)}$. The relevant equations for these being

$$x^{(k+1)} = x^{(k)} + \alpha r^{(k)} = [I - \alpha D^{-1} A] x^{(k)} + \alpha D^{-1} b, \qquad (2.4)$$

$$x^{(k+1)} = x^{(k)} + \alpha_k r^{(k)} = [I - \alpha_k D^{-1} A] x^{(k)} + \alpha_k D^{-1} b \qquad (2.5)$$

which are the Simultaneous Displacement and Richardson methods, respectively. The constants α, α_k, are given by simple formulae in terms of the extreme eigenvalues of the matrix A i.e., for the eigenvalue spectrum $a < \lambda_i < b$, the methods provide superior convergence rates which can be expressed (in terms of the P condition number $P = b/a$ of A) as $2/P$ and $2/\sqrt{P}$ respectively. (Evans, 1967).

If storage space permits, then methods involving two previous iterates

$\mathbf{x}^{(k)}$, and $\mathbf{x}^{(k-1)}$ by way of a three term recurrence relationship can be expressed as

$$Dx^{(k+1)} = Dx^{(k)} + \alpha \left[\mathbf{b} - A\mathbf{x}^{(k)}\right] + \beta D \left[\mathbf{x}^{(k)} - \mathbf{x}^{(k-1)}\right], \qquad (2.6)$$

and

$$Dx^{(k+1)} = Dx^{(k)} + \alpha_k \left[\mathbf{b} - A\mathbf{x}^{(k)}\right] + \beta_k D \left[\mathbf{x}^{(k)} - \mathbf{x}^{(k-1)}\right], \qquad (2.7)$$

with simple formulae again giving the values for the two acceleration parameters α, β, α_k, β_k which provide the maximum convergence to the solution for the Richardson and Chebyshev 2nd order methods respectively which is again of the order of $2/\sqrt{P}$.

The Gauss–Siedel method which has gained widespread success because of its improved convergence rate over the basic method (2.3) is obtained by utilising the more recently calculated point values $x_i^{(k+1)}, i = 1, 2, \ldots n - 1$ immediately within the same iteration cycle (not a later one as in equation (2.3)). This technique can not only save valuable storage space but also there is a decisive speeding up of the iteration. The method is defined by

$$(D - L)\mathbf{x}^{(k+1)} = U\mathbf{x}^{(k)} + \mathbf{b} \qquad (2.8)$$

and its rate of convergence depends upon the spectral radius of $(D - L)^{-1}U$. However, a basic result when A is symmetric and positive definite $(U = L^T)$ is Ostrowski's theorem, which says that the Gauss–Seidel iteration (2.8) always converges and when the convergence rate of the method is speeded up by extrapolation, then the method given by

$$\mathbf{x}^{(k+1)} = \mathbf{x}^{(k)} + \omega D^{-1} \left(L\mathbf{x}^{(k+1)} + U\mathbf{x}^{(k)} - D\mathbf{x}^{(k)} + \mathbf{b}\right), \qquad (2.9)$$

also converges for $0 < \omega < 2$. However, for general A, it is almost impossible to optimise the iteration further and no guide lines other than experimental exist for determining the extrapolation or over-relaxation factor ω.

A particular successful instance of (2.9) exists for a special important class of matrices A i.e., those derived from finite difference approximations to self adjoint elliptic partial differential equations on a rectangular grid. Young (1954) has shown that for such matrices (possessing special property A) and for certain orderings of the equations (consistent orderings) the spectral radius of the iteration operator of (2.9) can be optimised. In that instance, a functional relationship between the eigenvalues of $(D - \omega L)^{-1} \left((1 - \omega) D + \omega U\right)$ and $D^{-1}(L + U)$ exist which enables the optimum ω to be explicitly determined. The successive over-relaxation method (S.O.R.) then becomes a powerful method which is particularly simple to use and easy to program.

If the matrix A is arranged so that D includes not only the diagonal terms but possibly some off-diagonal terms as well, then we can prove that the method (2.3) is convergent. Also, the convergence rate is increased by taking more off-diagonal elements into D. Thus, for matrices of this type, block iterative methods are advantageous, provided the blocks are suitably chosen. So by partitioning A into the form as in (2.2) and let

$$
D \equiv \begin{bmatrix}
D_1 & & & \\
& D_2 & & 0 \\
& & \ddots & \\
& 0 & & \\
& & & D_m
\end{bmatrix}
\tag{2.10}
$$

where the D_i are square submatrices on the main diagonal. With this alternative formulation, all the previously discussed methods given by equations (2.3) to (2.9) become block methods. In particular the block Gauss–Seidel method

$$
Dx^{(k+1)} = Lx^{(k+1)} + Ux^{(k)} + b
\tag{2.11}
$$

requires the solution of equations involving the sub-matrices $D_1, D_2, \ldots D_k$ at each step of the iteration. Recently, emphasis has been concentrated on discovering new forms of blocks, which if chosen as large as possible as well as giving equations which are easy to solve, results in a faster iterative method. In Benson and Evans (1972), a new form of block method was introduced which has stimulated further work in this area and has led to some interesting new algorithms. (Benson and Evans, 1973a, 1973b).

Essentially, the new blocks are of the form

$$
D_i = \begin{bmatrix}
b_1 & c_1 & & & & a_1 \\
a_2 & b_2 & c_2 & & & \\
& & \ddots & \ddots & 0 & \\
& & & \ddots & \ddots & \\
& 0 & & & \ddots & c_{n-1} \\
c_n & & & & a_n & b_n
\end{bmatrix}
\tag{2.12}
$$

and arise from peripheral orderings of the grid points of a network on which the solution of a self-adjoint elliptic partial differential equation is sought. Particular success has been obtained in the solution of exterior problems which will be reported upon in a later paper.

3. The Application of Preconditioning to a Large Order Sparse Matrix

It is well known that the asymptotic rate of convergence of the basic iterative methods discussed in Section 2 for symmetric positive definite matrices depends inversely on the ratio of the eigenvalue of maximum modulus λ_1 to the eigenvalue of least modulus λ_N which is the P-condition number of the coefficient matrix. Thus, in the quest for a new technique of accelerating convergence, a sensible approach is to attempt to minimise (or reduce to as small as possible) the condition number of the coefficient matrix. This was proposed initially by Evans (1967). The essential parts of the theory are re-iterated here.

Turing (1948), first recognised that a linear system need possess a 'condition number' and that it should depend symmetrically on both A and A^{-1} or specifically on the product of their norms. He thus defined the $\overline{M}$ and $\overline{N}$ condition numbers as follows:

$$\overline{M}(A) = N \max_{i,j} |a_{i,j}| \max_{i,j} |\alpha_{i,j}|,$$

$$\overline{N}(A) = N^{-1} \left(\sum_{i,j} a_{i,j}^2 \right)^{\frac{1}{2}} \left(\sum_{i,j} \alpha_{i,j}^2 \right)^{\frac{1}{2}}, \tag{3.1a}$$

where the terms $(\alpha_{i,j})$ are the inverse of matrix $A = (a_{i,j})$ of order N. In contrast, the results of Von Neumann and Goldstine (1947) on the rounding errors in the Gaussian elimination process were interpreted in terms of the P-condition number (P = Princeton), i.e.

$$P = \lambda_1/\lambda_N \tag{3.1b}$$

In general, for any matrix norm $\| . \|$, we can define its condition number as

$$K(A) = \|A\| . \|A^{-1}\|. \tag{3.2}$$

Where the norms satisfy the relations,

$$\|A\|_1 = \max_j \sum_i |a_{i,j}|,$$

$$\|A\|_\infty = \max_i \sum_j |a_{i,j}|,$$

and $\|A\|_2 = (\text{max. eigenvalue of } A^T A)^{\frac{1}{2}}.$

In the latter case, we call $K_2(A)$ the spectral condition number, and for A real and symmetric, then it can be shown that $K_2(A) = |\lambda_1|/|\lambda_N|$, the previously called P-condition number.

It is also possible to consider mixed condition numbers (Bauer, 1963) such as

$$K_{12}(A) = \|A\|, \|A^{-1}\|_2 \tag{3.3}$$

where $\| \ \|_1$ and $\| \ \|_2$ are 2 different matrix norms i.e. Euclidean, spectral, infinity, etc, but at present there is little evidence as to which to choose as the best indicator of conditioning.

In the numerical work appertaining to this research a variety of condition numbers $P(A)$, $\overline{M}(A)$, $\overline{N}(A)$ and $K(A)$ were considered and in almost every case, fairly broad agreement between the condition numbers as good indicators of the condition or ill conditioning of a linear system was achieved. This will be evident from the numerical results presented in this chapter.

The concept of a minimum condition number (if it exists) is an important one. Since the given system (2.1) is theoretically equivalent to the system,

$$PAQy = c, \tag{3.4}$$

with $c = Pb$, $Qy = x$ and P, Q are non-singular matrices. Thus, the question as to the existence of matrices P and Q for which

$$K(PAQ) \text{ is a minimum,} \tag{3.5}$$

or even the criteria,

$$K(PAQ) < K(A) \tag{3.6}$$

to be satisfied is certainly worthy of detailed attention.

In order to even attempt to seek a solution, it seems of practical computational interest to restrict the form of the P and Q matrices since the matrix product (PAQ) has to be evaluated. A simple choice is for P and Q to be diagonal matrices, for which, the transformation from (2.1) to (3.3) is then a scaling and Bauer (1964) discusses the problem of optimal scaling in the context of the various matrix norms.

An alternative choice is for P and Q to be triangular matrices. Although the question of how best to select them is as yet unanswered, we shall develop this idea further by considering them to be comprised of the existing triangular components of the original matrix with some slight modifications.

The given system (2.1) is first transformed to its symmetric form with unit diagonal entries i.e.

$$D^{-\frac{1}{2}}AD^{-\frac{1}{2}}(D^{\frac{1}{2}}x) = D^{-\frac{1}{2}}b,$$

i.e.,

$$\hat{A}y = (I - \hat{L} - \hat{U})y = d, \tag{3.7}$$

where $\hat{L}$, $\hat{U}$, d and y are defined to be $D^{-\frac{1}{2}}LD^{-\frac{1}{2}}$, $D^{-\frac{1}{2}}UD^{-\frac{1}{2}}$, $D^{-\frac{1}{2}}b$ and $D^{\frac{1}{2}}x$ respectively. This transformation corresponds to a form of scaling or equilibration and improves the condition of the system slightly. (Forsythe and Moler, 1967)

Now, triangular matrices P and Q are sought which will reduce the condition number of the system (3.7) even further. One such form worthy of consideration is when the P and Q matrices are

$$P = (I - \omega\hat{L})^{-1} \quad \text{and} \quad Q = (I - \omega\hat{U})^{-1}. \tag{3.8}$$

By inspection, P and Q can be seen to be modified forms of the triangular components of $\hat{A}$ as given by (3.7) and hence can easily be obtained in all cases.

Thus, the system (3.7) can be rewritten as

$$(I - \omega\hat{L})^{-1} \hat{A}(I - \omega\hat{U})^{-1} [(I - \omega\hat{U})\mathbf{y}] = (I - \omega\hat{L})^{-1}\mathbf{d} \tag{3.9}$$

which with the aid of intermediate transformation vectors $\mathbf{z}$ and $\mathbf{b}_\omega$ given by

$$\mathbf{z} = (I - \omega\hat{U})\mathbf{y}, \quad \mathbf{b}_\omega = (I - \omega\hat{L})^{-1}\mathbf{d} \tag{3.10}$$

and a parameter ω to be defined later, simplifies (3.7) to a new or modified linear system of the form,

$$(I - \omega\hat{L})^{-1} \hat{A}(I - \omega\hat{U})^{-1} \mathbf{z} = \mathbf{b}_\omega$$

or

$$B_\omega \mathbf{z} = \mathbf{b}_\omega. \tag{3.11}$$

Since matrix symmetry has been preserved in both the transformation (3.7) and (3.11), B_ω is thus a symmetric, positive definite matrix. The parameter ω can also be seen to play an important part for when $\omega = 0$, the system reduces to its original form (3.7) and for $\omega = 1$, the system becomes that involved in the Aitken or Gauss–Seidel forward–backward iterative method (Bodewig, 1959) which we know possesses more favourable convergence properties than the Simultaneous Displacement method. Thus, in the context of this theory, we allow ω to play the role of a preconditioning parameter such that as ω varies within a restricted range $0 < \omega < W$ (say), a minimum value of the condition number of B_ω is obtained.

Theoretical and experimental results (Evans. 1967) have shown that the modified or preconditioned system (3.11) does possess a minimum condition number for a certain value of the parameter ω in the range $0 < \omega < 2$. However, this result has only been established for relatively simple forms of matrices i.e., those derived from discrete approximations to ordinary and partial differential equations and integral equations. However, the preconditioning theory as developed here has been applied to very many matrices derived from diverse origins and extremely promising results have been obtained. Recently (Evans, 1937b) established further theoretical and heuristic arguments to substantiate the claim that for a restricted class of matrices a formula to obtain the optimal preconditioning parameter $\bar{\omega}$ can be given and at this optimal value, the P-condition number is minimised to an order of magnitude equivalent to the square root of its original value at $\omega = 0$.

Since the preconditioned system (3.11) is symmetric and positive definite, we can immediately apply the basic iterative methods of Section 2 to the preconditioned system at the optimal value of ω i.e. $\bar{\omega}$. This ensures that the methods will converge at the fastest speeds attainable. Thus, working with the transformed variable z, we have the Preconditoned Simultaneous Displacement method, given by

$$z^{(k+1)} = z^{(k)} + \alpha(b_{\bar{\omega}} - B_{\bar{\omega}} z^{(k)}), \qquad (3.12)$$

the Preconditioned Second Order Richardson method,

$$z^{(k+1)} = z^{(k)} + \alpha(b_{\bar{\omega}} - B_{\bar{\omega}} z^{(k)}) + \beta(z^{(k)} - z^{(k-1)}), \qquad (3.13)$$

and the Preconditioned Second Order Chebychev method,

$$z^{(k+1)} = z^{(k)} + \alpha_k(b_{\bar{\omega}} - B_{\bar{\omega}} z^{(k)}) + \beta_k(z^{(k)} - z^{(k-1)}). \qquad (3.14)$$

In each case, the iteration is continued to convergence in the variable z before the transformations

$$y = (I - \bar{\omega}\hat{U})z \quad \text{and} \quad x = D^{-\frac{1}{2}}y \qquad (3.15)$$

to the required final solution is carried out.

To assess the effectiveness of the preconditioning theory developed here, two problems involving the solution of a very large order sparse matrix derived from the finite difference solution of partial differential equations were analysed and the reuslts compared. The problems were:

1. Two dimensional biharmonic equation using a 13 point finite difference equation over a region involving the unit square with prescribed boundary values and normal second derivatives for mesh sizes $h^{-1} = 7, 10, 20$. It is well known from previous results that the discretised biharmonic operator leads to very ill conditioned linear systems.

2. Three dimensional Laplace operator using a 7 point difference formula for mesh sizes $h^{-1} = 5, 10, 20$ within the unit cube with specified boundary values. This problem leads to particularly large systems of equations of order 64, 729 and 6,859 respectively.

The structure of the coefficient matrix for each problem is shown in Figs. 1(a) and (b) and both are positive definite, sparse and ill conditioned, thus providing valuable test cases for the preconditioning theory.

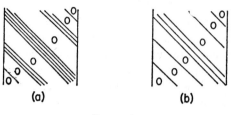

(a)   (b)

FIGURE 1

The performance of the preconditioned iterative methods (3.12), (3.13) and (3.14) on the chosen model problems are shown in the accompanying tables and diagrams. Table I gives the largest and smallest eigenvalues and P-condition numbers for the biharmonic operator with mesh size $h^{-1} = 20$. Clearly, a minimum value for the P-condition number is achieved and this is portrayed for a smaller mesh size in Fig. 2. Similar but less spectacular

TABLE 1. Tabulation of the maximum and minimum eigenvalues and P-condition numbers for the coefficient matrix B_ω versus the preconditioning parameter ω for the Biharmonic operator on a 20×20 rectangular grid.

ω preconditioning parameter	λ_1 maximum eigenvalue	λ_N minimum eigenvalue	$P = \lambda_1/\lambda_N$ P-condition number
0	3·15216	0·001645	1916·2067
0·2	2·13342	0·001739	1226·8085
0·4	1·53845	0·001826	842·5246
0·6	1·19034	0·001859	640·3120
0·8	1·04163	0·002004	519·7754
1·0	1·00000	0·002409	415·1100
1·2	1·04163	0·003385	307·7194
1·4	1·19046	0·005385	221·0696
1·5	1·33333	0·007332	181·8508
1·6	1·56249	0·010519	148·5398
1·7	1·96071	0·015661	125·1970
1·8	2·77342	0·026595	104·2835
1·85	3·57758	0·031349	114·1210
1·9	5·05815	0·035298	143·2985
1·95	8·15428	0·037495	217·4765

results were obtained for the Laplace operator and Fig. 3 shows the P-condition numbers plotted for various values of the preconditioning parameter ω for the three chosen mesh sizes. Finally, Table 2 compares the number of iterations required with and without preconditioning. (Fig. 4). Since the results with optimal preconditioning are vastly superior in iteration

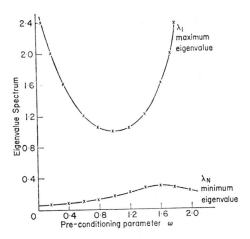

FIGURE 2

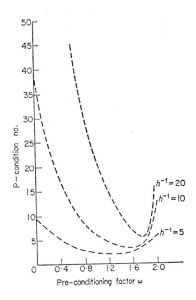

FIGURE 3

TABLE 2. Table giving the P condition numbers and the number of iterations required to achieve an accuracy of 5×10^{-6} for the Preconditioned iterative methods for values of the preconditioning parameter $\omega = 0$ (basic methods) and $\omega = \bar{\omega}$, (optimal preconditioning).

Problem	Grid size h^{-1}	Precond- itioning parameter ω	P condition number P	Precond- itioned Simult. Disp. method	2nd order Precond- itioned Richardson method	2nd order Precond- itioned Chebyshev method
				Number of iterations		
	7	0	48·49	142	17	23
	10	0	286·44	290	40	41
Biharmonic	20	0	1916·21	1432	124	120
operator	7	1·4	4·33	18	8	8
	10	1·6	13·39	54	15	14
	20	1·8	104·28	174	40	36
	5	0	9·47	35	8	15
	10	0	39·86	120	32	30
Laplace	20	0	161·47	480	65	59
operator	5	1·3	1·65	8	8	7
	10	1·6	2·81	11	10	8
	20	1·8	5·42	21	13	14

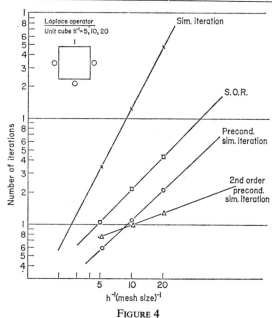

FIGURE 4

count, it is necessary to investigate the feasibility of the proposed computational algorithms and whether the extra arithmetic work involved does not
off set any increase in convergence rate which may have been achieved.

Computational considerations concerning the determination of the
preconditioned matrix B_ω or the vector $B_\omega z$ figure prominently into the
reasons for restricting the choice of P and Q to be inverse triangular in form.
It can be shown that these forms permit simple forward and back subsitution
processes which are easily facilitated on a computer in single or double
precision arithmetic. Furthermore, these operations can also be shown to
preserve any quality of sparsity in the original matrix A whether it is stored in
its usual compact form as a square array in the computer memory or in
generated form on a network of grid points. If A is stored in a compact form,
then the determination of the vector $B_\omega z$ is obtained in the following manner.

$$
B_\omega z =
\begin{bmatrix}
1 & & 0 \\
& \ddots & \\
-\omega l_{i,j} & & 1
\end{bmatrix}^{-1}
\begin{bmatrix}
1 & & -U \\
& \ddots & \\
-L & & 1
\end{bmatrix}
\begin{bmatrix}
1 & & -\omega u_{i,j} \\
& \ddots & \\
0 & & 1
\end{bmatrix}^{-1}
\begin{bmatrix}
z_1 \\
\vdots \\
z_i \\
\vdots \\
z_N
\end{bmatrix}
$$

$$(3.16)$$

$$
\underbrace{(I - \omega L)^{-1}}_{\text{Forward substitution process}}
\underbrace{\quad A \quad}_{\text{Matrix–vector multiplication process}}
\underbrace{(I - \omega U)^{-1} \qquad z}_{\text{Back substitution process}}
$$

The simple algorithms for carrying out these operations are:

the back substitution process,

$$
\mathbf{x} = (I - \omega U)^{-1}\mathbf{z}
$$

$$
x_N = z_N \tag{3.17}
$$

$$
x_j = z_j + \omega \sum_{i=j+1}^{N} u_{j,i} x_i \quad \text{for} \quad j = N-1, N-2, \ldots 1.,
$$

matrix vector multiplication,

$$\mathbf{y} = A\mathbf{x}, \tag{3.18}$$

$$y_i = \sum_{j=i}^{N} a_{i,j} x_j \quad \text{for} \quad i = 1, 2, \dots N.,$$

and forward substitution process,

$$\mathbf{v} = (I - \omega L)^{-1}\mathbf{y}$$

$$v_1 = y_1 \tag{3.19}$$

$$v_j = y_j + \omega \sum_{i=1}^{j-1} l_{j,i} v_i \quad \text{for} \quad j = 2, 3, \dots N.$$

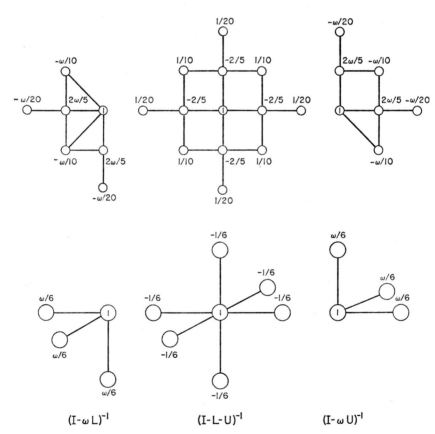

FIGURE 5. Computational molecules for generating the preconditioned matrix vector $B_\omega z$ for the Biharmonic and Laplace operators.

Alternatively, if A is a generated rather than a stored matrix then it has been shown previously that the vector $B_\omega z$ can be obtained from the application of three simple computational molecules applied on the given grid of points which for the chosen problems are shown in Fig. 5. The details of these operations have been given elsewhere (Evans, 1973a). To conclude, the application of preconditioning can lead to a two-fold increase in arithmetical work which must be offset against the greatly increased convergence rates obtained. However, as the experimental results show for large ill conditioned systems, an order of magnitude improvement can be obtained.

4. The Application of Preconditioning to a Small Order Dense Matrix

In a different context, Von Neumann and Goldstine (1947) in a classic paper showed that if we invert a matrix A which is symmetric and positive definite by the Gaussian elimination process and obtain the matrix X as the result, then the rounding errors incurred during the computation are bounded and can be expressed as

$$|\mu| \leqslant 14\cdot24\,P(A)N^2\varepsilon, \tag{4.1}$$

where μ is the eigenvalue of largest modulus of the error matrix $I - AX$, N the order of the matrix A and ε is the smallest number recognisable to the machine (i.e. 2^{-t} for a machine word of t binary digits). When A is symmetric but non-positive definite, then the result becomes

$$|\mu| \leqslant 36\cdot58\,P(A^T A)N^2\varepsilon, \tag{4.2}$$

where

$$P(A^T A) \geqslant [P(A)]^2.$$

Next, by using norms we estimate the error δx on $\mathbf{x}$ the solution of a linear system in which small perturbations on the elements in both the matrix A and the right-hand side vector b have been carried out. Thus, by definition, we have

$$(A + \delta A)(x + \delta x) = b + \delta b, \tag{4.3}$$

from which we can obtain δx in the form,

$$\delta x = (I + A^{-1}\delta A)^{-1} A^{-1}(\delta b - \delta Ax). \tag{4.4}$$

When expressed in spectral norms (4.4) becomes

$$\|\delta x\|_2 \leqslant \|(I + A^{-1}\delta A)^{-1}\|_2 \cdot \|A^{-1}\|_2 \cdot \|\delta b - \delta Ax\|_2 \tag{4.5}$$

where $\|A\|_2$ is the spectral norm and is defined as the maximum eigenvalue of $(A^T A)^{\frac{1}{2}}$.

If we now assume that $\|A^{-1}\| . \|\delta A\| < 1$, so that $I + A^{-1}\delta A$ is non-singular and since for subordinate norms we can use the result

$$\frac{1}{1 + \|A^{-1}\delta A\|} \leqslant \|I + A^{-1}\delta A\| \leqslant \frac{1}{1 - \|A^{-1}\delta A\|}, \qquad (4.6)$$

then the absolute error δx can be given as

$$\|\delta x\| \leqslant \frac{1}{1 - \|A^{-1}\| . \|\delta A\|} . \|A^{-1}\| . (\|\delta b\| + \|\delta A\| . \|x\|). \qquad (4.7)$$

whilst for the relative error, we have

$$\frac{\|\delta x\|}{\|x\|} \leqslant \|A\| . \|A^{-1}\| \left\{ \frac{\|\delta b\|}{\|A\| . \|x\|} + \frac{\|\delta A\|}{\|A\|} \right\} \frac{1}{1 - \|A^{-1}\| . \|\delta A\|}. \qquad (4.8)$$

If we let $k = \|A\| . \|A^{-1}\|$, $\delta_1 = \delta A\|/\|A\|$ and $\delta_2 = \|\delta b\|/\|b\|$, then the relative error can be written in the simpler form,

$$\frac{\|\delta x\|}{\|x\|} \leqslant k(\delta_1 + \delta_2)/(1 - k\delta_1) \qquad (4.9)$$

in which the role of k (or $\|A\| . \|A^{-1}\|$) as an indicator of the relative errors incurred in the solution of a linear system when small perturbations arise in the coefficients is clearly observed.

Thus, from the results given by (4.1) and (4.9) it is reasonable to infer that the accurate inversion or solution of matrices possessing large condition numbers can involve considerable difficulty and may necessitate arithmetic working involving double precision numbers.

Earlier in this section, the preconditioning concept was put forward with some considerable success as an acceleration device for the iterative solution of large order, sparse, ill conditioned matrices. In a different context, we can similarly apply the preconditioning idea to determine the accurate solution of small order dense ill conditioned matrices. For instance, instead of solving a given ill conditioned system (2.1) by an elimination process which may involve multiple precision arithmetic working, we evaluate the alternative precon-ditioned system (3.8) and solve using a similar method but at the optimal preconditioning parameter $\bar{\omega}$ and using single precision working. For this value, we know the condition number to be a minimum. Thus, the rounding errors incurred in the solution process as given by (4.1) will be minimised. Then, the final more accurate solution can be retrieved using the transform-ations given by (3.15).

The validity of these proposals is best assessed by way of illustration and the example chosen is that of the solution of a linear system involving the Hilbert matrix defined by

$$A = (a_{i,j}), \quad \text{where} \quad a_{i,j} = \frac{1}{i+j}, \quad i, j = 1, 2, \ldots N. \quad (4.10)$$

This is an extremely difficult numerical problem for which to obtain accurate results since the matrix A is exponentially ill-conditioned and for $N > 8$, it is well known that multiple precision arithmetic working is necessary to obtain even one significant figure of accuracy.

However, we shall consider the system (2.1) where matrix A is the (7×7) segment of the infinite Hilbert matrix and

$$b^T = (1, 1, \ldots 1)$$

This system is known to have the exact integer solution, given by

$$x^T = (56, -1512, 12600, -46200, 83160, -72072, 24024) \quad (4.11)$$

(Wilkinson, 1967).

We now proceed to evaluate the preconditioned system (3.8) and then analyse numerically the resulting system. The results obtained are shown in the accompanying tables.

The tabulation of the maximum and minimum eigenvalues of the preconditioned matrix B_ω and a comparison of the P, $\overline{M}$ and $\overline{N}$ condition numbers for specific values of the preconditioning parameter ω in the range $0 < \omega < 2$ is given in Table 3. The validity of the proposed preconditioning concept is clearly shown in the condition numbers for criteria (3.6) is attained for all values of $\omega > 0$ and the minimum values achieved by the P and $\overline{N}$ condition numbers are underlined. Then, the preconditioned linear system (3.11) was solved using the Gaussian elimination scheme employing single precision arithmetic working and the solution vector $x_i, i = 1, 2, \ldots N$ obtained was compared with the known integer solution X_i and values of the

$$\text{relative Euclidean error norm } \|E\|_2 = \left\{ \sum_{i=1}^{N} (x_i - X_i)^2 / X_i^2 \right\}^{\frac{1}{2}},$$

$$\text{the maximum error norm } \|E\|_\infty = \max_i |x_i - X_i|, \quad (4.12)$$

$$\text{and error sum norm } \|E\|_1 = \sum_{i=1}^{N} |x_i - X_i|$$

TABLE 3. Values of the maximum and minimum eigenvalues, and the P, $\bar{M}$ and $\bar{N}$ condition numbers versus the preconditioning parameter for the Hilbert (7×7) matrix.

Precondition parameter ω	Maximum eigenvalue λ_1	Minimum eigenvalue λ_N	P-condition number $P = \lambda_1/\lambda_N$	N condition number $\bar{N}$	M condition number $\bar{M}$
0	6·4355135	$0·69015637 \times 10^{-8}$	$9·3247180 \times 10^{8}$	$1·3380665 \times 10^{8}$	$4·8429190 \times 10^{8}$
0·2	2·6261723	$0·84965815 \times 10^{-8}$	$3·0908576 \times 10^{8}$	$4·4924388 \times 10^{7}$	$3·2937520 \times 10^{8}$
0·4	1·5608273	$0·10696886 \times 10^{-7}$	$1·4591417 \times 10^{8}$	$2·1467015 \times 10^{7}$	$3·0503575 \times 10^{8}$
0·6	1·1904719	$0·13775039 \times 10^{-7}$	$8·6422397 \times 10^{7}$	$1·2677513 \times 10^{7}$	$2·3106101 \times 10^{8}$
0·8	1·0416667	$0·18198985 \times 10^{-7}$	$5·7237626 \times 10^{7}$	$8·3377430 \times 10^{6}$	$1·6739379 \times 10^{8}$
1·0	1·0000000	$0·24664801 \times 10^{-7}$	$4·0543608 \times 10^{7}$	$5·8680772 \times 10^{6}$	$1·2956071 \times 10^{8}$
1·1	1·0101010	$0·28936243 \times 10^{-7}$	$3·4907815 \times 10^{7}$	$5·0386286 \times 10^{6}$	$1·1952018 \times 10^{8}$
1·2	1·0416667	$0·34031538 \times 10^{-7}$	$3·0608863 \times 10^{7}$	$4·4077400 \times 10^{6}$	$1·0988947 \times 10^{8}$
1·3	1·0989010	$0·39965590 \times 10^{-7}$	$2·7496179 \times 10^{7}$	$3·9516291 \times 10^{6}$	$1·0066885 \times 10^{8}$
1·4	1·1904726	$0·46576446 \times 10^{-7}$	$2·5559542 \times 10^{7}$	$3·6672176 \times 10^{6}$	$9·1857756 \times 10^{6}$
1·5	1·3332440	$0·53389665 \times 10^{-7}$	$2·4971950 \times 10^{7}$	$3·5781331 \times 10^{6}$	$8·3456663 \times 10^{7}$
1·6	1·5611834	$0·59516712 \times 10^{-7}$	$2·6231009 \times 10^{7}$	$3·9546523 \times 10^{6}$	$7·5465257 \times 10^{7}$
1·7	1·9467588	$0·63754467 \times 10^{-7}$	$3·0535253 \times 10^{7}$	$4·3675111 \times 10^{6}$	$6·7883874 \times 10^{7}$
1·8	2·6513117	$0·65019465 \times 10^{-7}$	$4·0777200 \times 10^{7}$	$5·8293533 \times 10^{6}$	$6·0711521 \times 10^{7}$
2·0	6·9200628	$0·58152764 \times 10^{-7}$	$1·1899800 \times 10^{8}$	$1·7008833 \times 10^{7}$	$4·7597248 \times 10^{7}$

TABLE 4. Values of the Relative Euclidean Norm, Max. Error Norm and Error Sum Norm of the solution vector versus the preconditioning parameter ω for the Hilbert (7×7) matrix

Preconditioning parameter ω	Rel. Euclidean norm	Max. error norm	Error sum norm
0	$0 \cdot 68921355 \times 10^{-3}$	$0 \cdot 58281642 \times 10^{2}$	$0 \cdot 16693410 \times 10^{3}$
0·2	$0 \cdot 72250044 \times 10^{-4}$	$0 \cdot 61149993 \times 10^{1}$	$0 \cdot 17529601 \times 10^{2}$
0·4	$0 \cdot 10600021 \times 10^{-3}$	$0 \cdot 89627525 \times 10^{1}$	$0 \cdot 25663882 \times 10^{2}$
0·6	$0 \cdot 10882085 \times 10^{-4}$	$0 \cdot 92087089 \times 10^{0}$	$0 \cdot 26425385 \times 10^{1}$
0·8	$0 \cdot 51019915 \times 10^{-5}$	$0 \cdot 43143868 \times 10^{0}$	$0 \cdot 12358472 \times 10^{1}$
1·0	$0 \cdot 12558652 \times 10^{-5}$	$0 \cdot 10625491 \times 10^{0}$	$0 \cdot 30450066 \times 10^{0}$
1·1	$0 \cdot 73965627 \times 10^{-6}$	$0 \cdot 62492414 \times 10^{-1}$	$0 \cdot 17873998 \times 10^{0}$
1·2	$0 \cdot 20277181 \times 10^{-6}$	$0 \cdot 17147632 \times 10^{-1}$	$0 \cdot 49160234 \times 10^{-1}$
1·3	$0 \cdot 12987501 \times 10^{-5}$	$0 \cdot 10977093 \times 10^{0}$	$0 \cdot 31408327 \times 10^{0}$
1·4	$0 \cdot 49976562 \times 10^{-7}$	$0 \cdot 42276074 \times 10^{-2}$	$0 \cdot 12131553 \times 10^{-1}$
1·5	$0 \cdot 53371244 \times 10^{-6}$	$0 \cdot 45383661 \times 10^{-1}$	$0 \cdot 13023007 \times 10$
1·6	$0 \cdot 12565888 \times 10^{-6}$	$0 \cdot 10590467 \times 10^{-1}$	$0 \cdot 30335815 \times 10^{-1}$
1·7	$0 \cdot 12914819 \times 10^{-5}$	$0 \cdot 10944292 \times 10^{0}$	$0 \cdot 31485420 \times 10^{0}$
1·8	$0 \cdot 53527207 \times 10^{-5}$	$0 \cdot 45359352 \times 10^{0}$	$0 \cdot 13047195 \times 10^{1}$
2·0	$0 \cdot 52790661 \times 10^{-4}$	$0 \cdot 44627511 \times 10^{1}$	$0 \cdot 12771547 \times 10^{2}$

TABLE 5. Comparison of the exact solution values obtained for no preconditioning ($\omega = 0$) and optimal preconditioning ($\omega = 1 \cdot 4$).

	Exact Solution	Solution at $\omega = 0$	Solution at $\omega = 1 \cdot 4$
	56	$0 \cdot 55931152 \times 10^{2}$	$0 \cdot 55999994 \times 10^{2}$
	-1512	$-0 \cdot 15104398 \times 10^{4}$	$-0 \cdot 15119998 \times 10^{4}$
	12600	$0 \cdot 12588777 \times 10^{5}$	$0 \cdot 12599999 \times 10^{5}$
	-46200	$-0 \cdot 46163771 \times 10^{5}$	$-0 \cdot 46199997 \times 10^{5}$
	83160	$0 \cdot 83101718 \times 10^{5}$	$0 \cdot 83159996 \times 10^{5}$
	-72072	$-0 \cdot 72026326 \times 10^{5}$	$-0 \cdot 72071996 \times 10^{5}$
	24024	$0 \cdot 24010102 \times 10^{5}$	$0 \cdot 24023999 \times 10^{5}$
Rel. Euclidean error norm	0	$0 \cdot 68921353 \times 10^{-3}$	$0 \cdot 42976562 \times 10^{-7}$
Max. error norm	0	$0 \cdot 58281642 \times 10^{2}$	$0 \cdot 42276074 \times 10^{-2}$
Error sum norm	0	$0 \cdot 16693410 \times 10^{3}$	$0 \cdot 12131553 \times 10^{-1}$

evaluated. These are tabulated and given in Table 4. In each case, the error
norm is reduced by a factor of 10^{-4} from its value at $\omega = 0$ (no preconditioning) to its value at $\omega = 1\cdot4$ (optimal preconditioning). In addition, the
solutions at the values $\omega = 0$ and $\omega = 1\cdot4$ are given in Table 5 and verify
further that four more significant figures of accuracy are given when optimal
preconditioning to the system is applied. Finally in Tables 6 and 7, the
error matrix $I - AX$ with and without preconditioning is displayed with
their respective maximum absolute row and column sums. Some of these
results have already been presented (Hatzopoulos, 1972) and are the subject
of a forthcoming paper (Hatzopoulos and Evans, 1973).

Finally, the accurate computation of the preconditioned matrix B_ω can
also be obtained from simple algorithms of forward and back substitution
processes on the rows and columns of A. Single precision arithmetic working
was employed throughout with double length accumulation of inner products.
The algorithms employ forward substitution processes,

$$C = (I - \omega L)^{-1}A \qquad (4.13)$$

for $j = 1, 2, \ldots N$

$$c_{i,j} = a_{i,j}$$

$$c_{k,j} = a_{k,j} - \omega \sum_{i=1}^{k-1} l_{k,i} c_{i,j} \qquad (4.14)$$

for $k = 2, 3, \ldots N$; whereas the further operation

$$B_\omega = C(I - \omega U)^{-1} \qquad (4.15)$$

can either be completed via a similar algorithm to the above on the trans-
posed system

$$B_\omega^T = (I - \omega U)^{-T} C^T \qquad (4.16)$$

or by working on the rows instead of columns, in which case, we have the
back substitution processes,

$$B_\omega = C(I - \omega U)^{-1} \qquad (4.17)$$

for $i = 1, 2, \ldots N$

$$b_{i,1} = c_{i,1}$$

$$b_{i,k} = c_{i,k} - \omega \sum_{j=1}^{k-1} b_{i,j} u_{j,k} \qquad (4.18)$$

for $k = 2, 3, \ldots N$,

The extra work involved in evaluating B_ω is $O(N^3)$ multiplication and is
probably a prohibiting factor in continuing further interest in this application.

TABLE 6. The Error matrix $I - AX$ without preconditioning, $(\omega = 0)$ with values of the maximum absolute row and column sums.

−0·31255768 − 5	0·11223112 − 4	−0·30766608, − 3	0·26428906, − 3	−0·11836918, − 2	0·28388718, − 3	−0·28307047, − 3
−0·52479349, − 5	0·26398557, − 4	−0·37123765, − 3	0·54471971, − 3	−0·13742460, − 2	0·60665311, − 3	−0·32830917, − 3
−0·35822517, − 5	0·20749991, − 4	−0·36099627, − 3	0·17649872, − 3	−0·11256249, − 2	0·32857571, − 3	−0·31528096, − 3
−0·40261011, − 5	0·11122666, − 4	−0·35041292, − 3	0·18209510, − 4	−0·10004090, − 2	0·20207809, − 3	−0·23418204, − 3
−0·22128097, − 5	0·83989595, − 5	−0·25689931, − 3	0·75720014, − 4	−0·41860441, − 2	0·16563649, − 3	−0·17414910, − 3
−0·43395871, − 5	0·14958145, − 4	−0·39962628, − 3	0·38525299, − 3	−0·11086258, − 2	0·36939056, − 3	−0·29350835, − 3
0·30994419, − 5	0·15258789, − 4	−0·30517578, − 3	0·12207031, − 3	−0·85449219, − 2	0·00000000, 0	−0·2746582C, − 3

Max. abs. row sum $= 0·32562121 \times 10^{-2}$.

Max. abs. col. sum $= 0·70656942 \times 10^{-2}$

TABLE 7. The Error matrix $(I - B_\omega Z)$ with optimal preconditioning ($\omega = 1\cdot4$) and values of the maximum absolute row and column sums.

−0·40367013, −7	0·14317054, −6	−0·14540891, −5	−0·18480342, −6	0·27952207, −5	−0·18122676, −4	−0·25903804, −5
−0·49457530, −8	−0·18440187, −6	−0·18165244, −6	−0·30003789, −6	−0·50891019, −5	−0·94231262, −6	−0·15895125, −5
−0·10237080, −7	0·30803272, −7	−0·47839421, −6	−0·11905123, −6	0·13743672, −5	−0·48206287, −5	0·16618698, −5
−0·42407337, −8	−0·13034165, −8	−0·16809194, −6	−0·76179276, −7	−0·29591756, −6	−0·75904450, −6	0·14991355, −5
−0·38409900, −8	0·96293309, −8	−0·14859811, −6	−0·47487304, −7	0·35388803, −6	−0·13668582, −5	0·30536534, −5
−0·20485369, −8	0·51378234, −8	−0·81957235, −7	−0·37245990, −7	0·95857473, −7	−0·49780647, −6	0·16757906, −6
−0·17176403, −8	0·38853402, −8	−0·66156540, −7	−0·24810327, −7	0·17533598, −6	−0·76101240, −6	0·11541124, −6

Max. abs. row sum = $0\cdot22999365 \times 10^{-4}$

Max. abs. col. sum = $0\cdot27270339, 10^{-4}$.

However, in extremely ill conditioned systems this process can be used to advantage in obtaining solutions from the preconditioned system employing only single precision working whereas computations on the original system may necessitate arithmetic working involving multiple precision.

5. Approximate Factorisation of the Coefficient Matrix A

Since the application of direct methods to the large systems we are considering is impractical, iterative methods are usually used. Unfortunately, the standard iterative methods are also deficient in this area. The Jacobi and Gauss–Seidel methods are quite slow even on simple problems whilst the S.O.R. method is dependent on the problem and may also be slow. The A.D.I. method is generally the most efficient of them all. However, it requires the determination of a set of iteration parameters and moreover loses much of the fast convergence properties it possesses when the solution domain is irregular.

The method developed in this section is based on factorisation techniques where sparse lower and upper triangular matrices L_s and U_s (the approximate triangular factors of the coefficient matrix A) are determined in an easy manner.

We consider the quasi-linear diffusion equation of the form.

$$\phi_t = (K\phi_x)_x + (K\phi_y)_y, \qquad K = K(x, y) \tag{5.1}$$

in the region
$$\bar{R} = R \times [0 < t \leqslant T],$$
where
$$R = \{(x, y); \qquad 0 < x, y < 1\}$$

with the initial condition,

$$\phi(x, y, 0) = f(x, y), \qquad (x, y) \in R, \tag{5.2}$$

and the boundary condition,

$$\phi(x, y, t) = g(x, y, t), \qquad (x, y, t) \in \partial R \times [0 \leqslant t \leqslant T], \tag{5.3}$$

where ∂R is the boundary of R.

The region R is now covered by a rectilinear net with mesh spacings h_x, h_y and k in the x, y and t directions and mesh points (x_i, y_j, t_r) where

$$x_i = ih_x, \qquad i = 0, 1, \ldots, m; \qquad y_j = jh_y, \qquad j = 0, 1, 2, \ldots, p;$$
$$t_r = rk, \qquad r = 0, 1, \ldots, T/k.$$

Average central difference approximations to the partial derivatives in (5.1) are now used to derive a Crank–Nicolson type finite difference formula in two space dimensions. Thus, we can write the finite difference discretisation of eqn (5.1) on the chosen grid as a series of five point linear finite difference equations of the form:

$$v_{i,j}\phi_{i,j-1,r+1} + a_{i,j}\phi_{i-1,j,r+1} + b_{i,j}\phi_{i,j,r+1} + c_{i,j}\phi_{i+1,j,r+1} + u_{i,j}\phi_{i,j+1,r+1}$$

$$= d_{i,j,r} \qquad \text{for } 1 \leqslant i \leqslant m - 1 \text{ and } 1 \leqslant j \leqslant p - 1, \qquad (5.4)$$

where

$$v_{i,j} = -kK_{j-\frac{1}{2}}/2h_y^2; \quad u_{i,j} = -kK_{j+\frac{1}{2}}/2h_y^2; \quad a_{i,j} = -kK_{i-\frac{1}{2}}/2h_x^2;$$
$$c_{i,j} = -kK_{i+\frac{1}{2}}/2h_x^2; \quad b_{i,j} = 1 + k[(K_{j-\frac{1}{2}} + K_{j+\frac{1}{2}})/2h_y^2$$
$$+ (K_{i-\frac{1}{2}} + K_{i+\frac{1}{2}})/2h_x^2];$$

and

$$d_{i,j,r} = \phi_{i,j,r} + k[K_{i+\frac{1}{2}}(\phi_{i+1,j,r} - \phi_{i,j,r}) - K_{i-\frac{1}{2}}(\phi_{i,j,r} - \phi_{i-1,j,r})]/2h_x^2$$
$$+ k[K_{j+\frac{1}{2}}(\phi_{i,j+1,r} - \phi_{i,j,r}) - K_{j-\frac{1}{2}}(\phi_{i,j,r} - \phi_{i,j-1,r})]/2h_y^2.$$

When we group the above system of finite difference equations into matrix form, we obtain a quindiagonal matrix of order n ($n = mp$) and of semi-bandwidth p of the form

$$A\phi = d, \qquad (5.5)$$

or

which has to be solved to give the required solution to the problem at each time step.

A parallel investigation into the current solution processes involving the diffusion equation with one space dimension reveals the fact that extensive use is made of the tridiagonal matrix algorithm (Varga, 1962) to solve the linear system involved. However, in the case of the quindiagonal matrix of semibandwidth p no such compact algorithmic solution is known to exist. However, we can derive one which is admirably suitable for our purposes by using the algorithm derived in Evans (1972) for successive peripheral over-relaxation in an echelon process as indicated by the partitioned dotted lines in the matrix.

Thus, the algorithm for the solution of a quindiagonal linear system of semi bandwidth p which can be seen to be a natural extension to the tridiagonal algorithm is given below. We compute the following quantities recursively:

for $i = 1$,

$$g_1 = c_1/b_1, \qquad h_{1,p} = u_1/b_1, \qquad f_1 = d_1/b_1, \tag{5.6}$$

$$G_{p,1} = v_p, \qquad D_{p,1} = b_p, \qquad g_p = c_p \quad \text{and} \quad F_{p,1} = d_p;$$

for $i = 2, 3, \ldots, p - 1$,

$$w_i = b_i - a_i g_{i-1}; \quad g_i = c_i/w_i; \quad f_i = (d_i - a_i f_{i-1})/w_i,$$

$$h_{i,p+k-2} = - a_i h_{i-1,p+k-2}/w_i, \qquad \text{for} \quad k = 2, 3, \ldots, i,$$

$$h_{i,p+i-1} = u_i/w_i,$$

$$G_{p,i} = - g_{i-1} G_{p,i-1}; \qquad D_{p,i} = D_{p,i-1} - G_{p,i-1} h_{i-1,p},$$

$$F_{p,i} = F_{p,i-1} - G_{p,i-1} f_{i-1}; \qquad g_p = g_p - G_{p,i-1} h_{i-1,p+1},$$

$$h_{p,p+k} = h_{p,p+k} - G_{p,i-1} h_{i-1,p+k}, \qquad \text{for} \quad k = 2, 3, \ldots, i;$$

for $i = p$

$$D_{p,p} = [D_{p,p-1} - (G_{p,p-1} + a_p)(g_{p-1} + h_{p-1,p})],$$

$$f_p = [F_{p,p-1} - (G_{p,p-1} + a_p)f_{p-1}]/D_{p,p},$$

$$g_p = [g_{p,p-1} + a_p)h_{p-1,p+1}]/D_{p,p},$$

$$h_{p,p+k-1} = [h_{p,p+k-1} - (G_{p,p+k-1} + a_p)h_{p-1,p+k-1}]/D_{p,p};$$

for $k = 3, 4, \ldots, p - 1$

$$h_{p,2p-1} = u_p/D_{p,p},$$

for $i = p + 1, p + 2, \ldots, n,$

    for $j = i - p + 1,$

       $G_{i,j} = v_i, \quad D_{i,j} = b_i, \quad F_{i,j} = d_i \quad$ and $\quad G_i = c_i,$

    for $j = i - p + 2, i - p + 3, \ldots, i - 1,$

$$G_{i,j} = G_{i,j} - [g_{j-1} + h_{j-1,j}]G_{i,j-1}, \quad a_i = a_i - G_{i,j-1}h_{j-1,i-1},$$

$$F_{i,j} = F_{i,j-1} - G_{i,j-1}F_{j-1}, \quad g_i = g_i - G_{i,j-1}h_{j-1,i+1},$$

$$D_{i,j} = D_{i,j-1} - G_{i,j-1}h_{j-1,i}, \quad G_{i,k} = G_{i,k} - G_{i,j-1}h_{j-1,k}$$

$$\text{for} \quad k = j + 1, \ldots i - 2,$$

$$h_{i,i+k} = h_{i,i+k} - G_{i,j-1}h_{j-1,i+k}, \quad \text{for} \quad k = 2, \ldots, p - 1$$

    for $j = i,$

$$D_{j,j} = [D_{j,j-1} - (G_{j,j-1} + a_j)(g_{j-1} + h_{j-1,j})],$$

$$f_j = [F_{j,j-1} - (G_{j,j-1} + a_j)f_{j-1}]/D_{j,j},$$

$$g_j = [g_j - (G_{j,j-1} + a_j)h_{j-1,j+1}]/D_{j,j}, \quad h_{j,j+p-1} = u_j/D_{j,j},$$

$$h_{j,j+k-1} = [h_{j,j+k-1} - (G_{j,j-1} + a_j)h_{j-1,j+k-1}]/D_{j,j};$$

$$\text{for} \quad k = 3, 4, \ldots, (p - 2).$$

The vector components $\phi_i \, (i = 1, 2, \ldots, n)$ of the solution of (5.5) are given recursively by a back substitution process expressed simply as

$$\phi_n = f_n, \tag{5.7}$$

for $i = n - 1, n - 2, \ldots, 1$

$$\phi_i = f_i - g_i\phi_{i+1} - \sum_{r=i+1}^{i+p} h_{i,r}\phi_r.$$

The above recursive sequence of equations is simply the Gaussian elimination process without interchanges (diagonally dominant matrix) expressed in algorithmic form. It is well known that such an elimination process transforms the original equations into another set of equations for which the transformed matrix is upper triangular. Further, it can be shown that the elimination process is valid provided that none of the leading minors of A, i.e., $b_i - a_i g_{i-1}$ etc. are zero. Since the matrix A derived from the finite difference discretisation of a self-adjoint partial differential equation is symmetric, and positive definite, pivoting techniques are unnecessary, thus preserving the band structure of the original matrix throughout the reduction process. Then, since the elimination procedure is effectively equivalent to multiplying the original matrix A by a lower triangular matrix L, to produce an upper triangular matrix U, we have

$$LA = U \tag{5.8}$$

and

$$LA\phi = U\phi = Ld = f, \tag{5.9}$$

are the equations from which the results are obtained by back substitution. In the notation used in the algorithm, we have the following layouts for the L and U matrices,

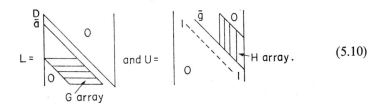

FIGURE 6

The algorithm (5.6)–(5.7) has a compact form which could be of universal use when coded and inserted in a computer program library. However, there are certain unfavourable features which we now enumerate and then attempt to eliminate.

Firstly, it consumes too much storage capacity for although the G, F and D arrays and $\bar{a}$ vector spaces can be overwritten, the g vector, f vector and H array spaces have to be strictly preserved. Secondly, the sparseness of the original matrix A has been irrevocably lost in the transformation to upper triangular form U and this shows itself in the inconvience of having to store the H array in matrix form as well as the time consuming summation product term in the back substitution process. The amount of work involved is also prohibitively high, i.e.,

$$O(p^2n) \quad \text{multiplications for} \quad n \gg p.$$

This algorithm was applied to many of the standard partial differential equations involving two space dimensions of Mathematical Physics and the contents of the H and G arrays scrutinised, for matrices of order 50 and with bandwidths of 10, 15, 20, 30 and 40 respectively. In particular, the error norms of the approximate solutions x_r, i.e., $[\Sigma (X - x_r)^2]^{\frac{1}{2}}$ obtained by including terms only in the bandwidth is expressed graphically by Fig. 7. These results clearly show that the error norm drops 50% in value between retaining two and three terms in the bandwidth. In addition, owing to the leveling off of each of the curves, there seems little point in retaining more than about four fill in terms of the bandwidth. In particular, for every case it was noticed that after the four outermost elements in each column of the H array, the magnitude of the remaining terms decreased rapidly as the matrix diagonal was approached. Thus, a large percentage of the fill-in terms are less than two per cent of the original extreme value occuring in the same position in the initial matrix A. Hence, it is a reasonable approach to re-design the algorithm (5.6)–(5.7) so that only the four outermost terms are retained in the G and H arrays, the remaining terms being just not computed at all. Consequently, a near or approximate factorisation of the matrix is achieved in which both sparseness is retained and storage requirements reduced to a minimum, for the H array can then be stored compactly in four vector spaces. Thus, we see

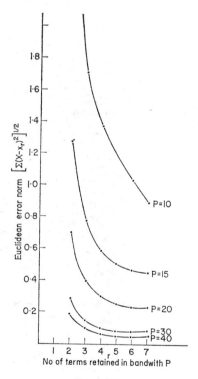

FIGURE 7

an approximate sparse elimination process can be carried out in a similar way as before. In particular, we have,

$$L_s A \approx U_s, \tag{5.11}$$

and the layout of the L_s and U_s matrices are as follows:

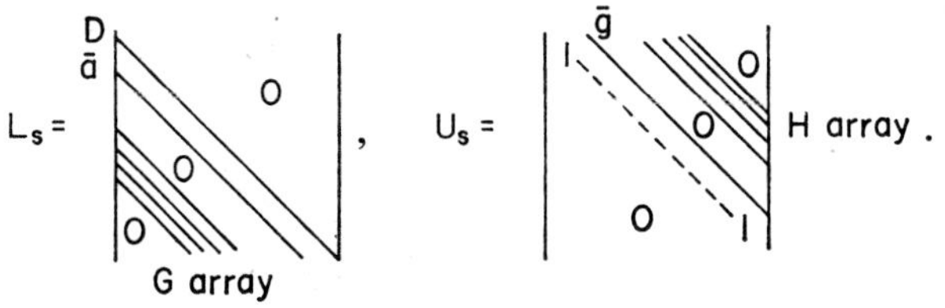

L_s =
D
ā
O
O
O
G array
U_s =
ḡ
I
O
O
O
I
H array .

(5.12)

FIGURE 8

The approximate elimination algorithm (henceforth called the sparse matrix elimination scheme) so obtained for retaining r outermost off-diagonal entries can still be expressed in the same compact form as before. We again calculate the quantities recursively:

for $i = 1$,

$$\begin{aligned} &g_1 = c_1/b_1, \quad h_{1,p} = u_1/b_1, \quad f_1 = d_1/b_1, \\ &G_{p,1} = v_p, \quad D_{p,1} = b_p, \quad g_p = c_p \quad \text{and} \quad F_{p,1} = d_p; \end{aligned} \tag{5.13}$$

for $i = 2(1)p-1$,

$$\begin{aligned} &w_i = b_i - a_i g_{i-1}, \quad g_i = c_i/w_i, \quad f_i = (d_i - a_i f_{i+1})/w_i, \\ &h_{i,k} = -a_i h_{i-1,k}/w_i, \quad \text{for} \quad k = i+p-r, \ldots, i+p-2; \\ &h_{i,p+i-1} = u_i/w_i, \\ &G_{p,i} = -g_{i-1}\, G_{p,i-1}, \quad D_{p,i} = D_{p,i-1} - G_{p,i-1}\, h_{i-1,p}, \\ &F_{p,i} = F_{p,i-1} - G_{p,i-1} f_{i-1}, \quad g_p = g_p - G_{p,i-1}\, h_{i-1,p+1}, \\ &h_{p,p+k} = h_{p,p+k} - G_{p,i-1}\, h_{i-1,p+k}, \quad \text{for} \quad k = p-r, \ldots, i; \end{aligned}$$

$$\begin{aligned} &g_{p-1} = g_{p-1} + h_{p-1,p} \\ &h_{p-1,p} = 0; \end{aligned}$$

for $i = p$,

$$D_{p,p} = [D_{p,p-1} - (G_{p,p-1} + a_p)(g_{p-1} + h_{p-1,p})],$$

$$f_p = [F_{p,p-1} - (G_{p,p-1} + a_p)f_{p-1}]/D_{p,p},$$

$$g_p = [g_p - (G_{p,p-1} + a_p)h_{p-1,p+1}]/D_{p,p},$$

$$h_{p,p+k-1} = [h_{p,p+k-1} - (G_{p,p-1} + a_p)h_{p-1,p+k-1}]/D_{p,p},$$

for $k = p - r + 1, \ldots, p - 1,$

$$h_{p,2p-1} = u_p/D_{p,p};$$

for $i = p + 1(1)n$,

for $j = i - p + 1$,

$$G_{i,j} = v_i, \quad D_{i,j} = b_i, \quad F_{i,j} = d_i \quad \text{and} \quad G_i = c_i;$$

for $j = i - p + 2(1)\,i - 1$,

$$G_{i,j} = G_{i,j} - (g_{j-1} + h_{j-1,j})G_{i,j-1}, \quad a_i = a_i - G_{i,j-1}\,h_{j-1,i-1},$$

$$F_{i,j} = F_{i,j-1} - G_{i,j-1}f_{j-1}, \quad g_i = g_i - G_{i,j-1}\,h_{j-1,i+1},$$

$$D_{i,j} = D_{i,j-1} - G_{i,j-1}\,g_{j-1,i},$$

$$G_{i,k} = G_{i,k} - G_{i,j-1}\,h_{j-1,k}, \quad \text{for} \quad k = j+1, j+2, \ldots, i-2,$$

$$h_{i,i+k} = h_{i,i+k} - G_{i,j-1}\,h_{j-1,i+k}, \quad \text{for} \quad k = p - r, \ldots, p - 1;$$

for $j = i$,

$$D_{j,j} = [D_{j,j-1} - (G_{j,j-1} + a_j)(g_{j-1} + h_{j-1,j})],$$

$$f_j = [F_{j,j-1} - (G_{j,j-1} + a_j)f_{j-1}]/D_{j,j},$$

$$g_j = [g_j - [G_{j,j-1} + a_j)h_{j-1,j+1}]/D_{j,j},$$

$$h_{j,j+k-1} = [h_{j,j+k-1} - (G_{j,j-1} + a_j)h_{j-1,j+k-1}]/D_{j,j},$$

for $k = p - r +, \ldots, p - 1,$

$$h_{j,j+p-1} = u_j/D_{j,j}.$$

The back substitution process is expressed simply as

$$\phi_n = f_n,$$

for $i = n - 1(-1)n - p + r + 1$,

$$\phi_i = f_i - g_i\phi_{i+1}, \tag{5.14}$$

for $i = n - p + r(-1)n - p + 1$,

$$\phi_i = f_i - g_i \phi_{i+1} \sum_{j=i+p-r}^{n} h_{i,j} \phi_j,$$

for $i = n - p(-1)1$

$$\phi_i = f_i - g_i \phi_{i+1} - \sum_{j=i+p-r}^{i+p-1} h_{i,j} \phi_j.$$

Thus, we have developed a sparse matrix elimination scheme in which the storage requirements and computational effort has been kept to a minimum. The amount of arithmetic work needed to implement this algorithm for $n > p$ is $O(n)$ multiplications and divisions, but if the coefficients of the matrix, i.e., a_i, b_i, c_i, u_i and v_i $(i = 1, 2, \ldots n)$ do not change, then for subsequent applications the work reduces to $O(6n)$ multiplications.

We now introduce an iterative procedure for solving numerically the usual five term linear system,

$$A\Phi = d$$

associated with (5.1). The iteration method (Simultaneous Displacement) we shall use has the following form.

$$L_s^{-1} U_s(\Phi^{(k+1)} - \Phi^{(k)}) = \alpha(d - A\Phi^{(k)}), \tag{5.15}$$

where L_s and U_s are the triangular matrices involved in the sparse elimination scheme discussed previously, α a predetermined acceleration parameter or sequence of parameters and the superscript k is an iteration index.

By making use of the well known concepts $r^{(k)} = d - A\Phi^{(k)}$, and $\delta\Phi^{(k+1)} = \Phi^{(k+1)} - \Phi^{(k)}$, a more convenient computational form to (5.15) can be expressed as

$$L_s^{-1} U_s \delta\Phi^{(k+1)} = \omega r^{(k)}, \tag{5.16}$$

or

$$U_s \delta\Phi^{(k+1)} = \omega L_s r^{(k)}. \tag{5.17}$$

This now corresponds closely to the algorithmic form given by (5.13)–(5.14). Thus, for a fixed choice of α, and an initial estimate to the solution $\phi^{(0)}$ a sequence of approximate solutions $\Phi^{(1)}$, $\Phi^{(2)}$, $\Phi^{(3)}$, $\ldots$, $\Phi^{(k)}$ can be obtained by using the algorithm (5.13–5.14).

In addition, 2nd order methods of the form,

$$L_s^{-1} U_s(\phi^{(k+1)} - \phi^{(k)}) = \alpha(d - A\phi^{(k)}) + \beta(\phi^{(k)} - \phi^{k-1}) \tag{5.18}$$

and

$$L_s^{-1} U_s(\phi^{(k+1)} - \phi^{(k)}) = \alpha_k(d - A\phi^{(k)}) + \beta_k(\phi^{(k)} - \phi^{(k-1)}) \tag{5.19}$$

for the Richardson and Chebyshev methods can be formulated in a similar manner.

Initial results obtained from these methods using a fixed value of the acceleration parameter, α and a Chebyshev sequence α_n for the usual model problem are given in the accompanying Table 8 and indicate performances very similar to the Stongly Implicit Method (Dupont 1968), (Stone 1968). Intuitively, one would expect this to be so, for the methods differ only in their solution process techniques, the former uses triangular resolution whilst the later method uses Gaussian elimination.

TABLE 8. Results for the Sparse Elimination algorithm when used to solve the discretised Laplace problem within the unit square with two mesh sizes giving sparse matrices of order 99 and 361 respectively.

Method	h^{-1} mesh size	Basic method Accel. factors α	β	No. of iterations	Sparse elimination method Accel. factors α	β	No. of iterations
1st order simultaneous displacement method	10	1·0	0	120	1·18	0	15
	20	1·0	0	120	1·45	0	33
2nd order Richardson method	10	1·53	0·53	32	0·98	1·04	12
	20	1·73	0·73	65	0·95	1·05	30
2nd order Chebyshev method	10	factor sequence obtained from Evans (1967).		30	factor sequence obtained from Evans (1967).		12
	20			59			30

The advantage to be gained in using an iterative method of solution (i.e. the sparse elimination scheme rather than a direct method, the full elimination scheme) for this type of problem is that the solution only differs slightly from plane to plane. Hence, the solution at the previous time step is a good initial approximation to commence the iteration scheme (5.15), which with the chosen acceleration parameters enables the solution at each step to be obtained correct to an accuracy of 5×10^{-6} in usually five iterations or less.

Current work on this topic involves the application of the Strongly Implicit method in sparse algorithmic form to multi-dimensional problems and to higher order equations yielding more complicated band structure type matrices, i.e., Biharmonic equation, and n dimensional partial differential equations, $n \geqslant 3$. However, as the amount of sparseness decreases, so will the complexity of the sparse LU factorisation or elimination process increase to the extent that it will become too intricate and too involved to handle without an inordinately large amount of extra computational effort. (Weinstein *et al.*, 1969). In addition, Saylor (1973) has reported success in achieving a second order symmetric factorisation with promising results.

It is puzzling to understand the motivation behind this quest to seek the sparse L and U factors of a complicated sparse matrix, because there are available from the matrix itself, copies of the component L and U matrices which are, by definition, sparse, and which could be used in lieu, for similar purposes. These original L and U factors are available with absolutely no work involved and can be obtained from the net itself. This approach has been shown in Section 3 to lead to a powerful class of iteration procedures applicable to the solution of sparse linear systems.

6. Eigensystems of Sparse Matrices

A significant problem in computational linear algebra is finding reliable fast and accurate methods for computing some or all of the eigenvalues $\lambda_1, \lambda_2, \ldots \lambda_N$ of a real N dimensional sparse matrix along with some of the corresponding eigenvectors. For some sparse matrices, in particular those with narrow band form, satisfactory algorithms are already available and these have been dealt with by Reid (1974) in his talk on direct methods.

Briefly, the iterative methods are designed to form sequences of vectors converging to eigenvectors of the matrix A, usually corresponding to the extreme eigenvalues. The basic use of the matrix in these methods is to form the matrix vector product $A\mathbf{v}$, on being given an initial vector $\mathbf{v}$. Usually, for sparse matrices, not even the nonzero elements are stored away as these can be generated when required and all that is needed is a simple procedure for forming the matrix vector product. Obviously, methods which leave the original matrix unchanged are more immediately attractive and easily implemented on a computer. The appeal of such methods as regards storage and time per step is obvious and also their generality makes possible the solution of more general linear operators than matrices.

Direct iteration (power method) with a single vector is the most familiar of these methods, and here convergence is usually to the eigenvector corresponding to the dominant eigenvalue. Deflation could then possibly be used to find the next dominant pair. The trouble with this method is that is it slow, restricted to very few extreme eigenvalues and if more than one is wanted it is cumbersome and even inaccurate for close eigenvalues. Useful generalisations of this method which iterate with several vectors have been developed by Bauer (1958), Jennings (1967), Rutishauser (1969) and others. It is quite clear that this is a very useful method of finding some extreme eigenvalues and eigenvectors of both symmetric and unsymmetric matrices with good accuracy in reasonable time. The obvious drawbacks of such methods are the uncertainty as to how many vectors will be needed and the difficulty of storing several vectors for very large matrices. The fact that only extreme eigenvalues are only found is seldom a drawback as this is usually what is required. It appears, also, that no rounding error analyses have been carried out on the latest techniques.

The remaining direct matrix vector product techniques are based on the fact that if v_1 is an arbitrary vector, and $v_{i+1} = Av_i$, then there will be a vector v_{m+1} ($m \leqslant n$) which is expressible as a linear combination of the preceding v_i. Krylov (Faddeev and Faddeeva, 1963) based a method on these vectors $v_1, v_2 \ldots v_{m+1}$ while the generalised Hessenberg matrices were attempts at producing more accurate methods using related sequences (Wilkinson, 1965). Another ingenious method by Lanczos (1950) has recently been subject of renewed interest by Paige (1972) who has shown that it is perhaps the most appealing of all possible methods for very large sparse matrices. Unfortunately, the original method in its use had a certain defect in its practical application, for the onset of rounding errors in the calculations made it almost impossible to obtain orthogonal vectors without the time and space consuming process of re-orthogonalisation. This had led indirectly to its neglect in favour of the more recent Givens, Householder and Hessenberg methods (Wilkinson, 1965). However, the work of Paige (1972) has sought to reappraise the Lanczos method without using re-orthogonalisation and has given some remarkable computational results which perhaps will be the spur to renew the interest of further researchers in this sadly neglected but nevertheless important area of numerical analysis.

References

Bauer, F. L. (1957). Das Verfahren der Treppeniteration und verwandte Verfahren zur Lösung algebraischer Eigenwertprobleme *Z.A.M.P.* **8**, 214–235.

Bauer, F. L. (1963). Optimally scaled matrices. *Num. Math.* **5**, 73–87.

Benson, A. and Evans D. J. (1972). The successive peripheral block overrelaxation method. *J. Inst. Maths Applics* **9**, 68–79.

Benson, A. and Evans D. J. (1973a). An algorithm for the solution of periodic quindiagonal systems of linear equations. *Comput. J.* **16**, 278–279.

Benson, A. and Evans, D. J. (1973b). A normalised algorithm for the solution of symmetric periodic quindiagonal systems of linear equations. *Comp. Stud. Rep.* 3. L.U.T.

Bodewig, E. (1959). "Matrix Calculus". North Holland, Amsterdam.

Dupont, T. (1968). A factorisation procedure for the solution of elliptic difference equations. *SIAM J. Num. Anal.* 5, 753–782.

Evans, D. J. (1967). The use of pre-conditioning in iterative methods for solving linear equations with symmetric positive definite matrices. *J. Inst. Maths Applics* **4**, 295–314.

Evans, D. J. (1972) A new iterative procedure for the solution of sparse systems of linear difference equations. *In* "Sparse Matrices and their Applications" (Rose, D. J. and Willoughby R. A., Eds.) pp. 89–100. Plenum Press New York.

Evans, D. J. (1973a). The analysis and application of sparse matrix algorithms in the finite element method. *In* "The Mathematics of Finite Elements and Applications" (J. R. Whiteman, Ed.). pp. 427–447. Academic Press, London and New York.

Evans, D. J. (1973b). Comparison of the convergence rates of iterative methods for solving linear equations. Presented at the Carathéodory Centenary Symposium, Greek Mathematical Society, Athens.

Faddeev, D. K. and Faddeeva, V. N. (1963). "Computational Methods of Linear Algebra". W. H. Freeman.

Forsythe, G. E. and Moler, Cleve B. (1967). "Computer Solution of Linear Algebraic Systems". Prentice-Hall, Englewood Cliffs, New Jersey.

Hatzopoulos, M. (1972). "The Use of Pre-conditioning for Solving Ill-conditioned Linear Equations". M.Sc. Thesis, Loughborough University (unpublished).

Hatzopoulos, M and Evans, D. J. (1973). "On the Direct Solution of Pre-conditioned Linear Equations". *Comp. Stud. Rep.* **17**. L.U.T.

Householder, A. S. (1964). "The Theory of Matrices in Numerical Analysis". Blaisdell, New York.

Jennings, A. (1967). A direct iteration method of obtaining latent roots and vectors of a symmetric matrix. *Proc. Camb. Phil. Soc.* **63**, 755–765.

Lanczos, C. (1950). An iteration method for the solution of the eigenvalue problem of linear differential and integral operators. *J. Res. nat. Bur. Stand.* **45**, 255–282.

Paige, C. C. (1972). Computational variants of the Lanczos method for the eigenproblem. *J. Inst. Maths Applics* **10**, 373–381.

Reid, J. K. (1974). This Volume, pp. 29–47.

Rutishauser, H. (1969). Computational aspects of F. L. Bauer's simultaneous iteration method. *Num. Math.* 13, 4–13.

Saylor, P. E. (1973). Second order, strongly implicit, symmetric, factorisation methods for the solution of elliptic difference equations. *SIAM J. Num. Anal.* To be published.

Stone, H. L. (1968). Iterative solution of implicit approximations of multi-dimensional partial differential equations. *SIAM J. Num. Anal.* **5**, 530–558.

Turing, A. M. (1948). Rounding-off errors in matrix processes. *Quart. J. Mech. Appl. Math.* **1**, 287–308.

Varga, R. S. (1963). "Matrix Iterative Analysis". Prentice-Hall, Englewood Cliffs, New Jersey.

Von Neumann, J. and Goldstine, H. H. (1947). Numerical inverting of matrices of large order. *Bull. Amer. Math. Soc.* **53**, 1021–1099.

Weinstein, H. G., Stone, H. L. and Kwan, T. V. (1969). Iterative procedure for solution of systems of parabolic and elliptic equations in three dimensions. *I. and E.C. Fundamentals*, **8**, 281–287.

Wilkinson, J. H. (1965). "The Algebraic Eigenvalue Problem". Clarendon Press, Oxford.

Wilkinson, J. H. (1967). The solution of ill-conditioned linear equations. *In* "Mathematical Methods for Digital Computers" (Ralston, A. and Wilf, M., Eds.). Vol. 2. John Wiley and Sons, New York.

Young, D. (1954). Iterative methods for solving partial difference equations of elliptic type. *Trans. Amer. Math. Soc.* **76**, 92–111

5. Sparse Inverse in the Factored Form and Maintaining Sparsity During Simplex Iterations

G. MITRA

*Department of Statistics and Operational Research,
Brunel University, Uxbridge, Middlesex, England.*

1. Introduction

Some recent works on the sparse representation of the inverse of LP basis matrices have shown considerable improvement over the earlier methods. Hellerman and Rarick (1971) have described an algorithm for identifying structure and reinversion which is fast and also leads to an extremely sparse representation of the inverse. Brayton *et al.* (1969) and Tomlin and Forrest (1971) address themselves to the question of maintaining sparsity at every step of the simplex iteration. The computational results reported in Hellerman and Rarick (1971) and Tomlin and Forrest (1971) are noteworthy.

On reflection, however, two opposite trends between the Tomlin and the Hellerman schemes become evident. By Hellerman's method it is quicker to reinvert and a more sparse inverse is produced than in the earlier methods: hence inversion is carried out more frequently. Tomlin, however, continues to maintain the sparsity of the inverse basis originally expressed in the U^{-1} L^{-1} elimination form. This is achieved by deleting some elements of the transformation matrices whose product constitutes the U^{-1} representation, and replacing one of these with a newly created transformation matrix. In Tomlin's scheme therefore the non-zero build up is not significant, and iteration time does not go up steeply; as a result reinversion is less frequent.

In the present paper it is first demonstrated (Section 2) that any sparse update scheme (Brayton *et al.* 1969; Tomlin and Forrest, 1971) based on *LU* decomposition will not apply to the inverse representation provided by the Hellerman scheme.

Hellerman's algorithm reorders the matrix in the block lower triangular form with as many diagonal matrices as possible. A factorization of this

85

structure is outlined which leads to the convenient computation of a sparse inverse. In Section 3, a method of compactly updating a fully lower-triangular matrix is considered. In Section 4 a method of compactly updating the Heller-man inverse using the concepts developed in Section 3 is described. Some concluding remarks are made in Section 5. The scheme is being currently implemented in the XDLA mathematical programming system for ICL 1900 series computers. The results of the investigations to verify the advantages, if any, of this scheme will be reported in Harrison *et al.* (in preparation).

2. Structure of the Basis Matrix and the Derivation of its Factors†

For an $m \times m$ matrix B if a lower triangular form L is found by reordering the rows and columns, then L is the most desirable form for computing the inverse. For the inverse may be obtained by simply pivoting down the diagonal of the L-matrix and no more non-zero elements than the original L and hence the B-matrix non-zeros may be created. An algorithm to structure B into equivalent L may be found in Hellerman and Rarick (1971) and Orchard-Hays (1968).

However, very few of the basis matrices may be fully reordered into an equivalent L form; hence all the present day inversion schemes by the appli-cation of the above algorithm puts as many columns in the L form as possible. At the termination of the algorithm which reorders the columns explicitly and the rows implicitly the B matrix is always partitioned as,

$$B = \begin{bmatrix} L_{11} & & \\ B_{21} & B_{22} & \\ B_{31} & B_{32} & L_{33} \end{bmatrix} \tag{1}$$

B_{22} is often referred to as the 'bump' matrix and the columns in L_{11}, B_{21}, B_{31} as 'above the bump columns' and the columns in L_{33} 'below the bump columns'; L_{11}, L_{33} are of course lower triangular matrices.

B as partitioned in (1) may be factorised,

$$B = \begin{bmatrix} L_{11} & & \\ B_{21} & B_{22} & \\ B_{31} & B_{32} & L_{33} \end{bmatrix} = \begin{bmatrix} L_{11} & & \\ B_{21} & I & \\ B_{31} & & I \end{bmatrix} \times \begin{bmatrix} I & & \\ & B_{22} & \\ & & I \end{bmatrix} \times \begin{bmatrix} I & & \\ & I & \\ & B_{32} & I \end{bmatrix}$$
$$\times \begin{bmatrix} I & & \\ & I & \\ & & L_{33} \end{bmatrix} \tag{2}$$

† See Orchard-Hays (1968) and Beale (1970).

If the inverses (in the product form) of each of these factors are computed, only B_{22} leads to non-zero build up; for the others no more non-zeros are created than in the original matrix. Beale has suggested a scheme for re-ordering (implicitly) the partition of B in (1), from which the elimination form of the B^{-1}, $B^{-1} = U^{-1} L^{-1}$ is easily computed†.

Rewrite B as,

$$
B = \begin{bmatrix} L_{11} & & \\ _rB_{31} & _{cr}L_{33} & _rB_{32} \\ B_{21} & & B_{22} \end{bmatrix} \tag{3}
$$

where $_rB_{31}$, $_rB_{32}$, are the corresponding B_{31}, B_{32} submatrices with the rows taken in the reverse order. For the matrix $_{cr}L_{33}$ both the rows and the columns are taken in the reverse order.

The B matrix may now be expressed in a factored form from which the elimination form is easily obtained.

$$
B = \begin{bmatrix} L_{11} & & \\ _rB_{31} & _{cr}L_{33} & _rB_{32} \\ B_{21} & & B_{22} \end{bmatrix} = \begin{bmatrix} L_{11} & & \\ _rB_{31} & I & \\ B_{21} & & I \end{bmatrix} \times \begin{bmatrix} I & & \\ & I & \\ & & L_{22} \end{bmatrix}
$$

$$
\times \begin{bmatrix} I & & \\ & I & _rB_{32} \\ & & U_{22} \end{bmatrix} \times \begin{bmatrix} I & & \\ & _{cr}L_{33} & \\ & & I \end{bmatrix} \tag{4}
$$

where $B_{22} = L_{22} U_{22}$, thus to compute the inverses of the middle two factors it is necessary to carry out Gaussian elimination of B_{22}. In (3) and hence in (4) observe that $_{cr}L_{33}$ is an upper triangular matrix. From the first two of these factors the $L^{-1} \equiv (L_m^{-1} L_{m-1}^{-1} \ldots L_m^{-1})$ of the matrix is computed and written to the forward eta file, from the last two taken in that order, but pivoting up the main diagonal from right-hand corner $U^{-1} \equiv (U_1^{-1} U_2^{-1} \ldots U_m^{-1})$ is created and written to the backward eta file.

Advanced mathematical programming systems such as UMPIRE, XDLA, OPHELIE are all known to employ this elimination form of inverse, or some variant. The Hellerman, Rarick (1971) algorithm starts by structuring the B matrix into the partitions shown in (1). Within the bump matrix B_{22} they discover further bumps called external bumps with their right-hand edges defined by external spikes. We shall consider this scheme for a problem with

---

† The factorisation $B = LU$ is often called decomposition into triangular factors; from this the inverse representation $B^{-1} = U^{-1}L^{-1} = U_1^{-1}U_2^{-1} \ldots U_m^{-1}L_m^{-1}L_{m-1}^{-1} \ldots L_1^{-1}$ follows. This form of inverse representation is also referred to as the elimination form of inverse; "elimination" since the L^{-1}, U^{-1} may be obtained by Gaussian Elimination. As opposed to the full Gauss–Jordan transformation, nothing before the current row or column of the diagonal pivotal element is updated (Brayton et al., 1969; Tomlin and Forrest, 1971; Beale, 1970; Markowitz, 1957; Dantzig, 1963).

two external bumps, we shall carry out a reordering to demonstrate that no EFI representation of the Hellorman inverse is possible.

By the application of the structuring algorithm in (Hellerman and Rarick, 1971) let B be partitioned as,

$$
B = \begin{bmatrix} L_{11} & & & \\ D_{21} & D_{22} & & \\ D_{31} & D_{32} & D_{33} & \\ D_{41} & D_{42} & D_{43} & L_{44} \end{bmatrix}
\tag{5}
$$

Comparing (1) with (5) it follows that,

$$
B_{21} = \begin{bmatrix} D_{21} \\ D_{31} \end{bmatrix}, B_{31} = D_{41}, B_{22} = \begin{bmatrix} D_{22} \\ D_{32} & D_{33} \end{bmatrix}; B_{32} = [D_{42}, D_{43}]; L_{33} = L_{44}.
$$

B as expressed in (5) may be factored as,

$$
B = \begin{bmatrix} L_{11} & & & \\ D_{21} & I & & \\ D_{31} & & I & \\ D_{41} & & & I \end{bmatrix} \times \begin{bmatrix} I & & & \\ & D_{22} & & \\ & & I & \\ & & & I \end{bmatrix}
$$

$$
\times \begin{bmatrix} I & & & \\ & I & & \\ & D_{32} & I & \\ & D_{42} & & I \end{bmatrix} \times \begin{bmatrix} I & & & \\ & I & & \\ & & D_{33} & \\ & & & I \end{bmatrix}
$$

$$
\times \begin{bmatrix} I & & & \\ & I & & \\ & & I & \\ & & D_{43} & I \end{bmatrix} \times \begin{bmatrix} I & & & \\ & I & & \\ & & I & \\ & & & L_{44} \end{bmatrix}
\tag{6}
$$

Hellerman's procedure of creating transformation matrices consists of pre-assigning pivots in L_{11}, D_{22}, D_{33}, L_{44}, in the first, second, fourth and sixth factors. In the third and fifth factors unit (diagonal) pivots are used; the etas are created in exactly the same order in which the factors are presented. Note that only the second and fourth factors may lead to the build up of more non-zero elements in the etas than there are non-zeros in the corresponding matrices. In Hellerman's scheme the inverse of the submatrices D_{22}, D_{33} are computed in the product form. The submatrices D_{22}, D_{33} may be LU

decomposed, $D_{22} = L_{22} U_{22}$ and $D_{33} = L_{33} U_{33}$ so that the matrix is further factorised as,

$$
B = \begin{bmatrix} I_{11} & & & \\ D_{21} & I & & \\ D_{31} & & I & \\ D_{41} & & & I \end{bmatrix} \times \begin{bmatrix} I & & & \\ & L_{22} & & \\ & & I & \\ & & & I \end{bmatrix}
$$

$$
\times \begin{bmatrix} I & & & \\ & U_{22} & & \\ & & I & \\ & & & I \end{bmatrix} \times \begin{bmatrix} I & & & \\ & I & & \\ & D_{32} & I & \\ & D_{42} & & I \end{bmatrix}
$$

$$
\times \begin{bmatrix} I & & & \\ & I & & \\ & & L_{33} & \\ & & & I \end{bmatrix} \times \begin{bmatrix} I & & & \\ & I & & \\ & & U_{33} & \\ & & & I \end{bmatrix}
$$

$$
\times \begin{bmatrix} I & & & \\ & I & & \\ & & I & \\ & & D_{43} & I \end{bmatrix} \times \begin{bmatrix} I & & & \\ & I & & \\ & & I & \\ & & & L_{44} \end{bmatrix} \tag{7}
$$

Brayton *et al.* (1969) by an analysis which involves Boolean operations on a 0–1 matrix, and also by experiments have demonstrated that the Elimination Form of Inverse (EFI) is sparser than the Product Form of Inverse (PFI). Experience with proper LP systems has also verified this claim in as much as the inverse obtained from the EFI in (4) turns out to be sparser than the PFI obtained from (2).

Based on these observations it may be claimed that this approach will lead to a sparser inverse representation than that due to Hellerman. Inverse representation that may be obtained from (7) will now be called Partial Elimination Form of Inverse (PEFI).

If, instead of a partial elimination form a full elimination form of the B matrix is sought this leads to the update of subdiagonal matrices such as D_{32} and the consequent loss of sparsity. Let B as expressed in (5) be reordered as,

$$
B = \begin{bmatrix} L_{11} & & & \\ {}_r D_{41} & {}_{cr} L_{44} & {}_r D_{42} & {}_r D_{43} \\ D_{21} & & D_{22} & \\ D_{31} & & D_{32} & D_{33} \end{bmatrix} \tag{8}
$$

or as,

$$
B = \begin{bmatrix} L_{11} & & & \\ {}_r D_{41} & {}_{cr} L_{44} & {}_r D_{43} & {}_r D_{42} \\ D_{31} & & D_{33} & D_{32} \\ D_{21} & & & D_{22} \end{bmatrix} \tag{9}
$$

Observe that either form is comparable to (3), and the subscript r implies that the rows in these submatrices are in the reverse order. By simple pivoting down the diagonal of the matrix (8) or (9) and carrying out Gaussian Elimination and then pivoting up the diagonal again the factors of $L^{-1} U^{-1}$ are created and the elimination form is obtained. Although preassignment of pivots is possible in each of the diagonal submatrices it will lead to the update of subdiagonal matrices D_{32}, etc. Hence the Hellerman inverse may be only put into partial EFI as in (7) but not a full EFI. A method of compactly updating this inverse form is presented in Section 4, which assumes the intial block triangular structure obtained by Hellerman.

3. Updating the Inverse of a Fully Lower Triangular Matrix

A method of compactly updating a fully lower triangular matrix is described in this section. The compact update of the partial EFI described in the next section is based on the scheme developed in this section.

Given the $m \times m$ lower triangular matrix L,

$$
L = \begin{bmatrix}
l_{11} & & & & \\
l_{21} & l_{22} & & & \\
\vdots & & \ddots & & \\
\vdots & \vdots & & l_{kk} & \\
& & & & \ddots \\
l_{m1} & l_{m2} & & l_{mk} & l_{mm}
\end{bmatrix}, \tag{10}
$$

its inverse may be expressed as,

$$
L^{-1} = L_m^{-1} L_{m-1}^{-1} \cdots\cdots L_1^{-1}, \tag{11}
$$

where

$$
L_k^{-1} = \begin{bmatrix}
1 & & & & \\
& 1 & & & \\
& & \ddots & & \\
& & & 1/l_{kk} & \\
& & & -l_{ik}/l_{kk} & \ddots \\
& & & -l_{mk}/l_{kk} & & 1
\end{bmatrix} = I - \frac{1}{l_{kk}}(l_k - e_k)\, e_k' \tag{12}
$$

The above notation is described in detail in Brayton *et al.* (1969) and Tomlin and Forrest (1971), and note that e_k is the unit vector with the kth component unity, e_k is the kth column of the L matrix, and the product in (12) is an outer product of two m-vectors leading to an $m \times m$ matrix.

Consider now the inverse of L_{a_k}, the matrix obtained by replacing the column l_k of the matrix by the column a_k:

$$L_{a_k} = \begin{bmatrix} l_{11} & & a_{1k} & & \\ l_{21} & l_{22} & a_{2k} & & \\ \vdots & \vdots & \vdots & & \\ & & a_{kk} & & \\ & & \vdots & \ddots & \\ l_{m1} & l_{m2} & a_{mk} & & l_{mm} \end{bmatrix}, \tag{13}$$

In the standard product form update the new inverse will be obtained as,

$$L_{a_k}{}^{-1} = (T_k^p)^{-1} L^{-1} = (T_k^p)^{-1} L_m{}^{-1} \dots L_1{}^{-1} \tag{14}$$

where $t_k^p = L^{-1} a_k$ is the updated column of a_k and

$$(T_k^p)^{-1} = I - \frac{1}{t_{kk}} (t_k^p - e_k) e_k' \tag{15}$$

In (14), (15) the subscript k indicates it is the pivot row and the superscript p that it is product form.

If one pretends that instead of full product form update an *ad hoc* reinversion is being carried out for L_{a_k} with a_k pivoting in row k in the kth step, the inverse may be expressed as

$$L_{a_k}{}^{-1} = L_m{}^{-1} \dots L_{k+1}^{-1} (T_k^c)^{-1} L_{k-1}^{-1} \dots L_1{}^{-1}, \tag{16}$$

where

$$t_k^c = L_{k-1}^{-1} \dots L_1{}^{-1} a_k,$$

and

$$(T_k^c)^{-1} = I - \frac{1}{t_{kk}^c} (t_k^c - e_k) e_k'$$

The superscript c this time stands for the compact update scheme. Note that all the L factors are the same as in (11) and $L_k{}^{-1}$ is deleted and replaced by $(T_k^c)^{-1}$.

If a second vector a_s replaces the sth column of L_{a_k} then the inverse $L_{a_k a_s}^{-1}$ may be expressed in the product form as

$$L_{a_k a_s}^{-1} = (T_s^p)^{-1} L_{a_s}{}^{-1} = (T_s^p)^{-1} (T_k^p)^{-1} L_m{}^{-1} \dots L_1{}^{-1} \tag{17}$$

where $(T_s^p)^{-1}$ is computed by relations of the type (14) and (15). In the compact update scheme three cases need to be considered,

$\dots s > k$; in this case

$$L_{a_k a_s}^{-1} = L_m{}^{-1} \dots (T_s^c)^{-1} \dots (T_k^c)^{-1} \dots L_1{}^{-1} \tag{18}$$

where $t_s^c = L_{s-1}^{-1} \dots (T_k^c)^{-1} \dots L_1{}^{-1} a_s$ and $(T_s^c)^{-1}$ is the corresponding transformation matrix formed out of this column using a relationship of the type (13).

... $s = k$; in this case

$$L_{a_k a_s}^{-1} = L_m^{-1} \ldots (T_s^c)^{-1} \ldots L_1^{-1}, \tag{19}$$

where $t_s^c = L_{s-1}^{-1} \ldots L_2^{-1} L_1^{-1} a_s$, and $(T_s^c)^{-1}$ is the corresponding transformation matrix formed out of the t_s^c column by the relationship of the type (15).

... $s < k$; in this case

$$L_{a_k a_s}^{-1} = L_m^{-1} \ldots (T_k'^c)^{-1} \ldots (T_s^c)^{-1} \ldots L_1^{-1}, \tag{20}$$

where $(T_s^c)^{-1}$ is computed as in the last case, and

$$t_k'^c = L_{k-1}^{-1} \ldots (T_s^c)^{-1} \ldots L_1^{-1} a_k, \tag{21}$$

from which the transformation matrix $(T_k'^c)^{-1}$ follows. In this case $(T_k'^c)^{-1}$ needs to be newly updated and $(T_k'^c)^{-1} \neq (T_k^c)^{-1}$.

In all the compactly updated forms of the inverse (16), (18), (19), (20) there are m (hence a fixed number of) transformation matrices which imply the deletion of the corresponding L_k^{-1}, L_s^{-1} matrices. The new etas themselves are transformed by a fewer premultiplying etas than in the PFI; hence the overall non-zeros should be less than the corresponding PFI. The method of compactly updating a nearly triangular inverse matrix by the relationships of the type (18), (19), (20) may be extended to any number of neighbouring matrices; but this approach will be efficient only if the number of updates are very much smaller than the total number of rows or columns in the matrix. For a problem with more than a thousand rows and where inversion takes place every fifty to sixty iterations such an assumption is reasonable. At reinversion the matrix may not be fully structured in the L-form but the Hellerman inverse of course puts it into block lower triangular form. In the next section it will be outlined how this compact update scheme for a fully lower triangular matrix may be extended to the update of the inverse of large sparse matrices displaying block lower triangular structure.

4. Compact Update of the Hellerman Inverse or the Partial Elimination Form of the Inverse

Consider the decomposition of the matrix B', where B' differs from the matrix B in (5) by only one column which is in the third column partition and has entries in all the row partitions of the matrix.

$$B' = \begin{bmatrix} L_{11} & & \bar{P} & \\ D_{21} & D_{22} & \bar{Q} & \\ D_{31} & D_{32} & \bar{D}_{33} & \\ D_{41} & D_{42} & \bar{D}_{43} & L_{44} \end{bmatrix} \qquad (22)$$

$\bar{P}$, $\bar{Q}$ are therefore submatrices with only nonzero column and $\bar{D}_{33}$, $\bar{D}_{43}$ submatrices are different from the submatrices D_{33}, D_{43} by one column only. B' may be factored as,

$$B' = \begin{bmatrix} L_{11} & & & \\ D_{21} & I & & \\ D_{31} & & I & \\ D_{41} & & & I \end{bmatrix} \times \begin{bmatrix} I & & & \\ & D_{22} & & \\ & & I & \\ & & & I \end{bmatrix}$$

$$\times \begin{bmatrix} I & & & \\ & I & & \\ & D_{32} & I & \\ & D_{42} & & I \end{bmatrix} \times \begin{bmatrix} I & & & \\ & I & & \\ & & D_{33}' & \\ & & & I \end{bmatrix}$$

$$\times \begin{bmatrix} I & & P' & \\ & I & Q' & \\ & & I & \\ & & D_{43}' & I \end{bmatrix} \times \begin{bmatrix} I & & & \\ & I & & \\ & & I & \\ & & & L_{44} \end{bmatrix} \qquad (23)$$

Where

$$P' = L_{11}^{-1}\bar{P}$$
$$Q' = D_{22}^{-1}(\bar{Q} - D_{21}L_{11}^{-1}\bar{P})$$
$$D_{33}' = (\bar{D}_{33} - D_{31}L_{11}^{-1}\bar{P} - D_{32}D_{22}^{-1}(\bar{Q} - D_{21}L_{11}^{-1}\bar{P}))$$
$$D_{43}' = (\bar{D}_{43} - D_{41}L_{11}^{-1}\bar{P} - D_{42}D_{22}^{-1}(\bar{Q} - D_{21}L_{11}^{-1}\bar{P})) \qquad (24)$$

Comparing (23) with (6) it follows that the inverse of B',

$$(B')^{-1} = \begin{bmatrix} I & & & \\ & I & & \\ & & I & \\ & & & L_{44} \end{bmatrix}^{-1} \times \begin{bmatrix} I & & P' & \\ & I & Q' & \\ & & I & \\ & & D_{43}' & I \end{bmatrix}^{-1}$$

$$\times \begin{bmatrix} I & & & \\ & I & & \\ & & D_{33}' & \\ & & & I \end{bmatrix}^{-1} \times \begin{bmatrix} I & & & \\ & I & & \\ & D_{32} & I & \\ & D_{42} & & I \end{bmatrix}^{-1}$$

$$\times \begin{bmatrix} I & & & \\ & D_{22} & & \\ & & I & \\ & & & I \end{bmatrix}^{-1} \times \begin{bmatrix} L_{11} & & & \\ D_{21} & I & & \\ D_{31} & & I & \\ D_{41} & & & I \end{bmatrix}^{-1} \qquad (25)$$

will differ from the inverse representation of B^{-1} by the fourth and the fifth factor, counting the factors in the reverse order this time.

Note that although the expressions for the submatrices in (24) look involved these are simply updated from their corresponding B' matrix values by the premultiplication by the inverse of the earlier factors; also observe that only one column in these matrices is updated by this process.

Let a_k be the new column of the B' matrix and let $_1a_k, _2a_k, _3a_k, _4a_k$, be the parts of it in the four different partitions and let $_1\alpha_k, _2\alpha_k, _3\alpha_k, _4\alpha_k$ be the updated (by relation in (24)) parts of it in the four different partitions making up the appropriate columns in the matrices P', Q', D_{33}', D_{43}'. The method of updating the inverse of the two factors, fourth and fifth may now be considered.

Taking the fifth factor first, the update

$$
\begin{bmatrix} I & & & \\ & I & & \\ & & I & \\ & & D_{43} & I \end{bmatrix}^{-1} \rightarrow \begin{bmatrix} I & & P' & \\ & I & Q' & \\ & & I & \\ & & D_{43}' & I \end{bmatrix}^{-1} . \tag{26}
$$

may be carried out by deleting the eta with unit pivot in row k and replacing it by an eta vector

$$
A_k^{-1} = I - ([_1\alpha_k', _2\alpha_k', 0, _4\alpha_k',]') \cdot e_k' \tag{27}
$$

The update of the fourth factor requires transforming D_{33}^{-1} to $(D_{33}')^{-1}$.

If the full B^{-1} is expressed in the original Hellerman form we have by simple product form technique.

$$
(D_{33}')^{-1} = (T_k^p)^{-1} (D_{33})^{-1} \tag{28}
$$

where $t_k^p = (D_{33}^{-1}) (_3\alpha_k)$ and T_k^p is obtained by the relationship given in (15). However, if the modified Hellerman scheme as suggested in Section 2 is followed to obtain a PEFI for B^{-1}, then the compact update schemes as in Brayton et al. (1969) and Tomlin and Forrest (1971) may be applied to produce the update of D_{33}^{-1}, i.e., $(D_{33}')^{-1}$. This is because in this case a full EFI of the D_{33} submatrix is available such that $D_{33}^{-1} = U_{33}^{-1} L_{33}^{-1}$.

It appears that a scheme due to Brayton et al. (1969) fits in the same way as the repeated sequential update scheme outlined in Section 3. For simplicity, the subscripts of the D_{33} submatrix is dropped and we concern ourselves with the problem of updating: $(D')^{-1}$ from $D^{-1} = U^{-1} L^{-1}$ where D' is a neighbouring matrix of D with one column of D replaced by $_3\alpha_k$. Assume that D is a $q \times q$ submatrix and in order to indicate that the transformations corresponding to U^{-1}, L^{-1} start at the middle of the whole set of transformations for B introduce the relative index r so that D^{-1} may be expressed as,

$$
D^{-1} = U_{r+1}^{-1} U_{r+2}^{-1} \dots U_{r+q}^{-1} L_{r+q}^{-1} \dots L_{r+1}^{-1} ; \tag{29}
$$

this also implies that rows $r + 1$ to $r + q$, and columns $r + 1$ to $r + q$ find pivots in this submatrix. The compactly updated $(D')^{-1}$ where $_3\alpha_k$ pivots in row k may be expressed as, (in what follows assume $k = r + \xi$)

$$(D')^{-1} = U_{r+1}^{-1} U_{r+2}^{-1} \ldots T_{r+\xi}^{-1} \ldots U_{r+q}^{-1} L_{r+q}^{-1} \ldots L_{r+1}^{-1} \qquad (30)$$

where

$$t_{r+\xi} = U_{r+\xi+1}^{-1} \ldots U_{r+q}^{-1} L_{r+q}^{-1} \ldots L_{r+1}^{-1} (_3\alpha_k)$$

and

$$t_{r+\xi} = I - (1/t_{r+\xi,r+\xi}) (t_{r+\xi} - e_k) e_k'. \qquad (31)$$

Consider now a matrix which has two columns a_k, a_s which are different from the B matrix; i.e., the column a_s in B'' replaces the sth column of the B' matrix. All the relationships deduced between (22) and (25) holds for the B'' matrix, where

$$B'' = \begin{bmatrix} L_{11} & & \bar{P} & \\ D_{21} & D_{22} & \bar{Q} & \\ D_{31} & D_{32} & \bar{D}_{33} & \\ D_{41} & D_{42} & \bar{D}_{43} & L_{44} \end{bmatrix} \qquad (32)$$

Observe that the equations (22), (25) are now expressed in terms of P'', Q'', D_{33}'', D_{43}'', $\bar{P}$, $\bar{Q}$...etc.

Again the fourth and fifth factors will need to be updated to obtain $(B'')^{-1}$.

Taking the fifth factor first, the update

$$\begin{bmatrix} I & & P' & \\ & I & Q' & \\ & & I & \\ & & D_{43}' & I \end{bmatrix}^{-1} \rightarrow \begin{bmatrix} I & & P'' & \\ & I & Q'' & \\ & & I & \\ & & D_{43}'' & I \end{bmatrix}^{-1} \qquad (33)$$

may be carried out in the same way as in (26) by deleting the eta with unit pivot in row s and replacing it by

$$A_s^{-1} = I - ([_1\alpha_s', {}_2\alpha_s', 0, {}_3\alpha_s']') e_s', \qquad (34)$$

where $_i\alpha_s$, $i = 1, 2, 3, 4$ are the updated columns in P'', Q'', D_{33}'', D_{43}'' obtained from the corresponding partitions of a_s and using the relationship (24).

To update the fourth factor consider the three following cases (in what follows assume $s = r + \sigma$).

(a) $s < k$; in this case

$$(D'')^{-1} = U_{r+1}^{-1} \ldots T_{r+\sigma}^{-1} \ldots T_{r+q}^{-1} U_{r+\xi}^{-1} L_{r+q}^{-1} \ldots L_{r+1}^{-1} \qquad (35)$$

where

$$t_{r+\sigma} = U_{r+\sigma}^{-1} \ldots T_{r+\xi}^{-1} \ldots U_{r+q}^{-1} \ldots L_{r+q}^{-1} \ldots L_{r+1}^{-1}(_3\alpha_s)$$

and

$$T_{r+\sigma}^{-1} = I - (1/t_{r+\sigma,r+\sigma})(t_{r+\sigma} - e_s)e_s'$$ (36)

and $U_{r+\sigma}^{-1}$ is deleted.

(b) $s = k$; in this case

$$(D'')^{-1} = U_{r+1}^{-1} \ldots T_{r+\sigma}^{-1} \ldots U_{r+q}^{-1} L_{r+q}^{-1} \ldots L_1^{-1}$$ (37)

where $T_{r+\sigma}^{-1}$ is calculated exactly as in (31) and $T_{r+\xi}^{-1}$ is deleted.

(c) $s > k$; in this case

$$(D'')^{-1} = U_{r+1}^{-1} \ldots (T_{r+\xi}')^{-1} \ldots T_{r+\sigma}^{-1} \ldots U_{r+q}^{-1} L_{r+q}^{-1} \ldots L_{r+1}^{-1}$$ (38)

where

$$t_{r+\sigma} = U_{r+\sigma+1}^{-1} \ldots U_{r+q}^{-1} L_{r+q}^{-1} \ldots L_{r+1}^{-1} \,{}^{-1}(_3\alpha_s)$$

$$t_{r+\xi}' = U_{r+\xi+1}^{-1} \ldots T_{r+\sigma}^{-1} \ldots U_{r+q}^{-1} L_{r+q}^{-1} \ldots L_1^{-1}(_3\alpha_k)$$

and $T_{r+\sigma}^{-1}$, $(T_{r+\xi}')^{-1}$ are obtained by relationships of the type (31).

This scheme therefore applies to update of one or more vectors pivoting in one or more diagonal square submatrices. As this is an *ad hoc* inverse scheme to obtain the new transformation matrices a premultiplication by the inverse of the earlier factors is necessary.

5. Conclusions

A method of extending the Hellerman inverse by putting it into a Partial Elimination Form of Inverse has been described. A method of compactly updating this form is proposed. The method of Update of the inverse (25) of the block triangular matrix, and the method of updating the submatrices within it (26), (30), (33), (35), (37), (38) are very similar to the simple method outlined in Section 3, (16), (18), (19), (20). In our opinion this scheme is attractive because,

(i) it does not require a full $U^{-1} L^{-1}$ representation of the inverse, which representation is less sparse than PEFI,

(ii) no backward transformation is necessary to create row transformations (see Tomlin and Forrest, 1971),

(iii) if implemented in a GUB scheme special GUB iterations (Beale, 1970) will not pose a problem as they would in (Tomlin and Forrest, 1971).

The only drawback of the scheme seems to be that it requires repeated update of new transformation matrices; although these may be carried out during the Forward Transformation process itself. The problem of implementing this scheme in the XDLA system for the ICL 1900 machine and the results of the experimental investigation will be discussed in a forthcoming report (Harrison *et al.*).

Acknowledgements

The author would like to thank Mr. Z. Herzenshtein of the Applications and Dedicated Systems Division of ICL/DATASKIL for his permission to publish this work which was carried out while the author worked as a consultant in his division. Thanks are also due to the members of the mathematical programming group in that division for their continuing interest and help in this project.

References

Hellerman, E. and Rarick, D. (1971). Reinversion with the preassigned pivot procedure. *Mathematical Programming* **1**, 195–216.

Brayton, R. K., Gustavson, F. G. and Willoughby, R. A. (1969). "Some Results on Sparse Matrices". RC-2332, IBM Research Center, Yorktown, Heights, N.Y.

Tomlin, J. A., Forrest, J. J. H. (June, 1971). "Updating Triangular Factors of the Basis to Maintain Sparsity in the Product Form Simplex Method". Presented to NATO Conference ESLINORE.

Orchard-Hays, W. (1968). "Advanced Linear Programming Computing Techniques", McGraw-Hill, New York.

Beale, E. M. L. (1970). Sparseness in linear programming. *In* "Large Sparse Sets of Linear Equations" (J. K. Reid, Ed.), pp. 1–15. Academic Press, London and New York.

Markowitz, H. M. (1957). The Elimination Form of Inverse and its application to Linear Programming. *Management Sci.* **3**, 255–269.

Dantzig, G. B. (1963). Compact basis triangulation for the Simplex Method. *In* "Recent Advances in Mathematical Programming" (R. L. Grave and P. Wolfe, Eds). pp. 125–132. McGraw-Hill, New York.

Harrison, M., Mitra, G. and Palmer, R. (1973). "The Implementation of a Sparse Inverse Scheme in the Factored Form and Compact Update During Simplex Iterations; and some Experimental Results". DATASKIL Report (in preparation).

Beale, E. M. L., (1970). Advanced Algorithmic Features for General Mathematical Programming Systems, Integer and Non Linear Programming (J. Abadie, Ed.), pp. 87–137. North Holland, Amsterdam.

Discussion: Sparse Matrices

PROF. EVANS. In the least squares problem i.e.,

$$A^T A x = A^T b$$

you advocate the technique of using the factorisation $A = LU$ and premultiplying both sides by L^T to obtain the new system

$$(L^T L) Ux = L^T b.$$

Could you discuss the condition of this system as compared with the original one?

DR. REID. The second system is better conditioned because it has been obtained from the first by analytic multiplication of U^{-T}. We aim for our pivotal strategy to result in $L^T L$ being well-conditioned so that any ill-conditioning is confined to U. Unfortunately, no useful bound for the conditioning of $L^T L$ is available *a priori* but numerical experience is encouraging.

DR. WILKINSON. We have not had any trouble at NPL with the ill-conditioning of $L^T L$.

DR. FLETCHER. A colleague (W. W. Bradbury) and myself (*Num. Math.* **9**, 259–267, 1966) suggested the obvious idea of solving sparse eigenvalue problems by maximising the Rayleigh quotient, using the method of conjugate gradients. Does the panel know of any comparisons of this sort of work with that which they have described? (I seem to remember a recent paper by a Scandinavian numerical analyst on this subject.)

PROF. EVANS. When computing eigenvalues and eigenvectors of large sparse matrices, it is impracticable to use any of the powerful transformation methods available for dense stored matrices. Instead, one has to rely upon some kind of direct iteration involving the matrix. A reliable algorithm of this kind is simultaneous iteration (Rutishauser, H., pp. 284–302 "Handbook of Automatic Computation", Vol. 2). Other powerful algorithms are based on orthogonalisation as in the Lanczos method or the optimisation of the Rayleigh quotient with the conjugate gradient algorithm as you mentioned. These algorithms give a sequence of eigenvalue approximations which converge faster than the vector approximations. I believe an investigation of all these different algorithms is currently underway at the University of Umea, Sweden under the direction of Axel Ruhl.

MR. FORD. (a) What effect would "PAGING" have on the efficiency of the algorithms you have just described? (b) Have you thought of either writing your own

99

handling software work in conjunction with a known local paging algorithm or do you feel this is an unfair strategy when working on a multiprogramming machine? (i.e. other users will have access to the core etc.).

DR. REID. (a) Paging would allow my present program (Curtis and Reid, 1971 algorithm Z) to handle larger problems which would be an enormous advantage to a user with an urgent need to solve a very large problem. The first phase, in which a linked list is used while choosing pivots, would run slowly because of the essentially random way that the non-zeros are referenced. In later phases, in which a new matrix with the same pattern or a new right-hand side is handled, the non-zeros are held by columns so I see no reason why a paging machine should not be almost as efficient as if specially written code were in use to handle backing-store transfers. For the first phase I think it would be better to use a pivotal strategy that does not require the sparsity pattern to be kept updated (e.g. Curtis and Reid, 1971, algorithm X). (b) I don't work with a paging machine so I have not considered these questions.

DR. J. A. MEIJERINK (*Shell Labs., Rijswijk, Netherlands*). I think that the eigen-values of your preconditioned matrix are equal to 1 plus the eigenvalues of the SSOR (a constant* iteration matrix). So by doing your preconditioning k-line-wise I think, you will obtain again better condition numbers.

PROF. EVANS. Although the Preconditioning and SSOR methods appear to be similar I do not agree with your remarks. For instance, for $A \equiv I - L - U$, then the iteration matrix for the Preconditioning method can be shown to be

$$I - (I - \omega L)^{-1} A(I - \omega U)^{-1}$$

which by a similarity transformation can be shown to have the same eigenvalues as the matrix

$$I - (I - \omega U)^{-1}(I - \omega L)^{-1} A.$$

Similarly, the SSOR method can be shown to have the iteration matrix,

$$I - \omega(2 - \omega)(I - \omega U)^{-1}(I - \omega L)^{-1} A.$$

Thus they appear only to be equal when $\omega = 1$.

However, numerical results obtained for the block Preconditioning method where the block submatrices consist of $1, 2, ..., k$ lines give better condition numbers thus confirming your final remark.

DR. T. B. M. NEILL (*P.O. Research Dept.*). In electrical networks one may either obtain a very sparse matrix as in a nodal analysis, or a much smaller but denser matrix, as in a state space analysis. Does the Panel consider the advantages of lower order outweigh the disadvantages of extra density?

DR. REID. I think the concensus of opinion is in favour of treating the network equations by sparsity techniques without doing any preliminary analysis. This approach works well because of the great amount of sparsity present. State analysis is, I understand, out of favour because of the excessive amount of manipulation involved in the generation of the state equations.

PROF. EVANS. My view is similar for sparse matrices of a simple regular form permit easier analysis by way of extrapolation or over-relaxation than a smaller order denser matrix.

MR. THOMAS. Could you give any guide lines as to when we should use a direct method and when to use an iterative method in the numerical solution of elliptic p.d.e.'s?

DR. REID. If finite-differences or simple finite elements are used then the matrices are banded and very sparse (see Section 6). In three dimensions there is little doubt that iterative methods are likely to be more economic. For example if Laplace's equation in a cube is solved by the usual 7-point finite difference formula on an $S \times S \times S$ grid then direct solution requires about $S^7/7$ multiplications whereas SOR needs about $S^4/1 \cdot 3$ multiplications per decimal. In two dimensions the decision is not so clear cut and depends on the fineness of the grid and how well the particular matrix adapts to iterative solution. For Laplace in an $S \times S$ square direct solution requires about $S^4/4$ multiplications and SOR requires about $S^3/1 \cdot 3$ multiplications per decimal.

   If very large and complicated finite elements are used then the matrices are less sparse so that iterative methods are less favourable. In these cases I would therefore expect that direct methods would sometimes be preferable in three dimensions and almost always be preferable in two dimensions.

DR. J. A. ENDERBY (*U.K.A.E.A., Risley*). If the structure of the matrix is banded or step-banded except for a comparatively small number of coefficients in a small number of columns (rows) which fall outside the band, the elimination algorithm should avoid disturbing the band structure where it exists. In such cases any re-ordering carried out in an analysis phase of the calculation is likely to do more harm than good.

DR. REID. Are you sure that the Markowitz strategy would not perform well on your pattern? Of course it is true that here is a substantial computational cost in applying such a strategy and where a good ordering is known beforehand, as in your case, it is probably best simply to use it.

MR. C. G. ESSERY (*Hawker Siddely Aviation*). Could Dr. Reid compare the coded-zero matrix method with the three methods described in the morning session. By coded-zero, I mean holding integers indicating the beginnings and ends of all blocks of consecutive zeros in each column.

DR. REID. This is very comparable with structure 1 of Chapter 5 and would be almost as convenient. Which is the more economical of storage would depend on the actual sparsity pattern. It should be borne in mind that structure 1 is already very economical with just one integer being associated with each non-zero. On the IBM 360/370 integers may be two bytes long and the non-zeros are held in four or (more usually) eight bytes. I do not think your scheme offers any advantage over structure 1 apart from the possibility of saving integer storage.

DR. MITRA. One of the most recent methods of compact storage of sparse matrices utilizes a technique employed by compiler writers in dealing with numeric constants in computer languages. The scheme is best illustrated by an example.

Consider the following 5×5 sparse matrix which should be stored by columns and which has a total of 13 non-zero quantities

$$\begin{bmatrix} 1\cdot 0 & 4\cdot 0 & & & \\ 5\cdot 0 & 1\cdot 0 & 4\cdot 0 & & \\ & 4\cdot 0 & 1\cdot 0 & 4\cdot 0 & \\ & & 4\cdot 0 & 1\cdot 0 & 5\cdot 0 \\ & & & 4\cdot 0 & 1\cdot 0 \end{bmatrix}$$

A usual scheme to represent the vectors in the matrix is illustrated in Fig. 1.

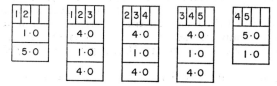

FIGURE 1

This assumes that four integer row indices and one floating point coefficient value may be stored per word of computer storage.

Because the non-zero quantities 1·0, 4·0, 5·0 etc. (depending on the problem) are likely to repeat in practice this can be first entered in a look up table. A pointer to the look up table can then be used in the vector structure, cf. Fig. 2.

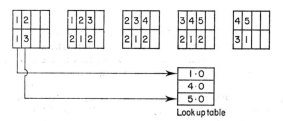

FIGURE 2

With a large repetition of these non-zero values the saving in computer storage can be considerably more.

To give an idea of the sort of numbers which are met in real life I can quote an LP problem with about 97,000 non-zero elements in the matrix for which the look up table is only 4500 entries long.

MR. D. GELDER (*Pilkington Bros. Limited*). (1) Can the speaker suggest means of publicising the advantages of band matrix methods for 2-dimensional P.D.E.'s, and making them easy to use? (2) Is the disappointing performance of partial factorisation with Chebyshev acceleration due primarily to the loss of a real eigenvalue spectrum?

Dr. Reid. (1) I can only suggest that you put a good subroutine in your library. (2) I suspect you may be correct. Consequently I have developed with a colleague, Dr. A. Benson, a symmetric factorisation which is currently under investigation.

Dr. Wilkinson. I would like to make some comments on Paige's work on Lanczos method (for eigenvalues) without re-orthogonalisation. The impression may have been given that re-orthogonalisation serves no purpose. This is certainly not true; re-orthogonalisation is essential if one wants to find the complete eigensystem. However he did show that the process without re-orthogonalisation does enable one to find *some* eigenvalues accurately and showed why a surprisingly small number of iterations often prove to be adequate. His work certainly gives Lanczos a new lease of life on sparse matrices.

6. Numerical Quadrature. A Survey of the Available Algorithms

VALERIE A. DIXON†

1. Introduction

It is now 2,000 years since Archimedes used a form of quadrature to approximate the area of a circle in order to obtain upper and lower bounds for π. Since then, and in particular since the advent of computers, a vast amount of literature has been written on quadrature methods and significant advances are still being made.

This survey has three aims:

(i) to give an up-to-date account of the material that is now available,

(ii) to compare some of the methods in the circumstances to which they are relevant; and

(iii) by way of a summary, to suggest the essential constituents of a versatile quadrature library.

2. General Background

In designing quadrature schemes our aims are twofold. On the one hand it is important that there should be available an array of powerful tools that, when coupled with the knowledge that can match the relevant method to the integral in hand, can efficiently provide an estimate of the integral and some idea of how accurate this estimate is. Moreover, since the late sixties, there has been a trend towards making these quadratures *automatic*, in the sense that each quadrature algorithm is capable of making decisions for itself, thereby lifting much of the burden from the user. Such a scheme is usually called an *automatic integrator*.

† The author is a member of Oxford University, supported on a grant from U.K.A.E.A. (Culham Laboratory) and is at present a guest worker in the Division of Numerical Analysis and Computing, National Physical Laboratory.

On the other hand, in order to relieve the user of having to think at all, there has been an effort to supply general purpose automatic schemes that can each cope with a wide variety of integrals.

This survey will concentrate on automatic schemes, both specialised and general.

2.1. *Automatic Schemes* (*what the user sees*)

An automatic scheme appears to the user as a "black box" (Fig. 1) which, when supplied only with the necessary details of any integral, i.e.

(i) the limits of integration;

(ii) a method of evaluating the integrand for any argument within the range;

(iii) a requested error-bound;

(iv) some "safety-valve" or limit to the amount of computation that may take place,

performs a computation; the user being generally completely unaware of the details. Eventually, and preferably quickly, the black box does one of two things: *either* it produces a reliable estimate of the integral (and by "reliable" we mean that the estimate must be at least as accurate as the user requested or else the scheme is said to have *failed*), *or* it admits that it has not managed

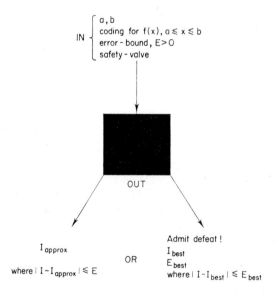

FIG. 1. "Black box" for the evaluation of $I = \int_a^b f(x)\, dx.$

to achieve this accuracy after carrying out the allowed amount of computation. In this case, in order not to waste any effort, it is useful if the scheme can disclose the best estimate that it did achieve (if any) and how good it thinks this estimate is.

Note that the requested error bound may be stated in absolute or relative terms or even as a combination of both. For convenience we restrict attention here to absolute errors only.

It is worthwhile pausing here to consider a few points.

Of course, the aim of "relieving the user of having to think" is highly controversial (Davis and Rabinowitz, 1967; Lyness, 1969a). In the introduction to their excellent book, Davis and Rabinowitz comment on the serious errors that can occur when numerical integration is used in a blind fashion. Furthermore, even a small amount of deliberation over any problem may suggest a method of simplifying it considerably:

"One good thought may be worth a hundred hours on the computer" (Davis and Rabinowitz, 1967).

However, there will always remain a body of users who are either unable or unwilling to provide this effort and it is obviously better for them to use a general scheme which can cope with a diversity of problems, rather than one of the specialised tools in perhaps inappropriate circumstances.

Another problem is that a completely reliable automatic integrator simply does not exist; for any scheme bases its estimate of an integral on a finite sample of integrand values and so the accuracy of the estimate will depend upon how truly the behaviour of the integrand is represented by this sample (Fig. 2). In short, for every automatic scheme it is possible to construct an example, often quite innocent in appearance, for which that scheme will *fail* in the sense described above. Such examples are not confined to the drawing-board but occur quite often in practice!

Note that the smaller the sample the greater the chance of misinterpretation so that any automatic scheme, which builds up a picture of the integrand progressively, is likely to be unreliable in its early stages.

2.2. *Automatic Schemes* (*what the user never sees!*)

Inside the black box an automatic scheme has three main components:

(i) One (or a family of) quadrature rules.

(ii) Some method(s) of estimating the errors incurred by these rules.

(iii) A strategy, which decides how to continue the computation, in the light of the results already obtained, with the ultimate objective of providing an estimate which has the requested accuracy.

Immediately, the objectives of efficiency and reliability are seen to come into conflict; for it is but rarely in practice that we can devise error bounds for a quadrature formula which are both rigorous and sharp. Any useful bounds that we are able to construct will be approximate and so will possess a certain degree of unreliability. In order to make a scheme more reliable, more conservative error estimates have to be used so that reliability is almost always achieved at the expense of efficiency. Fortunately most of us are prepared to sacrifice some efficiency if we thereby obtain more confidence in our answer.

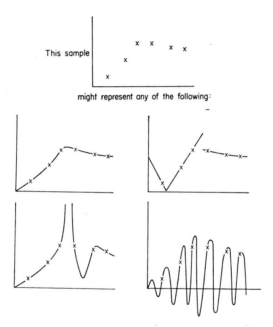

FIG. 2. The difficulty of determining the behaviour of an integrand from a sample of values.

Before considering individual rules it is worth making some general remarks about the strategy component. This is of particular importance since a good strategy will enhance the usefulness of a quadrature rule by providing reliable results, perhaps for a wide class of problem. On the other hand a poor strategy may limit the scope of the scheme or may lead to results which are so unreliable that the rule is rendered virtually useless.

An automatic scheme is classed as *adaptive* if the choice of the points at which the integrand is evaluated is based on or "adapted to" the behaviour of the integrand. Otherwise the method is termed *non-adaptive* or *fixed*.

Clearly, in cases where the range of integration contains a region where the integrand is badly behaved, the method which discovers this and concentrates its attention in that region will obtain more representative information about the integrand and hence a better estimate of the integral than one whose abscissae are pre-assigned.

There are many ways in which such a concentration may be achieved by an adaptive method. One (O'Hara and Smith, 1969) is to attack the range of integration from the left. At any stage the next interval over which to apply the rule is chosen in the light of the information already obtained. This poses the problem of how to start the process and also leads to what de Boor (1971a) calls "Achilles' disease" when some extreme form of integrand behaviour, for example a discontinuity or near singularity, is approached in ever decreasing steps. In fact, the scheme may give up entirely at this point, expecially if the requested error-bound is small. Although in this case we are left without any approximation to the whole integral, the point of failure should be communicated to the user who may be able to utilise this information.

Another method suggested by Cranley and Patterson (1971) is the following. At any step in the computation the range will have been divided into some number of sub-intervals. If the error requirements are met then the applications of the quadrature rule over each of these sub-intervals are aggregated to form the required estimate. Otherwise the sub-interval that makes the largest contribution to the error is subdivided (most probably halved) and the situation for the new number of sub-intervals is appraised. This approach may make large demands on storage but has the advantage that no sub-interval is excluded from further subdivision at any time.

Ideally, we might also expect an automatic scheme to recognise any trouble-spots and, wherever possible, to advise the user of their nature and approximate location in case he wishes to take alternative action.

Finally let us consider the problem of rounding errors. We would expect an automatic scheme to take all possible steps to guard against the build-up of rounding errors during the computation, for example by using double precision for the computation of weighted sums of integrand values. Of course, rounding errors in the evaluation of the integrand are outside the control of such a scheme. Thus it should be alert to the possibility that it might be asked to integrate *noisy data*. This situation could arise, for instance, if the integrand were defined by experimentally determined values or by some computation which gives rise to discretisation errors. If noise is recognised (and this is not always easy) and if the error requirement is within the noise level, the scheme should adjust the error requirement to above the noise level and should inform the user that it has done so. Otherwise the computation will continue until the safety-valve cuts in, with no gain in accuracy but with a large wastage of computing time. Lyness (1969 a, 1969b) is so far one of the few authors to have tackled the noise problem for quadrature. The first paper contains a full discussion of the problem set in the context of automatic schemes.

The ideal automatic scheme described above, that can cope satisfactorily with our requirements of efficiency, reliability and (in some cases)

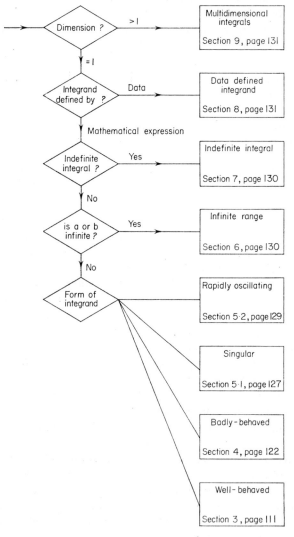

Fig. 3. Classification of $I = \int_a^b f(x)\, dx$.

versatility and that can guard against some of our blunders would be a very rare animal indeed. In the following sections we consider some of the available automatic schemes.

The first type of scheme mentioned above, the powerful tool, is in most cases proposed for a particular class of integrand and for this reason it is convenient to break up the field of possible integrals into idealised regions. Fig. 3 gives a chart which does this very simply and which indicates which section to consult for a certain type of problem.

3. Well-Behaved Integrand and a Finite Range

The simplest type of integral to evaluate is that of a well-behaved integrand over a finite range. By a "well-behaved integrand" we mean one that can be approximated by a polynomial of reasonable degree. This implies that the integrand is continuous and bounded and possesses a sufficient number of continuous and bounded derivatives. In addition we must exclude from this definition any integrand that varies rapidly over some part of the range, for example a highly oscillatory function. Let us assume that the integrand can be evaluated at any point within the range (if not, see Section 8).

For the evaluation of such an integral we shall concentrate on fixed schemes (adaptive methods can be used to evaluate these integrals but they are generally less efficient in this case).

Since almost all quadratures for the evaluation of

$$I = \int_a^b f(x) \, dx \tag{3.1}$$

are essentially a weighted sum of a number (say N) of integrand values, the approximate result may be written in the form

$$I_N = \sum_{j=1}^{N} w_j f(x_j). \tag{3.2}$$

Fixed schemes, as defined in the previous section, are those where the *abscissae* x_j are determined only by the rule that we apply and do not depend in any way upon $f(x)$. (The w_j are called the *weights*.) Fixed automatic methods use a sequence of N-point rules, from a particular family of formulae, which provide successively better approximations to I as N is increased. If the abscissae for any N include those for the previous N, no integrand values are wasted as the scheme progresses and such a sequence is termed *common-point*.

For a fixed scheme, in the absence of a calculable error estimate for the particular family of rules used, it is usual to assess the accuracy attained at any stage by comparing successive estimates of the integral. This has serious drawbacks since:

(i) If the process is converging slowly the difference between successive estimates may be much smaller than the error in either: accepting this difference as an error estimate will lead to failure.

(ii) If the sequence converges quickly the later member is generally much more accurate than this difference would suggest: the error estimate will be very conservative and more work will be done than is really necessary.

(iii) The chance of failure is large for the first few steps (discussed in Section 2.1). Some startling examples of this are given by Clenshaw and Curtis (1960). This can generally be overcome by refusing to accept as final any result which is based on a small sample of points.

Fixed quadratures that have been available since the pre-computer era are those of Newton–Cotes (17th century) and Gauss–Legendre (19th century). More recent methods are Romberg (1955), Clenshaw–Curtis (1960) and Patterson (1968).

3.1. Newton–Cotes Rules

The Newton–Cotes formulae are a familiar family for which the N-point formula is exact for polynomials of degree N (if N odd) or $N - 1$ (if N even). The best known members are the trapezium rule ($N = 2$) and Simpson's rule ($N = 3$). Although the abscissae are equally spaced and the weights are easy to form, this family does not provide a good basis for an automatic scheme for the following two reasons.

The first is that for some functions, which are analytic in the range of integration, the process of applying a sequence of N-point rules may diverge as $N \to \infty$ (although Davis (1955) has proved that the process will converge if the integrand is analytic in a certain elliptic region containing the interval of integration).

The other gives rise to more practical difficulties. For $N > 7$ the weights are of differing size and fluctuate in sign so that rounding errors build up. Although Oliver (1971a) notes that N must be quite large before this effect becomes serious, these two disadvantages, coupled with the low order of the family have been sufficient to exclude a sequence of Newton–Cotes formulae from consideration in automatic schemes.

The low-order formulae, however, can be extremely useful; for instance rules with N less than 11 have been favoured by the designers of adaptive automatic schemes (next section). In addition, most libraries contain routines for the trapezium and Simpson's rules, expressed in compound form, and it is worth making a short digression here to note the circumstances in which the compound trapezium rule is particularly useful.

The Euler–Maclaurin summation formula gives the correction to the compound trapezium rule in terms of the odd derivatives evaluated at the end points only. For an integral of the form (3.1), where $f(x)$ has a continuous $(2k + 1)$th derivative on $[a, b]$, we may write it as follows (see for example Davis and Rabinowitz, 1967, p. 55):

$$\int_a^b f(x)\, dx = h \sum_{i=0}^{N}{}'' f(a + ih) - \sum_{i=1}^{k} h^{2i} \frac{B_{2i}}{(2i)!} \left[f(b)^{(2i-1)} - f(a)^{(2i-1)} \right]$$
$$+ O(h^{2k+1}) \qquad (3.3)$$

where

$$h = (b - a)/N$$

and

$$B_{2i} = i\text{th Bernoulli number } (B_2 = \tfrac{1}{6}, B_4 = -\tfrac{1}{30}, \text{etc}).$$

We see that if the odd derivatives at each end of the range are equal, the trapezium rule will converge extremely rapidly. This is true, for instance, if $f(x)$ is periodic with period $(b - a)$ (see Davis and Rabinowitz, 1967, pp. 57–58 for examples). Alternatively, if the derivatives are zero or extremely small the same will be true and this can be useful when the range is infinite (same reference, pp. 93–94 for examples).

3.2. *Gauss–Legendre Rules*

The Gauss–Legendre formulae have the advantage of extremely high accuracy; their order $2N - 1$ is the maximum possible for an N-point formula and this determines the N points to be the zeros of the Legendre polynomial of degree N. Thus the abscissae and weights are, in general, irrational numbers which have to be stored within any algorithm. (Tables of the abscissae and weights are available from Stroud and Secrest (1966) for values of N up to 512.) Other advantages are that the weights are always positive and that a sequence of N-point formulae will always converge for a function which is continuous and bounded over the range of integration.

Unfortunately these formulae are also unlikely to provide a basis for an automatic scheme since no useful error bounds are available and since it is impossible to construct a common-point sequence. (In fact no two rules have any points in common except the midpoint if both rules are odd.)

Of course, it could be that the extremely high accuracy more than compensates for the wastage in function values—however no sequence of rules can be devised that is competitive with Patterson's family, for instance (see Oliver (1972), where what is probably the best Gauss–Legendre sequence is compared with Patterson's family over a number of examples).

3.3 *Patterson's Family*

In 1965 Kronrod showed how to add a further $N + 1$ points to an N-point Gauss–Legendre formula to produce a $(2N + 1)$-point formula of degree $3N + 1$ (N even) or $3N + 2$ (N odd). These extra $N + 1$ points interlace the original ones.

However, the new estimate I_{2N+1} can only be used to give a better bound on the accuracy of I_N for, although I_{2N+1} is itself much more accurate, we are unable to use the same procedure to determine the extent of its accuracy. This means that if I_N does not satisfy the error requirements we must waste all of the $2N + 1$ integrand values. There is no efficient basis for an automatic scheme here.

However, in 1968 Patterson extended the ideas of Kronrod and showed how to add a further $N + 1$ points to *any* N-point formula to produce a formula with order as above. As an example of the technique he produced a family of rules starting from the 3-point Gauss–Legendre rule and ending with one having 255 points. Since this is a common-point family of fairly high order which possesses good stability and convergence properties it is ideal for an automatic scheme.

It is an easy matter to construct an automatic routine based on this family since the abscissae and weights are readily available (Patterson 1968). ALGOL and FORTRAN versions of such a scheme have recently been added to the N.A.G. library.

3.4. *Romberg Quadrature*

Although this method of quadrature was not expressed in recursive form until Romberg published his account in 1955, the basic idea has been known for 300 years. (Christian Huyghens used it in 1654 to improve the estimates of π obtained by Archimedes.)

The method is particularly simple and the basic algorithm may be accomplished in under 30 lines of ALGOL. Moreover the method lends itself to mathematical analysis and these must be the reasons why it has achieved such popularity since the early sixties, for it has little to recommend it in terms of performance.

The basic Romberg algorithm relies on the h^2 expansion of the error of the trapezium rule, which is given by the Euler–Maclaurin formula in (3.3). The coefficients of the powers of h^2 do not depend in any way upon h, so that for a given integral we may write

$$\int_a^b f(x)\,dx = T_0(h) + a_1 h^2 + a_2 h^4 + a_3 h^6 + \ldots, \tag{3.4}$$

where the a_i are independent of h. The scheme combines two trapezium estimates to knock out the term in h^2; i.e. if

$$T_1(h/2) = \frac{4\,T_0(h/2) - T_0(h)}{3} \tag{3.5}$$

then

$$\int_a^b f(x)\,dx = T_1\left(\frac{h}{2}\right) + b_1 h^4 + b_2 h^6 + \dots. \tag{3.6}$$

The next step is to combine two of these new estimates to eliminate the term in h^4; i.e. if

$$T_2(h/4) = \frac{16\,T_1(h/4) - T_1(h/2)}{15} \tag{3.7}$$

then

$$\int_a^b f(x)\,dx = T_2\left(\frac{h}{4}\right) + c_1 h^6 + c_2 h^8 + \dots \tag{3.8}$$

and so on, as shown in Fig. 4.

$$
\begin{array}{llll}
T_0(h) & & & \\
& \searrow & & \\
T_0(h/2) & \rightarrow T_1(h/2) & & \\
& & \searrow & \\
T_0(h/4) & \rightarrow T_1(h/4) & \rightarrow T_2(h/4) & \\
& & & \searrow \\
T_0(h/8) & \rightarrow T_1(h/8) & \rightarrow T_2(h/8) & \rightarrow T_3(h/8)
\end{array}
$$

etc.

FIG. 4. The T-table for Romberg quadrature.

This process gives a common-point sequence which is stable and which converges if $f(x)$ is sufficiently continuous. The serious drawback is that the number of points must be doubled to increase the order of the process by 2 so that the amount of computation increases exponemtially and soon becomes prohibitive. In addition, if $f(x)$ does not possess a sufficient number of continuous derivatives the h^2 expansion of the trapezium rule is no longer valid and the method becomes hopelessly inefficient. It is not surprising that many modifications of the basic method have been suggested and these have been aimed at the three main areas:

(i) Other sequences of h values, to reduce the exponential growth of computation (Bulirsch, 1964).

(ii) Other error expansions of the trapezium rule, to make the method useful for a wider class of functions (Rutishauser, 1963; Bulirsch and Stoer, 1967; Fox, 1967; Fox and Hayes, 1970; Hunter, 1967; Shanks, 1972; Kahaner, 1972,

(iii) New basic rule (Meir and Sharma, 1965; Lyness, 1972).

Most of these modifications have been discussed in a recent survey paper by Oliver (1971b) so we shall only mention the two most useful ones here.

The optimum sequence of h, for which the amount of computation grows more slowly and yet which is reasonably stable to round-off, is that proposed by Bulirsch (1964) viz

$$h = \tfrac{1}{2}, \tfrac{1}{3}, \tfrac{1}{4}, \tfrac{1}{6}, \tfrac{1}{8}, \tfrac{1}{12}, \ldots.$$

The other modification is due to Bulirsch and Stoer (1967) who proposed that the error expansion of the trapezium rule should be expressed as a rational function of two polynomials in h^2. An example of the effect of these modifications is given in Fig. 5.

In the comparisons at the end of Section 3 we shall incorporate both of these and call the resulting scheme "modified Romberg".

Some of the algorithms which are available for versions of Romberg quadrature are given in Fig. 6.

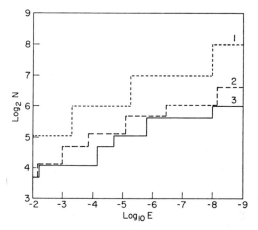

FIG. 5. A comparison of the number, N, of integrand evaluations required to achieve an absolute error, E, for the three types of Romberg quadrature applied to $\int_{-1}^{1} dx/(1 + x^2)$

1. Polynomial extrapolation with $h = (1/2, 1/4, 1/8, 1/16, \ldots)$ (Basic Romberg)
2. Polynomial extrapolation with $h = (1/2, 1/3, 1/4, 1/6, \ldots)$
3. Rational extrapolation with $h = (1/2, 1/3, 1/4, 1/6, \ldots)$ ("Modified Romberg").

3.5. *Clenshaw–Curtis Quadrature*

In the Clenshaw–Curtis (1960) method the range is transformed to $[-1, 1]$ then the integrand $f(t)$ is approximated by a finite Chebyshev series of order N,

$$f(t) = \sum_{i=0}^{N}{}'' a_i T_i(t),\dagger \qquad -1 \leqslant t \leqslant 1.$$

The coefficients of the Chebyshev polynomials are found by collocating with $f(t)$ at the $N + 1$ points

$$\cos\frac{j\pi}{N}, \qquad j = 0, 1, \ldots, N,$$

then the series is integrated term by term.

This method forms a good foundation for an automatic scheme, for by doubling N at each stage a common-point family of rules is generated which is particularly stable to round-off and which always converges if $f(t)$ is bounded and piecewise continuous.

There are also two advantages which the other methods that we have considered have not had. Once the approximate coefficients have been obtained, it is just as easy to compute the indefinite integral as it is the definite. Secondly, since the coefficients of the Chebyshev series are available, it is fairly easy to use them to construct some estimate of the error involved, so that it is unnecessary to proceed to a higher degree formula to check the result (Clenshaw and Curtis, 1960; Fraser and Wilson, 1966; O'Hara and Smith, 1968; Havie, 1969; Gentleman, 1972).

Set against these advantages are two criticisms that have been made of the method. The first is that the Chebyshev recurrence relation used in calculating the coefficients and in evaluating the integral is numerically unstable. A method of overcoming this, which involves a modification to Reinsch's method, has recently been devised by Curtis (see Appendix).

Secondly, the arithmetic cost of calculating the coefficients is large. This can be overcome by either pre-computing and storing the weights and abscissae for the weighted-sum form (3.2) (Fraser and Wilson, 1966) or by employing a fast Fourier transform (FFT) method to compute the coefficients (Gentleman, 1972).

The basic method is available in ALGOL from N.A.G., NPL or CACM Algorithm 279 (Hopgood and Litherland, 1966) and in FORTRAN from N.A.G. A FFT version is available in ALGOL from NPL and in FORTRAN from CACM Algorithm 424 (Gentleman, 1972).

---

† The T_i here are the Chebyshev polynomials of the first kind and should not be confused with the trapezoidal sums, T_i, of the previous section. It is unfortunate that both are standard notation in their separate contexts.

Version	Language	Algorithm Name	Author(s)	Source
Basic Romberg	ALGOL	rombergintegr	BAUER F L	CACM Alg. 60
	ALGOL	havieintegrator	KUBIK R N	CACM Alg. 257
	ALGOL	ROMINT	FAIRWEATHER	CACM Alg. 351
	ALGOL	ROMBERG	GRAM C	BIT, VOL 4, 54–60
	ALGOL	DO1ABA		NAG
	FORTRAN	QUAD	DUNKL C F	DAVIS & RABINOWITZ 1967
	FORTRAN	DO1ABF		NAG
Using Bulirsch's sequence for h	ALGOL	romnevint	BULIRSCH R	BULIRSCH 1964
Using Bulirsch's sequence for h and rational extrapolation ("Modified Romberg")	ALGOL	quadrature	BULIRSCH & STOER	BULIRSCH & STOER 1967

Fig. 6. Published algorithms for Romberg-type quadratures.

3.6. *Comparison of Fixed Schemes for Well-Behaved Integrands over a Finite Range*

Now let us examine the practical performance of these fixed schemes.

The Romberg and Clenshaw–Curtis methods have been in the field for over a decade and there is plenty of evidence, both numerical and theoretical, to show that the "modified" Romberg method is only comparable with that of Clenshaw–Curtis for particularly well-behaved integrands and undemanding error requirements. For the remainder of cases it is generally considerably less efficient (O'Hara and Smith, 1968; Oliver, 1971b and 1972; Gentleman, 1972). Fig. 7 shows a comparison which is typical of the results obtained in a series of tests at NPL. (For the Romberg method the convergence criterion is agreement to within E of three successive values along the main diagonal of Fig. 4, as recommended by Davis and Rabinowitz, 1967.)

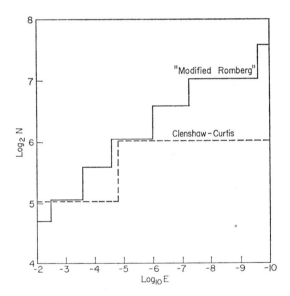

FIG. 7. A comparison of the number, N, of integrand evaluations required to achieve an absolute error, E, for "Modified" Romberg and Clenshaw–Curtis quadratures applied to $\int_{-1}^{1} dx/(x^2 + \frac{1}{4})$.

In making such a comparison we follow common practice by using N, the number of integrand evaluations required to achieve a given tolerance E, as a measure of the efficiency of a method. This measure, of course, takes no account of the amount of internal "housekeeping" carried out by the method.

However, for large N it is generally true that the time spent in obtaining integrand values is dominant, while for small N the distinction is not really important since, *ipso facto*, the evaluation of the integral is a simple matter.

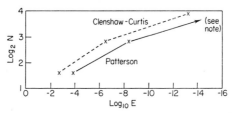

FIG. 8. A comparison of Patterson and Clenshaw–Curtis methods for $\int_0^1 dx/(1+x^2)$ (Note: for Patterson's method the accuracy achieved with 15 points is in excess of 16 digits.

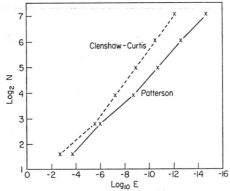

FIG. 9. A comparison of Patterson and Clenshaw–Curtis methods for $\int_0^1 x^{3/2}\,dx$.

There is not as much information available on the relative merits of the Patterson and Clenshaw–Curtis formulae. The only published results (Cranley and Patterson, 1971; Oliver, 1972) compare the accuracy of the two methods "point for point", i.e. take no account of the fact that for Patterson's family the next higher rule must also be evaluated to check the error while for Clenshaw–Curtis the use of a good error bound will eliminate this. Fig. 8 and 9 compare their performance "point for point" on two simple examples, Figs 10 and 11 on two which are more difficult. (The lines joining the points have no significance; they serve only to link the points belonging to each method.) These examples are taken from Cranley and Patterson (1971).

On the other hand, Fig. 12 shows how the picture changes when the practical implementation of the methods is taken into account. Here, as in

Figs 5 and 7, the number of integrand evaluations needed by the automatic implementation to satisfy the appropriate convergence criterion is plotted against the requested absolute error. The error estimate used in the Clenshaw–Curtis scheme is that suggested by Clenshaw and Curtis (1960) for a Chebyshev expansion that converges fairly rapidly. (As in Figs 5 and 7 the lines are again significant.) This figure should be compared with Fig. 9.

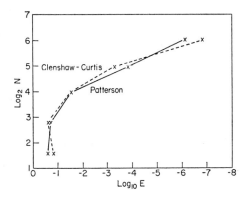

FIG. 10. A comparison of Patterson and Clenshaw–Curtis methods for

$$\int_0^1 \frac{4dx}{1 + 256(x - 3/8)^2}$$

(For $N = 127$ the accuracy is in excess of 16 digits for both methods.)

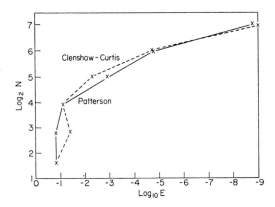

FIG. 11. A comparison of Patterson and Clenshaw–Curtis methods for

$$\int_0^1 \frac{dx}{1 + \frac{1}{2}\sin 10\pi x}.$$

A routine based on either of these methods would be a valuable addition to any program library and, since the difference in their performance is slight, it would be partial to recommend one in preference to the other.

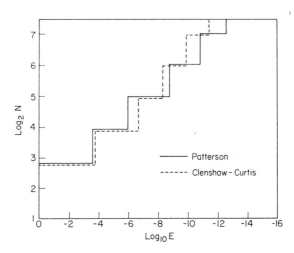

FIG. 12. A comparison of the number, N, of integrand evaluations required to achieve an absolute error, E, for the "automatic" implementations of Patterson and Clenshaw–Curtis quadratures applied to $\int_0^1 x^{3/2}\, dx$ (compare with Fig. 9).

4. Badly-Behaved Integrands over a Finite Range

4.1. *Available Schemes*

We have seen that the well-behaved integrands can be integrated satisfactorily by whole interval formulae. However, if the integrand behaves in a non-polynomial manner in some part of the range (e.g. discontinuous integrand or first derivative, rapidly oscillating integrand), these methods become extremely inefficient. They have to take enough points to fit a sufficiently high order polynomial to the integrand *over the whole range* and it takes them a long time to reach this stage.

It is in this area that general adaptive routines become necessary and Fig. 13 gives a list of some of the available ones. Since it would be a lengthy task to discuss these individually we give only a general summary.

Whereas fixed schemes use a series of rules over one interval, adaptive schemes generally use one rule over a series of subintervals. This rule is usually of low order so that assessments may be made rapidly and so that few, if any, integrand values are wasted when an interval is subdivided. The Newton–Cotes formulae are useful here, since their abscissae are equally

Type of Rule	Number points	Name	Language	Author(s)	
Newton–Cotes	3	SQUANK	F	LYNESS	1970
	3	SIMPSON	A,F	McKEEMAN & TESLER	1963
	5	INT5PT	A	MILLER	1971
	7	QNC7	F	KAHANER	1971
	10	QUAD	F	KAHANER	1971
Gauss	5 & 7	GAUSS	F	MELENDEZ & KAHANER	
	3	GAUSS[1]	F	ROBINSON	1971
	10	AIND[2]		PIESSENS	1973
Clenshaw–Curtis		ADAPQUAD	A	OLIVER	1972
		SPLITABS[1, 3]	F	O'HARA & SMITH	1969
	7	——[1]	—	CRANLEY & PATTERSON	1971
Romberg		RBUN	F	BUNTON	1970b
		CADRE	F	DE BOOR	1971

Fig. 13. General adaptive quadrature routines. [1] Method and results published but no coding. [2] I am grateful to B. Einarsson who brought this routine to my attention after the conference. [3] A Clenshaw–Curtis 7-point/Romberg 9-point hybrid.

spaced, and we include two methods based on Simpson's rule and three based respectively on the 5-, 7- and 10 point rules (SQUANK is not designed to cope with discontinuous or highly oscillatory integrands nor with those having a discontinuity in one of their first four derivatives. It is thus not as generally applicable as the others in Fig. 13, but is included because it is the only published routine which contains an automatic "noise detector".)

We have already seen that the disadvantage of the Gauss–Legendre formulae is that it is difficult to utilise previously computed integrand values. The first GAUSS routine estimates the accuracy of the 5-point Gauss rule by comparing it with the 7-point Gauss rule so that eleven evaluations are wasted when subdivision occurs. In AIND the accuracy of the 10-point Gauss rule is estimated by comparison with the 21-point Kronrod rule so that 21 evaluations are wasted on subdivision. Robinson's GAUSS scheme is ingeniously designed to eliminate the wastage which has hitherto been inherent in Gaussian methods.

The method uses the 3-point Gauss formula in any interval and at each stage, if subdivision is necessary, this interval is divided into three more in such a way that each old Gauss point becomes the middle Gauss point in one of the new intervals (Fig. 14). There are not sufficient results available to enable any fair comparisons to be made but the author (Robinson, 1971) states that GAUSS is reliable and compares favourably with SQUANK and SIMPSON.

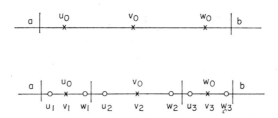

FIG. 14. Robinson's subdivision method for 3-point Gauss–Legendre formula.

ADAPQUAD (Oliver, 1972, 1971c) is another interesting scheme. It is "doubly adaptive" in that it can choose both the order of the Clenshaw–Curtis rule and the interval over which to apply it. ADAPQUAD does this by inspecting the rate of decrease of the Chebyshev coefficients. In this way it can provide whole-interval formulae for well-behaved integrands or low order formulae over small intervals for the nastier ones. Oliver has shown (1972) that for well-behaved integrands ADAPQUAD compares well with the fixed whole-interval methods that were discussed in Section 3.

There are not as many adaptive routines available using Romberg-type quadratures as there were fixed ones. CADRE (De Boor, 1971b) is another interesting scheme which uses "cautious extrapolation". This is basically Romberg's process but the routine is "trained" to recognise the characteristic convergence pattern in the T-Table (Fig. 4) which results from certain types of integrand behaviour. CADRE can recognise, and correct the extrapolation for, jump discontinuities and algebraic end-point singularities in the integrand. The user is informed whenever the scheme detects integrand behaviour of one of these types.

4.2. *Comparison of Adaptive Schemes*

A comparison of these schemes is hampered by the absence of any standard procedure for testing and comparing quadrature routines. This is, of course, also true for fixed schemes (although the Davis–Rabinowitz (1954) error coefficient σ_R provides a means of comparison) but here the problem is complicated by the presence of the strategy component which exerts its influence on both reliability and efficiency. In consequence it is impossible to find any common ground for a complete comparison of each routine listed in Fig. 13 with all the others.

A good starting point is, however, a comprehensive series of tests carried out by Kahaner (1971) on SQUANK, SIMPSON, QNC7, QUAD, GAUSS (the Melendez and Kahaner version), SPLITABS and RBUN. He found that the 'best buys' for a general purpose library routine were QNC7, QUAD and SPLITABS which each combined good reliability with good efficiency.

De Boor (1971b) used exactly the same tests on CADRE, which proved to be more reliable than the best of Kahaner's set and generally more efficient, except at finer tolerances.

Piessens (1973) also used Kahaner's tests on AIND and states that AIND is also more reliable than Kahaner's best and that its efficiency is "somewhat better". The figure given for the reliability of AIND is identical to that of CADRE, but there are no detailed results given for AIND which prevents us from comparing the efficiencies of these two routines.

Oliver (1972) compared ADAPQUAD with SPLITABS on over 2,000 examples and found ADAPQUAD to be more efficient but less reliable.

INT5PT has been in general library use at NPL for eight years and has proved extremely reliable. It compares well with the other routines for crude and moderate tolerances but its efficiency is not as high for the finer tolerances.

Figure 15 shows an example of how ADAPQUAD, SPLITABS and INT5PT cope with an integrand which has a discontinuous slope (example taken from Oliver, 1972). The results of the Patterson scheme are also given, to indicate the greater efficiency of an adaptive method in this case. It is for this type of integrand, where the Chebyshev series is so slowly convergent, that the reliability of a Clenshaw–Curtis based scheme decreases.

If an improvement could be effected in such cases these schemes would become particularly useful.

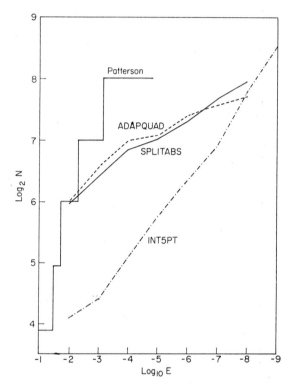

FIG. 15. A comparison of quadrature methods for $\int_0^6 \phi(x)\,dx$, where

$$\phi(x) = \left\{ \begin{array}{l} e^x, x \leqslant 1/2 \\ e^{1-x}, x > 1/2 \end{array} \right\}.$$

Information on the Cranley–Patterson model is only available for an easy set of examples over which it compares satisfactorily with the other routines.

To summarise, any of best seven (i.e. ADAPQUAD, AIND, CADRE, INT5PT, QNC7, QUAD, SPLITABS) can cope reliably and efficiently with many different types of integrand and would provide a good general library routine. (These adaptive schemes can, of course, be used on well-behaved integrands although they are generally inferior there to the whole-interval methods.)

There is probably a lesson to be learned here about the optimum order of a rule for use in adaptive quadrature. It used to be thought that "the lower the order the better" and Simpson's rule was particularly favoured. Experience has shown that if the order is too low the scheme becomes a lengthy struggle with small intervals and the chances of misinterpretation are large. On the other hand, if the order is too high, excessive time is spent on an interval before it is rejected. These examples indicate that, for combined reliability and efficiency, the optimum order would seem to be nearer 10.

5. Special Cases of Bad Behaviour

The last two sections have covered the cases that occur most often in practice. In the remainder of the survey we discuss recent developments in some of the remaining areas.

All the methods discussed so far have difficulty in coping with two particular types of bad behaviour. These are integrable singularities and rapid oscillations.

5.1. *Integrable Singularity*

If there is an integrable singularity in some part of the range there are analytic techniques that might be applied (Davis and Rabinowitz, 1967) but let us lay these aside and ask the question "what can we do numerically$_\kappa$". By far the easiest thing to do is to ignore the difficult behaviour altogether and to use an automatic scheme optimistically. (If it is necessary to evaluate the integrand at the singularity itself, some arbitrary finite value is supplied.) For fixed schemes this is rather a hit and miss process and if a scheme converges at all it does so very slowly (Davis and Rabinowitz, 1965). An adaptive method is more likely to provide the required estimate but the computation will generally be extremely lengthy. Alternatively, if the position and nature of the singularity are known, it may be possible to utilise one of the Gauss–Jacobi type formulae. The problem then is that it becomes necessary to provide a comprehensive set of library routines covering different types of singularity.

Recently a method has been proposed by Iri, Moriguti and Takasawa (1970) for dealing with almost any type of integrable end-point singularity. In a forthcoming report Burton and Miller investigage some generalisations of this method which appear very promising.
Let

$$I = \int_{-1}^{1} f(x)\, dx , \tag{5.1}$$

and make the substitution

$$x = \phi(t),$$

where

$$\phi'(t) = \frac{1}{k} \exp\left(\frac{-a}{(1-t^2)^p}\right),$$ (5.2)

k is a normalisation factor and a and p are parameters whose values are selected for optimum performance on a wide variety of functions. Then

$$I = \int_{-1}^{1} f(\phi(t))\,\phi'(t)dt$$ (5.3)

The integrand in (5.3) has the useful property that it vanishes together with all its derivatives at the end-points of the range, no matter what the type of end-point singularity in $f(x)$. We have already seen in Section 3.1 that the trapezium rule is particularly useful in this case. Applying it with the range divided into N intervals, we obtain the approximate formula

$$I_{\text{Approx}} = \frac{2}{N}\sum_{j=1}^{N-1} w_j f(x_j)$$ (5.4)

where

$$w_j = \phi'(2j/N)$$ (5.5)

and

$$x_j = \phi(2j/N)$$ (5.6)

The main advantage of this approach is that once a and p have been chosen by the designer of the algorithm, the same family of rules is used in all circumstances i.e. for any type of singularity. (Note also that the method can be used for integrands which have a different type of singularity at each end of the range.)

Moreover, this is a common-point family of rules since in progressing from a formula with N intervals to one with $2N$ intervals all the previous function values *and* weights are used.

In practice it is best to pre-compute and store the weights and abscissae. The only drawback is that some of the abscissae are very near the end-points of the range and the user may have to exercise some care in evaluating the integrand there, to prevent loss of accuracy or even overflow.

Burton and Miller are investigating the optimum choice of the parameters a and p and also other transformations with similar properties.

Figure 16 gives three examples computed with $a = 16$, $p = 1$. Here the approximate number of correct figures obtained is shown as a function of the number of points used. In the first example the integrand has the same form of singularity at each end of the range. The second example is much more difficult and contains a rapidly oscillating trigonometric factor. The final example is included to show that, although the method is designed with singular integrands in mind, it can be used fairly economically on well-behaved ones. Of course, its performance on well-behaved integrands does not measure up to that of the fixed whole interval formulae which are designed specifically for that purpose.

	Number Points	$-\log_{10} E$
	5	1·77
	7	3·67
	11	4·79
Ex.1. $\displaystyle\int_0^1 \frac{dx}{\sqrt{x(1-x)}} = \pi$	15	5·94
	23	7·28
	31	8·96
	47	m/c acc*

	5	1·43
Ex.2. $\displaystyle\int_0^\infty x^{-0\cdot7} e^{-0\cdot4x} \cos 2x \, dx$	11	0·34
	23	2·12
	47	2·83
$\displaystyle= \int_0^1 t^{-0\cdot6} (-\ln|t|)^{-0\cdot7} \cos(2\ln|t|) \, dt$	63	3·36
	95	4·65
	127	6·08
	191	7·95
$\simeq 2\cdot2$	255	10·15
	383	m/c acc

	5	2·76
	7	4·08
Ex.3. $\displaystyle\int_0^1 \frac{dx}{1 + e^x} \simeq 0\cdot38$	11	6·36
	15	7·53
	23	10·52
	31	m/c acc

FIG. 16. Three examples of the application of the generalisation of the Iri, Moriguti, Takasawa method computed with a = 16, p = 1.

* machine accuracy is approximately 11 digits.

5.2. Rapid Oscillations

Highly oscillatory integrands occur, for example, when Fourier transforms are computed. If the rapid oscillation is caused by a high frequency sine or cosine factor, e.g. in

$$\int g(x) \sin mx \, dx,$$

there is a standard technique that can be used, proposed originally by Filon (1928). In this method the non-oscillatory part $g(x)$ is approximated piecewise by a low order polynomial. The product of the polynomial and the sine factor is then integrated analytically. This process can be made the basis of an automatic scheme.

In Filon's method quadratic arcs are used to approximate $g(x)$ over equal intervals. (Most libraries contain a version of this method.) This approach is useful whenever $g(x)$ is fairly smooth. If, however, $g(x)$ varies rapidly over some part of the range, the method becomes uneconomical since the small interval which is necessary to give a good approximation over the rapidly varying part must also be used over the remainder of the range. Recently Linz (1972) has provided a FORTRAN routine which applies Filon's formula in an adaptive manner. This method can be used with economy on a much wider class of integrand.

Other authors have suggested using higher order polynomials to approximate $g(x)$. Einarrson (1968) devised a method using cubic splines. More recently Piessens and Poleunis (1971) have used a truncated Chebyshev series. This method is considerably more involved than Filon's but the gain in accuracy is substantial. Piessens and Poleunis note that it is easy to construct an automatic integrator based on this method.

Abramovici (1973) has made use of the Fast Fourier Transform technique and has obtained results which are much better than those of Filon's method, especially for large values of m.

6. Infinite Range

All the quadratures considered so far have been for integrals with a finite range. For integrals with an infinite range the situation is fraught with difficulties. In the first place, it is impossible to attach any validity to the result of any approximate scheme in the absence of theoretical information about the convergence of the integral itself. Most of the available techniques can easily be misused to provide a finite approximation to a divergent integral!

Once convergence has been proved, it may be possible to use the Gauss–Laguerre or Gauss–Hermite formula or to use a mixture of analytic and numerical techniques (Davis and Rabinowitz, 1967). One such technique is to transform the integrand to a finite range. This often introduces a singularity at one of the end-points which may be treated by a version of the Iri–Moriguti–Takasawa method.

7. A Note on the Evaluation of Indefinite Integrals

If the integral is indefinite, e.g.

$$I(x) = \int_a^x f(t)dt, \qquad a \leqslant x \leqslant b$$

the best approach is to use a collocation technique, as employed in the Clenshaw–Curtis method, to obtain the coefficients of a Chebyshev approximation to the integrand over the range $[a, b]$. Once these coefficients have been determined the integrated series can be summed for any selected value of x. (Notice that both the even and odd coefficients are required in this case whereas the Clenshaw–Curtis method needs only the even ones.)

8. Integrand Defined by a Set of Data Points

So far we have discussed those integrands which can be evaluated at any point in the range. If the integrand is only available in the form of a table with arbitrary spacing, it may not be possible to use any of the methods already considered.

If the quadrature is part of a lengthy computation which includes some type of fit to the data then the approximate integral can be obtained quite cheaply by integrating the fit (this is particularly simple if B-splines are in use). Otherwise it is best to approximate the data by low-order piecewise polynomials (Davis and Rabinowitz, 1967). Hennion (1962) gives an ALGOL procedure AVINT which uses overlapping quadratics and thus incorporates some smoothing.

Another method due to Gill and Miller (1970) uses cubic interpolation of the data and provides an indication of the reliability of the result by comparing it with the corresponding result obtained with piecewise quartics. An ALGOL routine INT4PT is available together with a version designed for indefinite integrals. (These routines are not automatic. Generally it is best to make use, at the outset, of all of the limited amount of information that is available.)

9. Multiple Integrals

The problems of quadrature become considerably more complicated when we turn to the evaluation of multiple integrals. Now we have not only to consider a wide variety of integrands but also an infinite variety of regions over which to integrate them.

If the region is sufficiently simple it is possible to express the multiple integral as an iterated one and to apply a one-dimensional rule repeatedly. Practically this can be an expensive process since for a k-point rule applied to n dimensions the amount of computation is proportional to k^n. Even for triple integrals this amount may become unmanageable.

In the last decade much effort has been devoted to deriving formulae of the form

$$\int_{B_n} w(\mathbf{x})f(\mathbf{x})d\mathbf{x} = \sum_{i=1}^{N} A_i f(\mathbf{v}_i)$$

where B_n denotes the n-dimensional region of integration and $\mathbf{x}$, $\mathbf{v}_i$ are n-dimensional vectors. The most comprehensive collection of these, and of product rules, for some of the simpler regions B_n, is to be found in Stroud (1971). In the last chapter of this book a number of FORTRAN routines are given but the only automatic one, written by Lyness and McHugh, uses Romberg-type extrapolation of the midpoint rule over an n-cube and does not appear to be very efficient.

The only published adaptive scheme of which the author is aware is by Genz (1972) and is covered in a later chapter. The method uses the ε-algorithm to extrapolate the results obtained from a basic (symmetrical) rule and can be applied to integrands which have a singularity on the boundary of the region of integration. The scheme can be used for any region B_n which can be transformed onto the unit n-cube.

If the region is irregular, so that none of the above methods is applicable there are two approaches that can be used. The first is to approximate the irregular region by a series of subregions of regular shape, over which the integral can be evaluated. The other is to contain the irregular region within some regular one and to set the integrand to zero outside the boundary. In either case the region close to the boundary will require careful attention, particularly if the integrand is troublesome there. Both of these processes can be used in an adaptive manner.

Genz has given a good summary of the state of the art in multiple integration in the introduction to his paper (1972). He states:

"The numerical evaluation of multidimensional integrals has always been a difficult problem because of the large amount of computational work necessary, but because of the increasing demand for the evaluation of such integrals and the appearance of faster and faster computers much analysis has been done in the past few years to develop techniques which are suitable for use with computers and at the same time minimise the necessary amount of computer work".

We are now beginning to see the results of this effort but there is obviously plenty of scope for future work in this area.

10. Summary

The following table summarises the conclusions of this survey by suggesting an appropriate type of routine for each of the types of integral considered above. A library which contains at least one routine for each entry should be able to handle efficiently most of the problems that arise in normal circumstances:

(i) For well-behaved integrands include routines for both Patterson and Clenshaw–Curtis methods.

(ii) For badly-behaved integrands (and as a general routine for use when little is known about the integrand) include one of the best adaptive routines (ADAPQUAD, AIND, CADRE, INT5PT, QNC7, QUAD, SPLITABS) or one of a similar standard.

(iii) For singular integrands, include a routine based on a version of the Iri–Moriguti–Takasawa method.

(iv) For integrands which contain a high frequency sine (cosine) factor include an adaptive Filon-type method.

(v) For integrals over an infinite range which are CONVERGENT include Gauss–Laguerre and Gauss–Hermite formulae (can also use (iii) after appropriate transformation).

(vi) For indefinite integrals include a routine which finds the Chebyshev series of the integrand and then the coefficients of the integrated series. Include also a routine which sums a Chebyshev series.

(vii) For integrands defined by irregularly spaced data include a routine based on piecewise, low-order polynomial approximation, e.g. AVINT, INT4PT.

(viii) For multiple integrals include an adaptive routine for an integral over an n-dimensional cube (this will only cover the simplest cases, the rest will probably have to be dealt with individually).

(ix) For special cases include a set of Gauss–Legendre formulae.

In conclusion, it must be stressed that the usefulness of such a library will be seriously impaired unless the user is given adequate guidance on how to select the correct method to use in order to solve his problem.

Acknowledgements

I should like to thank A. R. Curtis, G. F. Miller and A. J. Burton of NPL for many useful discussions (the former also for supplying the material for the Appendix).

I should also like to thank P. J. Davis for permission to quote from "Numerical Integration", and B. T. Hinde who carried out many of the computations.

References

Abramovici, F. (1973). The accurate calculation of Fourier integrals by the Fast Fourier Transform technique. *J. Comput. Phys.* **11**, 28–37.
Bauer, F. L. (1961). Algorithm 60—Romberg integration. *Comm. ACM* **4**, 255. See also *Comm. ACM* **5**, 168 and *Comm. ACM* **7**, 420.

Bulirsch, R. (1964). Bemerkungen zur Romberg-integration. *Numer. Math.* **6**, 6–16.
Dulirsch, R. and Stoer, J. (1967), Numerical quadrature by extrapolation. *Numer. Math.* **9**, 271–278.
Bunton, W. (1970). (See Kahaner (1971) for details of FORTRAN Subroutine RBUN.)
Burton, A. J. and Miller, G. F. (1974). (This work will be published as an NPL divisional report.)
Clenshaw, C. W. and Curtis, A. R. (1960). A method for numerical integration on an automatic computer. *Numer. Math.* **2**, 197–205.
Cranley, R. and Patterson, T. N. L. (1971). On the automatic numerical evaluation of definite integrals. *Comput. J.* **14**, 189–198.
Davis, P. J. (1955). On a problem in the theory of mechanical quadratures. *Pacific J. Math.* **5**, 669–674.
Davis, P. J. and Rabinowitz, P. (1954). On the estimation of quadrature errors for analytical functions. *M.T.A.C.* **8**, 193–203.
Davis, P. J. and Rabinowitz, P. (1965). Ignoring the singularity in numerical integration. *J. SIAM Ser. B. Numer. Anal.* **2**, 367–383.
Davis, P. J. and Rabinowitz, P. (1967). "Numerical Integration", Blaisdell, London.
Davis, P. J. and Rabinowitz, P. (1972). On the nonexistence of simplex integration rules for infinite integrals. *Maths. Comp.* **26**, 687–688.
De Boor, C. (1971a). On writing an automatic integration algorithm. *In* "Mathematical Software" (Ed. J. R. Rice), ACM Monograph Series. pp. 201–209. Academic Press, London and New York.
De Boor, C. (1971b). CADRE: An algorithm for numerical quadrature. *In* "Mathematical Software" (Ed. J. R. Rice), ACM Monograph Series, pp. 417–449, Academic Press, London and New York.
Dunkl, C. F. (1967). See Davis and Rabinowitz (1967, p. 199).
Einarsson, B. (1968). Numerical calculation of Fourier integrals with cubic splines. *BIT*, **8**, 279–286.
Fairweather, G. (1969). Algorithm 351—Modified Romberg quadrature. *Comm. ACM*, **12**, 324.
Filon, L. N. G. (1928). On a quadrature formula for trigonometric integrals. *Proc. Roy. Soc. Edinburgh*, **49**, 38–47.
Fox, L. (1967). Romberg integration for a class of singular integrands. *Comput. J.* **10**, 87–93.
Fox, L. and Hayes, L. (1970). On the definite integration of singular integrands. *SIAM Rev.* **12**, 449–457.
Fraser, W. and Wilson, M. W. (1966). Remarks on the Clenshaw–Curtis quadrature scheme. *SIAM Rev.* **8**, 322–327.
Gentleman, W. M. (1969). An error analysis of Goertzel's (Watt's) method for computing Fourier coefficients. *Comput. J.* **12**, 160–165.
Gentleman, W. M. (1972). Implementing Clenshaw–Curtis quadrature. I Methodology and experience. *Comm. ACM.* **15**, 337–342; II Computing the cosine transformation. *Comm. ACM*, **15**, 343–346; Algorithm 424—Clenshaw–Curtis quadrature. *Comm. ACM*, **15**, 353.
Genz, A. (1972). An adaptive multidimensional quadrature procedure. *Comput. Phys. Comm.* **4**, 11–15.
Gill, P. E. and Miller, G. F. (1970). "An Algorithm for the Integration of Unequally Spaced Data." DNAC report No 93, National Physical Laboratory, Teddington, Middlesex.

Gram, C. (1964). ALGOL programming contribution No 8—Definite integral by Romberg's method. ALGOL Procedure. *BIT* **4**, 54–60. See also *BIT* **4**, 118–120.

Havie, T. (1969). On a modification of the Clenshaw–Curtis quadrature formula. *BIT* **9**, 338–350.

Hennion, P. E. (1962). Algorithm 77—Interpolation, Differentiation and Integration. *Comm. ACM* **5**, 96. See also *Comm. ACM* **5**, 348; *Comm. ACM* **6**, 446–447, 663; Davis and Rabinowitz (1967, 22–23, 193).

Hopgood, F. R. A. and Litherland, C. (1966). Algorithm 279—Chebyshev quadrature. *Comm. ACM* **9**, 270.

Hunter, D. B. (1967). Romberg's method for certain integrals involving a singularity. *BIT* **7**, 200–205.

Iri, M., Moriguti, S. and Takasawa, Y. (1970). On a Numerical Integration Formula. *Kokyuroko* (*Records of Studies*), *the Research Institute of Mathematical Sciences, Koyoto University*, **91**, 82–117, (See also Takahasi, H. and Mori, M. Error estimation in the numerical integration of analytic functions. *Rep. Compt. Centre, Univ. Tokyo,* **3**, 41–108.

Kahaner, D. K. (1971). Comparison of numerical quadrature formulas. *In* "Mathematical Software" (Ed. J. R. Rice), ACM Monograph Series, pp.229–259. Academic Press, London and New York.

Kahaner, D. K. (1972). Numerical quadrature by the ε-algorithm. *Maths. Comp.* **26**, 689–693.

Kronrod, A. S. (1965). "Nodes and Weights of Quadrature Formulas". English translation from Russian, Consultants Bureau, New York.

Kubik, R. N. (1965). Algorithm 257—Havie integrator. *Comm. ACM* **8**, 381.

Linz, P. (1972). Algorithm 427—Fourier cosine integral. *Comm. ACM* **15**, 358–360.

Lyness, J. N. (1969a). The effect of inadequate convergence criteria in automatic routines. *Comput. J.* **12**, 279–281.

Lyness, J. N. (1969b) Notes on the adaptive Simpson quadrature routine. *J. ACM* **16**, 483–495.

Lyness, J. N. (1970). Algorithm 379—SQUANK (Simpson quadrature used adaptively-noise killed) *Comm. ACM* **13**, 260.

Lyness, J. N. (1972). An algorithm for Gauss–Romberg integration. *BIT* **12**, 194–203.

Lyness, J. N. and McHugh, B. J. J. (1963). Integration over multidimensional hypercubes. I. A progressive procedure. *Comput, J.* **6**, 264–270.

McKeeman, W. M. and Tesler, L. (1963). Algorithm 182—Non-recursive adaptive integration. *Comm. ACM* **6**, 315. See also FORTRAN version, SIMP, in Davis and Rabinowitz (1967, p.198).

Meir, A. and Sharma, A. (1965). On the method of Romberg quadrature. *J. SIAM Ser. B. Numer. Anal.* **2**, 250–258.

Miller, G. F. Details of ALGOL procedure INTSPT available from the author, DNAC, National Physical Laboratory, Teddington, Middlesex.

O'Hara, H. and Smith, F. J. (1968). Error estimation in Clenshaw–Curtis quadrature formula. *Comput. J.* **11**, 213–219.

O'Hara, H. and Smith, F. J. (1969). The evaluation of definite integrals by interval subdivision. *Comput. J.* **12**, 179–182.

Oliver, J. (1971a). The calculation of definite integrals using high order formulae. *Comput. J.* **14**, 301–306.

Oliver, J. (1971b). The efficiency of extrapolation methods for numerical integration. *Numer. Math.* **17**, 17–32.

Oliver, J. (1971c). A practical strategy for the Clenshaw–Curtis quadrature method. *J. Inst. Maths. Applics*, **8**, 53–56.

Oliver, J. (1972). A doubly-adaptive Clenshaw–Curtis quadrature method. *Comput. J.* **15**, 141–147.

Patterson, T. N. L. (1968). The optimum addition of points to quadrature formulae. *Maths. Comp.* **22**, 847–856.

Piessens, R. (1973). "An Algorithm for Automatic Integration." Report TW 13, April 1973, Applied Mathematics and Programming Division, Katholieke Universiteit Leuven.

Piessens, R. and Poleunis, F. (1971). A numerical method for the integration of oscillatory functions. *BIT* **11**, 317–327.

Robinson, I. G. (1971). Adaptive Gaussian integration. *Aust. Comput. J.* **3**, 126–129.

Romberg, W. (1955). Vereinfacte numerische Integration. *Det. Kong. Norske Videnskabers Selskabs Forhandlinger*, **28**, 30–36.

Rutishauser, H. (1963). Ausdehnung des Rombergschen Prinzips. *Numer. Math.* **5**, 48–54.

Shanks, J. A. (1972). Romberg tables for singular integrands. *Comput. J.* **15**, 360–361.

Stroud, A. H. (1971). "Approximate Calculation of Multiple Integrals." Prentice-Hall.

Stroud, A. H. and Secrest, D. (1966). "Gaussian Quadrature Formulas." Prentice-Hall.

Appendix

Summation of a Chebyshev series when the argument can be written $t = \cos\theta$, where θ is known. (A modification of Reinsch's method proposed by A. R. Curtis.)

In the Clenshaw–Curtis (1960) method it is necessary to sum a Chebyshev series of the form

$$S(t) = \sum_{r=0}^{n}{}' a_r T_r(t), \qquad -1 \leqslant t \leqslant 1$$

in order to evaluate the coefficients of the Chebyshev series approximation to the integrand. Clenshaw and Curtis outlined a recurrence method for this summation as follows:

The numbers $c_n, c_{n-1}, \ldots, c_0$ are calculated successively using the relation

$$c_r = 2t\, c_{r+1} - c_{r+2} + a_r, \tag{A1}$$

where $c_{n+1} = c_{n+2} = 0$. The sum of the series is then given by

$$S(t) = \tfrac{1}{2}(c_0 - c_2).$$

Now if $|t| < \tfrac{1}{2}$ this recurrence is stable but if $|t| > \tfrac{1}{2}$, especially if $|t|$ is close to unity, a build-up of error can occur in the coefficients c_r. Gentleman (1969) quotes a modification of the recurrence due to Reinsch (unpublished) which claims to avoid this instability. In this case the recurrence relation (A1) is written in the form (for $t > 0$),

$$c_r - c_{r+1} = 2(t - 1)c_{r+1} + (c_{r+1} - c_{r+2}) + a_r.$$

Defining

$$d_r = c_r - c_{r+1},$$

we obtain the recurrence relations

$$\left.\begin{aligned} d_r &= 2(t - 1)c_{r+1} + d_{r+1} + a_r \\ c_r &= d_r + c_{r+1} \end{aligned}\right\} \quad r = n - 1, n - 2, \dots, 0 \qquad \text{(A2)}$$

where $c_n = d_n = a_n$. The sum of the series is then given by

$$S(t) = \tfrac{1}{2}(d_0 + d_1).$$

If $t < 0$, define

$$d_r = c_r + c_{r+1}$$

to obtain recurrence relations analogous to (A2), i.e.

$$\left.\begin{aligned} d_r &= 2(t + 1)c_{r+1} - d_{r+1} + a_r \\ c_r &= d_r - c_{r+1} \end{aligned}\right\} \quad r = n - 1, n - 2, \dots, 0 \qquad \text{(A3)}$$

and

$$S(t) = \tfrac{1}{2}(d_0 - d_1).$$

It is found in practice that Reinsch's modification makes no difference if one simply forms $t - 1$ or $t + 1$ from the given $t = \cos \theta$ since figures are lost through cancellation when $|t|$ is near unity. However in the Clenshaw–Curtis method the value of θ is known so that it is possible to express $t - 1$ as

$$\cos \theta - 1 = \frac{\cos^2 \theta - 1}{\cos \theta + 1} = -\frac{\sin^2 \theta}{\cos \theta + 1} = -2 \sin^2 \theta/2. \qquad \text{(A4)}$$

$t - 1$ is now correct to working accuracy and the Reinsch recurrence succeeds in preventing build up of error.

7. Algorithms for Integral Equations

G. F. Miller

Division of Numerical Analysis and Computing,
National Physical Laboratory,
Teddington, Middlesex, England.

1. Introduction

The subject of integral equations is an extremely complex one embracing a considerable area of both mathematics and numerical analysis. Moreover, it overlaps at various points with other fields, notably ordinary and partial differential equations, linear algebra and optimization. This very complexity may help to account for the shortage of algorithms which undoubtedly exists in this field—provided that by an "algorithm" we understand a coded set of instructions intelligible to a computer (cf. Chapter 4, p. 49). We must here confess to being in something of a dilemma. On the one hand, merely to describe such algorithms as exist would scarcely provide an adequate view of the subject as a whole. On the other, a detailed review of the innumerable *methods* ("algorithms" in a broader sense) available for the solution of the many different types of integral equation would be a mammoth task quite beyond the scope of this lecture.

We shall therefore adopt a middle course. First, in Section 2, we attempt a rudimentary classification of the various types of equation and comment on aspects of their numerical solution. This will enable us to consider, in Section 3, some of the implications of trying to provide a comprehensive set of algorithms, whether and to what extent such a goal is attainable or even desirable, and how users' needs can in general best be met. Existing algorithms, briefly reviewed in Section 4, can now also be seen in better perspective. Finally, in Section 5, we describe some work in progress or envisaged at the National Physical Laboratory, aimed at filling some of the gaps.

2. Classification of Integral Equations

Fredholm equation of second kind

Let us begin our enumeration with what is perhaps the most fundamental and also the most straightforward type of equation, the so-called Fredholm equation of the second kind:

$$f(x) - \lambda \int_a^b K(x, y) f(y) \, dy = g(x), \qquad a \leqslant x \leqslant b. \tag{1}$$

Here the parameter λ, the kernel $K(x, y)$ and the function $g(x)$ are given, and the problem is to determine the unknown function $f(x)$. It is characteristic of an equation of "second kind" that $f(x)$ occurs both outside and under the sign of integration. For brevity we may write the equation in the operator form

$$(I - \lambda K) f = g. \tag{2}$$

A great many physical problems give rise to equations of this type. For example two-point boundary value problems for second-order ordinary differential equations can be reduced to this form; so also can a large class of boundary-value problems for elliptic partial differential equations, provided that in two-dimensional cases it is understood that the path of integration is a closed contour, while in three-dimensional cases it is to be replaced by a surface, etc. In addition there are, of course, many problems which arise directly as Fredholm integral equations and cannot be formulated as differential equations.

The customary and natural method of solution involves replacement of the integral by a suitable quadrature formula. Whether $f(x)$ is approximated in terms of its values at particular points or in the form of a series of basis functions with unknown coefficients, the problem reduces to the solution of a system of linear equations—a task for which many algorithms are available. Provided that λ does not lie too close to an eigenvalue of K, error bounds can be obtained without difficulty. A useful survey of methods and error analysis is to be found in Atkinson (1973), see also Sections 4 and 5.

Eigenvalue problem

Closely associated with the Fredholm equation of second kind is the eigenvalue problem obtained by setting $g(x) \equiv 0$ in eqn (1); that is, the problem of determining values of λ, and associated functions $\phi(x)$, such that the equation

$$(I - \lambda K) \phi = 0 \tag{3}$$

possesses a non-trivial solution.

Naturally there is a close connection between this and the algebraic eigenvalue problem to which, after suitable approximation, it usually reduces. Here, as in most problems in the numerical solution of integral equations, one relies heavily on algorithms for processes in linear algebra. Thus anyone who has an integral equation to solve, while he may not be able to find a ready-made algorithm which will solve the problem in its entirety, is by no means without algorithmic resources.

Volterra equations of second kind

Next, if we simply change the upper limit of the integral in (1) from b to x we derive the so-called Volterra equation of the second kind

$$f(x) - \lambda \int_a^x K(x, y) f(y) \, dy = g(x). \tag{4}$$

This is broadly analogous to an initial-value problem for a differential equation, of which it may be regarded as a generalization. Hence the numerical methods employed for its solution are usually of the marching or step-by-step type.

It may be remarked that there is no eigenvalue problem associated with this equation since the Volterra integral operator has no eigenvalues.

Fredholm equation of first kind

Another, completely different type of equation is obtained by dropping the term $f(x)$ and setting $\lambda = -1$ in eqn (1), namely

$$\int_a^b K(x, y) f(y) \, dy = g(x), \tag{5}$$

or briefly

$$Kf = g.$$

The range of x is not necessarily the same as that of y and may be taken to be $c \leqslant x \leqslant d$. The integral operator K, being completely continuous has an infinite string of eigenvalues (singular values in unsymmetric cases) with zero as limit point. The problem is thus roughly comparable with that of solving a large ill-conditioned system of linear equations $Ax = b$, where the matrix A has many small eigenvalues (singular values). By deleting the $f(x)$ term we have removed the member which was holding the equation stable and we are left with an ill-posed problem. Problems of this type are notoriously difficult to handle because in general a solution does not exist, and if it does it will be extremely sensitive to small perturbations in the data, g. This means, in effect, that we cannot usually "solve" an equation of the first kind numerically in the conventional sense of obtaining a function which is demonstrably close to the exact solution; we can only seek a "best" approximate solution according to some appropriate criterion.

Equations of the first kind arise in a variety of forms and in many different fields of physics, etc. (for a review of applications see Nedelkov, 1972). Whereas it used to be the fashion to dismiss these out of hand, their importance is now being increasingly recognised and there has been a flood of papers on the topic in recent years. Most of the many methods which have been proposed are based on the application of suitable constraints to prevent the solution from being contaminated by the effects of noise in the data. See, for example, Twomey (1965) and Turchin *et al.* (1971) for expository accounts and further references.

Volterra equation of first kind

Similarly by omitting the term $f(x)$ from the Volterra equation of second kind we obtain the corresponding equation of first kind. This is likewise an ill-posed problem. However, it can sometimes be converted into an equation of the second kind by differentiation. For a discussion and method of computation see Linz (1969).

Further classification

It will already be apparent that there exists a considerable diversity of types of integral equation. However, there are several other modes of classification which may have an important bearing on the choice of method and which we now briefly consider.

(i) There may be one equation or a system of equations. Dual and triple Fredholm equations and fairly large systems of Volterra equations are not uncommon.

(ii) A problem may involve one or more dimensions. In the latter case one is faced with the task of integrating over a curve, surface or region, and the method and error analysis may be greatly complicated. In practice this equation is often closely bound up with the treatment of singularities; see (v) below.

(iii) The region of integration may be finite or infinite. If it is infinite, it may be possible to deal with the situation by a mere truncation, but there will often be fundamental difficulties which call for preliminary analysis and special methods.

(iv) A problem may be either linear or nonlinear. The importance of the distinction in both theory and computation needs no emphasis. In practice, nonlinear equations are usually solved by a method of successive approximation based on some form of local linearization. A valuable collection of papers on the subject is to be found in Anselone (1964); for a concise account see also Rall (1969).

(v) The kernel may be singular or nonsingular. A variety of types of singularity is encountered in practical problems, and each type needs special treatment.

In addition when constructing algorithms it is desirable, both from the point of view of computational efficiency and on theoretical grounds, to accord special treatment to equations whose kernels have particular properties. Thus we may distinguish the following cases:

(vi) Equations with symmetric kernels: $K(x, y) = K(y, x)$, which have properties akin to those of algebraic equations with symmetric matrix operators.

(vii) Equations with kernels of convolution type: $K(x - y)$.

(viii) Equations with periodic kernels (such as arise, for example, from integration round a closed contour).

Our list is far from exhaustive. It could, for example, be extended in the direction of integro-differential equations and other functional equations, but this would take us too far afield.

3. Algorithms or Methods?

There is an extensive literature devoted to the numerical treatment of the various types of integral equation enumerated above (for a comprehensive bibliography see Noble, 1971) but, as we have said, very few concrete algorithms are available. This may be partly due to the fact that one can get along reasonably well with an armoury of methods for representing integrals, coupled with a collection of algorithms for solving the algebraic equations which arise.

In fact there is a good deal to be said for *not* trying to produce complicated algorithms in which these two elements are fused together. Because of the great variety of types of integral (to which Valerie Dixon has drawn attention in her excellent survey) it is difficult to allow for every contingency in an algorithm, whereas if suitable methods are to hand it may be comparatively easy to prepare programs for the solution of particular problems. Therefore we suggest that there are many situations in which the user is best served by providing him with good *methods* which he can then adapt to meet particular needs.

On the other hand there are a few standard types of integral equation for which the provision of library algorithms seems both practicable and worthwhile. The main candidates would appear to be; linear Fredholm equations of the second kind and the associated eigenvalue problem, with provision for kernels of special form; and linear or nonlinear Volterra equations of the second kind, with or without singularities, and systems of such equations.

4. Existing Algotithms

These needs are met to some extent by existing algorithms. We here briefly describe the three published ALGOL procedures of Elliott and Warne (1967), Pouzet (1964) and Rumyantsev (1965):

(i) *Procedure of Elliott and Warne*

This solves a linear Fredholm equation of the second kind of the form of eqn (1), or a Volterra equation of the form (4), the kernel $K(x, y)$ being supposed nonsingular. A finite Chebyshev series expansion

$$f(x) = \sum_{i=0}^{n} a_j T_j(\xi), \qquad \xi = \frac{2x - a - b}{b - a}$$

is assumed for $f(x)$ in the range $a \leqslant x \leqslant b$, and a system of linear equations for the unknown coefficients a_j is obtained by approximating the equation at selected points x_i. The integrals which arise are evaluated by also expanding $K(x_i, y)$ as a Chebyshev series and then integrating its product with each $T_j(y)$. Thus for the full applicability of the method $K(x, y)$ should possess continuous y-derivatives up to a fairly high order. However, special provision is made for the commonly occurring case of a simple discontinuity in $\partial K(x, y)/\partial y$ at $y = x$, and for that in which $K \equiv 0$ for $y > x$ (yielding a Volterra equation). The user is also enabled to effect economies if the solution is known to be either odd or even.

No error indication is provided by the algorithm but in practice it is often possible to obtain a good estimate of the error by varying the order of the Chebyshev series approximations.

Unfortunately the published procedure (Elliott and Warne, 1967) contains a serious error; line 7 on page 220 should read

$$D[kp] := (C[kp - 1] - C[kp + 1]) \times 0\cdot 5/kp;$$

(ii) *Procedure of Pouzet*

This solves a single nonlinear Volterra integral equation of a very general type:

$$\phi(x) = F\left(x, \int_{x_0}^{x} g(x, s, \phi(s)) \, ds\right),$$

where F and g are well-behaved functions. The algorithm employs two types of method commonly applied to the solution of ordinary differential equations, namely

(a) one-step methods of Runge–Kutta type, and

(b) multi-step methods of Adams type.

Their extension to integral equations is treated in an earlier paper of the author (Pouzet, 1963). The user has the choice of (a) or (b); moreover, the order of the method is at his disposal provided that he can supply the appropriate set of coefficients. The coefficients actually given correspond to order 4 for method (a) and order 5 for method (b). If (b) is selected, (a) must in any case be used to obtain starting values. The user is required to choose a suitable interval of integration and no error estimate is provided.

This procedure also contains an error. On page 170 on the third line following the *comment*, N should be replaced by Q.

The algorithm is useful by virtue of its considerable generality; it could readily be adapted to solve systems of equations (see Pouzet, 1963). On the other hand it would appear to be uneconomical in application to linear equations, particularly those of convolution type, and has the weakness that it applies the same extrapolatory-type formulae over ranges where the integrand is known as over those where it is as yet unknown.

(iii) *Procedure of Rumyantsev*

This procedure solves a system of linear Volterra equations of the second kind. The unknown functions are approximated by piecewise quadratic polynomials. In this case the user is required to specify accuracy parameters, namely bounds on the residuals for each equation, and the interval is broken down automatically until this specification is met.

5. Some Work in Progress

A major deficiency of the existing algorithms described in Section 4 is their inability to deal effectively with singular kernels. This is therefore one of the aspects to which we have devoted most attention at NPL.

As a starting point we have taken the method of El Gendi (1969) for non-singular equations. This is theoretically similar to that of Elliott and Warne but considerably simpler to apply. It is based on the use of a quadrature formula.

$$\int_{-1}^{1} \phi(x)\, dx \approx \sum_{j=0}^{n} C_j^{(n)} \phi(x_j),$$

in which the points x_j are the Chebyshev points, $x_j = \cos(\pi j/n)$ and the weights are such that the formula is exact if $\phi(x)$ is a polynomial of degree n.

If we apply it to the integral eqn (1) we obtain, when $x = x_i$,

$$\int_{-1}^{1} K(x_i, y) f(y) \, dy \approx \sum_{j=0}^{n} C_j^{(n)} K(x_i, x_j) f(x_j) \tag{6}$$

(we suppose for simplicity that the range has been normalized to $(-1, 1)$); hence the integral equation can be reduced to an approximating system of linear algebraic equations. This method, too, can be adapted to take account of a simple discontinuity in $K(x, y)$ or its derivative at $y = x$.

It can also be extended to various types of singular equation. Thus, given an absolutely integrable weighting function $w(y)$, coefficients $C_j^{(n)}$ can be found (Kussmaul, 1972) such that the approximate formula

$$\int_{-1}^{1} w(y) L(x_i, y) f(y) \, dy \approx \sum_{j=0}^{n} C_j^{(n)} L(x_i, x_j) f(x_j) \tag{7}$$

is valid, provided only that the product $L(x, y) f(y)$ behaves like a polynomial of degree n for each x_i.

Since in practice the position of the singularity usually varies with x, we need also formulae for integrals containing a weighting function of type $w(x, y)$. It is possible to construct such formulae; naturally they differ from (7) in that $C_j^{(n)}$ is replaced by $C_{ij}^{(n)}$. An example is provided in the paper by Erdogan and Gupta (1972) who, in treating a class of problems in elasticity, encounter Cauchy singular integrals with a weighting function $w(x, y) = (1 - y^2)^{\pm\frac{1}{2}}/(x - y)$. We have also treated the case of a kernel with the logarithmic singularity $(1 - y^2)^{-\frac{1}{2}} \log |x - y|$; details will be reported elsewhere.

An attractive feature of the approach here described is that it is easily applicable to (systems of) integral equations exhibiting more than one type of singularity, since all the formulae involve, for the same choice of n, the same set of points x_i. Hence algorithms for the solution of a wide variety of equations may readily be constructed.

Acknowledgement

I am indebted to my colleague, Miss Susan Hill, for her substantial help in the writing and testing of algorithms.

References

Anselone, P. M. (Ed.) (1964). "Nonlinear Integral Equations". University of Wisconsin Press, Madison.

Atkinson, K. E. (1973). Report of Indiana University. (To appear in proceedings of 1971 Fall National Meeting of SIAM, Madison, Wisconsin.)

El Gendi, S. E. (1969). *Comput. J.* **12,** 282–287.

Elliott, D. and Warne, W. G. (1967). *I.C.C. Bulletin* **6,** 207–224.

Erdogan, F. and Gupta, G. D. (1972). *Quart. Appl. Maths* **29,** 525–534.

Kussmaul, R. (1972). *Computing* **9,** 159–164.

Linz, P. (1969). *Comput. J.* **12,** 393–397.

Nedelkov, I. P. (1972). *Comput. Phys. Commun.* **4,** 157–164.

Noble, B. (1971). A bibliography on "Methods for solving integral equations"; Vol. 1: Subject listing; Vol. 2: Author listing. MRC Tech. Summary Reports 1176 and 1177, University of Wisconsin, Madison.

Pouzet, P. (1963). *Rev. Franc. Trait. Inf. (Chiffres)* **6,** 79–112.

Pouzet, P. (1964). *Rev. Franc. Trait. Inf. (Chiffres)* **7,** 169–173.

Rall, L. B. (1969). "Computational Solution of Nonlinear Operational Equations". John Wiley and Sons, New York.

Rumyantsev, I. A. (1965). *USSR Comput. Math. and Math. Phys.* **5,** 218–224.

Twomey, S. (1965). *J. Franklin Inst.* **279,** 95–109.

Turchin, V. F., Kozlov, V. P. and Malkevich, M. S. (1971). *Soviet Phys. Uspekhi* **13,** 681–702.

8. Testing and Evaluation of Some Subroutines for Numerical Quadrature

BO EINARSSON

*Research Institute of National Defence (FOA),
Tumba, Sweden.*

1. Introduction

Some Fortran subroutines for numerical quadrature have been tested at the Ordnance Laboratory of the Research Institute of the Swedish National Defence. The purpose of this article is to suggest a measure, called quality, that gives an idea of the reliability of a quadrature subroutine. Some comments on the tested routines are also given.

Three commercial subroutines for calculating the integral $\int_a^b f(x)\,dx$ with the Romberg scheme have been compared with the Clenshaw–Curtis quadrature of *Comm. ACM* (Algorithm 424), Gentleman (1972b). The three commercial Romberg routines were DRMBIU from IMSL (1972), QATR from SSP (IBM 1969), and the adaptive routine QAR from SL-MATH (IBM 1971). The subroutine ROMINT from *Comm. ACM* (Algorithm 351), Fairweather (1969,) was also included in the test. The calculations were performed in single precision on an IBM 360/75 with the Rice test-package of 50 different integrals, see Gentleman (1972a) or Casaletto, Pickett, and Rice (1969).

As input relative accuracies of 0·1, 0·01, 0·001, 0·0001, 0·00001 and 0·000001 were used and the output produced consisted of the approximate answer, the number of function evaluations, and the estimated error. The last two values required minor changes in DRMBIU, QATR, and QAR.

After the calculation of the answer the computer calculated a quality Q defined by

1^0. If the obtained error is less than the allowed error, then $Q = 3$. The allowed error is here defined as the requested relative accuracy times the *exact* value of the integral. If the obtained error is greater than the allowed error, then $Q = 1$.

2^0. If the estimated error is greater than the obtained error, then Q is increased by 1.

3^0. If the estimated error is greater than the allowed error, in this case defined as the requested relative accuracy times the *computed* value of the integral, the computer considers that it has failed in the calculation, and signals this by subtracting $\frac{1}{2}$ from Q if $Q = 4$ but by adding $\frac{1}{2}$ if $Q = 1$ or 2.

The quality Q is perhaps easier to understand from Table 1.

TABLE 1. Definition of the quality Q.

	Convergence	Non-convergence
*Obt. error $\leqslant$ Tol. * Exact value*		
Est. error $\geqslant$ obt. error	4	3·5
Est. error $<$ obt. error	3	3·0
*Obt. error $>$ Tol. * Exact value*		
Est. error $\geqslant$ obt. error	2	2·5
Est. error $<$ obt. error	1	1·5

"Convergence" is defined from Est. error $\leqslant$ Tol. * obt. value. All these quantities are available without knowledge of the exact value. "Non-convergence" gives an indication that the computation has failed, this implies increased quality if the requested accuracy is not obtained, but decreased quality if it in fact is obtained.

2. Evaluation

In the performed test, all functions were given as FUNCTION subprograms and approximately the same maximum number of function evaluations were used for all methods. Both the functions and the quadrature routines were used as black boxes, no use of special information on the functions was used to decide step sizes and similar parameters. The exact value of an integral was used only for calculating the obtained error and the quality.

One page of the computer output is reproduced as an appendix. For every method $6\frac{1}{4}$ pages of output was obtained like this and the quality concept was introduced in order to compress the obtained information.

Since I consider the relative accuracy 10^{-5} to be the most revelant one in single IBM precision, a summary of the results for this case is given in Table 2, where the number of integrals calculated with quality Q is printed.

TABLE 2. The number of integrals calculated with quality Q.

Q	March 1971 DRMBIU	September 1971 DRMBIU	QATR	QAR	ROMINT	CCQUAD
4·0	18	22	22	29	27	22
3·5	0	2	0	0	1	1
3·0	15	19	16	14	15	19
2·5	0	0	0	4	1	2
2·0	0	0	0	0	0	0
1·5	0	0	8	0	1	2
1·0	17	7	4	2	5	4
0·0	0	0	0	1	0	0
Average of Q	2·7	3·2	3·0	3·4	3·3	3·2

The quality 0 is given if the computation requires too much CPU time. This occurred with the last integral of the Rice test-package, $\int_0^1 \sin(100\pi x)\,dx = 0$, and the routine QAR. This integral will be discussed later in the paper.

This comparison gives the impression that DRMBIU or QATR is a bad choice, and that QAR or ROMINT is the best choice, but we also have to consider the number of function evaluations. In the first line of Table 3 I give the average number of function evaluations for "Extra nice" integrands (No. 1–21, 24, 28 and 35), in the second line the total number of evaluations for all integrands, and in the third line the number of integrands for which more than 1025 evaluations were necessary. In the fourth line I repeat the average quality and in the last line the ratio quality/average number is given.

From Table 3 it follows that the five different subroutines required about the same number of function evaluations for extra nice integrands and that there was no great difference in the quality of the compared routines. We also find that quality/average number is a useless concept, since the old version of DRMBIU gave the highest (best) value of this ratio.

By using $b - a$ as the maximum step size in DRMBIU, I did not make full use of the parameter HMAX, therefore the interval was often divided only once. However, in QATR the original interval is divided at least four times, if the dimension of the auxiliary storage variable is at least five. Neither did I use a non-zero value of the corresponding parameter K in QAR.

TABLE 3. Values for comparison of the subroutines.

	March 1971 DRMBIU	September 1971 DRMBIU	QATR	QAR	ROMINT	CCQAD
Average for extra nice integrands	12	18	22	20	19	22
Total number for all integrands	4814	145189	32018	125109+?	262022	28454
Number of difficult integrands	0	9	3	9+1	11	7
Quality	2·7	3·2	3·0	3·4	3·3	3·2
Quality/Average number	0·22	0·18	0·14	0·17	0·17	0·15

The ? symbol refers to the case with quality 0. The computation was then terminated before completion.

All subroutines except DRMBIU were successful for the integrand No. 45 $(f(x) = [10x])$, while no subroutine gave a correct answer for integrand No. 47, $(f(x) = 0$ for $0·49 < x < 0·50$ and $-1000(x^2 - x)$ elsewhere).

The obtained error decreased with decreasing required relative accuracy, except in some cases where it increased by a factor less than two when the relative accuracy was changed from 10^{-5} to 10^{-6}. In some exceptional cases the error increase was larger or occured also for larger relative accuracies.

Regarding the estimated errors I have noticed that those from QAR, ROMINT, and CCQUAD are rather realistic, while those from QATR are too optimistic. The estimates in DRMBIU (March 1971 version) had the property of giving the value zero quite often (for the relative accuracy 10^{-6} all except two estimates were zero), but the estimates in the September 1971 version are satisfactory. (The routine was modified by Cody's version of Håvies scheme.).

3. Comments on Integral Number 50

This integrand, which is $\sin(100\pi x)$, is a pathological case with strong oscillations of the integrand over the interval $[0, 1]$. The adaptive routine QAR divides the interval into several subintervals in order to find intervals over which the integral is non-zero and can be calculated with the requested relative accuracy. Therefore the (internal) maximum value of function evaluations of about 524288 was used. I would like to have the maximum number of function evaluations (or interval divisions) as an extra input parameter. A parameter of that kind exists in DRMBIU, QATR, ROMINT, and CCQUAD. With the proposed change the possibility of getting lost in QAR while executing a large program system containing quadrature is significantly diminished.

TABLE 4. Calculation of integral No. 50.

Routine	Error code	Function evaluations	Answer
DRMBIU	0	3	$-4{\cdot}3 \times 10^{-5}$
QATR	1	33	$-3{\cdot}9 \times 10^{-6}$
ROMINT	1	65537	$-3{\cdot}7 \times 10^{-7}$
CCQUAD	0	4375	$+1{\cdot}8 \times 10^{-7}$
QAR 0·1	0	1281	$-6{\cdot}0 \times 10^{-7}$
0·01	0	2289	$-4{\cdot}5 \times 10^{-7}$
0·001	10	256465	$-6{\cdot}1 \times 10^{-7}$

The results in Table 4 were obtained at the calculation of integral No. 50 with the five different routines. For the first four, the results were essentially the same for all relative accuracies, while for QAR results are given for three different requested relative accuracies. The only acceptable results are those of QATR and ROMINT, since these signal a problem with the error code. The numbers 65537 and 4375 are the maximum number of function evaluations with the used versions of ROMINT and CCQUAD, respectively. The numbers 3 and 33 are the minimum numbers for DRMBIU and QATR, respectively.

It can also be noted that if the integrand $\sin(100\pi x)$ is translated to $\sin(100\pi(x + 0{\cdot}005)) = \cos(100\pi x)$, the value of the integral will still be zero, but the value of the integrand at the three points $x = 0, \frac{1}{2}$, and 1 will be 1. The expected value of a numerical calculation of the integral is therefore one, since the first two attempts with a trapezoidal formula will give identical results.

For integrands with strong oscillations special precautions must be made, either by using special methods, as suggested by Filon (1928), or by using a stepsize small enough.

4. Comments on the Subroutines

In this section some specific comments on the five subroutines are given.

Comments on DRMBIU

(a) Inform the user how to obtain the estimated error (T1).
For example, add the following card:

$$T1 = ZERO \qquad\qquad DURM0\,475$$

Change the input–output list by adding T1.

(b) I find it rather difficult for the user to handle the connection between the parameters HMIN and HMAX and the dimension of the work area WK. If the dimension of WK is too small, the routine will store values of WK in unknown storage locations, probably resulting in serious errors. I would prefer that IORD1 is added to the input list as the dimension of WK and that the calculated value IORD is changed by IORD = MIN0 (IORD, IORD1 − 1).—The allocation of storage statement for WK has been modified in Edition 3 of the IMSL Library 1.

Comments on QATR and QAR

Inform the user how to obtain the estimated error. Add an input parameter to QAR that limits the number of function evaluations.

Comments on ROMINT

It is more convenient to have the integrand $F(x)$ in the parameter list. This routine claims to be less sensitive to the accumulation of rounding errors than the customary one.

In the appendix, a page of the output from the text of ROMINT is reproduced. The parameter MAXE is on entry the maximum number of extrapolations wanted, on exit the actual number of extrapolations performed. If the maximum number of extrapolations has been performed without the desired accuracy being obtained, the exit value is zero.

Comments on CCQUAD

The great disadvantage with this subroutine is that it requires a large working space for the cosine transform CSXFRM. On the other hand the cosine transform is returned from the subroutine and can be used to give an approximation to the indefinite integral of the integrand in the interval.

5. Concluding Remarks

The qualities of the tested routines were rather similar and I am not able to give the preference to anyone of them. I am very surprised that the two non-commercial routines behaved so well. In certain connections where the adaptive nature is important, the subroutine QAR from SL-Math is favourable.

Several comparisons of subroutines for numerical quadrature have been published, for example Davis and Rabinowitz (1967), Casaletto, Pickett, and Rice (1969), Cranley and Patterson (1971), Kahaner (1971), and Oliver (1971).

Other articles of interest in connection with evaluations of quadrature routines are those of de Boor (1971a, b), Wilf (1967), Gentleman (1969), Lipow and Stenger (1972), and Lyness (1972). An interesting article with many references is the survey of Dixon (1973).

Acknowledgements

I would like to thank IBM Sweden for making the Program Product QAR from SL-Math available for the evaluation. Valuable comments on preliminary versions of the paper have been given by Mr. Sven Axemo.

References

de Boor, C. (1971a). On writing an automatic integration algorithm. *In* Rice (1971) pp. 201–209.

de Boor, C. (1971b). CADRE, an algorithm for numerical quadrature. *In* Rice (1971) pp. 417–449.

Casaletto, J., Pickett, M., and Rice, J. (1969). A comparison of some numerical integration programs. *SIGNUM Newsletter* **4**, (3), 30–40.

Cranley, R. and Patterson, T. N. L. (1971). On the automatic numerical evaluation of definite integrals. *Comput J.* **14**, 189–198.

Davis, P. J. and Rabinowitz, P. (1967). "Numerical Integration". Blaisdell Publishing Company, Waltham, Mass.

Dixon, V. A. (1973). Numerical quadrature: A survey of available algorithms. These Proceedings, pp. 105–137.

Fairweather, G. (1969). Algorithm 351, modified Romberg quadrature. *Comm. ACM* **12**, 324–325 and **13**, 263.

Filon, L. N. G. (1928). On a quadrature formula for trigonometric integrals. *Proc. Roy. Soc. Edinburgh* **49**, 38–47.

Gentleman, W. M. (1969). Off-the-shelf black boxes for programming. *IEEE Transactions on Education* **12**, 43–50.

Gentleman, W. M. (1972a). Implementing Clenshaw–Curtis quadrature, I, Methodology and experience. *Comm. ACM* **15**, 337–342.

Gentleman, W. M. (1972b). Algorithm 424, Clenshaw–Curtis quadrature. *Comm. ACM* **15**, 353–355 and **16**, 490.

IBM (1969). System/360 Scientific Subroutine Package, Version III, Programmer's Manual GH 20–0205–3 with Technical Newsletter N 20–1944, pp. 297–298.

IBM (1971). IBM System/360 and System/370, IBM 1130 and IBM 1800, Subroutine Library—Mathematics, User's Guide SH 12–5300–0, pp. 400–403, 422–424.

IMSL (1972). IMSL Library 1, Reference Manual IMSL LIB1-0002, p. DRMBIU.

Kahaner, D. K. (1971), Comparison of numerical quadrature formulas. *In* Rice (1971) pp. 229–259.

Lipow, P. R. and Stenger, F. (1972). How slowly can quadrature formulas converge? *Math. Comp.* **26**, 917–922.

Lyness, J. N. (1972). Guidelines for automatic quadrature routines. *In* "Information Processing 71, Proceedings of the IFIP Congress 71". (C. V. Freiman, Ed.). Vol. 2, pp. 1351–1355. North-Holland Publishing Company, Amsterdam.

Oliver, J. (1971). The efficiency of extrapolation methods for numerical integration. *Num. Math.* **17**, 17–32.

Ralston, A. and Wilf, H. S. (1967). "Mathematical Methods for Digital Computers". Vol. 2, John Wiley and Sons, New York.

Rice, J. R. (Ed.) (1971). "Mathematical Software". Academic Press, New York and London.

Wilf, H. S. (1967). Advances in numerical quadrature. *In* Ralston and Wilf (1967) pp. 133–144.

Appendix

ROMINT

INT. NO.	REQ. REL. ERROR	ESTIMATED ERROR	OBTAINED ERROR	QUALITY	MAXE	N	ANSWER
41	1.0E −01	1.937E −03	4.318E −04	4	1	5	4.004318E −01
	1.0E −02	1.937E −03	4.318E −04	4	1	5	4.004318E −01
	1.0E −03	2.492E −04	5.347E −05	4	2	9	4.000534E −01
	1.0E −04	7.153E −06	1.192E −06	4	4	33	4.000012E −01
	1.0E −05	1.192E −06	−5.960E −08	4	5	65	3.999999E −01
	1.0E −06	2.682E −07	−4.172E −07	1	6	129	3.999996E −01
42	1.0E −01	2.241E −03	1.079E −04	4	2	9	1.489795E −01
	1.0E −02	5.484E −05	1.752E −05	4	3	17	1.488891E −01
	1.0E −03	5.484E −05	1.752E −05	4	3	17	1.488891E −01
	1.0E −04	1.439E −05	2.861E −06	4	4	33	1.488744E −01
	1.0E −05	4.768E −07	−1.788E −07	4	6	129	1.488714E −01
	1.0E −06	0.0	−2.384E −07	1	7	257	1.488713E −01
43	1.0E −01	1.075E −03	−1.218E −04	4	1	5	2.855924E −01
	1.0E −02	1.075E −03	−1.218E −04	4	1	5	2.855924E −01
	1.0E −03	4.557E −05	−4.649E −06	4	2	9	2.857096E −01
	1.0E −04	3.457E −06	−4.768E −07	4	3	17	2.857138E −01
	1.0E −05	2.384E −07	−2.384E −07	4	4	33	2.857140E −01
	1.0E −06	2.384E −07	−2.384E −07	4	4	33	2.857140E −01
44	1.0E −01	3.613E −04	−1.144E −05	4	2	9	6.550330E −02
	1.0E −02	3.613E −04	−1.144E −05	4	2	9	6.550330E −02
	1.0E −03	4.947E −06	−7.749E −07	4	3	17	6.551397E −02
	1.0E −04	4.947E −06	−7.749E −07	4	3	17	6.551397E −02
	1.0E −05	5.960E −07	−1.788E −07	4	4	33	6.551456E −02
	1.0E −06	2.980E −08	−1.788E −07	1	5	65	6.551456E −02
45	1.0E −01	3.333E −01	1.667E −01	4	1	5	4.666666E +00
	1.0E −02	3.845E −02	3.827E −02	4	3	17	4.538271E +00
	1.0E −03	2.379E −03	2.378E −03	4	7	257	4.502378E +00
	1.0E −04	2.966E −04	2.966E −04	4	10	2049	4.500297E +00
	1.0E −05	3.624E −05	3.624E −05	4	13	16385	4.500036E +00
	1.0E −06	8.583E −06	8.583E −06	2.5	0	65537	4.500009E +00
46	1.0E −01	0.0	0.0	4	1	5	1.500000E +00
	1.0E −02	0.0	0.0	4	1	5	1.500000E +00
	1.0E −03	0.0	0.0	4	1	5	1.500000E +00
	1.0E −04	0.0	0.0	4	1	5	1.500000E +00
	1.0E −05	0.0	0.0	4	1	5	1.500000E +00
	1.0E −06	0.0	0.0	4	1	5	1.500000E +00
47	1.0E −01	0.0	2.500E +00	3	1	5	1.666666E +02
	1.0E −02	0.0	2.500E +00	1	1	5	1.666666E +02
	1.0E −03	0.0	2.500E +00	1	1	5	1.666666E +02
	1.0E −04	0.0	2.500E +00	1	1	5	1.666666E +02
	1.0E −05	0.0	2.500E +00	1	1	5	1.666666E +02
	1.0E −06	0.0	2.500E +00	1	1	5	1.666666E +02
48	1.0E −01	4.146E −03	4.609E −03	3	3	17	3.114614E −01
	1.0E −02	5.026E −04	−7.094E −04	3	6	129	3.061434E −01
	1.0E −03	2.188E −04	−4.721E −05	4	8	513	3.068056E −01
	1.0E −04	8.017E −06	5.424E −06	4	12	8193	3.068582E −01
	1.0E −05	4.470E −06	−1.073E −06	3.5	0	65537	3.068517E −01
	1.0E −06	4.470E −06	−1.073E −06	2.5	0	65537	3.068517E −01

9. Some Extrapolation Methods for the Numerical Calculation of Multidimensional Integrals

ALAN C. GENZ

Mathematical Institute,
University of Kent at Canterbury
Canterbury, England.

1. Introduction

In this paper I will discuss some methods for the numerical evaluation of the integral given by

$$If = \int_0^1 \int_0^1 \cdots \int_0^1 f(x_1, x_2, \ldots, x_n) \, dx_1 dx_2 \ldots, dx_n. \tag{1}$$

All practical methods for evaluating If numerically involve using an approximation of the form

$$\sum_{i=1}^m w_i f(X_i), \quad \text{with} \quad \sum_{i=1}^m w_i = 1, \quad X_i = (x_{1i}, x_{2i}, \ldots, x_{ni}).$$

One of the first such methods to be developed was a natural generalization of an effective one-dimensional method. If a one-dimensional quadrature rule is given by

$$S_m f_1 = \sum_{i=1}^m w_i f_1(x_i),$$

a natural generalization to the n variable problem is given by the product rule

$$S_m f = \sum_{i_1=1}^m w_{i_1} \sum_{i_2=1}^m w_{i_2} \cdots \sum_{i_n=1}^m w_{i_n} f(x_{i_1}, x_{i_2}, \ldots, x_{i_n}).$$

Usually a practical procedure begins by forming $S_m f$ for m small and gradually increasing m until comparison between successive values in the sequence $\{S_m f\}$ suggests that convergence has been obtained.

159

The product rule methods often work very well when the one-dimensional basic rule is chosen appropriately and $f(X)$ is sufficiently well behaved but they have as their main disadvantage the fact that the number of function evaluations (m^n for $S_m f$) grows very rapidly when n is larger than say 3 or 4. If one estimate for If is obtained involving m^n function evaluations and is not believed to be a good one a new estimate will generally require $(m + 1)^n$ new function evaluations and might only suggest how good the previous estimate was. This problem of the rapid growth in the number of function evaluations makes the simple product rule methods very impractical for problems when n is large and the integrand $f(X)$ not well behaved.

A second line of approach to the practical problem of evaluating If began with the development of the Monte-Carlo methods which initially approximated If by

$$S_N f = \frac{1}{N} \sum_{i=1}^{N} F(R_i)$$

where R_i was a vector with n pseudo random components. This line of approach avoided the problem of the large number of function evaluations needed to go from one estimate of If to the next but generally had much slower convergence than the product rule methods.

Significant improvements along both lines of approach have brought us into a present position where, in the first case, the use of extrapolation, specially developed n dimensional rules, and coordinate transformations has led to the development of methods which have reduced somewhat the large growth rate in the number of necessary function evaluations. In the second case more sophisticated ways of choosing the evaluation points R_i, and more sophisticated methods of combining the estimates $S_N f$ have led to methods with better convergence properties. For large n methods developed in the second category are still thought to be the only practical methods.

Reviews and discussions of general as well as practical developments in both areas are given by David and Rabinowitz (1967, Chapter 5), Haber (1970), and Stroud (1972). Some fairly recent developments of practical methods in the second category are given by Cranley and Patterson (1970), Lautrup (1971), Keast (1972), Gallaher (1973), and Tsuda (1973). In the first category some specific references to practical methods are Lyness and McHugh (1963), Sag and Szekeres (1964), Stenger (1971) and Genz (1972).

In this paper I will consider three related methods in the first category designed to reduce the growth rate of the number of necessary functional evaluations without sacrificing too much in the way of convergence. The methods will involve obtaining a large number of estimates for If and combining them using various extrapolation techniques to produce improved estimates for If.

2. The Basic Sequence of Approximations to If

The three methods to be discussed later will use the sequence of n dimensional product midpoint rules defined by

$$S_M f = 2^{-[M]} \sum_{i_1=1}^{2^{m_1}} \sum_{i_2=1}^{2^{m_2}} \cdots \sum_{i_n=1}^{2^{m_n}} f\left(\frac{2i_1 - 1}{2^{m_1} + 1}, \frac{2i_2 - 1}{2^{m_2} + 1}, \cdots, \frac{2i_n - 1}{2^{m_n} + 1}\right) \qquad (2)$$

where $M = (m_1, m_2, \ldots, m_n)$, $[M] = m_1 + m_2 + \ldots + m_n$.

These approximations to If are to be computed in the following order. The one approximation with $[M] = 0$ will be computed first, then the n approximations with $[M] = 1$, and so on. During stage l,

$$\binom{l + n - 1}{n - 1}$$

sequence elements in the sequence $\{S_M f\}$ are generated each of which has required 2^l function evaluations. At the end of stage l, a total of

$$\binom{l + n}{n}$$

sequence elements will have been generated requiring the total number of function evaluations given by

$$N_l^{(2)} = \sum_{k=0}^{l} 2^k \binom{k + n - 1}{n - 1}.$$

A comparison of the general growth rate in the number of function evaluations given by this number and the general growth rate for a simple product rule method:

$$N_l^{(1)} = \sum_{k=0}^{l} (k + 1)^n$$

is given for some representative values of l and n in Table 1 below.

As can be seen $N_l^{(2)}$ is generally smaller than $N_l^{(1)}$ and the difference between the two increases as n gets larger, so the growth rate has been reduced to what is hoped will be a more manageable practical value.

There are many ways with which to use the information in the sequence $\{S_M f\}$ and the three methods to be discussed in the following sections are some that seem to work reasonably well in practice.

TABLE 1. $N_l^{(1)}$, $N_l^{(2)}$ (approximately) with $k = 1000$.

l	n			
	4	6	8	10
1	17, 9	65, 13	257, 17	1·0k, 21
2	98, 49	794, 97	6·8k, 161	60k, 241
4	979, 769	21k, 2·5k	460k, 64k	1000k, 13k
6	4·7k, 7·9k	180k, 40k	7900k, 140k	35000k, 400k
8	15k, 66k	980k, 470k		
10	40k, 470k			

The theory for all three methods is based on the asymptotic expansion for $S_M f$ (Lyness and McHugh, 1970) given by

$$S_M f \sim I f + \sum_{j=1}^{d} \sum_{[K]=j} c_K(f) h_1^{k_1} h_2^{k_2}, \ldots, h_n^{k_n} + O(2^{-2(d+1)[M]}) \qquad (3)$$

with

$$h_i = 2^{-2m_i}, \sum_{[K]=j} = \sum_{k_1=0}^{j} \sum_{k_2=0}^{j-k_1} \cdots \sum_{k_{n-1}=0}^{j-k_1-\ldots-k_{n-2}}, k_n = j - k_1 - \ldots - k_{n-1}.$$

The coefficients $c_K(f)$ depend on mixed partial derivatives of the integrand f, so the expansion exists whenever f has existent mixed partial derivatives in the integration region with total order $\leqslant 2d$. The important point when using (3) for the purposes of extrapolation is that these coefficients are independent of M.

3. Method 1: A Multivariable Recursive Interpolation Method

This method is based on a direct application of the multivariable recursive interpolation scheme developed by McKinney (1972). Let $F(H_M) = F(h_1, h_2, \ldots, h_n) = S_M f$, with $h_i = 2^{-2m_i}$. Because $F(H_M)$ is approximately a multivariable polynomial, a natural extrapolation method for determining $I f$ would be to form an interpolation polynomial $F'(H_M)$ for $F(H_M)$ and then to evaluate $F'(H_M = (0, 0, \ldots, 0))$. McKinney's recursive interpolation scheme allows this to be done in a practical situation.

First, the ordering on M must be specified exactly. Following McKinney, let

$$_M S_k = \sum_{i=1}^{k} m_i;$$

then $N < M$ if and only if

(a) $_NS_n < {_M}S_n$ or

(b) $_NS_k < {_M}S_k$ and $_NS_i = {_M}S_i$ for some integer k such that $0 < k < n$ and all integers i such that $k < i \leqslant n$.

This ordering imposes a one-to-one mapping of the integer n-tuples $(m_1, m_2, \ldots, m_n)$ onto the non-negative integers given by

$$M = \sum_{k=1}^{n} \left(\frac{_MS_k + k - 1}{k} \right)$$

So we have $0 = (0, 0, \ldots, 0)$, $1 = (0, 0, \ldots, 0, 1)$, $2 = (0, 0, \ldots, 0, 1, 0)$, and so on. In practice, the successor M' to M is

$$M' = (m_1 + 1, m_2 - 1, m_3, \ldots, m_n) \quad \text{if} \quad m_2 \neq 0.$$

If

$$m_i = 0 \quad \text{for} \quad i = 2, 3, \ldots, k$$

then

$$M' = (0, 0, \ldots, 0, m_1 + 1, m_{k+1} - 1, m_{k+2}, \ldots, m_n).$$

McKinney's interpolation method applied to the sequence $\{S_M\}$ becomes the following:
for

$$M = 1, 2, 3, \ldots$$

form

$$R_M f = R_{M-1} f + a_M f \cdot \phi_M(0)$$

with

$$R_0 f = S_0 f \tag{4}$$

$$a_M f = \left(S_M f - \left(R_0 f + \sum_{K=1}^{M-1} a_K f \cdot \phi_K(H_M) \right) \right) \Big/ \phi_M(H_M)$$

$$H_M = (2^{-2m_1}, 2^{-2m_2}, \ldots, 2^{-2m_n}) = (h_1, h_2, \ldots, h_n)$$

$$\phi_K(H_M) = \prod_{i=1}^{n} \prod_{j=1}^{k_i} (h_i - 2^{-2(j-1)})$$

For

$$M = \binom{n+l}{l} - 1,$$

$R_M f$ is the value at $H = (0, 0, \ldots, 0)$ of the unique interpolation polynomial of total degree d which interpolates the first

$$\binom{n+l}{l}$$

elements in the sequence $\{S_M f\}$. So $R_M f$ is an approximation to If with the first

$$\binom{n+l}{l}$$

terms (not including If) in the asymptotic expansion (3) eliminated. This method is in some sense a generalization of the Romberg method for evaluating one dimensional integrals.

This method produces a sequence of approximations $\{R_M f\}$ converging to If subject to suitable conditions on f. A practical error estimate for this method is given by

$$E_M f = \sum_{i=1}^{n} (R_M f - R_{M'(i)} f)/n_m,$$

where

$$M'(i) = (m_1, m_2, \ldots, m_{i-1}, m_i - 1, m_{i+1}, \ldots, m_n),$$
$$R_{M'(i)} f = R_M f, \quad \text{if} \quad m_i = 0,$$
$$n_m = \text{number of } m_i \neq 0 \text{ in } M.$$

The overall growth in the number of function evaluations for this method is given by $N_l^{(2)}$ if one wishes to compare it with some of the simple product methods.

At the end of stage l, $N_l^{(2)}$ function evaluation will have been necessary and the method will have integrated exactly any linear combination of the

$$\binom{n+2l}{2l}$$

monomials of total degree less than or equal to $2l$. But the method can be terminated whenever the error is below a desired tolerance. To obtain each new sequence element requires only 2^l function evaluations at stage l, so for example if after $N_l^{(2)}$ function evaluations the specified accuracy has not been obtained this does not necessarily mean that the number of function evaluations must be increased to $N_{l+1}^{(2)}$.

The method could also be used with a product midpoint rule which uses only l points per iteration at stage l with only slight modification of eqns (4) if the function was exceptionally smooth, or the method could be modified to use a slightly higher order basic product rule.

The main difficulties in the practical application of the method are that the numbers $R_M f$ and $a_M f$ must be stored in arrays which must have some limit in size, and the increasing amount of time needed to calculate the functions $\phi_K(H_M)$ for large n, although there was no difficulty with these two problems for the examples to be presented in Section 6. It is also possible that the calculation of $\phi_K(H_M)$ might be optimised.

4. Method 2: A Multinomial Expansion Coefficient Method

This method was initially motivated by a suggestion from Chisholm (1973). It involves forming a sequence of approximations to If for $l = 0, 1, 2, \ldots$ given by

$$S_A^{(l)}f = \frac{1}{n^l} \sum_{[M]=l} \frac{l!}{m_1! \, m_2! \ldots, m_n!} S_M f.$$

An extrapolation method is then applied to $\{S_A^{(l)}\}$.

The form of extrapolation which is appropriate for the sequence $\{S_A^{(l)}\}$ is indicated by the following theorem.

THEOREM 1. *If*

$$F(H) = A + \sum_{K=1}^{K'} b_K h_1^{\alpha k_1} h_2^{\alpha k_2} \ldots h_n^{\alpha k_n}$$

and

$$A^{(l)} = \frac{1}{n^l} \sum_{[M]=l} \frac{l!}{m_1! \ldots, m_n!} F(H_M)$$

with

$$H_M = (2^{-m_1}, 2^{-m_2}, \ldots, 2^{-m_n}),$$

then

$$A^{(l)} = A + \sum_{K=1}^{K} b_K \beta_K^l$$

with

$$\beta_K = (2^{-\alpha k_1} + 2^{-\alpha k_2} + \ldots, 2^{-\alpha k_n})/n.$$

Proof.

$$A^{(l)} = \frac{1}{n^l} \sum_{[M]=l} \frac{l!}{m_1! \, m_2! \ldots, m_n!} F(H_M)$$

$$= A + \sum_{K=1}^{K'} b_K \frac{1}{n^l} \sum_{[M]=l} \frac{l!}{m_1! \ldots, m_n!} (2^{-\alpha k_1})^{m_n} \ldots (2^{-\alpha k_n})^{m_n}$$

$$= A + \sum_{K=1}^{K} \frac{1}{n^l} (2^{-\alpha k_1} + 2^{-\alpha k_2} + \ldots + 2^{-\alpha k_n})^l$$

$$= A + \sum_{K=1}^{K} b_K \beta_K^l.$$

This completes the proof, and the theorem can be directly applied to the asymptotic expansion (3) with $\alpha_{k_j} = 2k_j$. So $S_A^{(l)}f$ has the asymptotic form

$$S_A^{(l)} \sim If + \sum_{[K] \leq d} c_K(f)\beta_K^{\,l} + O\left(\beta_{\binom{n+d}{d}+1}^{\,l}\right) \tag{5}$$

with

$$\beta_K = \left(\frac{2^{-2k_1} + 2^{-2k_2} + \ldots 2^{-2k_n}}{n}\right).$$

If all the terms in the sum on the right-side of (5) with β_K equal are combined, then (5) can be re-written as

$$S_A^{(l)} \sim If + \sum_{j=1}^{j'} d_j(f)\delta_j^{\,l} + O(\delta_{j+1}^{\,l}) \tag{6}$$

where the numbers $d_j(f)$ are appropriate sums of the $c_K(f)$ and δ_j are the unique β_K determined by taking partitions with at most n parts of the integers $1, 2, \ldots$ to form the exponents $k_1, k_2, \ldots, k_n$. If $k_1, k_2, \ldots, k_n$ is the jth partition in some ordering of all the partitions with at most n parts of the positive integers then

$$\delta_j = \left(\frac{2^{-2k_1} + \ldots + 2^{-2k_n}}{n}\right).$$

For example, with $n = 3$ the first few (k_1, k_2, k_3) and their respective δ_j obtained by selecting the partitions as they occur in the ordering described in Section 3 are given by

K	$(0,0,1)$,	$(0,0,2)$,	$(0,1,1)$,	$(0,0,3)$,	$(0,1,2)$,	$(1,1,1)$,	$(0,0,4)$
δ_j	3/4	11/16	1/2	43/64	7/16	1/4	171/256

Once an ordering for the sequence $\{\delta_j\}$ is determined an extrapolation method similar to the one used for the one dimensional Romberg quadrature method can be applied.
Let

$$T_0^{(l)} = S_A^{(l)} \sim If + \sum_{j=1}^{j'} d_j^{(0)}\delta_j^{\,l}, \quad \text{with} \quad d_j^{(0)} = d_j(f)$$

and form for $l = 0, 1, \ldots, j', k = 1, 2, 3, \ldots, l$

$$T_k^{(l)} = T_{k-1}^{(l+1)} + \delta_k(T_{k-1}^{(l+1)} - T_{k-1}^{(l)})/(1 - \delta_k). \tag{7}$$

A simple inductive proof shows that

$$T_k^{(l)} = If + \sum_{j=k+1}^{j'} d_j^{(k)}\delta_j^{\,l} \quad \text{for} \quad k < j'$$

with

$$d_j^{(k)} = \left(\frac{\delta_j - \delta_1}{1 - \delta_1}\right)\left(\frac{\delta_j - \delta_2}{1 - \delta_2}\right) \cdots \left(\frac{\delta_j - \delta_k}{1 - \delta_k}\right) d_j^{(0)},$$

so this extrapolation method eliminates the first k terms in the asymptotic expansion (6) given $S_A^{(0)}, S_A^{(1)}, \ldots, S_A^{(k)}$.

An obvious problem here which has not yet been solved is how to choose the best ordering for the sequence $\{\delta_j\}$. Some of the δ_j's are very similar to others even though they occur much later in any obvious ordering. One possibility would be to choose δ_{k+1} such that $|d_i^{(k)}/d_i^{(0)}|$ has maximum value for $k + 1 = 1$ over some large range of i. This was tried on some examples but there seemed to be no real improvement over the simple procedure of selecting the δ_j associated with the ordering of K described in Section 3. The examples given in Section 6 were produced using this second technique.

An extrapolation method which might avoid this difficulty is the ε-algorithm (Wynn, 1956).
Let

$$\varepsilon_0^{(l)} = S_A^{(l)}$$

and form for $l = 0, 1, \ldots; k = 1, 2, \ldots,$

$$\varepsilon_{k+1}^{(l)} = \varepsilon_{k-1}^{(l+1)} + (\varepsilon_k^{(l+1)} - \varepsilon_k^{(l)})^{-1}$$

with

$$\varepsilon_{-1}^{(l)} = 0.$$

The analysis of the use of this extrapolation method is more complicated, but when the δ_j are well separated it eliminates roughly half as many terms in the asymptotic expansion given the same number of elements in the sequence $\{S_A^{(l)}\}$ as the method defined by eqn (7). This extrapolation method did not work as well as the first method in the examples tested but it might be expected to work better when the integrand f is not smooth enough for the asymptotic expansion to have a form as simple as that given by eqn (3).

5. Method 3: A Generating Function Method

This method is developed from a multidimensional sequence to generating function transformation. Let the multivariable mixed partial backward differences be given by

$$\nabla^{(n)} S_M f = \sum_{k_1=0}^{1} \sum_{k_2=0}^{1} \cdots \sum_{k_n=0}^{1} (-1)^{[K]} S_{M\theta K} f$$

where $M\theta K = (m_1 - k_1, m_2 - k_2, \ldots, m_n - k_n)$; $S_{M\theta K} f = 0$ if $m_j - k_j < 0$ for any j. A generating function for the sequence $\{S_M f\}$ can then be formed and is given by

$$F_M(x_1, x_2, \ldots, x_n) f = \sum_{k_1=0}^{m_1} \sum_{k_2=0}^{m_2} \cdots \sum_{k_n=0}^{m_n} \nabla^{(n)} S_K f \cdot x_1^{k_1} \cdot x_2^{k_2} \cdots x_n^{k_n}$$

This is an n-variable generalization of the more familiar

$$F_{m_1}(x) = S_0 + (S_1 - S_0) x + (S_2 - S_1) x^2 + \ldots (S_{m_1} - S_{m_1-1}) x^{m_1}$$

Clearly $F_{m_1}(1) = S_{m_1}$. Induction of n shows generally that

$$F_M(1, 1, \ldots, 1) f = S_M f.$$

Now $F_M(X)$ involves $m_1, m_2, \ldots, m_n$ terms from the sequence $\{S_M f\}$. A portion of $F_M(X)$ to be used for the purposes of this investigation will be expressed in the form

$$F^{(l)}(X) f = \sum_{K=0}^{\binom{n+l}{l}-1} \nabla^{(n)} S_K f x_1^{k_1} x_2^{k_2} \cdots x_n^{k_n}. \tag{9}$$

This function involves for a given l only the first

$$\binom{n+l}{l}$$

terms in the sequence $\{S_M f\}$. The sequence to be used for extrapolation purposes is obtained by defining $S_B^{(l)} f = F^{(l)}(1, 1, \ldots, 1) f$. The form given by eqn (9) for $S_B^{(l)} f$ is not particularly suitable for computational purposes but a somewhat lengthy combinatorial argument which will not be repeated here shows that $S_B^{(l)} f$ can be re-written in the form

$$S_B^{(l)} f = \sum_{j=0}^{n-1} (-1)^j \binom{n-1}{j} S_C^{(l-j)} f, \tag{10}$$

where

$$S_C^{(i)} f = \sum_{[K]=i} S_K f; S_C^{(i)} f = 0 \quad \text{if} \quad i < 0.$$

The asymptotic form for $S_B^{(l)}f$ can be expressed by

$$S_B^{(l)}f \sim If + \sum_{j=1}^{d} \rho_j^l \sum_{j'=0}^{d'_j} r_{j,j'}(f)l^{j'} + O(2^{-2(d+1)}) \tag{11}$$

where $\rho_j = 2^{-2j}$. This form is established by the consideration of the effect of the transformation defined by eqn (10) on various classes of terms in the asymptotic expansion (3) for $S_M f$. To begin with the constant term If has coefficient as a result of eqn (10) equal to

$$\sum_{j=0}^{n-1} (-1)^j \binom{n-1}{j} \binom{n-1+l-j}{l-j}$$

which equals 1. A proof of this can be found in Riordan (1968, Chapter 1). The detailed analysis necessary to consider all of the terms in the asymptotic expansion (3) will not be given here. Generally associated with each $C_K(f)$ in (3) is a factor

$$2^{-2K \cdot M}, \quad \text{with} \quad K \cdot M = k_1 m_1 + k_2 m_2 + \ldots + k_n m_n.$$

When summed over $[M] = l$ and transformed according to eqn (10) the effect is

$$\sum_{j=0}^{n-1} (-1)^j \binom{n-1}{j} \sum_{m_1=0}^{l-j} \sum_{m_2=0}^{l-j-m_1} \cdots \sum_{m_{n-1}=0}^{l-j-m_1-\ldots-m_{n-2}} 2^{-2K \cdot M}.$$

This will produce a sum of geometric terms with polynomials in l as factors.

The point of this analysis is that the form given by eqn (11) is an exponential cum polynomial sum for which the ε-algorithm is an effective extrapolation method (Wynn, 1972). So method 3 consists of generation the sums $S_C^{(l)}f$ from the basic sequence $S_M f$ and applying the $n-1$ order backward difference transformation (10), followed by the ε-algorithm. This method is the most straightforward of the three methods to use although the theory for it involves fairly complicated combinatorial analysis. This method should be a method which will work for some functions that are not smooth enough to have an asymptotic expansion exactly like that given by eqn (3). If, for example, the powers associated with each $C_K(f)$ are given by non-integral values the form of eqn (11) remains the same even though the ρ_j will change, so the ε-algorithm should still be effective.

6. Examples

The first three examples in this section are taken from the book by Stroud (1973, p. 124) and the last from the paper by Cranley and Patterson

(1970, p. 71). For comparison the $(l + 1)^n$ point Gaussian product rule approximation to If is given along with the result from methods 1, 2 and 3. Example 1 involves the function

$$f_1(x_1, x_2, x_3) = 8/(1 + 2(x_1 + x_2 + x_3))$$

with $If_1 = 2{\cdot}15214283 \ldots$. The results are given in Table 2.

TABLE 2.

l	G_l	Method 1	Method 2	Method 3
1	2·147...	2·12...	2·12...	2·09...
2	2·159...	2·146...	2·145...	2·151...
3	2·15213...	2·1509...	2·154...	2·1519...
4	2·1521425...	2·1518...	2·1529...	2·1523...
5	2·15214281...	2·15208...	2·15217...	2·15219...
6	2·15214283...	2·15213...	2·152147...	2·15217...
Total points	784		2,815	

The Gaussian product rule is clearly better in this case as is expected for a fairly smooth function in only three variables.

Example 2 involves the function

$$f_2(x_1, x_2, x_3, x_4) = \exp\left(|x_1 + x_1 - 1| + |x_2 + x_2 - 1| + |x_3 + x_3 - 1| \right. $$
$$\left. + |x_4 + x_4 - 1|\right)$$

with $If_2 = 139{\cdot}4754\ldots$. The results are given in Table 3.

TABLE 3.

l	G_l	Method 1	Method 2	Method 3
1	161·0...	71·3...	71·3...	57·5...
2	118·5...	133·1...	136·9...	101·2...
3	146·3...	149·1...	150·2...	158·4...
4	130·7...	139·6...	133·7...	140·5...
5	142·7...	138·4...	137·4...	139·43...
6	134·7...	139·8...	137·3...	139·49...
Total points	4,676		7,737	

Here the Gaussian rules behave poorly whereas method 3 does much better, as is expected because of the discontinuous derivatives in f_2 at $(0, 0, 0, 0)$.

Example 3 involves the function

$$f_3(x_1, x_2, x_3, x_4, x_5) = \exp\left(-x_1, x_2, x_3, x_4, x_5\right)$$

with $If_3 = 0{\cdot}970657191388\ldots$. The results are given in Table 4.

TABLE 4.

l	G_l	Method 1	Method 2	Method 3
1	0·97065...	0·9700...	0·9700...	0·969...
2	0·97065719...	0·9705...	0·9705...	0·9702...
3	0·970657191386...	0·970649...	0·97057...	0·9707...
4	0·970657191384...	0·9706577...	0·970641...	0·970642...
5		0·9706568...	0·97066...	0·970655...
Total points	4,425		5,503	

Here again the Gaussian rules do very well because the function is very well-behaved.

Example 4 involves the function

$$f_4(x_1, x_2, x_3, x_4, x_5, x_6) = ln^2\big((x_1, x_2, x_3)/(x_4, x_5, x_6)\big) \cdot x_1, x_2, x_3, x_4, x_5, x_6$$

with $If_4 = 0{\cdot}0234375\ldots$. The results are given in Table 5.

TABLE 5.

l	G_l	Method 1	Method 2	Method 3
1		0·03...	0·03...	0·022...
2		0·025...	0·026...	0·025...
3	0·024...	0·024...	0·024...	0·024...
4		0·0236...	0·0239...	0·02346...
5	0·0236...	0·02349...	0·0237...	0·02344...
Total points	67,171		10,625	

In this example method 3 does much better than the Gaussian rules and with fewer function evaluation points. Methods 1 and 2 are also better. The results for method 3 are also better than those for the methods of Sag and Szekeres (1964) and Cranley and Patterson (1970) who also tested this particular example.

Conclusions

Three methods for calculating If were developed which have a manageable growth rate in the number of required functional evaluations and are fairly easy to use in practice. Method 3 is probably the best of the three methods as a general method because of its ease of use and wider range of applicability. Method 1, however, should be particularly well-suited for moderately well-behaved integrands when the Gaussian product rules are inappropriate. Method 2 has not performed as well generally as methods 1 and 3 but it is possible that a better choice of extrapolation parameters could improve its behaviour.

What still needs to be done is to select an appropriate set of test examples and then to thoroughly test the large number of methods that now exist to see which methods are generally best for particular classes of functions $f(X)$ or all classes of functions $f(X)$.

References

Chisholm, J. S. R. (1973). Private communication.
Cranley, R. and Patterson, T. N. L. (1970). *Num. Math.* **16,** 58–72.
Davies, P. J. and Rabinowitz, P. (1967). "Numerical Integration". Blaisdell Publishing Company, Waltham, Mass.
Gallaher, L. J. (1973). *Comm. ACM* **16,** 49–50.
Genz, A. (1972). *Computer Phys. Comm.* **4,** 11–15.
Haber, S. (1970). *SIAM Review* **12,** 481–525.
Keast, P. (1972). University of Toronto Department of Computer Science Technical Report No. 40.
Lautrup, B. (1971). Proceedings of Colloquium on Advanced Computing Methods in Theoritical Physics, CNRS, Marseille.
Lyness, J. and McHugh, B. J. J. (1963). *Computer J.* **6,** 264–270.
Lyness, J. and McHugh, B. J. J. (1970). *Num. Math.* **15,** 333–344.
McKinney, E. H. (1972). *Math. Comp.* **26,** 723–735.
Riordan, J. (1968). "Combinatorial Identities". John Wiley and Sons, New York.
Sag, J. W. and Szekeres, G. (1964). *Math. Comp.* **18,** 245–253.
Stenger, F. (1971). *Math. Comp.* **25,** microfiche supplement.
Stroud, A. H. (1971). "Approximate Calculation of Multiple Integrals". Prentice-Hall, Englewood Cliffs, New Jersey.
Tsuda, T. (1973). *Num. Math.* **20,** 377–391.
Wynn, P. (1956). *MTAC* **10,** 91–96.
Wynn, P. (1972). University of Montreal Centre of Mathematical Research Report 244.

Discussion: Numerical Quadrature

PROFESSOR L. M. DELVES, (*Liverpool University*). Can Mrs. Dixon or Dr. Einarsson comment on the use of integrand packages (e.g. that of Casaletto, Pickett and Rice) to test quadrature routines. How closely can they be thought of as representative of real life?

MRS. DIXON. I am glad this question has arisen since I feel strongly about both the problem of testing quadrature routines and the Casaletto, Pickett and Rice (CPR) test package. Now that many good automatic routines are available the problem of comparing them all will become extremely difficult unless the procedure for testing each new routine is standardised to some extent. A natural step is to provide a test package of integrals on which each routine can be tried. The problems are then:

(i) to devise a concise set of examples which cover the types of behaviour that arise in normal circumstances, and

(ii) to draw valid conclusions from the results obtained from this package.

O'Hara and Smith (1968, 17 examples), Kahaner (1971, 21 examples) and CPR (1969, 50 examples) have devised integrand packages which have all subsequently been used by other authors to test and compare new routines. The O'Hara and Smith package is small but comprehensive. Kahaner's package was chosen to give a good representation of the quadrature work-load at his own computer installation. On the other hand the CPR package, potentially having more scope because of its larger content, is in my opinion a rather strange collection of examples which are hardly representative of real life. It is very unbalanced since 30 of the integrals are extremely well-behaved (20 of these are polynomials) and of the remainder, 18 are quite difficult (10 of these are extremely difficult e.g.

$$\int_0^1 [10x]\, dx, \qquad \int_0^{2\pi} x \sin 30x \cos 50x\, dx).$$

Moreover there is no attempt to sort these integrals into types (e.g. well-behaved, oscillatory, discontinuous etc.) or to grade them in order of difficulty.

An integrand package which covers all types of behaviour should only be fully used for testing general-purpose routines. It is unfortunate that the very existence of such a package encourages the indiscriminate testing of any automatic routine regardless of the fact that the routine may only be designed to cope with certain types of behaviour. This makes interpretation of the results very difficult.

I should like to see a standard procedure for testing quadrature routines adopted in the near future. A new package might be devised incorporating the best examples of the packages already mentioned and divided into sections each dealing with a certain type of behaviour. The results would then indicate the strong and weak points of a general-purpose routine in addition to the overall picture of its performance. Routines designed to cope with particular types of integrand behaviour would only be tested on the examples in the relevant sections. In order to provide a larger sample of tests without making the package unwieldy a transformation suggested by O'Hara and Smith (1968) could be used, i.e.

$$t = \frac{(\beta + 1)\, x + \beta - 1}{(\beta - 1)\, x + \beta + 1}, \qquad -1 \leqslant x \leqslant 1.$$

The integrand is continuously deformed as the parameter β varies, while the range remains unchanged.

References

Casaletto, J., Picket, M. and Rice, J. (1969). A comparison of some numerical integration programs. *SIGNUM Newsletter* **3**, 30–40.

Kahaner, D. K. (1971). Comparison of numerical quadrature formulas. *In* "Mathematical Software" (Ed. J. R. Rice). ACM Monograph Series. Academic Press, London and New York.

O'Hara, H. and Smith, F. J. (1968). Error estimation in Clenshaw–Curtis quadrature formula. *Comput. J.* **11**, 213–219.

DR. EINARSSON. I agree with the opinion of Mrs. Dixon that the Rice package contains too many polynomials and that functions with singularities just outside the integration interval should be included. I would also like to have cases with $a > b$ and $a = b$ included in a new package.

PROF. DELVES. The "Japanese" algorithm referred to by Mrs. Dixon is based on a method which has been discovered many times, and has been used in multi-dimensional quadrature by Sag and Szekeris around 1964. Does Mrs. Dixon or Mr. Genz have any comments on this work?

MRS. DIXON. I am not acquainted with this paper, though I know that there has been other work on rather similar lines, for instance, that of Schwarz in *J. Comput. Phys.* **4**, (1969), 19–29. Whoever first invented them, methods of this type are certainly proving effective in dealing with integrals possessing end-point singularities.

MR. GENZ. Most transformation methods have the disadvantage that the transformation involves additional and sometimes rather significant computational work. The method of Sag and Szekeres did well on the examples given in their paper and should probably be tested more thoroughly and compared with other methods.

PROF. DELVES. An alternative way of attempting to beat the dimensionality effect is that used by Cranley and Patterson. Has Mr. Genz any comparisons to make with his own method?

MR. GENZ. Example 4 from my lecture (p. 171) used an integrand also used by Cranley and Patterson. Also, method 3 (p. 168) using approximately 10,000 points did better than the methods of Cranley and Patterson and Sag and Szekeres on this particular example, although there are of course other examples where the method of Cranley and Patterson is better. Now that a significant number of methods have been developed what is needed is a comprehensive testing and comparison of the various methods.

PROF. DELVES. Essentially all of the algorithms presented by Mr. Miller for integral equations used a direct expansion of the solution in terms of, for example,

Chebyshev polynomials, rather than using a collocation method based directly on a numerical quadrature rule. Is this purely chance, or do such methods have overriding advantages in practice?

MR. MILLER. It is not easy to draw a distinction between the two types of method; for example, the El Gendi method can be regarded as based either on collocation at the Chebyshev points or on the use of an expansion in Chebyshev polynomials, and the solution can be obtained almost equally easily in terms of function values or series coefficients. Methods based on expansion of the solution have much to commend them. Provided that the solution has suitable behaviour they are both accurate and economical. They have also the attractive feature that the evaluation of the associated moment integrals can be carried out independently of the actual process of solution, by whatever method is appropriate.

DR. A. R. GOURLAY (*Loughborough University*). It might be worth considering the work of Lambert and Shaw published in *Maths. of Comp.* **10** (1965), 456–462, for the quadrature of functions with singularities.

MRS. DIXON. Is this to be taken as an observation or a question? If the latter, then the answer is that it is almost certainly not worth considering in an automatic routine since the method requires values of derivatives of the integrand as well as values of the integrand itself. (The method was originally proposed for the solution of differential equations but the authors claim that it is applicable to quadrature).

MRS. DIXON. Can NAG comment on the relative efficiencies of their automatic implementations of the Patterson and Clenshaw–Curtis quadrature methods. The result from our test examples (which include both well-behaved and badly-behaved integrands) show that there is little to choose between our automatic implementations of the two methods. The Clenshaw–Curtis method is marginally preferable. The error-bound used in the Clenshaw–Curtis method is $E_N^{(a)}$ of O'Hara and Smith (1968).

MR. HAGUE. The NAG contributor for quadrature (Dr. M. Kennedy of Queens, Belfast) works with Dr. Smith. We believe that the NAG quadrature testing software is based on the test set developed by Smith and O'Hara. There appeared little difference in the performance of the NAG routines (e.g. between versions of Clenshaw–Curtis and Cranley–Patterson) on these test sets.

MR. FORD. If possible, the results of NAG testing in quadrature will be provided for publication in the conference proceedings. The NAG contributor and validator for quadrature are not present at the meeting.

10. Initial and Boundary Value Routines for Ordinary Differential Equations

J. WALSH

Department of Mathematics,
Manchester University, Manchester, England.

1. Types of Problem

The problem of solving ordinary differential equations numerically arises in many fields of scientific computing, including engineering, physics, chemistry, applied mathematics, biology, and economics. Because the programmer may not be an expert mathematician, there is always a demand for simple routines to integrate ordinary differential equations, which do not require any detailed knowledge of the mathematical theory. From the early days of computing, Runge–Kutta routines have been provided as a standard facility, sometimes built in to the compiler, or wired in to the fixed store. Experience has shown the limitations of these methods in speed, accuracy, and stability, and considerably improved techniques have been developed in the last few years. But although the methods are more sophisticated, there is still a need to provide routines which are simple and automatic in operation for the general user. Because the theory of ordinary differential equations is considerably more complicated than, for example, the theory of linear algebraic equations, we cannot hope to provide algorithms which are as comprehensive as the best linear algebra routines. So one of the problems of the algorithm writer is to decide how far the routine should go in attempting to deal automatically with numerical difficulties, and how best to help the user when the routine fails.

The first requirement is to classify the different types of ordinary differential equations which arise in practice. The following properties are relevant in various degrees to the problem of numerical solution: whether the system is

(i) linear or nonlinear,

(ii) first-order or higher-order,

(iii) initial-value or boundary-value,

(iv) well-posed or inherently unstable,

(v) stiff or non-stiff,

(vi) singular at certain points or nonsingular.

The distinction between linear and nonlinear problems will not be important for our present discussion, because linear equations arise fairly infrequently in practice, and they are not usually treated as a special case. However, in boundary-value problems and in stiff equations, linearity is an important property, which can be used to advantage in constructing algorithms. A comprehensive program library would certainly include linear versions of a number of methods for these problems. A similar situation holds for differential equations of various orders. It is well known that all ordinary differential equations can be reduced to the first-order form

$$y_i' = f_i(x, y_1, y_2, ..., y_n), \qquad i = 1, 2, ..., n, \qquad (1)$$

by simple substitutions, provided they can be solved explicitly for the highest derivatives. However, general methods for solving (1) are not necessarily efficient when the system is derived from higher-order equations, and better methods can be devised for special forms such as

$$y'' = f(x, y, y'), \qquad (2)$$

particularly when some of the lower derivatives are absent. A few cases have been looked at in detail, e.g. Runge–Kutta methods for second-order equations, and a large library might include some routines for special forms. For simplicity, we shall confine ourselves here to systems of the form (1), assumed to be nonlinear.

The distinction between initial-value and boundary-value problems is of course fundamental in numerical methods of solution (except for certain collocation methods, which use the same technique in both cases). For initial-value problems, the solution is usually constructed in a step-by-step manner from the data at an initial point. Boundary-value problems may be of simple or generalized type. To illustrate, consider the following example, the equations for the flight of a projectile,

$$\left. \begin{array}{l} y' = \tan \phi \\ V' = -(g/V) \tan \phi - kV/\cos \phi \\ \phi' = -g/V^2 \end{array} \right\}, \qquad (3)$$

where $y' = dy/dx$, etc. Here x and y are the horizontal and vertical distances of the projectile from some origin, V is the velocity, and ϕ the angle made by the direction of flight with the horizontal. The gravitational constant is g, and the coefficient of the air-resistance term is k.

Suppose we are given the initial values of y, V, and ϕ; then we have a simple initial-value problem and we can integrate forwards to find the motion of the projectile over a range R. Alternatively, if we want to find the initial angle required to hit a target at a given range R, we have a simple boundary-value problem. More generally, the system may be considered as having nine parameters:

> initial values of y, V, ϕ at $x = 0$,
>
> final values of y, V, ϕ at $x = R$,
>
> values of the range R and the coefficients g, k.

Given any six of these, we can find the other three. If R, g, or k is among the unknown parameters, the system is a generalized boundary-value problem. For instance, suppose the initial and final values of y and V are given, and the values of k and R are known; then we can solve the generalized problem to find the value of g.

The class of generalized problems includes the determination of eigenvalues, and the solution of differential equations with certain types of singularity (see Section 4). For all boundary-value problems, it is seldom possible to guarantee in advance that a solution exists. (The existence theorems that are known have very restrictive conditions.) Consequently in numerical work it is difficult to distinguish between a problem which has no solution and one in which the solution is hard to find, e.g. because no good starting approximation is available.

Returning to initial-value problems, an important property of a system is its stability with respect to perturbations of the initial data. The classical definition of stability requires that the effect of perturbations in the initial conditions should die away as x increases. More precisely, suppose the exact solution is y, and the perturbed solution is z; the system has absolute stability if there exists a δ such that

$$|y(0) - z(0)| < \delta \Rightarrow |y(x) - z(x)| < \varepsilon \qquad (4)$$

for any $\varepsilon > 0$, and for all x. This condition is too stringent for most practical problems. In a floating-point computation we often want to maintain a fixed number of significant figures, so we are concerned with the *relative* effect of perturbations. We may define relative stability by replacing condition (4) with

$$|y(0) - z(0)| < \delta \Rightarrow |y(x) - z(x)| < \varepsilon\,|y(x)| \qquad (5)$$

for all x, or for all x in a given range. (This still leads to difficulties if y is oscillatory.) If a problem is not stable, either absolutely or relatively, almost any method of solution is likely to give a wrong answer, and it is not easy to detect the error automatically.

Instability may also be induced by the numerical method used, and this happens most often in the case of stiff equations. Suppose we linearize (1) with respect to an approximate solution $\mathbf{y}^{(0)}$. This gives

$$\mathbf{y}' = J\mathbf{y} + \mathbf{f}(x, \mathbf{y}^{(0)}) - J\mathbf{y}^{(0)}, \tag{6}$$

where J is the Jacobian matrix of partial derivatives

$$\left| \frac{\partial f_i}{\partial y_j} \right|,$$

evaluated at $\mathbf{y} = \mathbf{y}^{(0)}$. If J has large positive eigenvalues, the solution or complementary function increases rapidly, and we may have inherent instability. In any case we shall need a small step-length to preserve accuracy in the integration. If J has large negative eigenvalues the system is stiff, and the solution contains rapidly decaying transients or complementary functions. These disappear quickly from the exact solution as x increases; nevertheless in the numerical solution a very small step-length is needed to represent them correctly, if we use explicit methods of integration. A large step-length causes these components to be magnified, and gives induced instability.

Problems of this type require special methods of solution. Unfortunately it is not easy to decide in advance whether a given system is stiff or not, unless the user knows something about the complementary functions or the transient solutions of his problem. However, stiffness is soon noticeable if an unsuitable method of integration is used, because either the step-length becomes very small while the solution varies slowly, or the results are clearly unstable.

If the solution has discontinuities, all the usual numerical methods will fail, and the user must carry out some mathematical analysis of the problem. For singularities at the end-points, a local analytical solution can often be found from the first few terms of the series expansion. Within the range, if a discontinuity occurs in a derivative and not in the function, it may be possible to integrate through it by taking a sufficiently small step-length.

Singularities of the complementary function may cause trouble when the solution itself is well-behaved. To take a simple example, suppose we want to find the non-singular solution $J_0(x)$ of Bessel's equation

$$xy'' + y' + xy = 0, \tag{7}$$

starting with two conditions at $x = 8$ and integrating backwards. The numerical solution contains a component of the second solution $Y_0(x)$ because of perturbations, and this increases rapidly as we approach $x = 0$. There is nothing to indicate that the result is incorrect, because the truncation error can be kept to a reasonable level and there is no induced instability, but the computed solution will have a singularity at the origin. To exclude $Y_0(x)$, the user has to specify another condition at $x = 0$, e.g. that the solution or its derivative remains finite, and this implies that the equation should be solved as a boundary-value problem. (Another way of excluding the singular solution is to use a Chebyshev collocation method, which automatically gives a result with polynomial-like behaviour.) The algorithm writer cannot protect the user from errors and difficulties of this kind, and it is desirable to provide detailed documentation to explain some of the theoretical problems which can arise.

2. Methods for Initial-Value Problems

In assessing the various methods available for initial-value problems, we have to consider not only the type of problem, discussed in the previous Section, but also some practical aspects of the computation. The main features influencing the choice of method are:

  (i) the accuracy required,
  (ii) the length of range (more precisely the number of steps),
  (iii) the "cost" of evaluating the functions f_i.

All comparative studies seem to show that different methods may be more efficient for a particular problem when different accuracies are required. Efficiency is measured by the computing time needed for solution, assuming that the required accuracy is obtained. Thus the Runge–Kutta methods, particularly the fourth-order versions, are rather expensive for high-accuracy work, but very competitive with other methods when only a few figures are required. Again, methods of predictor–corrector type inevitably have a rather slow starting procedure; so although they may be very efficient over a large number of steps, they are not as good as Runge-Kutta methods if the time taken to get started is a substantial part of the calculation. It is not possible to define exactly the "break-even" point between one method and another, because it depends on the time taken to evaluate the functions f_i, and on the behaviour of the solution in a particular case.

A comprehensive report has recently been published by Hull et al. (1972), giving a detailed comparison of several methods for initial-value problems. This is the most systematic study that I know of, and it covers a large number of examples which are solved at three different accuracy levels. A certain amount of testing has also been done at Manchester in connection with the development of routines for the Nottingham Algorithms Group library. One of our conclusions is that, for the more complicated methods (e.g. Gear, Krogh, Nordsieck), the details of the implementation make a considerable difference to the assessment. A major problem with high-order methods is the perturbation of intermediate quantities (differences or estimated derivatives) by rounding and other errors. The precise form of the arithmetic, and the methods of estimating truncation errors and testing for convergence of the corrector iterations, may substantially alter the decisions about change of order or step-length, and thus affect the efficiency. Starting techniques are also important, except for very long ranges. There seems to be no theoretical basis for resolving some of the problems of implementation at present, and our current versions of the routines are the result of a good deal of practical experimentation.

The experience we have had with Krogh's method (Krogh, 1970, 1971) supports the conclusion of Hull, that it is the most economical method in terms of function evaluations over a long range, for non-stiff systems. It is certainly superior to the original fixed-order form of Nordsieck's method for almost all problems. Runge–Kutta routines are generally very effective for low-accuracy calculations and short ranges. The overheads are very small, and the routines are short and simple. Our general impressions are slightly more favourable towards Runge–Kutta methods than Hull's report. We have used mainly the Merson 4th-order form, which provides an error estimate with five function evaluations. It is generally believed that this tends to over-estimate the error, although England (1970) showed that it can under-estimate it in certain cases. Our tests indicate that the Merson estimate gives about the same accuracy and efficiency over a range as England's method, for low-accuracy calculations. (Hull uses the slightly slower method of repeating the calculation at twice the interval.) It is true that the theoretical conditions for justifying Merson's method are very restrictive, but the position is similar for a great deal of stability theory.

For stiff equations the methods of integration have to be partly implicit, to maintain stability with a reasonable value of h. Gear's variable-order method (Gear 1969) has been used extensively for such problems, and it is very much more efficient than a general non-stiff method. However its starting procedure can be rather slow, and it can run into considerable trouble at high orders because of rounding error. This problem is very dependent on the implementation and on the word-length of the machine, and the use of double-length arithmetic at certain points may be advantageous.

3. User's View of a Routine

In constructing general library routines, we need to bear in mind the great difference in experience and mathematical knowledge between different classes of users. A very sophisticated routine, with a large number of options and parameters, will be appreciated by the expert, but it will be rejected by the average user because of its complexity. It is important to persuade people to take advantage of up-to-date methods by providing good implementations, but for non-specialists a short and simple parameter list is one of the chief attractions of a routine. (This is partly because computing time is provided free in universities; if people had to pay for it, efficiency would be more appreciated.) The practical approach is to provide a standard routine with as few parameters as possible, and to make an annotated source text available for the experts, so that they can modify it.

The essential parameters for a routine include the number n of equations, the starting values for x and for y_i $(i = 1, 2, ..., n)$, the range over which integration is required, and the name of the routine which calculates the derivatives f_i. The user must also give some information about the accuracy he requires, and this leads to complications, because a single accuracy test is not suitable for all types of problem. In many cases the components y_i of the solution differ considerably in magnitude; the user could be asked to scale them appropriately, but it is simpler to ask him to provide a different error bound, e_i say, for each component. (A number of standard routines do not allow this option.) If the error estimate for the ith component is t_i, the simplest error test (absolute) is: $|t_i| < e_i$. This is unsatisfactory for problems where the solution varies greatly in magnitude over the range, and a relative error test is needed for such cases: $|t_i/y_i| < e_i$. This again may be unsatisfactory if y_i becomes small, and it fails if y_i passes through a zero. So a third form of test is needed, which can be

either

$$|t_i| < e_i \max(1, |y_i|),$$

or

$$|t_i| < e_i (1 + |y_i|).$$

This may be called a "mixed" error test. We have used the second form extensively in library routines, with the absolute and relative tests also provided as options.

Hull suggests that the error estimate t_i should be scaled to give the error per unit step before testing for accuracy, i.e. the quantity tested should be $|t_i/h|$, where h is the current step-length. This is a logical proceeding, and it provides some safeguard against the accumulation of error when the number of steps is large and h is small. However, we have encountered difficulties in using it, particularly in the Gear program. Whenever the step-length is reduced there is some disturbance in the higher differences, and therefore in the estimate of truncation error. If the error test becomes more stringent as h is reduced, it may fail repeatedly and bring the calculation to a halt.

A mechanism for changing the step is essential to enable the routine to meet the accuracy requirement. Predictor–corrector methods have a special starting procedure, which establishes the appropriate initial value for h. This part of the routine can be speeded up if the user is able to specify a suitable value of h on entry, perhaps taken from a previous calculation. Each change of step-length causes a perturbation in the solution, and so it is advisable not to change h too often. It is simple to specify a minimum number of steps between increases of h, but we cannot place any restriction on reducing h, because the error test must always be satisfied. To avoid frequent reduction, the step should be divided by a substantial factor when it has to be changed. We have used halving and doubling as the simplest strategy for step-changing; if h is altered by factors of 2, it is easy to ensure that the endpoint of the range is reached without any need for interpolation.

A practical problem in constructing library routines is whether any bound (upper or lower) should be placed on the values of h. A natural upper bound is the range of integration, but the user may want to put further restrictions on h because of his knowledge of the functions f_i. For example, if one of the components oscillates rapidly, he will want to ensure that h does not become too large to represent its behaviour properly. A lower bound on h is desirable for several reasons. A very small step-length (relative to the initial step) may indicate any of the following

    (i) the solution is approaching a singularity,

   (ii) the system of equations is becoming stiff,

   (iii) the accuracy requirement is too stringent.

In the first case, the user may anticipate trouble if he knows that f_i is discontinuous at some point; he can then set a very small lower limit on h in this region. In such a case it is difficult to guarantee that the error test is meaningful, and the user must check by repeating the calculation with a different accuracy limit. In the second case, the routine can automatically switch to a method for stiff equations, but it may be better to terminate the calculation and draw the user's attention to the problem. This is an area in which the expert would like to have more sophisticated options, but for general use I think the safest policy is to terminate the routine whenever h goes below some preset value (e.g. $10^{-4} \times$ its initial value).

In cases of failure, it is important that the user should be able to find out what has happened, and should have access to any data which may help him. Trivial cases of failure arise from inconsistencies in the input parameters, and these should be checked by the routine on entry. Once the integration has started, failure is usually indicated either by an arithmetic overflow (e.g. near a singularity), or by an excessively small value of h. A good computing system should have a trap on overflow which is accessible to the programmer, so that he can provide his own recovery procedure. (Strangely enough, not all machines have this facility.) When a failure occurs, I think the best policy in a general routine is to print an informative comment, following by the relevant data under suitable headings. However, many program libraries have a convention against printing in routines, and cases of failure are indicated by terminating the routine with an error marker set. This gives the user some information about the type of failure, but he does not have access to the current data unless it is included in the parameter list, or is kept in a common area of the store.

In future, it is likely that interactive systems will become more widespread, and it is to be hoped that routines will be designed which are more helpful to the user in giving him information about failures. A comprehensive system would display a lot of diagnostic information, and could also suggest possible causes and remedies for the trouble. It could draw the user's attention to other routines and make it easy for him to call them in, or it could refer him to text-books for further theoretical information.

4, Boundary-Value Problems

Algorithms for boundary-value problems have been less explored than those for initial-value problems. The two main methods of solution are to linearize the system and solve matrix equations, or to use a shooting method and solve nonlinear equations for the unknown parameters. The first method is generally faster in computing time, but it has considerable disadvantages as a basis for a general routine. The linearization cannot be done automatically, and so the user has to start by carrying out some analysis, which may be very complicated for large systems. If the linearized equations are approximated by finite differences, the process of setting up the matrix is not straightforward for general orders and boundary conditions. The process becomes more automatic if we reduce the system to the first-order form (1), and use the approximations given by Keller (1968, Chapter 3). This method is fairly effective, but it makes heavier demands on storage than direct approximation of the high-order form. Storage requirements are considerable for all finite-difference methods; the matrix equations are of high order and band form, and the band can be very wide if the system is large.

If collocation methods are used the equations again have to be linearized, and the solution is then expressed in terms of a polynomial expansion. The resulting matrix equations for the coefficients are not of band form, but the storage required is generally less than for finite-difference methods. A disadvantage of all matrix methods is that the user has to provide an initial estimate of the solution over the whole range, which is more difficult than simply estimating certain boundary values. (All these remarks refer to non-linear problems; matrix methods are a good deal easier for linear equations.)

The method of shooting and matching for solving boundary-value problems is usually slower, but it is easier to program in a general form, and also easier for the user to handle. Let us write the system as

$$y_i' = f_i(x, y_1, y_2, ..., y_n, p_1, p_2, ..., p_k), \qquad i = 1, 2, ..., n, \qquad (8)$$

where $p_1, p_2, ..., p_k$ are parameters occurring in the equations, some of which may be unknown. Suppose this is to be solved over a range $[a, b]$; then we can integrate from either end if we have the appropriate boundary conditions. We assume that we either know or can estimate the $2n$ boundary values of y_i, and the k values of the parameters p_j. Then we calculate a "forward" solution y_f from $x = a$ by initial-value methods, and similarly a "backward" solution y_b from $x = b$. The two solutions are compared at some matching point $x = r$ in the range. If they agree to the required accuracy, we have solved the problem; if not, we have a system of n nonlinear equations from which to improve our estimates of the unknown parameters. These equations are given by

$$\mathbf{F} \equiv \mathbf{y}_f(r) - \mathbf{y}_b(r) = 0. \qquad (9)$$

The function $\mathbf{F}$ depends on the $2n + k$ quantities $y_i(a)$, $y_i(b)$, $i = 1, 2, ..., n$, and $p_j, j = 1, 2, ..., k$; if at least $n + k$ of these are known, we can find the remainder by solving (9).

Equation (8) is not a completely general system, because there may be other parameters which do not occur explicitly in the differential equation. For example, the length of the range may be an unknown parameter, or there may be implicit parameters in the boundary conditions. An important case is that where the solution has a singularity at one of the end-points. Suppose y is known to be singular at $x = a$, and we can find a local analytical form, e.g.

$$y \sim \alpha + \beta \log (x - a) + \gamma(x - a)^{\frac{1}{2}}, \qquad (10)$$

where α, β, γ are unknown. We can regard these quantities as parameters of the system, and solve by shooting and matching as above. Instead of taking the boundary condition at $x = a$, we use (10) as the boundary condition at a point close to a, to give y in terms of the current estimates of α, β, γ.

Returning to the problem of solving (9), the most straightforward approach is to use some variant of Newton's method. This requires the calculation of the partial derivatives of $\mathbf{F}$ with respect to the parameters. If the parameters

are simple boundary values of y_i, the derivatives may be found by solving
the variational equations of the system, which are linear and have the form

$$\mathbf{q}' = J\mathbf{q}, \qquad J = \left[\frac{\partial f_i}{\partial y_j}\right], \tag{11}$$

with the appropriate boundary conditions. However, if (11) is used directly,
it is necessary to calculate the Jacobian matrix J explicitly, which may be
rather complicated.

A simpler and more general approach is to approximate the derivatives
of $\mathbf{F}$ by finite differences. We first solve the system (8) with estimated parameter values, and then re-solve it with each of the n parameter values perturbed in turn. The derivative of F_i with respect to the parameter p_k may be
approximated by

$$\frac{\partial F_i}{\partial p_k} \simeq \frac{F_i(p_k + \delta p_k) - F_i(p_k)}{\delta p_k}, \tag{12}$$

which is easily calculated. The Newton method now becomes a generalized
secant method; each step gives improved estimates of the parameter values,
and the calculation is repeated iteratively. The method is easily adapted to
deal with parameters of any type, however they occur in the system. In our
experience, the efficiency and rate of convergence of the secant method are
not significantly different from those of the exact Newton method.

Whichever method is used, convergence is usually dependent on having
a good starting approximation. If good estimates of the unknown parameters
are not available, we can use general root-finding techniques for $\mathbf{F} = 0$, or
try for example to minimize

$$\|\mathbf{F}\|^2 = F_1{}^2 + F_2{}^2 + \dots + F_n{}^2 \tag{13}$$

in order to get near the solution. A better policy is often to start from the
differential equation, and to perturb it into a form which is more easily
solved. Suppose we write eqn (8) in the following form

$$\mathbf{y}' = \varepsilon \mathbf{f}(x, \mathbf{y}, \mathbf{p}) + (1 - \varepsilon) \mathbf{g}(x, \mathbf{y}, \mathbf{p}), \tag{14}$$

which is equivalent to (8) when $\varepsilon = 1$. We choose the functions g_i so that
(14) is easy to solve for $\varepsilon = 0$. We then vary ε in stages from 0 to 1 to give
a sequence of problems, each of which can be solved fairly readily by using
the solution of the previous problem as a starting approximation. Many
variants of this approach have been suggested; elaborate methods can be
used for tracing the variation of the solution of (13) with ε, and we can
perturb the range in a similar manner. To make it generally applicable,
further analysis is needed to find suitable ways of choosing the functions g_i,

in order to ensure that all the intermediate problems of the sequence are solvable.

In shooting methods, it is often found that the system (8) is inherently unstable for step-by-step solution, and the calculation fails with overflow in the integration routine. (This is to be expected when the boundary-value problem arises from an elliptic equation, which is not well-posed as an initial-value problem.) Inherent instability may also occur when the starting approximation is very poor, so that the calculated solution is nowhere near the true solution. The difficulty may be reduced or overcome by dividing the range $[a, b]$ into a number of sub-intervals, and integrating the system separately over each. If the intervals are small enough, the instability will not be serious. The solutions are then matched at the points between intervals, giving a system of equations similar to (9) but considerably larger (Osborne, 1969). This method is known as multiple shooting; it is slightly more complicated for the user because he has to supply estimates of the solution at a number of intermediate points in the range, as well as at the end-points.

In our present state of knowledge, it is not possible to make very robust algorithms for solving boundary-value problems. As with most nonlinear problems, the approach has to be rather tentative, and the important thing is to give the user a framework within which he can experiment, when the problem is difficult. In spite of the limitations of the methods described, I think it is worth having such algorithms in a program library. If they are well-designed they can supply a lot of useful information even when they fail, and the average user is unlikely to do better if he is left to construct his own routines. It is particularly necessary in these problems to print monitoring information about the progress of the calculation, and to give all the relevant data if the routine fails, so that the user can decide what to try next. Again, an interactive system might be made very efficient for this type of work.

Acknowledgements

The development of algorithms for ordinary differential equations has been a joint effort by a group of people in Manchester, with major contributions from I. Gladwell, G. Hall, D. K. Sayers, and J. L. Siemieniuch.

References

England, R. (1970). Error estimates for Runge–Kutta type solutions to systems of ordinary differential equations. *Comput. J.* **12,** 166–160.

Gear, C. W. (1969). The automatic integration of stiff ordinary differential equations *In* "Proceedings IFIPS Congress". pp. 187–193. North Holland, Amsterdam.

Hull, T. E., Enright, W. H., Fellen, B. M. and Sedgwick, A. E. (1972). Comparing numerical methods for ordinary differential equations. *SIAM J. Num. Anal.* **9**, 603–637.

Keller, H. B. (1968). "Numerical Methods for Two-Point Boundary-Value Problems". Blaisdell Publishing Company, Waltham, Mass.

Krogh, F. T. (1970). "On Testing a Subroutine for the Numerical Integration of Ordinary Differential Equations". Jet Propulsion Lab. Section 314, Tech. Memo 217.

Krogh, F. T. (1971). "Algorithms for Changing the Stepsize Used by a Multistep Method". Jet Propulsion Lab. Section 314, Tech. Memo 275.

Osborne, M. R. (1969). On shooting methods for boundary-value problems. *J. Math. Appl.* **27**, 417–433.

Discussion: Ordinary Differential Equations

DR. REID. You mentioned the difficulties associated with recognising whether a differential equation is stiff. One way round this trouble is to use a stiffly-stable method such as Gear's all the time. I have heard that the loss of efficiency on non-stiff problems is not severe. Is this your experience?

DR. WALSH. My impression is that Gear's method would be less efficient in general for non-stiff problems, compared with a method like Krogh's.

DR. A. R. GOURLAY (*Loughborough University*). (1) I would agree with the remarks of John Reid that Gear's stiff algorithm is frequently very efficient on non-stiff systems. (2) I would disagree that the user should require to identify and cope with singularities or time cusps. The routine produced should be capable of handling any difficulties.

DR. WALSH. It is rather difficult for the routine to handle automatically any type of discontinuity, and I think it is as well for the user to be warned about the presence of singularities, even if the equation can be integrated through them.

DR. NEILL. Have you any experience in finding the asymptotic behaviour of an initial value problem with a periodic forcing function? This may be reduced to a boundary value problem.

DR. WALSH. No, we have not tried this particular problem, though the general boundary-value routine should be capable of dealing with it.

MR. A. N. RICHMOND (*Liverpool Polytechnic*). What has been your experience with Sarafyan's method for solving initial value problems?

DR. WALSH. The stability of methods of this type tends to be restricted, so they are unsuitable for stiff equations. For non-stiff problems, my impression is that the number of function evaluations is likely to be large (cf. Hull's report).

MR. R. W. McINTYRE (*Rolls Royce Limited*). Should printing be part of the routine? If so, users like to specify print intervals independent of the integration interval.

DR. WALSH. This is not difficult to arrange, but some libraries specify that routines should not initiate any printing.

MR. McINTYRE. What are your views of compound algorithms comprising several methods and an autoselection mechanism?

Dr. Walsh. With some reservations, this is a good idea but we have not experimented with compound algorithms ourselves. Gear refers to a compound form of his stiff and non-stiff methods in his recent book. There could be some difficulties near a singularity with any method of this type.

Dr. Einarsson. What do you think about the extrapolation method (Bulirsh–Stoer), that was very popular a few years ago?

Dr. Walsh. The report by Hull (Toronto) indicates that it is good if the functions f_i are easy to calculate, and that it is sometimes better than Krogh's method. The extrapolation method can not take care of discontinuities.

11. Nonlinear Optimisation: A Survey of the State of the Art

L. C. W. DIXON

Numerical Optimisation Centre,
The Hatfield Polytechnic, Hatfield, England.

1. Introduction

The unconstrained nonlinear optimisation problem is that of finding that value x of an n dimensional vector that minimises a function $f(x)$.

A very large number of algorithms have been suggested for the solution of the unconstrained optimisation problem and it is not the intention in this paper to attempt to describe them all. For a more complete survey of the field of suggested approaches the reader is referred to recent texts on the subject e.g. Dixon (1972a), Murray (1972a) and Ghani (1972). Instead a series of desirable properties will be stated and the convergency properties of a large number of the most successful algorithms, will be described within that framework. Details of the available implementations of these algorithms through institutions in the United Kingdom specialising in the provision of such algorithms will also be given. The choice of the algorithms described is of course a personal one and whilst it is hoped that the implementations included are both efficient and reliable the exclusion of an implementation from this discussion does not imply that in the author's opinion it is either unreliable or inefficient.

2. Definitions

The following notation will be used throughout this paper. The vector g will be used for the gradient vector, i.e.

$$g_i = \frac{\partial f}{\partial x_i}$$

and the matrix G for the Hessian matrix, i.e.

$$G_{ij} = \frac{\partial^2 f}{\partial x_i \partial x_j}.$$

The discussion will be restricted to functions that satisfy certain conditions and such functions will be termed well behaved.

Definition: *A well behaved function*

A function is stated to be well behaved for minimisation if

(i) a lower bound exists, i.e. $f(x) \geqslant L$ all x,   (2.1)

(ii) the Hessian matrix exists at all points x and is uniformly bounded

i.e. for all $\|z\| = 1, - M \leqslant z^T G(x) z \leqslant M$ (2.2)

(iii) the third derivatives of $f(x)$ exist at all points x.

(iv) a minimum point x^* exists and the Hessian there is well conditioned

i.e. for all $\|z\| = 1, 0 < m \leqslant z^T G(x^*) z \leqslant M$ (2.3)

The discussion will also be restricted in the main to descent methods.

Definition: *A descent method*

A descent method is defined as one that proceeds iteratively, and in which each iteration consists of two stages:

In the first a direction $p^{(k)}$ is selected and in the second a step size in that direction is determined. The iteration is therefore

$$x^{(k+1)} = x^{(k)} + \alpha p^{(k)}$$ (2.4)

and we can introduce d for the step taken during the iteration and then

$$d = x^{(k+1)} - x^{(k)} = \alpha p^{(k)}.$$ (2.5)

It will be assumed that an iteration terminates if an $x^{(k)}$ is found for which

$$\|g(x)\| < \varepsilon_0 \text{ for some preselected } \varepsilon_0 > 0.$$ (2.6)

3. Convergence

The convergency of descent methods has been considered in detail by Wolfe (1969, 1971) and combining his approach with an earlier result due to Goldstein and Price (1967) we may deduce the following theorem.

THEOREM 1. *If In the application of a descent method to a well behaved function, the step taken at a regular subsequence of iterations is chosen to satisfy conditions, I, II, and III below, and if on the other iterations the function value does not increase, then the iteration will terminate with $\|g(x)\| < \varepsilon_0$.*

Condition I

$$-p^{(k)T}g^{(k)} \geqslant \varepsilon_1 \|p^{(k)}\| \, \|g^{(k)}\|, \qquad \varepsilon_i > 0. \tag{3.1}$$

This implies that the direction of search has a significant component in the negative gradient direction.

Condition II

Either

$$|g^{(k+1)T}p^{(k)}| \leqslant \varepsilon_2 |g^{(k)T}p^{(k)}|, \tag{3.2}$$

or

$$|f(x^{(k)}) + g^T d - f(x^{(k+1)})| > \varepsilon_3 \, |g^T d|. \tag{3.3}$$

Either of these implies that the step taken in this direction is bounded away from zero.

Condition III

$$f(x^{(k)}) - f(x^{(k+1)}) \geqslant -\varepsilon_4 \alpha p^{(k)T}g^{(k)}. \tag{3.4}$$

This condition then implies that the reduction in function value is bounded away from zero.

Comment

It is only fair to state that the theorem stated above is more restrictive than that given by Wolfe who stated a number of alternative conditions.

In many of the algorithms that we will consider the direction of search $p^{(k)}$ will be defined by

$$p^{(k)} = -H^{(k)}g^{(k)} \tag{3.5}$$

for some matrix $H^{(k)}$.

If we represent the least eigenvalue of $H^{(k)}$ by $a^{(k)}$ and the greatest by $b^{(k)}$, then we may state the following theorem.

THEOREM 2. (Goldfarb, 1969, Murtagh and Sargent, 1969). *In algorithms in which the direction of descent $p^{(k)}$ is given by (3.5), Condition I of Wolfe's theorem is automatically satisfied if either*

$$a^{(k)}/b^{(k)} > \varepsilon_1 \quad \text{all} \quad (k) \tag{3.6}$$

or

$$0 < a \leqslant a^{(k)} \leqslant b^{(k)} \leqslant b \quad \text{all} \quad (k). \tag{3.7}$$

4. Rate of Convergence

In discussing the rate of convergence of an optimisation algorithm we will follow the approach of Dennis (1968, 1971). For well behaved functions we will usually be interested in establishing second order convergence, i.e. in showing that a scalar L exists such that

$$\|x^{(k+1)} - x^*\| < L \|x^{(k)} - x^*\|^2, \tag{4.1}$$

though frequently we have to be content with the weaker condition of superlinear convergence

$$\|x^{(k+1)} - x^*\| / \|x^{(k)} - x^*\| \to 0 \quad \text{as} \quad k \to \infty. \tag{4.2}$$

THEOREM 3. *If in a descent method, given*

$$d = x^{(k+1)} - x^{(k)}$$

we have

$$\|d + G(x^*)^{-1} g^{(k)}\| < L_1 \|x^{(k)} - x^*\|^2, \tag{4.3}$$

then a scalar L exists satisfying (4.1) *and the iteration has second order convergence.*

If the step is defined as

$$d = -H^{(k)} g^{(k)}, \tag{4.4}$$

then condition (4.3) *can be rewritten as*

$$\|(G(x^*)^{-1} - H^{(k)}) g^{(k)}\| < L_1 \|x^{(k)} - x^*\|^2, \tag{4.5}$$

which is satisfied if a scalar L_2 exists such that

$$\|G(x^*)^{-1} - H^{(k)}\| < L_2 \|x^{(k)} - x^*\|. \tag{4.6}$$

THEOREM 4. *If in a descent method*

$$\|d + G(x^*)^{-1} g^{(k)}\| / \|x^{(k)} - x^*\| \to 0, \tag{4.7}$$

then the method has Q superlinear convergence.

If the step is defined by (4.4) *then this becomes*

$$\|(G(x^*)^{-1} - H^{(k)}) g^{(k)}\| / \|x^{(k)} - x^*\| \to 0, \tag{4.8}$$

which is satisfied if

$$H^{(k)} \to G(x^*)^{-1}. \tag{4.9}$$

Comment

Simple algebra implies that the statements

$$\frac{\|(H^{(k)-1} - G(x^*)) (x^{(k+1)} - x^{(k)})\|}{\|x^{(k+1)} - x^{(k)}\|} \to 0$$

and

$$\frac{\|(H^{(k)-1} - G(x^*)) (x^{(k+1)} - x^{(k)})\|}{\|g^{(k)}\|} \to 0$$

stated by Dennis and More (1973) and McCormick and Ritter (1972) are equivalent to (4.8).

5. Quadratic Termination Vis-à-Vis Second Order Convergence

Definition: *Quadratic Termination*

An algorithm is said to have quadratic termination if it would minimise a quadratic function in a finite number of steps.

The sequence of steps that would minimise a quadratic function will be termed a major iteration. When this same sequence is applied to a non-quadratic function sufficient information would usually be obtained to identify a quadratic approximation function Q.A.F.

$$Q(x) = a + b_x^T + \tfrac{1}{2}x^T A x, \tag{5.1}$$

whose minimum would have been obtained during the iteration.

The sequence of steps involved in the major iteration will therefore have a resultant

$$d = -A^{-1} g_Q(x^{(k)}), \tag{5.2}$$

where $g_Q(x^{(k)})$ is the gradient of the Q.A.F. at $x^{(k)}$ the starting point of the major iteration.

THEOREM 5. *Major cycles establishing a Q.A.F.* (5.1) *have second order convergence if their resultant step d* (5.2) *satisfies condition* 4.3.

As an example of the use of the above theorem we may state:

THEOREM 6. *If* (i) *a method is used that constructs a set of conjugate directions* $t^{(j)}$ $j = 1, \ldots, n$ *of a matrix A and if*

(ii) *a step* $d^{(j)}$ *is taken along each of these directions and these steps remain within a region* $M\|x^{(k)} - x^*\|$ *and if*

(iii) *the vectors $y^{(j)}$ being the changes in gradient corresponding to $d^{(j)}$ are independent*

then

(i) $A = G^* + O(x^{(k)} - x^*),$ (5.3)

and

(ii) $g_Q(x^{(k)}) = g(x^{(k)}),$ (5.4)

and

(iii) *the step from $x^{(k)}$ to the minimum of the Q.A.F. satisfies equation 4.3 and the major iteration has second order convergence.*

6. Modified Newton Methods

(a) Exact Derivatives

When the second derivative matrix G is available the classical Newton–Raphson prediction states

$$x^{(k+1)} = x^{(k)} + \alpha p^{(k)},$$ (6.1)

where

$$G^{(k)}p^{(k)} = -g^{(k)}.$$ (6.2)

It follows from Section 3 that if (i) α is selected to satisfy Wolfe's Conditions and (ii) $G(x)$ is positive definite and the condition number is bounded at all points x, then the iteration will converge to a stationary point of F and as the function is, by (ii), convex this will be the global minimum. It also follows from Section 4 that Newton's method has second order convergence in the region in which $\alpha = 1$ is an acceptable point.

These results are discussed in more detail in Ortega and Rheinboldt (1971, Chapter 12) who cite numerous original references.

In practice the set of equations

$$G^{(k)}p^{(k)} = -g^{(k)}$$

is usually solved by the Choleski decomposition technique which is numerically stable when G is positive definite. When the matrix $G^{(k)}$ is non-positive definite an alternative strategy must be devised.

Two very different proposals have been made. Fiacco and McCormick (1968) suggested replacing the direction (6.2) by a linear combination of the eigenvectors associated with negative eigenvalues. For such a direction a point satisfying condition III of Wolfe's Theorem can be found even when $\varepsilon_1 = 0$ and the convergence to a local minimum (or at least to a point where $\|G\| \geqslant 0$) can be assured. The particular technique by which they avoid an eigen analysis has been criticised as numerically unstable (Murray, 1972a), and cannot be undertaken on all non-positive definite matrices. An implementation of this method is available in Lootsma (1972a) as MINIFUN/NFM/ALGOL60.

The more usual approach is to replace $G^{(k)}$ by a positive definite matrix P. Many suggestions have been made ranging from the obvious

$$P = I, \tag{6.3}$$

e.g. Dixon and Biggs (1970), to the more common

$$P = G^{(k)} + \mu I \tag{6.4}$$

first suggested by Levenberg (1944) and implemented in this context by Goldfeld, Quandt and Trotter (1966). The main difficulty with this proposal has always been the choice of a suitable μ. This has recently been discussed in detail by Hebden (1973) who has given an iterative method for obtaining a value of μ that not only makes P sufficiently positive definite but also ensures that $\alpha = 1$ is an acceptable point.

Murray (1972b), Gill and Murray (1972) have proposed an elegant method of modifying the Choleski decomposition of $G^{(k)}$ when $G^{(k)}$ is not a sufficiently positive definite matrix so that the outcome is a decomposition of a suitable positive definite matrix

$$P = G^{(k)} + E. \tag{6.5}$$

The directions of search so defined satisfy condition I of Section 2 and hence the algorithm will converge to a stationary point of F. An implementation is available in Gill, Murray and Picken (1972) NPL/MNA/ALGOL.

Methods based upon (6.3)–(6.5) have the disadvantage that they may terminate at a stationary point. As the second derivative matrix G is available a test can be undertaken at the termination point to ascertain whether the matrix there is positive definite and if not a suitable restarting point can be found by stepping along a combination of the eigenvectors associated with negative eigenvalues. Methods for determining such a direction efficiently are given by Gill, Murray and Picken (1972) and Hebden (1973). This does raise the question however of whether it might not be more efficient to move along such a direction whenever G is non-positive definite as intended by Fiacco and McCormick (1968). This could only be true on problems in which the function evaluation is very expensive as Murray (1972b) has estimated that the overhead cost would increase by a factor of 20.

All the above modifications retain second order convergence near the minimum as the methods all revert to the standard Newton method in the neighbourhood of the well behaved minimum.

(b) Estimated Derivatives

In practice obtaining analytic expressions for the second derivative matrix G is a chore and it is usually approximated by differences, i.e.

$$G_{ij} = \{g_i(x + he_j) - g_i(x)\}/h. \tag{6.6}$$

In infinite length arithmetic it is well-known that if h is chosen so that

$$|h^{(k)}| \leqslant \beta \|x^{(k)} - x^{(k-1)}\| \tag{6.8}$$

then the discrete Newton method retains superlinear convergence of order $(1 + \sqrt{5})/2$ (Ortega and Rheinboldt, 1971, p. 360). In practice however on a finite length machine the continuation of this policy would lead to large round off errors in the determination of G and Gill–Murray–Picken have recommended setting

$$h = 2^{-t/2}$$

where t is the number of bits in the word length of the computer employed. Implementations of modified Newton algorithms in which the Hessian is approximated by differences are available as

NPL/MNADIFF/ALGOL, MINIFUN/NFM/ALGOL,

NOC/MEANDER/TELCOMP (DIXON and BIGGS, 1970),

NOC/MEAND/BASIC (DIXON, 1973a).

7. Quasi-Newton Methods

The most common variation of the Modified Newton methods discussed in Section 6 are the quasi-Newton variable metric formulae. These were first proposed by Davidon (1959) and were based on the fact that on a quadratic function

$$y = Gd \quad \text{all} \quad k, \tag{7.1}$$

where

$$y = g^{(k+1)} - g^{(k)},$$

and

$$d = x^{(k+1)} - x^{(k)}.$$

Given a positive definite matrix $H^{(0)}$ the basic idea is to construct a sequence of matrices $H^{(k)}$ having the property that in some sense

$$H^{(k)} \to G^{-1},$$

by imposing the quasi-Newton condition

$$H^{(k+1)}y = d. \tag{7.2}$$

In the original variable metric algorithm, Fletcher and Powell (1963), this was achieved using the formula

$$H_{\mathrm{DFP}}^{(k+1)} = H^{(k)} - \frac{H^{(k)}y\,y^T H^{(k)}}{y^T H^{(k)} y} + \frac{dd^T}{d^T y}. \tag{7.3}$$

Then, directions of search were chosen so that

$$p^{(k)} = -H^{(k)}g^{(k)} \tag{7.4}$$

where theoretically the iterations were perfect, i.e. $\varepsilon_2 = 0$ in eqn (3.2).

Theoretical Results with Perfect Iterations

With *perfect* iterations four theoretical results have been established.

(i) Quadratic termination, Fletcher and Powell (1963). The algorithm will find the minimum of a positive definite quadratic function in at most n iterations.

(ii) N step second order convergence. This follows directly from Theorem 5. It was first shown by McCormick (1969) in relation to the reset algorithm but as N step quadratic termination is obtained for any positive definite matrix $H^{(0)}$ this restriction is unnecessary.

(iii) Convergence on convex functions, Powell (1971, 1972a). The algorithms will converge to the minimum of a convex function.

(iv) Superlinear convergence. Powell (1971).

BROYDEN's QUASI-NEWTON FAMILY

In Broyden (1967) a one-parameter family of variable metric formulae is introduced:

$$H_{\phi_1}^{(k+1)} = H_{\mathrm{DFP}}^{(k+1)} + \phi_1 v^{(k)} v^{(k)^T}. \tag{7.5}$$

where

$$v^{(k)} = \left(\frac{d}{d^T y} - \frac{Hy}{y^T Hy} \right). \tag{7.6}$$

In Dixon (1972b, 1973b) it is shown that with perfect iterations all members of family (7.5) generate the same sequence of points $x^{(k)}$ providing two degenerate values of ϕ_1 are avoided at each iteration.

It follows from this result that the above four properties are valid for all non-degenerate members of Broyden's family.

Convergence on non-convex functions

In practice perfect iterations are not possible on non-quadratic functions and α is chosen to satisfy theorem 1. Many implementations set ε_2 to a small non-zero value, which ensures that

$$d^T y > 0 \qquad (7.7)$$

and then the sequence of matrices $H^{(k)}$ remain positive definite providing $\phi_1 \geqslant 0$.

It has not however been established that these matrices satisfy the conditions of Theorem 2, so this does not imply convergence. In any case Gill and Murray (1972) have shown that with finite length arithmetic a positive definite matrix H needs not imply a downhill direction due to accumulated round off errors.

In the implementations at the N.O.C. we therefore reset

$$H^{(k)} = I \qquad (7.8)$$

whenever $p^{(k)}$ does not satisfy condition I of Section 3 and then ensure that α is chosen to satisfy the other conditions of Theorem 1.

In an attempt to decrease the adverse affects of round off error Gill and Murray (1972) have proposed the revised quasi-Newton method. In this the direction $p^{(k)}$ is determined from

$$B^{(k)}p^{(k)} = -g^{(k)} \qquad (7.9)$$

where $B^{(k)}$ is held as

$$L^{(k)}D^{(k)}L^{(k)T} \qquad (7.10)$$

where $L^{(k)}$ is a unit lower triangular matrix and $D^{(k)}$ a diagonal matrix.

In their method $p^{(k)}$ is calculated by solving successively

$$L^{(k)}z = -g^{(k)}$$

and

$$L^{(k)T}p^{(k)} = D^{(k)-1}z \qquad (7.11)$$

They derive a family of updating formula for $L^{(k)}$ and $D^{(k)}$ that corresponds to the Broyden family and whenever the diagonal matrix becomes ill-conditioned they modify the diagonal matrix so that its condition number does not exceed the bound (3.6).

With these modifications (7.8) or (7.9)–(7.11) the method is now guaranteed to converge to a stationary point of any well-behaved function.

The effect of practical linear search strategies

There is now a considerable body of experience Dixon (1972c), Lootsma (1972b), Gill, Murray and Pitfield (1972), Sargent and Sebastian (1972) that indiates that these methods are reliable and efficient and that the particular value of ϕ_1 suggested independently by Broyden (1970), Fletcher (1970), Shanno (1970) and Goldfarb (1970), namely

$$\phi_1 = \phi_{\text{BFS}} = y^T H y, \tag{7.12}$$

is the most efficient choice, particularly for large values of ε_2. These implementations nearly always include at least one interpolation per iteration to determine α to satisfy (3.2).

Implementations of the method using the updating formula (7.12) and estimating α by interpolation at each iteration include

MINIFUN/BFS/ALGOL 60 (Lootsma, 1972a)

NOC/VARMET/L = V = 2/BASIC (Dixon, 1972c)

while revised quasi-Newton methods are available as

NPL/QNMDER/ALGOL 60 (Gill, Murray and Pitfield, 1972).

Powell's Symmetric Method

A very different updating formula and step strategy were proposed by Powell (1970) in order to have a convergent algorithm without the need for these empirical modifications. If we let Γ denote an approximation to the Hessian matrix G and update Γ using

$$\Gamma^{(k+1)} = \Gamma^{(k)} + \frac{(y - \Gamma d)\,d^T + d(y - \Gamma d)^T}{d^T d} - \frac{dd^T(y^T d - d^T \Gamma d)}{(d^T d)^2} \tag{7.13}$$

then if the function were quadratic, we have for any arbitrary step d that

$$\Gamma^{(k+1)} - G^* = \left(I - \frac{dd^T}{d^T d}\right)(\Gamma^{(k)} - G^*)\left(I - \frac{dd^T}{d^T d}\right) \tag{7.14}$$

implying that the error in Γ steadily decreases for arbitrary steps.

Using the inverse of this formula as H, he generated a sequence of steps $d^{(k)}$ that satisfy condition I of Theorem 1 by biasing the direction towards the negative gradient, and also satisfy conditions on α equivalent to those stated in Theorem 1. The algorithm has the property of superlinear convergence on well behaved functions but does not have quadratic termination. This is available as

AERE/VAO6A/FORTRAN (Powell, 1970).

The numerical evidence comparing the performance of this algorithm with those based on (7.12) indicate however that it is less efficient (Fletcher, 1972a; Dixon, 1973c).

Acceptable point methods

In Broyden, Dennis and More (1972) it is shown that eventually iterations with the direct prediction $\alpha = 1$ have *superlinear convergence* with all three updating formulae DFP (7.3), BFS (7.12) and Powell (7.13). It is interesting to note that their proof implies

$$\frac{\|(G(x^*)^{-1} - H^{(k)}) g^{(k)}\|}{\|x^{(k)} - x^*\|} \to 0 \quad \text{i.e.} \quad (4.8)$$

but not that $H^{(k)} \to G(x^*)^{-1}$. (Condition 4.9).

Variants of the DFP and BFS algorithms described above that accept the point $\alpha = 1$ whenever it satisfies the conditions of Section 3 are available NOC/VARMET/L = 1/BASIC and AERE/VAO9A/FORTRAN (Fletcher, 1972a). Numerical results Dixon (1972c) indicate that while this policy is quite efficient when used with the BFS formula or with the combination of the BFS and DFP formula proposed by Fletcher it is disastrous when used with the DFP formula alone.

TOTAL E.F.E. for 9 functions	DFP	BFS
Interpolation	2333	1105
Acceptable point	3109	1149

This emphasises the fact that the significance of the property of superlinear or second order convergence depends on the radius of the region in which

$$\|x^{(k+1)} - x^*\|/\|x^{(k)} - x^*\| \leqslant \eta < 1 \quad \text{where} \quad \eta \sim 0.5. \quad (7.15)$$

The acceptance of a point $\alpha = 1$ which satisfies the conditions of Theorem 1 can lead to very slow convergence if applied outside this region.

Implementations that approximate α by interpolation may well also have superlinear convergence, Dennis and More (1973), and have a wider region of the type described above. A yet wider region of superlinear convergence may well be available due to Theorem 5 and the quadratic termination property.

Methods with quadratic termination

One such method has been available for some time namely symmetric rank-one updating formula (Murtagh and Sargent, 1970),

$$H^{(k+1)} = H + \frac{(d - Hy)(d - Hy)^T}{(d - Hy)^T y} \tag{7.16}$$

which has quadratic termination for arbitrary step sizes and hence (Theorem 5) often has N step second order convergence. NOC/VARMET/ V = 4/BASIC.

A second method has recently been given by Powell (1972b, c).

I have recently proposed a third alternative Dixon (1973c) which (i) generates conjugate directions without perfect iterations, (ii) generates the same sequence of matrices $H^{(k)}$ as a perfect iteration and hence, (iii) has cyclic second order convergence if the steps taken satisfy Theorem 5.

Implementations of the last two proposals are not generally available yet.

More general methods

In Huang (1970) a more general family of updating formulae were introduced, the symmetric members of which can be written as

$$H^{(k+1)} = H^{(k)} - \frac{Hyy^T H}{y^T Hy} + \rho \frac{dd^T}{d^T d} + \phi_1 vv^T.$$

He demonstrated that this family maintained quadratic termination for any value of ρ.

Biggs (1971) first suggested that the choice $\rho = 1$ was not appropriate on non-quadratic function since we would not expect

$$G^{(k+1)-1} y = d.$$

He has proposed two methods Biggs (1971, 1972) for estimating ρ based on non-quadratic properties of F determined during the iteration. His algorithm is the general purpose optimisation routine at the N.O.C. and is available as NOC/VMFUM/FORTRAN.

The numerical evidence indicates that estimating ρ in this way can greatly reduce the number of iterations required to minimise many functions. Over the 9 functions quoted by Biggs (1972) the number of iterations required with $\rho = 1$ was 672 (Biggs, 1971) while with estimated values of ρ this was reduced to 432 (Biggs, 1972).

8. Conjugate Gradient Algorithms

The conjugate gradient family of optimisation algorithms were introduced by Fletcher and Reeves (1964). The essential steps are to define the direction

$$p^{(k)} = - g^{(k)} + \beta p^{(k+1)} \tag{8.1}$$

and the step

$$d = x^{(k+1)} - x^{(k)} = \alpha p^{(k)}.$$

The main values of β that have been considered are

$\beta = g^{(k)^T} g^{(k)} / g^{(k-1)^T} g^{(k-1)}$ (Fletcher and Reeves, 1964)

$\beta = g^{(k)^T} y^{(k)} / p^{(k-1)^T} y^{(k)}$ (Hestenes and Stiefel, 1952)

$\beta = g^{(k)^T} y^{(k)} / g^{(k-1)^T} g^{(k-1)}$ (Polak and Ribiere, 1969)

It is usual to consider the performance of these algorithms in the reset mode, i.e. $\beta = 0$ when $k = 0, n, 2n \ldots$ and with perfect iterations. In this case it is fairly easy to show that the algorithms have the following properties:

(i) Quadratic Termination

(ii) Convergence to a stationary point (via Theorem 1)

(iii) At least N step 2nd ORDER Convergence

(see for instance Polak (1971), this also follows from Theorem 5).

The standard proofs of these properties are dependent on the iterations being perfect, whilst in practice α is usually chosen by interpolation until a point satisfying Theorem 1 is achieved. When α is relaxed in this way the direction (8.1) may not satisfy condition I and then it is usual to reset β to zero.

Implementations of this method are available as

AERE/VAO8A/FORTRAN Fletcher (1972b) and NOC/CONGRA/BASIC.

9. Non-Gradient Techniques

When analytic expressions for the gradient $g(x)$ are not available it is either possible to estimate their value numerically or to devise an algorithm that does not utilise this vector.

Numerical estimates of the derivatives can be utilised with revised quasi-Newton methods by using the modified routines NPL/QMNDIFF/ALGOL

Gill, Murray and Pitfield (1972); AERE/VA10/FORTRAN Fletcher (1972a); MINIFUN/BFS/ALGOL Lootsma (1973a); and by incorporating a subroutine NOC/OPND/FORTRAN or NOC/NUMDER/BASIC in with the VMFUM, VARMET or CONGRA routines.

These estimates of the derivatives are based on simple or central differences formula

$$g_i = \frac{f(x + he_i) - f(x)}{h} \quad \text{or} \quad g_i = \frac{f(x + he_i) - f(x - he_i)}{2h} \quad (9.1)$$

The choice of h has been discussed by Stewart (1967) and Murray (1972c) and must balance the truncation and round off errors. Murray has proposed setting h to a constant preselected value and switching from (9.1) to (9.2) when the step size approaches h and with this or similar strategies the algorithms are now relatively efficient but when the perfect iteration step size becomes of the same order of h premature termination can occur as the estimated negative gradient can point uphill. Even where line search strategies are modified to allow negative values of α the possibility of these rounding errors obviously destroy all the convergency properties derived with analytic gradients.

It used to be stated that an algorithm was convergent on a well-behaved function if it could be shown that a succession of linear searches took place along a set of independent directions. In Powell (1972d) an example is given on which the univariate search technique fails to converge and in consequence doubt has been cast on the convergence properties of most search techniques in which condition I of Theorem 1 cannot be tested.

The most well-known search technique that does not approximate the gradient was that suggested by Powell (1964) AERE/VA04/FORTRAN. Theoretical modifications to this have been suggested by Zangwill (1967) and more recently by Powell himself, Powell (1972e) and Brent (1973). Systematic comparisons of the performance of many variations of the basic ideas of Powell, Zangwill and Davies, Swann and Campey (Swann, 1964), have been carried out by Rhead (1971, 1972) and Brodlie (1972) and it appears that Brent's implementation which is listed in full in his book is the most efficient of these. It is interesting to note that when $n > 20$ it is possible to construct quadratic functions for which Powell's criteria for changing the initial search directions is never satisfied. This has been demonstrated theoretically and numerically by Professor Sargon at the London School of Economics (Sylwestrowicz, 1973). It is significant that this test is avoided by Brent in his implementation. It does not however compare favourably numerically with the approximate revised quasi-Newton results given by Fletcher (1972a) or Gill, Murray and Pitfield (1972). Brent's algorithm is unusual in that the set of linear directions is reorthogonalised after each

Q.A.F. cycle and he surmises that this may well imply second order convergence. If the Q.A.F. constructed could be shown to satisfy the conditions of Theorem 5 this would automatically follow.

Brent's approach is also unique in that he considers theoretically the difficulties that arise with search techniques when the round off error in the function evaluation routine exceeds the theoretical change in function value in an iteration. He comments that in these conditions the use of a pattern step (Rosenbrock, 1960, Hooke and Jeeves, 1960) is essential and incorporates a curvelinear pattern step between each Q.A.F. approximation. He also includes a linear pattern step whenever all the approximate line searches from a given point fail to give an improvement in the middle of a Q.A.F. approximation and states that this is essential if the minimum of ill-conditioned functions is to be obtained.

His comments are also supported by the results of Crombie (1972) who compared the performance of VA04, DFP and some pattern search techniques on a hybrid computer where the function evaluation was subject to random noise and showed that in these circumstances the line search routines were unreliable.

10. Numerical Supporting Evidence

Statement 1: The overhead cost per iteration for modified Newton methods is less than that for variable metric algorithms when $n < 6$, and does not display $O(n^3)$ behaviour for $n < 30$. The overhead cost for conjugate algorithms is always less than that for variable metric methods.

Evidence: The comparison curves for the NOC/BASIC algorithms are shown in Fig. 1.

Statement 2: Using numerical differences to estimate the Hessian matrix in Modified Newton methods does not increase the number of iterations.

Statement 3: Given the same linear search strategy Modified Newton algorithms require less iterations than quasi-Newton methods.

Evidence: The data quoted below is for the N.P.L. algorithms.

Function	Number of iterations		
	MNA	MNADIFF	QMNDER
Ros 2	21	21	31
Wood 4	37	37	75
Pow 4	16	16	37
Wat 6	11	11	32
Wat 9	12	12	69
Cheb 20	—	25	64

Statement 4: At each iteration most modified Newton algorithms require $n + 1$ gradient calculations to estimate the Hessian and hence the direction, whilst a quasi-Newton algorithm only requires one gradient calculation. If a gradient calculation is of the same order as the overheads the quasi-Newton approach should be more efficient.

Statement 5: As the accuracy of the linear search routine is relaxed the number of iterations required increases.

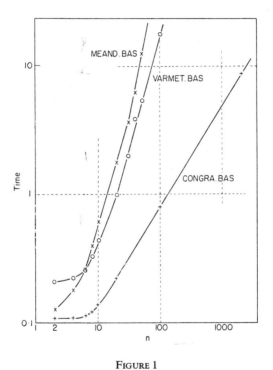

FIGURE 1

Statement 6: As the accuracy of the linear search routine is relaxed the number of function evaluations per iteration decreases.

Evidence: In Dixon (1972c) results are given for nine functions and four routines. An analysis of these results and similar ones implies that on average the relative number of iterations and the number of equivalent function evaluations per iteration are given by:

Line search routine	Accurate		Interpolated point		Acceptable point	
	Cubic	Parabolic	Cubic	Parabolic	Cubic	Parabolic
Rel. No. of iterations	1	1	1·15	1·33	1·93	1·93
No. of E.F.E./iter.	$5(n+1)$	$n+12$	$2·5(n+1)$	$n+3$	$1·5(n+1)$	$n+1·5$
Product	$5(n+1)$	$n+12$	$2·88(n+1)$	$1·33(n+3)$	$2·9(n+1)$	$1·93(n+1·5)$
$n=2$	15	14	9	7	9	7
$n = 10$	55	22	31	17	31	22
$n = 20$	155	32	60	31	60	41
$n = 30$	155	42	90	44	90	61

Statement 7: From the previous table it appears that when using parabolic interpolation the accuracy of the line search should be increased with n. For large n, parabolic interpolation is preferable to cubic interpolation.

Comment: A rigorous discussion of an efficient safeguarded parabolic interpolation technique is given in Brent (1973).

Statement 8: Functions exist for which the most appropriate polynomial has degree greater than two, e.g. the singular quartic function introduced by Powell. On such functions the appropriate step is

$$p^{(k)} = - (D - 1) G^{-1} g$$

where D is the degree of the appropriate polynomial (Jacobson and Oksman, 1972). On these functions acceptance of the Newton–Raphson step $\alpha = 1$ can cause very slow convergence.

Evidence: On Powell's quartic function if D is estimated by the Dominant Degree method (Biggs, 1971) and an initial step of $\alpha = D - 1$ taken then the number of iterations required is reduced from 21 to 5 (Dixon and Biggs, 1970).

Statement 9: Both when gradients are available and when they are not the variable metric approach is typically the most efficient on general functions.

		Equivalent function evaluations			Function evaluations	
n	Function	MEAND	VARMET	CONGRA	OPND	VAO4A
2	Ros 2	137	132	366	141	158
	Box 2	F	53	272	58	82
	Exp 2	95	53	84	63	43
	Pen	213	121	386	80	411
	Ros 8	115	71	45	102	110
3	Exp 3	95	67	600	89	102
4	Pow 4	241	136	390	209	191
	Wood 4	595	320	208	488	522
	Exp 4	242	152	1251	239	177
10	Test 10	1594	536	1158	544	1563

Statement 10: On symmetrical functions both variable metric and conjugate gradient algorithms can use the symmetry to converge in less than the expected number of iterations. This is presumably related to Broyden's (1970) result on the number of iterations required to minimise a quadratic function.

Evidence: Consider the function

$$F = \sum_{k=1}^{n/2} (x_{2k-1}^2 - x_{2k})^2 + (1 - x_{2k-1})^2$$

This is symmetric in that there are effectively only 2 independent types of directions. Experimentally the number of iterations is approximately independent of n.

	No. of iterations			No. of E.F.E.		
n	MEAND	VARMET	CONGRA	MEAND	VARMET	CONGRA
2	10	10	21	68	51	101
4	10	12	26	541	84	174
6	10	13	25	309	119	221
8	11	13	28	541	147	303
10	11	13	34	793	175	439
50	11	13	32	14,592	735	1739
100		12	34		1332	3590
150		13	32		2136	5036
300			41			12709
600			29			18074
1200			30			37285

In every case the function was reduced below 1E–9. The MEAND and VARMET runs were terminated when the standard student store allowance on The Hatfield Polytechnic Dec System 10 was exhausted. With this very cheap function for $n > 10$ the runs with CONGRA required least CPU time. My thanks are due to A. S. Whinfield for permission to include these results.

Statement 11: Functions that are sums of squared terms.

Many specialised algorithms have been written for minimising functions that are sums of squared terms, these include

AERE/VA02A/FORTRAN (Powell, 1965)   NOC/OPLS/FORTRAN

AERE/VA05A/FORTRAN (Powell, 1968)   NOC/OPLS/BASIC

AERE/VA07A/FORTRAN (Fletcher, 1971)

These algorithms are all based on the Gauss–Newton prediction. Given

$$F = \Sigma s_k^2 \quad \text{and} \quad J_{kj} = \partial s_k / \partial x_j$$

then

$$g_j = 2J_{kj}s_k \quad \text{and} \quad G_{ij} = 2J_{kj}J_{ki} + 2(\partial J_{kj}/\partial x_i)\, s_k$$

$$= 2J_{kj}J_{ki} + B_{ij}\,.$$

The Gauss–Newton prediction is obtained by neglecting B. Meyer (1970) has shown that the ultimate rate of convergence of Gauss–Newton methods is bounded by

$$\frac{\|x^{(k+1)} - x^*\|}{\|x^{(k)} - x^*\|} \leqslant \frac{\lambda_1}{\lambda_2} = \eta,$$

where λ_1 is the maximum eigenvalue of B and λ_2 is the minimum eigenvalue of $(J_T J)$. The method therefore only has superlinear convergence if

$$\|B(x^*)\| = 0$$

and this was true in the majority of functions tested by Box (1966) and Bard (1970) in their comparison studies which indicated that these routines are more efficient on these functions than general purpose routines.

McKeown (1973a) has recently published a series of practical problems in which the performance of the specialised algorithms was no better than the generalised routines. He has also shown McKeown (1973b) by constructing functions with increasing values of η that when $\eta > 0.5$ the general purpose routines are superior to the specialised routines.

Statement 12: When estimating numerical derivatives of functions that are sums of squared terms it is more accurate to estimate J and use

$$g = 2J^T s$$

than to estimate g directly. If the Jacobian is sparse we may evaluate g in less than $n + 1$ function evaluations by using the method outlined in Curtis, Powell and Reid (1972).

References

Bard, Y. (1970). *SIAM J. Numer. Analysis* **7**, 157–186.

Biggs, M. C. (1971). *J. Inst. Maths Applics* **8**, 315–327.

Biggs, M. C. (1972). "Some Further Experience With Minimisation Algorithms Which Make Use of Non-quadratic Properties of the Objective Function". The Hatfield Polytechnic, N.O.C. T.R. 35.

Box, M. F. (1966). *Comput. J.* **9**, 67–77.

Brent, R. P. (1973). "Algorithms for Minimisation Without Derivatives". Prentice-Hall, Englewood Cliffs, New Jersey.

Brodlie, K. W. (1972). "A New Method for Unconstrained Minimisation Without Evaluating Derivatives". IBM UKSC-0019.

Broyden, C. G. (1967). *Math. Comput.* **21**, 368–381.

Broyden, C. G. (1970). *J. Inst. Maths Applics* **6**, 79–90 and 222–231.

Broyden, C. G., Dennis, J. E. and More, J. J. (1972). "On the Local and Super-linear Convergence of Quasi-Newton Methods". Cornell University, Computer Science, T.R. 72–137.

Crombie, D. B. (1972). "Review of the Performance of Hill Climbing Strategies When Applied to a Hybrid Environment". M.Sc. Thesis in Control Engineering, The Hatfield Polytechnic.

Davidon, W. C. (1959). "Variable Metric Methods for Minimisation". A.E.C. R. & D. Report ANL–5990.

Dennis, J. E. (1968). *Num. Math.* **11**, 324–330.

Dennis, J. E. (1971). Towards a unified convergence theory for Newton-like methods. *In* (L. B. Rall, Ed.) "Nonlinear Functional Analysis and Applications". Academic Press, New York and London.

Dennis, J. E. and More, J. J. (1973). "A Characterisation of Superlinear Convergence and Its Applications to Quasi-Newton Methods". Cornell University, T.R. 73–157.

Dixon, L. C. W. and Biggs, M. C. (1970). "MEANDER—A Newton Based Procedure for *N*-dimensional Function Minimisation". Hatfield Polytechnic, N.O.C. T.R. 9.

Dixon, L. C. W. (1972a). "Nonlinear Optimisation". English University Press.

Dixon, L. C. W. (1972b). *Math. Prog.* **3** (3), 383–388.

Dixon, L. C. W. (1972c). The choice of step length, a crucial factor in the performance of variable metric algorithms. *In* (F. Lootsma, Ed.) "Numerical Methods for Nonlinear Optimisation". Academic Press, London and New York.

Dixon, L. C. W. (1973a). Experience using the library routine MEAND.BAS. (To appear).

Dixon, L. C. W. (1973b). *Math. Prog.* **3** (3), 345–358.

Dixon, L. C. W. (1973c). Conjugate directions without linear searches. *J. Inst. Maths Applics* **11**, 317–328.

Fiacco, A. V. and McCormick, G. P. (1968). "Nonlinear Programming". John Wiley and Sons, New York.

Fletcher, R. and Powell, M. J. D. (1963). *Comput. J.* **6**, 163–168.

Fletcher, R. and Reeves, C. M. (1964). *Comput. J.* **13**, 317–322.

Fletcher, R. (1970). *Comput. J.* **317**–322.

Fletcher, R. (1971). "A Modified Marquardt Subroutine for Nonlinear Least Squares". A.E.R.E. R 6799.

Fletcher, R. (1972a). "FORTRAN Subroutines for Minimisation by Quasi-Newton Methods". A.E.R.E.—R 7125.

Fletcher, R. (1972b). "A FORTRAN Subroutine for Minimisation by the Method of Conjugate Gradients". A.E.R.E.—R 7073.

Ghani, S. N. (1972). *Computer Aided Design* Vol. 4, No. 5.

Gill, P. E. and Murray, W. (1972). *J. Inst. Maths Applics* **9**, 91–108.

Gill, P. E., Murray, W. and Pitfield, R. A. (1972). "The Implementation of Two Revised Quasi-Newton Algorithms for Unconstrained Optimisation". N.P.L. NAC 11.

Gill, P. E., Murray, W. and Picken, S. M. (1972). "The Implementation of Two Modified Newton Algorithms for Unconstrained Optimisation". N.P.L. NAC 24.

Goldfarb, D. (1969). Sufficient conditions for convergence of a variable metric algorithm. *In* (R. Fletcher, Ed.) "Optimisation". Academic Press, London and New York.

Goldfarb, D. (1970). *Math. Comput.* **24**, 23–36.

Goldfeld, S. M., Quandt, R. E. and Trotter, H. F. (1966). *Econometrica* **34**, 541–551.

Goldstein, A. A. and Price, J. F. (1967). *Num. Math.* **10**, 184–189.

Hebden, M. D. (1973). "An Algorithm for Minimisation using Exact second Derivatives". A.E.R.E. T.P. 515.

Hestenes, M. and Stiefel, E. (1952). Methods of conjugate gradients for solving linear systems. *J. Res. Nat. Bur. Standards* **49**.

Hooke, R. and Jeeves, T. A. (1960). *J. Ass. Comput. Math.* **8**, 405–423.

Huang, H. Y. (1970). *J. Optim. Theory and Applic.* **5**, 405–423.

Jacobson, D. H. and Oksman, W. (1970). An algorithm that minimizes homogeneous functions of N variables in $N + 2$ iterations and rapidly minimizes general functions. Harvard University, Technical Report No. 618.

Levenberg, K. (1944). *Quart. App. Maths* **2**, 164–168.

Lootsma, F. A. (1972a). "The ALGOL 60 Procedure MINIFUN for Solving Nonlinear Optimisation Problems". Philips Research Laboratories, Report 27, 358–385.

McCormick, G. (1969). "The Rate of Convergence of the Reset Davidon Variable Metric Method". University of Wisconsin MRC. S.R. 1012.

McCormick, G. and Ritter, K. (1972). *Math. Prog.* **3**, 101–116.

McKeown, J. J. (1973a). A comparison of methods for solving nonlinear parameter estimation problems. *In* Proceedings 3rd I.F.A.C. Symposium on "Identification and Parameter Estimation". The Hague, 1973.

McKeown, J. J. (1973b). "Specialised versus General Purpose Algorithms for Minimising Functions that are Sums of Squared Terms". Hatfield Polytechnic, N.O.C. 50.

Meyer, R. R. (1970). Theoretical and computational aspects of nonlinear regression. *In* (Rosen, Mangasarian and Ritter, Eds) "Nonlinear Programming". Academic Press, London and New York.

Murray, W. (1972a). "Numerical Methods for Unconstrained Optimisation". Academic Press, London and New York.

Murray, W. (1972b). Second derivative methods. *In* Murray, W. (1972a), pp. 57–72.

Murray, W. (1972c). Failure, the causes and cures. *In* Murray, W. (1972a), pp. 107–122.

Murtagh, B. A. and Sargent, R. W. H. (1969). A constrained minimisation method with quadratic convergence. *In* (R. Fletcher, Ed.) "Optimisation". Academic Press, London and New York.

Murtagh, B. A. and Sargent, R. W. H. (1970). *Comput. J.* **13**, 2 185.

Ortega, J. M. and Rheinboldt, W. C. (1971). "Iterative Solution of Nonlinear Equations in Several Variables". Academic Press, London and New York.

Polak, E. and Ribiere, G. (1969). *Rev. Fr. Inform. Rech. Operation* 16–R1, pp. 35–43.

Polak, E. (1971). "Computational Methods in Optimisation". Academic Press, London and New York.

Powell, M. J. D. (1964). *Comput. J.* **7**, 155–162.

Powell, M. J. D. (1965). *Comput. J.* **7**, 303–307.

Powell, M. J. D. (1968). "VA05A". Harwell Subroutine Library.

Powell, M. J. D. (1970). A new algorithm for unconstrained optimisation. *In* Rosen, Mangasarian and Ritter, Eds) "Nonlinear Programming". Academic Press, London and New York.

Powell, M. J. D. (1971). *J. Inst. Maths Applics* **7**, 21–36.

Powell, M. J. D. (1972a). Some properties of the variable metric algorithms. *In* (F. Lootsma, Ed.) "Numerical Methods for Nonlinear Optimisation". Academic Press, London and New York.

Powell, M. J. D. (1972b). "Quadratic Termination Properties of a Class of Double Rank Minimisation Algorithms". A.E.R.E. T.P. 471.

Powell, M. J. D. (1972c). "Some Theorems on Quadratic Termination Properties of Minimisation Algorithms". A.E.R.E. T.P. 472.

Powell, M. J. D. (1972d). "On Search Directions for Minimisation Algorithms". A.E.R.E. T.P. 492.

Powell, M. J. D. (1972e). "Unconstrained Minimisation Algorithms Without Computation of Derivatives". A.E.R.E. T.P. 483.

Rhead, D. G. (1971). "Some Numerical Experiments on Zangwill's Method for Unconstrained Minimisation". Institute of Computer Science, W.P. ICSI 319.

Rhead, D. G. (1971b). "Further Experiments on Zangwill's Method". Institute of Computer Science, W.P. ICSI 347.

Rhead, D. G. (1971c). "Experiments on Step-lengths and Stopping Rules for the Linear Minimisations in Powell's Direct Search Method". Institute of Computer Science, W.P. ICSI 348.

Rhead, D. G. (1971d). "Two Variations of Powell's Method for Minimisation Without Evaluating Derivatives". Institute of Computer Science, W. P. ICSI 353.

Rhead, D. G. (1972). "On a New Class of Algorithms for Function Minimisation without Evaluating Derivatives". (Private communication).

Rosenbrock, H. H. (1960). *Comput. J.* **3**, 175–184.

Sargent, R. W. H. and Sebastian, D. J. (1972). Numerical experience with algorithms for unconstrained minimisation. *In* (F. Lootsma, Ed.) "Numerical Methods for Unconstrained Optimisation". Academic Press, London and New York.

Shanno, D. F. (1970). *Math. Comput.* **24**, 647–657.
Stewart, G. W. (1967). *J. Ass. Comput. Math.* **14**, 72–83.
Swan, W. H. (1964). I.C.I. Central Institute Research Lab. RN 64/3.
Sylwestrowicz, J. D. (1973). London School of Economics. (Private communication).
Wolfe, P. (1969). *SIAM Review* **11**, 226–235.
Wolfe, P. (1971). *SIAM Review* **13**, 185–188.
Zangwill, W. I. (1967). *Comput. J.* **10**, 293–296.

Discussion: Non-Linear Optimisation

MR. POWELL. The early variable metric methods, e.g. Davidon (1959), have the very nice property that, except for initial conditions, they are invariant under linear transformations of the variables. This property seems to me to be very desirable, because it obviates the need for the user to scale the variables so that they are all of about the same magnitude. Therefore I regret that some recent work, for instance, that which uses condition numbers, tends to lose this property. Please comment on this question.

MR. DIXON. The need for the introduction of modifications based on the condition number which affects the scale invariant nature of the path generated by variable metric algorithms, is due to the three factors:

(i) non-convex functions

(ii) imperfect line search routines

(iii) rounding errors.

Whilst the first two of these factors do not affect the scale invariant nature of the path, there is no proof that the path generated will terminate at a stationary point. The introduction of these modifications guarantee this.

The effects of rounding errors are of course scale dependent. The solution of a set of linear equations is theoretically invariant under linear transformations, but there is plenty of experience indicating that in finite length arithmetic the solution obtained depends on the scale.

In practice our routines reset H to I on very few iterations, probably about 1%. I hope that eventually it will be shown that the unmodified path generated on non-convex functions and with practical line search routines is convergent to a stationary point, but even so I would expect such modifications to be necessary in finite length arithmetic.

MR. P. E. GILL (*National Physical Laboratory*). Could you comment on the modification to the quasi-Newton methods so that the variables are scaled?

MR. DIXON. S. Oren (*Management Science*, 1973) has introduced a modification into the variable metric algorithms which he claims scales the variables. It is interesting to note that with perfect line searches his modification is effectively a choice of p in Huang's family. We have no experience of using this algorithm.

DR. HEATHER M. LIDDELL (*Queen Mary College*). I have found that for certain types of problem, occurring in filter design work and also in economic applications, variable metric methods do not always give good results, particularly in the initial stages, and it is better to use the Simplex method, and then possibly switch at a later stage. Has N.O.C. any algorithms available which use two methods for this type of problem?

MR. DIXON. There are classes of problems in which the function to be optimised contains ripples, i.e. local minima, in which variable metric algorithms tend to be attracted. Often, when these are ripples on the side of a larger valley, a pattern search routine can avoid the ripples and get nearer the bottom of the valley where a more sophisticated routine can then make better progress. We have a hybrid routine ACSIM (Dixon, 1973, *Computer Aided Design* **5**, No. 1) which combines a Nelder and Mead simplex approach with a modified Newton-Raphson technique; it also contains provisions for handling linear and nonlinear constraints. It is quite useful in 2–4 dimensions but I would not recommend it outside this range.

12. Algorithms for Curve and Surface Fitting

J. G. HAYES

Division of Numerical Analysis and Computing,
National Physical Laboratory,
Teddington, Middlesex, England.

1. Introduction

In this paper, the aim will be to survey available numerical algorithms for a
wide range of curve and surface-fitting problems. This problem description
will be taken to imply (a) discrete data, and (b) smoothing of that data:
thus in particular the paper will not be concerned with problems purely of
interpolation or with approximation of mathematical functions, in which
the value of the function at any value of the argument can be made
available to any required accuracy. Particular attention will be paid to those
areas for which computer algorithms in ALGOL or FORTRAN are
readily available. Where this is not the case, methods in the literature will be
referenced.

The basic problem considered is: given values $f_r, r = 1, 2, \ldots, m$, of the
dependent variable f, corresponding to values x_r of x, where x is a single
independent variable or a vector of several, fit to the f_r a function $f(x; \theta)$ of
known form but containing a vector θ of n disposable parameters.† Most
algorithms for solving this problem use the L_2 norm as the criterion for
closeness of fit, leading to the familiar least-squares solution. In this case we
minimize over θ the expression

$$\sum_{r=1}^{m} [f(x_r; \theta) - f_r]^2. \tag{1.1}$$

These algorithms will be treated in Section 2, and will be subdivided
according to the form of the fitting function. If this form is specified by the
context of the application, then, according to whether the form is linear or

---

† For simplicity of exposition we shall assume that the f_r are of equal weight; almost all
the methods of solution can be readily extended to the case of unequal weights, and indeed
many of the computer codes deal explicitly with this case.

219

nonlinear in the parameters θ, we have the general linear least-squares algorithms (Section 2.1) or specialized optimization algorithms (Section 2.2). It may be remarked that in practical applications the nonlinear situation is generally best avoided: the usual reason for fitting a nonlinear form is that its parameters have some meaningful physical significance and so need to be estimated, but in practice the problem is often so ill-conditioned that, even though a good fit to the data may be derived, the estimates obtained for the parameters have too large a statistical error for them to be meaningful. An equally good or better fit can usually be obtained, with much less effort, by using polynomials or splines, as in the next paragraph.

When the functional form is not specified in advance, as is perhaps more common, and the requirement is simply for an acceptable fit, polynomials or splines are normally used. These will be treated, for the case of one independent variable (the curve-fitting problem), in Section 2.3, and for the corresponding surface-fitting problem in Section 2.4. Both these functional forms are, of course, linear in their parameters and so a general linear least-squares algorithm could be employed. However, the use of splines leads to a least-squares problem of special form of which advantage can be taken. In the case of polynomials, also, it is almost always better to use a specialized algorithm. A particular exception is when the practical application requires the imposition of linear equality constraints of a type for which the specialized algorithms have not been adapted.

Algorithms based on the L_1 and L_∞ norms will be considered, for the linear fitting function, in Sections 3 and 4 respectively. With the L_1 norm we have to minimize over θ the expression

$$\sum_{r=1}^{m} |f(x_r; \theta) - f_r| . \tag{1.2}$$

With the L_∞ norm the corresponding expression is

$$\max_{1 \leqslant r \leqslant m} |f(x_r; \theta) - f_r|. \tag{1.3}$$

While there are statistical arguments, based on the form of the frequency distribution of the observational errors in the f_r, for choosing a particular norm, the choice is usually made on grounds of convenience: to reduce complexity in the computational problem. This consideration dictates the use of the L_2 norm in most cases. However, the L_1 norm has the characteristic, advantageous in some circumstances, of tending to be uninfluenced by a number of gross data errors: the L_∞ norm is appropriate when we wish to make the maximum residual as small as possible. Also, since the fitting problem in either of these two norms can be cast as a linear programming problem, each of them has an advantage when linear inequality constraints are to be imposed on the solution, in that the problem is still a linear programming problem, whereas the L_2 norm leads to a quadratic programming problem.

Finally, Section 5 will deal with a miscellany of other curve-fitting algorithms which do not fall into any of the above categories.

In giving references to the literature, I shall follow Fletcher (1972) and indicate by the use of capitals in the text those references which contain the ALGOL or FORTRAN code. Also the following abbreviations will be used to indicate the source of algorithms:

AEREH: Atomic Energy Research Establishment, Harwell.

NPL: National Physical Laboratory.

NAG: Numerical Algorithms Group, Oxford.

CACM: Communications of ACM.

CJ: Computer Journal.

HAC: Handbook for Automatic Computation: Vol. II (WILKINSON and REINSCH, 1971).

The letters (A) and (F) after the name of an algorithm or a reference will indicate ALGOL and FORTRAN respectively.

2. L_2 Norm

2.1. Linear Least Squares

This is an area in which many programs have been written, and in which extensive comparison tests have been carried out, in particular by Wampler (1969, 1970, 1973). While I have reservations about some of the test problems and the criterion of numerical accuracy used in this work, it constitutes a very valuable contribution to the subject and generally shows up well the quality of the various algorithms. I shall leave his papers to speak for themselves, quoting only the two programs which come out best in his tests, but adding some comparable programs which are more readily available in this country.

The fitting function in expression (1.1) now takes the form

$$f(x; \theta) = \sum_{i=1}^{n} \theta_i \phi_i(x), \qquad (2.1)$$

where the $\phi_i(x)$ are given functions of x. Our problem then is to find the least-squares solution of the over-determined system of linear equations

$$\Phi\theta = h, \qquad (2.2)$$

where Φ is the $m \times n$ matrix with elements $\phi_i(x_r)$, and θ and h are the vectors with elements θ_i and f_r respectively, with $i = 1, 2, \ldots, n$ and $r = 1, 2, \ldots, m$. Algorithms for this problem usually employ a different notation, in which Φ, θ and h are replaced by A, x and b respectively, so that (2.2) becomes

$$Ax = b. \tag{2.3}$$

We shall use this notation in the rest of this section. The time-honoured procedure is to obtain the solution directly from the "normal" equations

$$A^T Ax = A^T b.$$

It is well-known, and amply supported by Wampler's tests, that this procedure fares very badly with ill-conditioned systems of equations. Nevertheless, the method still has a place when the equations are known to be well-conditioned, since it is up to twice as fast as its more stable competitors. Appropriate computer algorithms are AEREH: MA09A(F) and NPL: ACCGENSOL(A). They both use Cholesky decomposition.

In general, however, the more stable algorithms, based on the use of orthogonal matrices, are to be preferred. In these, following Golub (1965), an orthogonal matrix Q is derived such that

$$QA = R = \begin{pmatrix} \tilde{R} \\ \cdots \\ O \end{pmatrix},$$

where $\tilde{R}$ is an upper-triangular matrix. The least-squares solution is then obtained by solving the triangular system

$$\tilde{R}x = \tilde{c}, \tag{2.4}$$

where $\tilde{c}$ contains the first n elements of the vector Qb, which we denote by c. The residual sum of squares is given by

$$\sum_{i=n+1}^{m} c_i^2. \tag{2.5}$$

Extensions to this basic procedure have been made in order to deal with linear equality constraints and to deal with the case when the matrix A is of rank $s < n$. In this latter situation there is an infinite number of solutions from which to choose. The two common choices are (a) the solution obtained by equating $(n - s)$ selected parameters to zero and solving for the remaining s parameters, and (b) the solution which has the smallest length, i.e. the smallest value of $x^T x$. I shall refer to these alternatives as the reduced-parameter solution and the minimal-length solution respectively.

The algorithm in BUSINGER and GOLUB (1965)(A), also available as HAC:I/8, uses for the matrix Q the product of a set of Householder matrices, and carries out interative refinement on the solution obtained. It is designed for the full-rank case, without constraints. A closely similar algorithm is NAG:FO1AX/FO4AM (A and F). There is also NAG: FO1AX/FO4AN (A and F) which omits the iterative refinement. Two other similar algorithms which omit the iterative refinement are AEREH:MA14A (F) and NPL:ORTFAC/ORTSOL (A). The former is able to deal with equality constraints and the latter with the rank-deficient case, deriving the minimal-length solution. This solution is also derived by NPL:GENERALSOL (A), in which the orthogonal decomposition of the previous algorithms has been replaced by an *LU* decomposition. The bases of both these NPL algorithms and their relative merits are discussed in Peters and Wilkinson (1970).

A further development has been an improved scheme for iterative refinement given by Björck (1967). This scheme has been included in the algorithms given in BJÖRCK and GOLUB (1967)(A) and BJÖRCK (1968) (A), both of which will deal with equality constraints. In place of House-holder transformations, the latter algorithm is based on modified Gram–Schmidt orthogonalization, which is of comparable stability. This algorithm deals also with the rank-deficient case and exists in two variants: one obtains the reduced-parameter solution and the other the minimal-length solution. FORTRAN versions of the first variant and of the Björck–Golub algorithm are available as WBASIC and FITBG respectively, from R. H. Wampler of the National Bureau of Standards in Washington. These two codes by Wampler are the only ones of those I have mentioned which compute the covariance matrix, the standard errors of the parameters and other results required in statistical applications.

The improved iterative refinement used in the algorithms of the previous paragraph produces a solution close to the exact solution even in ill-conditioned applications in which the random data errors are large, as is usual in data-fitting problems. The standard refinement breaks down in this situation. However, as Wilkinson remarks in WILKINSON and REINSCH (1971), there seems little point in carrying out iterative refinement at all when the data errors are large.

None of the algorithms so far mentioned will deal with rank deficiency in the constraint matrix. A method for doing this is included in Hayes and Halliday (1972).

GENTLEMAN (1972)(A) has used Givens' rotations in place of Householder transformations. A characteristic of this method is that the matrix *A* is brought into the computation a row at a time, a distinct advantage from a data-handling point of view. It also offers advantages with structured matrices. In the rank-deficient case, it gives a least-squares solution without the need to take special measures. The reduced-parameter solution is also easily obtained. Another version of this algorithm is available as NPL:FULLGIVENS (A). Finally, GOLUB and REINSCH (1970)(A) gives a Householder-based algorithm, available also as HAC:I/10 (A), which includes a singular-value analysis, a process recommended by a number of authorities for very ill-conditioned cases (see for example Lawson, 1971).

I have referenced many algorithms in this section. All except the first two, which solve the "normal" equations, should be satisfactory in most applications. It is, therefore, simply a matter of choosing the one most readily available which has the capability (such as dealing with constraints) required by the particular application.

2.2. Nonlinear Least Squares

In this area, my task has already been done for me by Fletcher (1972) and Powell (1972). We wish to minimize the sum of squares of nonlinear functions

$$F(x) = \sum_{r=1}^{m} [f_r(x)]^2, \qquad (2.6)$$

where x is the vector of the n disposable parameters and, with a further unfortunate clash with the notation in data-fitting applications, $f_r(x)$ represents $f(x_r; \theta) - f_r$ in eqn (1.1), for each $r = 1, 2, \ldots, m$.

Algorithms for this problem are iterative, deriving a sequence of points $x^{(1)}$, $x^{(2)}$, ..., which hopefully converges to a point x^* that minimizes $F(x)$. The classical approach is, at each iteration, to linearize each $f_r(x)$ about the current $x^{(k)}$ and carry out a linear least-squares calculation. This gives the Gauss–Newton iteration

$$x^{(k+1)} = x^{(k)} - 2\{B^{(k)}\}^{-1} \{J^{(k)T} f^{(k)}\}, \qquad (2.7)$$

where $f^{(k)}$ is the vector of the m function values $f_r(x^{(k)})$, $J^{(k)}$ is the $m \times n$ Jacobian matrix of first derivatives $\partial f_r(x^{(k)})/\partial x_j$, and $B^{(k)} = 2J^{(k)T} J^{(k)}$.

Unfortunately, the iteration can diverge, and to overcome this it is usual to employ the correction vector in (2.7) not as a specific step, but as a direction of search. However, this can also fail by converging to a non-stationary point at which J is singular.

Marquardt (1963) gave an algorithm which ensures convergence, at small additional cost, by allowing the possibility of adding a multiple of the unit matrix to $B^{(k)}$, so biasing the step direction towards the steepest-descent direction. Thus the iteration becomes

$$x^{(k+1)} = x^{(k)} - 2\{B^{(k)} + \lambda^{(k)} I\}^{-1} \{J^{(k)T} f^{(k)}\}, \qquad (2.8)$$

for some suitable value of the constant $\lambda^{(k)}$.

A Marquardt-type computer algorithm was given by FLETCHER (1971), also available as AEREH:VA07A (F) and as NAG:E04GA (A and F). An adaptation which does not require derivatives, appropriate to the case when the derivatives are costly to compute, is AEREH:VA05A (F), also available as NAG:E04FB (A and F). This algorithm does not include automatic scaling, as the previous one does, so scaling has to be taken care of separately.

If these algorithms are slow to converge, it will often be better to use a quasi-Newton method designed for general unconstrained optimization.

2.3. *Polynomials and Splines*

When the form of the approximating function is not dictated by the particular application, polynomials or splines are usually employed. A spline of degree N consists of a set of polynomial arcs, of degree N, joined together smoothly with continuity of function value and derivatives up to order $N - 1$. It is most usual to take $N = 3$, giving the cubic spline, since this works very well in practice and second-derivative continuity is sufficient for most applications. But when do we use polynomials and when splines? I think one can say that splines are the more versatile, and so, in the absence of special knowledge, carry the greater hope of success. On the other hand, the practical user is often pre-disposed towards what he sees as the simpler concept of polynomials. Recently I had the occasion, with Maurice Cox, to reconsider this question in the context of providing general guidance on curve fitting to the user with little previous experience. We were concerned with providing a means for representing for computer use the multitude of graphs and tables which appear in British Standards.

We recommended a process consisting of three parts. First, try a least-squares polynomial up to degree 5 or 6—after all, many curves require only quadratics. If this failed, possibly only because of too few points or a poor point-distribution, draw a curve by hand and read off 17 values at abscissae corresponding to the extremal points of the Chebyshev polynomial of degree 16, based on the data range. (Thus this could be applied also to graphical data.) Then, in a standard manner, derive the interpolating Chebyshev series and truncate appropriately.† If this also failed, try fitting a cubic spline by least squares. Fortunately, since much practical data is known only to graphical accuracy at best, the test for success or failure is easy—plot out the results. Even with more accurate data, it is usually possible to reduce the situation to graphical accuracy by subtracting a suitable low-degree polynomial (perhaps a least-squares polynomial) from both fit and data before plotting.

---

† It may be noted that this series, truncated at any particular degree, is the least-squares polynomial solution of that degree for the 17 points used.

In putting together the appropriate package of algorithms, we were of course concerned to make it as robust and fool-proof as possible. Robustness simply meant choosing good numerical algorithms. Making the package as fool-proof as possible was hopefully achieved by (a) providing a supporting discussion of practical considerations entailed in using it, and (b) including tests to check that the data satisfy all the requirements of the algorithms—for example, the spline algorithm tests the Schoenberg–Whitney conditions for the existence of a solution. This package will be discussed more fully by Maurice Cox in the next chapter, and will be available, with the supporting notes, in COX and HAYES (1973).

The polynomial algorithm in the package, NPL:POLYFIT (A), is based on the modification by Clenshaw (1960) of the stable numerical algorithm using orthogonal polynomials given by Forsythe (1957). Both algorithms deal with the polynomial fitting function

$$f(x) = b_0 + b_1 x + b_2 x^2 + \ldots + b_k x^k \tag{2.9}$$

in the form

$$f(x) = c_0 p_0(x) + c_1 p_1(x) + \ldots + c_k p_k(x), \tag{2.10}$$

with

$$\sum_{r=1}^{m} p_i(x_r) p_j(x_r) = 0 \quad \text{whenever} \quad i \neq j. \tag{2.11}$$

The p_i are computed by the recurrence relation

$$p_{i+1}(x) = 2(x - \alpha_{i+1}) p_i(x) - \beta_i p_{i-1}(x), \tag{2.12}$$

where α_{i+1} and β_i are constants depending on x_r, $p_i(x_r)$ and $p_{i-1}(x_r)$, $r = 1$, $\ldots, m$. A Forsythe-type algorithm provides the c_i, α_i and β_i (from which $f(x)$ can be computed for any x by means of the recurrence (2.12)), and sometimes also the coefficients b_i of (2.9). In the Clenshaw algorithm, all the polynomials concerned are represented by the coefficients in their Chebyshev-series expansion. Thus in particular, the function $f(x)$ is represented by the coefficients a_i in its Chebyshev expansion

$$f(x) = a_0 T_0(x) + a_1 T_1(x) + \ldots + a_k T_k(x), \tag{2.13}$$

where $T_i(x)$ is the Chebyshev polynomial of the first kind of degree i, and the x scale has been transformed so that the data values run from -1 to $+1$. (This transformation should always be carried out in any case.) We recommend the form (2.13), particularly from the point of view of numerical accuracy in evaluating $f(x)$.

Two Forsythe-type algorithms are ACRLII.VCUIA/PLU8A (F) and NAG:E02AB (A and F). For the latter, which incidentally includes an automatic choice of degree, the new (Mark 3) version should be used. There are many other algorithms of this type available in algorithms libraries. They may well be satisfactory provided the user transforms the independent variable to the range -1 to $+1$, if it is not done by the algorithm. (Forsythe used the range -2 to $+2$, dropping the factor 2 from (2.12), which is equivalent.) Also with these algorithms the derived coefficients b_i should relate to the transformed variable if the risk of severe loss of accuracy in the evaluation of $f(x)$ is to be avoided.

The polynomial fitting method can be extended to deal with fixed constraints, finite or infinite, on function values and derivatives (Clenshaw and Hayes, 1965). The use of the methods in practical application is discussed in Hayes (1970b). ·

The Chebyshev interpolation algorithm in the NPL package is NPL: CHEBCOEFFICIENTS (A).

Turning now to cubic splines, their most straightforward representation is

$$s(x) = \sum_{j=0}^{3} \alpha_j x^j + \sum_{i=1}^{h} \beta_i (x - \lambda_i)^3_+, \tag{2.14}$$

where

$$E_+ = \begin{cases} E, \text{ when } E \geqslant 0, \\ 0, \text{ when } E \leqslant 0, \end{cases}$$

the λ_i are the knots (joins between polynomial arcs), and the α_j, β_i are $h + 4$ disposable parameters. For the least-squares problem, however, it is numerically much more satisfactory to use instead the representation in terms of cubic B-splines, $M_i(x)$, namely

$$s(x) = \sum_{i=1}^{h+4} \gamma_i M_i(x). \tag{2.15}$$

The values of the B-splines at the data points can be computed either by means of divided differences, or by the stable recurrence provided independently by Cox (1972) and de Boor (1972). Either method enables us to derive the set of linear equations corresponding to eqn (2.3) with $n = h + 4$. This set has a special structure of which advantage can be taken when computing the least-squares solution.

The spline algorithm in the NPL package is NPL:CUBICSPLINEFIT (A) and there is also NPL:L2SPLINE (A), which fits splines of any degree. Both use the stable recurrence, which, because it can deal with coincident knots, allows the continuity at one or more knots to be reduced, if that is desired. Thus they can, for example, deal with applications in which a discontinuity in the first derivative is required at some point. A similar algorithm, but without this extra facility (since it uses the divided-difference scheme), is AEREH:VB05B (F). A development of the latter algorithm is AEREH:VB06A (F), also available as NAG:E02AA (A and F), which includes smoothing parameters at choice of the user (see Powell, 1970).

All the above spline algorithms leave the user to specify the knot positions: with a little experience satisfactory positions can often be found after one or two trials. The algorithm AEREH:VC03A (F), however, includes a scheme for choosing knot positions automatically (see Powell, 1970). It seems particularly suited to complicated curves with many peaks, plenty of data and similar behaviour throughout the range (Parker (1970) gives a number of examples). In some other cases, where the character of the desired curve differs widely from one part of the range to another, the utility of this algorithm is likely to be limited by the restriction it places on the rate at which the knot spacing can vary across the range. Another approach to choosing good knot-positions automatically was described by de Boor at the SIAM/SIGNUM meeting at Austin, Texas, in October 1972. The algorithm in DE BOOR and RICE (1968) tackles the problem of determining *optimum* positions for the knots. This problem, however, is highly non-linear and computationally expensive to solve. Moreover, one has to be content to find local optima, of which there may be many, so that good knot-positions cannot be guaranteed. In general, therefore, it is better to use one of the algorithms mentioned earlier.

2.4. *Surfaces*

The choice between polynomials and splines is less clear in the case of surfaces, largely because sufficient experience with bicubic splines has not yet been accumulated. The arrangement of the data points in the plane of the two independent variables introduces an extra factor in the surface case, and it would appear that splines might prove unsatisfactory with some arrangements which would be satisfactory for polynomials. The data distribution is an important consideration with either functional type, and in particular the choice of algorithm depends on whether the points are arbitrarily scattered, whether they lie on parallel lines, or, even more special, lie at the intersections of a rectangular grid.

For polynomials, these cases are discussed in Hayes (1970c). Cadwell and Williams (1961) give a method for the general case, and, for the rectangular grid case, Cadwell (1961) provides the basis of CACM:164. Clenshaw and Hayes (1965) give a method for the case of data on parallel lines. All three methods work in terms of orthogonal polynomials. The first two, however, produce the fitted polynomial in double power-series form

$$\sum\sum b_{ij}x^iy^j,$$

whereas the third gives it as a double Chebyshev series

$$\sum\sum a_{ij}T_i(x)T_j(y).$$

Methods are given for imposing constraints on function values and derivatives.

The corresponding form when bicubic splines are fitted is

$$\sum\sum \gamma_{ij}M_i(x)N_j(y),$$

where the M_i and N_j are two sets of cubic B-splines, one in each independent variable. Hayes and Halliday (1972) present an algorithm for general data sets which includes provision for imposing linear equality constraints. This currently provides the basis for four computer algorithms. Two of these are British Aircraft Corporation algorithms: ET0905A (F) and ET0905B (F). The first is core-based, and the second utilizes a disc. Both allow up to six independent variables. (It may be remarked here that all the surface algorithms readily extend to more variables.) The other two algorithms are NPL:DSP3FIT (A), using bicubic splines, and NPL:DSPNFIT (A), for general degree. They deal currently only with the two-variable, unconstrained case. In all the algorithms, the knots are at the disposal of the user, and this also applies to NPL:BISPLINERECT (A), which is specific to the rectangular grid case.

3. L_1 Norm

We shall consider only the linear case, in which the approximating function $f(x;\theta)$ in expression (1.2) takes the form

$$\sum_{i=1}^{n} \theta_i\phi_i(x), \tag{3.1}$$

where the θ_i are the elements of the vector θ and the $\phi_i(x)$ are given functions of the vector x. This problem can be formulated as a linear-programming problem, and this currently appears to be the best approach.

Based on this approach, the algorithm in BARRODALE and YOUNG (1966) (A) takes advantage of the special structure of the linear program for the L_1 problem. An improved version, which significantly reduces the number of iterations required, is described in Barrodale and Roberts (1973) and given in BARRODALE and ROBERTS (1972) (F), also available as AEREH:MA20A (F). A version in ALGOL 68 is being prepared.

Cox (1973) extends the above formulation of the linear L_1 problem to permit bounds to be set on the parameters θ_i and, adapting the Barrodale and Young algorithm, applies this to the particular case of fitting cubic splines with bounds on the second derivative of the spline at the knots. This provides the user with good control of the general shape of the spline: the algorithm is available as NPL:SP3FITCONSTRAINED.

4. L_∞ Norm

Again we shall consider only the linear case, in which the approximating function $f(x; \theta)$ in expression (1.3) takes the form (3.1). This problem also can be posed as a linear-programming problem, and an algorithm is given in BARRODALE and YOUNG (1966) (A). An improved version is in BARRODALE (1967) (A), and a further modification (in FORTRAN) will shortly be available. Of similar capability is AEREH:MA11B (F).

An alternative approach is the exchange algorithm of Stiefel (1959). There are close theoretical connections between the two approaches, through their implementations differ significantly in practice. The linear programming approach is the more versatile, since it does not even require the $\phi_i(x)$ of (3.1) to be linearly independent functions, whereas the exchange algorithm requires that every n rows of the $m \times n$ matrix A, composed of the values of $\phi_i(x_r)$, be linearly independent. An implementation of the exchange algorithm was given by Bartels and Golub (1968), available as CACM:328 (A). This uses LU decomposition with row interchanges and so will be more stable than the linear-programming algorithms, though significantly slower than the best of them.

The exchange algorithm can, however, be specially adapted to the case when the approximating function is a polynomial in one variable, and it is then particularly advantageous. Such an adaptation is CACM:409 (A), and, rather less versatile, CACM:318 (A), available also as NAG:E02AC (A and F).

5. Miscellany

When fitting a non-linear function by least squares, as discussed in Section 2.2, it often happens that some, perhaps most, of the parameters occur only linearly in the function. In such cases, the iterative scheme can be cast in terms of the non-linear parameters only, the linear parameters being determined at each iteration from a set of linear equations. This reduces the size of the non-linear problem and is usually advantageous. Algorithms based on this approach have been written, mainly by H. Späth, for various fitting functions which contain only one nonlinear parameter.

These algorithms, and the fitting functions they use are

CACM: 295 $a + be^{-cx}$

CACM: 375 ae^{-bx}

CACM: 376 $A \cos (Bx + C)$, rewritten as $\alpha \sin \gamma x + \beta \cos \gamma x$

CJ: 33 $a + bx + ce^{-dx}$

CJ: 37 $(a + bx)\,e^{-cx}$

They all require the user to provide a root-finder.

So far, in discussing the general curve-fitting problem, we have considered those methods of solution which minimize the L_1, L_2 or L_∞ norm for a specific form of the fitting function. A more general approach is to seek from a wide class of appropriately smooth functions† that function $f(x)$ which provides a minimum value of

$$J(f) = \int_{x_1}^{x_m} [f^{(k)}(x)]^2 \, dx, \tag{5.1}$$

subject to

$$E(f) = \sum_{r=1}^{m} [f(x_r) - f_r]^2 \leqslant S. \tag{5.2}$$

Here (x_r, f_r), for $r = 1, 2, \ldots, m$, are the data points, with x_1 and x_m respectively the smallest and largest of the x_r. Also $f^{(k)}(x)$ denotes the kth derivative of $f(x)$, and S is some chosen constant. In other words, accepting $J(f)$ as the measure of smoothness, we are looking for the smoothest function which lies acceptably close to the data points, as defined by (5.2) with some suitable choice for S. A knowledge of the inherent accuracy of the data would, of course, facilitate this choice.

The solution to this rather general problem is, in fact, a natural polynomial spline of degree $2k - 1$ (the practical implication of the "natural" spline is that its derivatives of all orders from k to $2k - 2$ are zero at both ends of the range, i.e. at $x = x_1$ and x_m). The value of k for which the smoothing criterion (5.1) is intuitively most acceptable is perhaps $k = 2$, leading to the natural cubic spline. This spline, however, has its second derivative zero at both ends of the range, giving a flatness in the curve at these points which would often not be satisfactory in practice.

Based on the above approach, REINSCH (1967) (A) gives an algorithm for $k = 2$, and WOODFORD (1970) (A) and LYCHE and SCHUMAKER

---

† Specifically, the class of all functions for which the integral in (5.1) exists and which have their $(k - 1)$th derivative absolutely continuous in $[x_1, x_m]$. The latter condition prevents such unsatisfactory solutions as a step function passing through all the data points, for which both $J(f)$ and $E(f)$ would be zero.

(1971) (A) give algorithms for general k. The last algorithm uses a representation in terms of a local basis, akin to B-splines, and should therefore be the most stable. All three algorithms involve the solution to the rather different problem

$$\text{minimize } J(f) + pE(f), \tag{5.3}$$

for some fixed value of p. They iteratively find the unique value of p for which the solution to (5.3) is the solution of the original problem. LYCHE and SCHUMAKER (1971) permits the alternative of solving (5.3) for a value of p specified by the user.

The advantage of the above approach in yielding the smoothest function (according to the criterion) is, however, accompanied by the severe disadvantage that the spline produced has knots at every data abscissa, and so has a very bulky representation. The method is therefore likely to have rather limited application to data fitting. REINSCH (1967) considers that its application is mainly to curve plotting.

References

Barrodale, I. (1967). Ph.D. Thesis, University of Liverpool.

Barrodale, I. and Roberts, F. D. K. (1972). Mathematics Department Report No. 69, University of Victoria, B.C.

Barrodale, I. and Roberts, F. D. K. (1973). *SIAM J. Numer. Analysis,* (to appear).

Barrodale, I. and Young, A. (1966). *Num. Math.* **8,** 295.

Bartels, R. H. and Golub, G. H. (1968). *Comm. ACM* **11,** 401.

Björck, A. (1967). *BIT* **7,** 257.

Björck, A. (1968). *BIT* **8,** 8.

Björck, A. and Golub, G. H. (1967). *BIT* **7,** 322.

Businger, P. and Golub, G. H. (1965). *Num. Math.* **7,** 269.

Cadwell, J. H. (1961). *Comput. J.* **3,** 266.

Cadwell, J. H. and Williams, D. E. (1961). *Comput. J.* **4,** 260.

Clenshaw, C. W. (1960). *Comput. J.* **2,** 170.

Clenshaw, C. W. and Hayes, J. G. (1965). *J. Inst. Maths Applics* **1,** 164.

Cox, M. G. (1972). *J. Inst. Maths Applics* **10,** 134.

Cox, M. G. (1973). Report NAC 23, National Physical Laboratory, Teddington.

Cox, M. G. and Hayes, J. G. (1973). Report NAC 26, National Physical Laboratory, Teddington.

De Boor, C. (1972). *J. Approx. Theory* **6,** 50.

De Boor, C. and Rice, J. R. (1968). Report CSD TR 21, Purdue University, Lafayette, Indiana.

Fletcher, R. (1971). Report R 6799, Atomic Energy Research Establishment, Harwell.

Fletcher, R. (1972). Section 8.2 in Murray (1972).

Forsythe, G. E. (1957). *J. Soc. Ind. Appl. Math.* **5,** 74.

Gentleman, W. M. (1972). Report CSRR 2068, University of Waterloo, Ontario.

Golub, G. H. (1965). *Num. Math.* **7,** 206.

Golub, G. H. and Reinsch, C. H. (1970). *Num. Math.* **14**, 403.

Hayes, J. G. (Ed.) (1970a). "Numerical Approximation to Functions and Data". University of London Athlone Press, London.

Hayes, J. G. (1970b). Chapter 5 in Hayes (1970a).

Hayes, J. G. (1970c). Chapter 7 in Hayes (1970a).

Hayes, J. G. and Halliday, J. (1972). Report NAC 22, National Physical Laboratory, Teddington.

Lawson, C. L. (1971). *In* "Mathematical Software" J. R. Rice (Ed.) Academic Press, London, New York.

Lyche, T. and Schumaker, L. L. (1971), (revised 1973). Report CNA 31, University of Texas at Austin.

Marquardt, D. W. (1963). *J. Soc. Ind. Appl. Math.* **11**, 431.

Murray, W. (Ed.) (1972). "Numerical Methods for Unconstrained Optimization". Academic Press, London, New York.

Parker, K. (1970). Chapter 9 in Hayes (1970a).

Peters, G. and Wilkinson, J. H. (1970). *Comput. J.* **13**, 309.

Powell, M. J. D. (1970). Chapter 6 in Hayes (1970a).

Powell, M. J. D. (1972). Section 3.2 in Murray (1972).

Reinsch, C. H. (1967). *Num. Math.* **10**, 177.

Stiefel, E. L. (1959). *In* "On Numerical Approximation", R. E. Langer, (Ed.). University of Wisconsin Press, Madison.

Wampler, R. H. (1969). *J. Res. Nat. Bur. Stand.* (*Math. Sciences*) **73B**, 59.

Wampler, R. H. (1970). *J. Amer. Statist. Assoc.* **65**, 549.

Wampler, R. H. (1973). Proceedings Computer Science and Statistics: 6th annual symposium on the interface, University of California, Berkeley, October 1972 (to appear).

Wilkinson, J. H. and Reinsch. C. H. (1971). "Handbook for Automatic Computation: Vol. II, Linear Algebra" Springer–Verlag, Berlin.

Woodford, C. H. (1970). *BIT* **10**, 501.

13. A Data Fitting Package for the Non-Specialist User

M. G. Cox

Division of Numerical Analysis and Computing,
National Physical Laboratory,
Teddington, Middlesex, England.

1. Introduction

In some problems of data fitting by least squares the user knows, perhaps from theoretical studies or physical knowledge, what type of mathematical function to employ in the approximation of his data. In such cases (see Chapter 12 by J. G. Hayes) he can make use of one of the standard methods such as modified Gram–Schmidt orthogonalization, Householder trans-formations or Givens' rotations (see, e.g., Peters and Wilkinson, 1970) if the problem is linear, or, in the non-linear case, one of the modern methods for minimizing a non-linear sum of squares (see, e.g. Fletcher, 1972).

In many other data-fitting problems the user has no prior knowledge of the "correct" form of the approximating function. In these cases it is necessary to employ a relatively arbitrary form of approximating function. We believe that many problems of this type can be handled adequately by just two simple classes of approximating functions, viz. polynomials and splines.

I shall describe briefly a polynomial and spline data-fitting package developed at NPL. The package is currently written in the form of a suite of ALGOL 60 procedures. It is hoped that a FORTRAN version can be made available at a later date.

The package includes algorithms for providing approximations to data which may be tabular, graphical or mathematical. Also included are algorithms for evaluating, differentiating and integrating the approximations obtained, for converting one representation into another (e.g. splines into piecewise polynomials) and for the incorporation of special end conditions and certain other types of constraint.

I shall concentrate on the five algorithms in the package which are aimed specifically at the non-specialist user. For fuller details of the numerical methods and the texts of the ALGOL procedures see Cox and Hayes (1973). Particular attention is paid in this paper to the actual design of the algorithms, and to their practical use.

2. The Five Basic Algorithms

The five basic algorithms in the package, briefly described here in terms of the parameters of their realization as ALGOL procedures, follow.

2.1. procedure *poly fit* ($m, k, x, y, w, a, s, ifail$)

2.1.1. Input Parameters

m	integer value	number of data points
k	integer value	maximum degree of polynomial
x	real array $[1:m]$	data abscissae x_r, $r = 1, 2, \ldots, m$
y	real array $[1:m]$	data ordinates y_r, $r = 1, 2, \ldots, m$
w	real array $[1:m]$	weighting factors w_r, $r = 1, 2, \ldots, m$

2.1.2. Output Parameters

a	real array $[0:k, 0:k]$	Chebyshev coefficients a_{ij}, $i = 0, 1, \ldots, k$; $j = 0, 1, \ldots, i$, in lower triangle of array
s	real array $[0:k]$	root mean square residuals s_i, $i = 0, 1, \ldots, k$
$ifail$	integer variable	error indicator; $= 0$ if successful use is made of the procedure, $= 1, 2$ or 3 if the input data violates certain restrictions (see Sections 3.1 and 3.2).

2.1.3. Brief Description

The procedure determines polynomial approximations of degrees $0, 1, \ldots, k$ of the set of data points (x_r, y_r) with weights w_r, $r = 1, 2, \ldots, m$. The approximation $p^{(i)}(x)$ of degree i has the property that it minimizes

$$\sigma_i = \sum_{r=1}^{m} \varepsilon_r^2,$$

where

$$\varepsilon_r = w_r \{ p^{(i)}(x_r) - y_r \}, \qquad r = 1, 2, \ldots, m.$$

Each polynomial is represented in Chebyshev-series form with normalized argument X. X lies in the range -1 to $+1$ and is related to the original variable x by the linear transformation

$$X = (2x - x_{min} - x_{max})/(x_{max} - x_{min}),$$

where x_{min} and x_{max} are respectively the smallest and largest values of x_r. The polynomial approximation of degree i is represented as

$$p^{(i)}(x) = a_{i0}T_0(X) + a_{i1}T_1(X) + \ldots + a_{ii}T_i(X),$$

where $T_j(X)$ denotes the Chebyshev polynomial of the first kind of degree j in X. The root mean square residual s_i corresponding to the approximation of degree i, defined by

$$s_i^2 = \sigma_i/(m - i - 1),$$

is computed for each $i = 0, 1, \ldots, k$. After selection of an appropriate degree (see Section 3.3.1) the polynomial may subsequently be evaluated using procedure *cheb series* (see Section 2.4).

2.2. procedure *cheb coefficients* (n, f, a)

2.2.1. Input Parameters

    n integer value   number of data points -1

    f real array $[0:n]$ data ordinates $f_r, r = 0, 1, \ldots, n,$
                                    corresponding to the abscissae $x_r = \cos(\pi r/n)$

2.2.2. Output Parameters

    a real array $[0:n]$ Chebyshev coefficients $a_i, i = 0, 1, \ldots, n$

2.2.3. Brief Description

The procedure determines a polynomial approximation $p(x)$ of degree n of the set of data points $(x_r, f_r), r = 0, 1, \ldots, n$. Here x_r are the "Chebyshev" points $\cos(\pi r/n)$. It is assumed that the user has normalized the range of his independent variable x so that $-1 \leqslant x \leqslant 1$. The polynomial is represented in its Chebyshev-series form

$$p(x) = a_0T_0(x) + a_1T_1(x) + \ldots + a_nT_n(x),$$

where $T_j(x)$ denotes the Chebyshev polynomial of the first kind of degree j in x. Truncation of the series after the term $a_iT_i(x)$ yields the least squares approximation of the data by a polynomial of degree i. After selection of an appropriate degree the polynomial may subsequently be evaluated using procedure *cheb series* (see Section 2.4).

2.3. procedure *cubic spline fit* $(m, ncap, x, y, w, k, c, ss, ifail)$

2.3.1. Input Parameters

m	integer value	number of data points
$ncap$	integer value	number of intervals N ($=$ number of interior knots $+ 1$)
x	real array $[1 : m]$	data abscissae $x_r, r = 1, 2, \ldots, m$
y	real array $[1 : m]$	data ordinates $y_r, r = 1, 2, \ldots, m$
w	real array $[1 : m]$	weighting factors $w_r, r = 1, 2, \ldots, m$
k	real array $[-3 : ncap + 3]$	knots $k_j, j = -3, -2, \ldots,$ $N + 3$ (only the interior knots k_j, $j = 1, 2, \ldots, N - 1$, need be applied by the user (see Section 2.3.3).

2.3.2. Output Parameters

c	real array $[1 : ncap + 3]$	B-spline coefficients c_j, $j = 1, 2, \ldots, N + 3$
ss	real variable	residual sum of squares σ
$ifail$	integer variable	error indicator; $= 0$ if successful use is made of the procedure, $= 1, 2, 3, 4$ or 5 if the input data violates certain restrictions (see Sections 3.1 and 3.2).

2.3.3. Brief Description

The procedure determines a cubic spline approximation of the set of data points (x_r, y_r) with weights w_r, $r = 1, 2, \ldots, m$. The interior knots $k_1, k_2, \ldots, k_{N-1}$ of the spline $s(x)$ are prescribed by the user (for guidance on choice of knots see Section 3.3.3). $s(x)$ has the property that it minimizes

$$\sigma = \sum_{r=1}^{m} \varepsilon_r^2,$$

where

$$\varepsilon_r = w_r\{s(x_r) - y_r\}, \qquad r = 1, 2, \ldots, m.$$

The procedure produces the coefficients c_i in the B-spline representation

$$s(x) = \sum_{i=1}^{N+3} c_i N_i(x),$$

where $N_i(x)$ denotes the normalized B-spline of degree 3 defined upon the knots $k_{i-4}, k_{i-3}, k_{i-2}, k_{i-1}$ and k_i.† The value of $\sigma(= ss)$ is also produced.

---

† In order to define the full set of B-splines required, eight additional knots, $k_{-3}, k_{-2}, k_{-1},$ $k_0, k_N, k_{N+1}, k_{N+2}$ and k_{N+3} are inserted automatically by the procedure. The first four of these knots are set equal to x_1 and the last four to x_m.

The fitted spline $s(x)$ may subsequently be evaluated using procedure *spdeg3* (see Section 2.5).

2.4. real procedure *cheb series* (n, a, x, ifail)

2.4.1. Input Parameters

n	integer value	degree of the polynomial
a	real array $[0:n]$	Chebyshev coefficients $a_i, i = 0, 1, \ldots, n$
x	real value	value of the argument $(-1 \leqslant x \leqslant 1)$

2.4.2. Output Parameters

cheb series	real variable	value of the polynomial $\sum_{i=0}^{n} a_i T_i(x)$
ifail	integer variable	error indicator; $= 0$ if successful use is made of the procedure, $= 1$ if $\lvert x \rvert > 1$.

2.4.3. Brief Description

This procedure evaluates the polynomial

$$p(x) = a_0 T_0(x) + a_1 T_1(x) + \ldots + a_n T_n(x)$$

for any value of x in the range $-1 \leqslant x \leqslant 1$. Here $T_j(x)$ denotes the Chebyshev polynomial of the first kind of degree j in x. Such a polynomial may have been produced by *poly fit* or *cheb coefficients*.

2.5. real procedure *spdeg3* (ncap, k, c, x, ifail)

2.5.1. Input Parameters

ncap	integer value	number of intervals N (= number of interior knots + 1)
k	real array $[-3 : ncap + 3]$	knots k_j, $j = -3, -2, \ldots, N + 3$ (the complete set of knots must be supplied†)
c	real array $[1 : ncap + 3]$	B-spline coefficients c_j, $j = 1, 2, \ldots, N + 3$
x	real value	value of the argument $(k_0 \leqslant x \leqslant k_N)$

† If *spdeg3* is used subsequent to *cubic spline fit* then the complete set of knots will automatically be available for use by *spdeg3*.

2.5.2. Output Parameters

    spdeg3   real variable   value of the spline $\sum\limits_{i=1}^{N+3} c_i N_i(x)$

    ifail   integer variable   error indicator; $= 0$ if successful use is made of the procedure, $= 1$ if $x < k_0$ or $x > k_N$

2.5.3. Brief Description

This procedure evaluates the cubic spline

$$s(x) = \sum_{i=1}^{N+3} c_i N_i(x)$$

for any value of x in the range $k_0 \leqslant x \leqslant k_N$. Here $N_i(x)$ denotes the normalized B-spline of degree 3 defined upon the knots k_{i-4}, k_{i-3}, k_{i-2}, k_{i-1} and k_i. Such a spline may have been produced by *cubic spline fit*.

3. Algorithm Design Considerations

In designing the procedures the following characteristics were considered (most of these are listed by Rice, 1971, p. 28):

     (i)   Domain of applicability
    (ii)   Diagnostics
   (iii)   Ease of use
   (iv)   Reliability
    (v)   Documentation
   (vi)   Portability
  (vii)   Flexibility
 (viii)   Modularity
   (ix)   Efficiency
    (x)   Extensibility.

It is not within the scope of this paper to discuss in depth each procedure in the package in terms of each of the above ten characteristics. I shall therefore concentrate on what I consider to be some of the more important considerations. Much of the discussion will relate to the routines *poly fit* and *cubic spline fit*. The other three procedures are somewhat simpler in form and in use and will not be discussed in great detail here.

3.1. Domain of Applicability

With any algorithm designed to solve a particular mathematical problem it is important that one (or preferably both) of the following two points is true.

(i) The user is aware of the *domain of applicability* of the algorithm, i.e. the restrictions (if any) that exist on the values of the input data.

(ii) As far as possible the algorithm itself should carry out checks upon the data supplied to it in order to see whether these restrictions are violated. Moreover, if the data *is* unsatisfactory in any way, the algorithm should, through its parameter mechanism, provide the user with suitable diagnostic information (also see Section 3.2).

Any one of three consequences may result from the use of invalid data. One possibility is that the procedure could "blow up", with the consequence that no results are produced at all. The second possibility is that results are produced which are completely erroneous and hence easily recognised as such by the user. The third possibility is that results are produced which "look reasonable" and therefore accepted as "correct". This last possibility is of course the most dangerous.

The restrictions on *poly fit* which are checked by the procedure itself are

(i) The weighting factors must be strictly positive.

(ii) The values of the independent variable x must be specified in non-decreasing order.

(iii) The number of *distinct* values of x must exceed the maximum degree k.

Those on *cubic spline fit* are, in addition to (i) and (ii) above

(iii) The number of distinct values of x must exceed the number of intervals N by at least 3.

(iv) The knots must be specified in non-decreasing order.

(v) The conditions specified by Schoenberg and Whitney (1953) must hold for at least one subset of the distinct values of x, i.e. there must be at least one subset of $N + 3$ strictly increasing values $x_{r_1}, x_{r_2}, \ldots, x_{r_{N+3}}$ such that

$$x_{r_1} < k_1 < x_{r_5},$$

$$x_{r_2} < k_2 < x_{r_6},$$

$$\cdots\cdots\cdots\cdots\cdots\cdots$$

$$x_{r_{N-1}} < k_{N-1} < x_{r_{N+3}}.$$

By comparison, the restrictions on the other three procedures in the package are moderate. They include, for instance, that the value of the argument supplied to *cheb series* or *spdeg3* lies in the appropriate range (see Sections 2.4.2 and 2.5.2).

Restriction (iii) on *poly fit* and restriction (v) on *cubic spline fit* are necessary to ensure the existence of a unique solution. Every linear least-squares problem has at least one solution, and in cases where the solution is not unique methods *can* be constructed for the determination of a particular solution, such as that of minimal length (see, e.g. Peters and Wilkinson, 1970). However, we believe that in most problems posed by non-specialist users, the occurrence of a non-unique solution would not have been anticipated by the user, and in all probability is a result of incorrect or poorly-chosen input data. We feel therefore that rather than allow the algorithm to proceed to find a particular solution the user should be informed of the non-uniqueness.

Restriction (ii) on both procedures could be omitted if an appropriate sort routine (e.g. Scowen, 1965) were included in the procedures themselves.

Both *poly fit* and *cubic spline fit* contain a sub-procedure *check data*. In each case this procedure carries out the necessary checks on the data and, if appropriate, sets a parameter to indicate which restriction has been violated (see Section 3.2). Procedure *check data* can be removed by the user from the main procedure if program storage space is at a premium, but *only* of course if it is known in advance that his data is satisfactory (see Section 3.8).

3.2. Diagnostics

In cases of failure the user inspects a parameter *ifail*, the value of which is related to the cause of failure. For example, if *cubic spline fit* has been used, *ifail* takes one of the values 1 to 5 according to which of the five restrictions on the procedure (see Section 3.1) has been violated. Similar remarks apply to *poly fit*, in which case *ifail* takes one of the values 1 to 3. In satisfactory cases *ifail* takes the value zero.

3.3. Simplicity of Use

It is not always possible to make procedures efficient (see Section 3.9), flexible (see Section 3.7) *and* simple to use, since these characteristics usually conflict to a greater or lesser extent. With the procedures under discussion a measure of success in this direction has been achieved, mainly as a result of the choices of Chebyshev polynomials and *B*-splines as basis functions for polynomials and splines, respectively.

Even though the procedures are intended for non-specialist users, we feel it important that certain crucial decisions should be made by the user himself. In polynomial fitting we think the user himself should decide, in light of the results produced, which degree of polynomial he is willing to accept as providing an adequate approximation, rather than allow the procedures to make such decisions based on relatively arbitrary criteria. We also believe that in the present state of the art in spline fitting it is usually better for the user to decide the number of knots and their positions. Automatic knot placement procedures (Powell, 1970; Dodson, 1972; de Boor, 1973) either tend to introduce many more knots than are strictly necessary to obtain an adequate approximation, or require detailed knowledge of a high derivative of the function underlying the data being approximated. In making these decisions the user should ideally interact with the procedures, i.e. the user is "in the loop", the machine performing the donkey-work under his supervision (see Section 4).

Some guidance on the selection of the degree in polynomial fitting and in choosing the number of knots and their positions in spline fitting is given in Sections 3.3.1 and 3.3.3 (also see Cox and Hayes, 1973).

We now discuss briefly the mode of use of each procedure.

3.3.1. procedure *poly fit*

The input parameters to be supplied by the user (see Section 2.1.1) are self-explanatory. If successful use has been made of the procedure (i.e. *ifail* $= 0$), then the user examines the output parameters (see Section 2.1.2) and either settles upon an appropriate polynomial or decides that polynomial approximations, at least of those determined, are inadequate. In testing the adequacy of a fitted polynomial the user will probably evaluate it for a range of values of x using *cheb series*, in order to examine its behaviour throughout the range, both at and between data points. At this stage he will be wise to employ visual aids such as a graph plotter or a display tube or, if these devices are not available, to plot by hand a graph of the fitted function.

The user will base his choice of degree on aspects such as the following. The Chebyshev coefficients tend to settle down, as the degree increases, to approximately constant values (to within the "noise level" of the data ordinates), once a reasonably satisfactory approximation has been obtained. Likewise, the root mean square residuals s_i also eventually settle down to an approximately constant value. Of course, the user may be prepared to accept a polynomial of lower order than that suggested by these considerations.

Note that a Chebyshev-series representation has a considerable advantage over the corresponding power series form in that the coefficients of the latter, even if the argument has been normalized to the range $-1 \leqslant x \leqslant 1$, rarely display a tendency to settle down to roughly constant values.

Moreover, the power series coefficients can become large relative to the magnitudes of the data ordinates, and hence loss of precision due to cancellation may occur in the subsequent evaluation of the approximating polynomial.

For fuller details of many of the practical aspects of polynomial fitting see Hayes (1970).

3.3.2. procedure *cheb coefficients*

The user would employ *cheb coefficients* in much the same way as he would *poly fit*. However, he need only supply the values of the dependent variable, since the values of the independent variable are the Chebyshev points $x_r = \cos(\pi r/n)$, $r = 0, 1, \ldots, n$. Weighting factors are not appropriate in this case.

cheb coefficients is somewhat easier to use than *poly fit* in that, as implied in Section 2.2.3, the Chebyshev coefficients do not change from degree to degree. This desirable property is a consequence of the use of the Chebyshev points as abscissae.

3.3.3. procedure *cubic spline fit*

All input parameters for this procedure are easily supplied apart perhaps for the values of N and k_j, $j = 1, 2, \ldots, N - 1$. As regards these numbers it is suggested, at least in the first instance, that the user estimates the number of intervals, i.e. the number of cubic pieces, which he feels could give rise to a sensible approximation. For instance he may use for N a value of $K(P + 1)$, where K is a small integer and P is the number of inflexion points of the underlying function, as indicated by the data. Although this rule is purely empirical, a value of K in the range 1–3 often, in our experience, enables an approximation close to graphical accuracy to be achieved. The knot positions themselves should be chosen on the basis that a fit with residuals of roughly equal size throughout the range tends to have knots grouped more closely in regions where the underlying function or its derivatives change more rapidly than elsewhere.

For full details of the advantages of *B*-splines as basis functions for splines and the method employed for their numerical evaluation, see Cox (1972). Suffice it to say here that they are bell-shaped functions with the compact support property that $N_i(x)$ is non-zero only for $k_{i-4} < x < k_i$.

The user may evaluate the approximation obtained using procedure *spdeg3*. Again he will find it useful to employ visual aids. He will then decide whether to accept the approximation as providing an adequate fit to his data. If he finds the fit unacceptable he may be able to improve the approximation in one of two ways. If the fit is markedly better in some regions than in others then he may adjust the knot positions so that there is a greater concentration of knots in the regions of poorer fit. If he feels the total number of knots is inadequate then he may insert as many extra knots as he considers necessary, perhaps after shifting the positions of the original knots. Finally, if the fit achieved is *more* accurate than required he may delete some of the knots. In all cases the user would then use *cubic spline fit* to re-fit the data by a spline based on the new knot set.

3.3.4. real procedure *cheb series*

The use of this procedure for evaluating a polynomial from its Chebyshev-series representation needs no explanation other than the details of the input and output parameters which are given in Sections 2.4.1 and 2.4.2.

3.3.5. real procedure *spdeg3*

Again no explanation of the use of this procedure for evaluating a cubic spline from its *B*-spline representation is necessary; the input and output parameters are listed in Sections 2.5.1 and 2.5.2.

3.4. Reliability

The reliability of procedures for data fitting is influenced by a number of factors including:

(i) the choice of internal and external representations of the approximating function,

(ii) the stability of the numerical methods employed,

(iii) checking of the data.

The third factor above has already been considered in Section 3.1. We now discuss briefly the procedures *poly fit*, *cheb coefficients* and *cubic spline fit* in terms of the first two factors.

3.4.1. Representation

Internally, *poly fit* represents the approximating polynomial as a linear combination of polynomials orthogonal with respect to summation over the given data set (Forsythe, 1957). The output parameters from the procedure are *not* the coefficients in this representation, since they are somewhat inconvenient for the user to work with, but rather the coefficients of the Chebyshev-series representation of the polynomial. The method of Clenshaw (1960) is used to produce the Chebyshev-series coefficients.

cheb coefficients produces the Chebyshev-series coefficients directly using a three-term recurrence relation originally given by Clenshaw (1955), with modifications suggested by Reinsch and Gentleman (see Gentleman, 1969). The form of the results is compatible with that of *poly fit*.

Both internally and externally *cubic spline fit* represents the spline as a linear combination of cubic *B*-splines (Cox, 1972; de Boor, 1972). The compact support property of *B*-splines gives rise to a computationally economical formulation of the spline-fitting problem, which also enables multiple knots to be employed (see Section 3.7.2).

3.4.2. Numerical Stability

poly fit is based upon a three-term recurrence relation for the generation of orthogonal polynomials (Forsythe, 1957). This approach obviates the need to set up and solve explicitly a linear system for the least-squares solution. No detailed error analysis of this method has yet been published. However, extensive use on a wide class of practical problems indicates that the method is usually extremely stable. It is possible, though, for numerical instabilities to appear in certain extreme situations. For example, in a test carried out by Clenshaw and Hayes (1965) with 200 equally-spaced data points, six decimal digits had been lost in the computation by degree 90. We rarely envisage requiring such high degrees, however, since the polynomials produced would not be competitive with splines, from the viewpoint of evaluation time of the resulting approximations (see Section 3.9).

cheb coefficients is based upon recurrence relations which produce directly the coefficients of a Chebyshev series which, if truncated after the term in $T_i(x)$, yields the least-squares approximation of degree i which approximates the data. An error analysis shows that the method employed is extremely stable. In cases where N is large, where $N + 1$ possesses convenient factors and where all or most of the $N + 1$ Chebyshev coefficients are required, then the Fast Fourier transform (Cooley and Tukey, 1965; Gentleman and Sande, 1966) could be used to produce the coefficients more efficiently; the current version of our procedure does not provide this option.

cubic spline fit essentially involves the setting-up and the least-squares solution of a linear system defining the coefficients c_i, $i = 1, 2, \ldots, N + 3$. The system is set up using a recurrence relation for *B*-splines which is unconditionally stable (Cox, 1972), even for multiple knots. The least-squares solution of the system is also obtained in a stable manner by using an orthogonalization method, viz. a variant of Givens' rotations due to Gentleman (1972a, 1972b).

3.5. Documentation

The documentation for the procedures has been produced in the same style as that of the Numerical Algorithms Group (see Chapter 20 of these proceedings), i.e. sections giving descriptions of the algorithm, its parameters, error indicators, timing, storage, accuracy, etc.

3.6. Portability

The package is written entirely in standard ALGOL 60 and hence could be used on any machine having a standard ALGOL 60 compiler.

No sophisticated use is made of the ALGOL language, e.g. there is no recursion, no use of Jensen's device, no switches etc. Hopefully therefore the algorithms could also be implemented with little or no change on some machines with compilers which implement only a subset of ALGOL (e.g. Dartmouth ALGOL compilers on General Electric and Honeywell machines).

There is no machine dependence. Constants are set by, e.g.,

$$pi := 4 \cdot 0 \times \arctan (1 \cdot 0).$$

There are no input/output statements; all messages to the user as regards the successful or unsuccessful use of the procedures are passed to him via the procedure parameter mechanism (see Section 3.2).

3.7. Flexibility

3.7.1. Interpolation

All three fitting procedures described here can also be used reasonably efficiently for polynomial or spline *interpolation* when, of course, the number of data values matches the number of parameters of the approximating function.

3.7.2. Splines with Multiple Knots

cubic spline fit can be used with simple knots or knots of multiplicity 2, 3 or 4. Thus, if a cubic spline with continuity of value and first derivative only is required, double knots are used in place of simple knots. If an approximation with a first derivative discontinuity at a prescribed point is required, a triple knot is placed at that point.

3.8. Modularity

The procedures have, where appropriate, been written in a modular manner. Such an approach makes the procedures more comprehendable and enables the slightly more experienced user to modify and extend them more easily. For instance, *cubic spline fit* contains the sub-procedures:

> *check data*—which performs detailed checks on the validity of the input parameters (see Section 3.1).

> *next interval*—which computes certain constants relating to the interval next to be considered.

b spline values—which computes the *B*-spline values corresponding to the current value of the independent variable.

If the user *knows* in advance that his data already satisfies the appropriate restrictions then, to save computing time, he can delete the call of *check data*; to save program storage space he can delete the declaration of *check data*. If he wishes to employ exponential splines or trigonometric splines (Jerome, 1973) in place of polynomial splines he can replace the body of *b spline values* as appropriate.

3.9. Efficiency

A serious attempt has been made to make the coding of the procedures reasonably efficient and the procedure working space small. No attempt has been made to *maximize* efficiency since such an objective would conflict with *modularity* (user-modifiability, see Section 3.8). In Table 1,

$$1 \ op. = 1 \text{ multiplication or 1 division,}$$

$$m = \text{number of data points,}$$

$$k = \text{degree of polynomial,}$$

$$N = \text{number of intervals.}$$

TABLE 1. Operation count and storage requirements
for the five procedures.

	Approximate no. of ops.	Approximate working space
poly fit	$\frac{1}{2}mk(k + 12)$	$3m$
cheb coefficients	n^2	9
cubic spine fit	$70m + 10N$	$4N$
cheb series	k	6
spedg3	18	16

Note that in terms of the number of operations, *cubic spline fit* is faster than *poly fit* for $k > 8$ and *spdeg3* is faster than *cheb series* for $k > 18$.

It is gradually becoming more widely recognized that when high-level languages such as ALGOL or FORTRAN are employed, a multiplication/ division count is often a poor statistic as regards comparison of execution times. The main reason for this is that the overheads associated with for- or DO-loops, together with the time to access array variables, tend to dominate the purely arithmetic operation times. The values in Table 1 should be interpreted therefore as a very rough guide only. Much more reliable

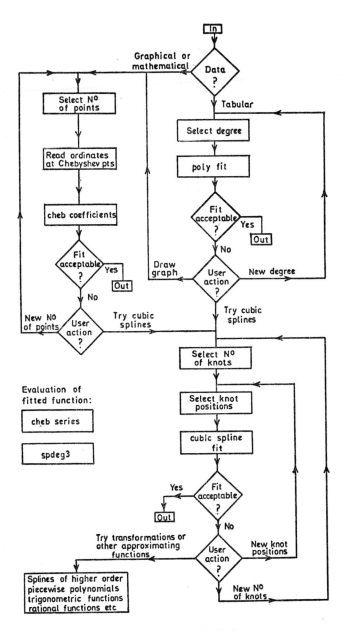

FIG. 1. Suggested method of use.

estimates of computation times and hence of comparative performance can be obtained using an approach due to Wichmann (1973). His method is based upon weighting appropriately each occurrence of a variable, arithmetic operation, etc. in a procedure or program, from which realistic estimates of running times can be obtained. The weights given by Wichmann are machine/compiler independent, and represent average execution times (in units of a basic machine) based upon a number of existing ALGOL compilers.

As an example, two different methods considered for the inner loop in *cheb coefficients* had multiplication counts of $4n$ and n, respectively, which, in terms of these figures alone, gave *theoretical* running times in the ratio 4 : 1. However, actual implementations of these methods gave running times in the ratio 1.3 : 1. The use of Wichmann's analysis predicted accurately the factor of 1.3.

Currently at NPL use is being made of the weighing analysis to provide reliable estimates of the performance of procedures.

3.10. Extensibility

Considerable thought has been given to the choice of input and output parameters for the procedures. As a consequence more advanced procedures such as arbitrary-order spline fitting and bivariate spline fitting have been and are being added to the package, without the need to change the structure of existing procedures.

4. Method of Use

We at NPL believe that data-fitting algorithms can never be *fully* automated. We feel that the user must make certain crucial decisions, the machine performing the purely arithmetic aspect of the computation (see Section 3.3). The approach we think a non-specialist user might care to adopt is illustrated in Fig. 1. We have suggested in the first instance that the user should attempt to obtain a polynomial approximation. If he were unsuccessful he should try cubic splines. If he *still* failed to obtain an acceptable fit he should consider the effects of applying appropriate transformations to the independent variable (Hayes, 1970) or try other approximating functions such as splines of higher order, trigonometric functions, rational functions etc., *or* consult an expert!

References

Clenshaw, C. W. (1955). A note on the summation of Chebyshev series. *Math. Tables and Aids to Computation* **9**, 118–120.

Clenshaw, C. W. (1960). Curve fitting with a digital computer. *Comput. J.* **2**, 170–173.

Clenshaw, C. W. and Hayes, J. G. (1965). Curve and surface fitting. *J. Inst. Maths Applics* **1**, 164–183.

Cooley, J. W. and Tukey, J. W. (1965). An algorithm for the machine computation of complex Fourier series. *Maths Comput.* **19**, 297–301.

Cox, M. G. (1972). The numerical evaluation of *B*-splines. *J. Inst. Maths Applics* **10**, 134–149.

Cox, M. G. and Hayes, J. G. (1973). "Basic Procedures for Curve Fitting". Report NAC 26. National Physical Laboratory, Teddington, Middlesex.

de Boor, C. (1972). On calculating *B*-splines. *J. Approx. Theory* **6**, 50–62.

de Boor, C. (1973). Good approximation by splines with variable knots. (To appear)

Dodson, D. S. (1972). Ph.D. Thesis. Computer Science Department, Purdue University, Lafayette, U.S.A.

Fletcher, R. (1972). A survey of algorithms for unconstrained optimization. *In* (W. Murray, Ed.) "Numerical Methods for Unconstrained Optimization", pp. 123–129. Academic Press, London and New York.

Forsythe, G. E. (1957). Generation and use of orthogonal polynomials for data-fitting with a digital computer. *J. Soc. Indust. Appl. Maths* **5**, 74–88.

Gentleman, W. M. (1969). An error analysis of Goertzel's (Watt's) method for computing Fourier coefficients. *Comput. J.* **12**, 160–165.

Gentleman, W. M. (1972a). "Least Squares Computations by Givens Transformations without Square Roots". Report CSRR–2062. University of Waterloo, Ontario, Canada.

Gentleman, W. M. (1972b). "Basic Procedures for Large, Sparse or Weighted Linear Least Squares Problems". Report CSRR–2068. University of Waterloo, Ontario, Canada.

Gentleman, W. M. and Sande, G. (1966). Fast Fourier transforms—for fun and profit. *In* "1966 Fall Joint Computer Conference, Volume 29, AFIPS", pp. 563–578. Spartan Books, Washington.

Hayes, J. G. (1970). Curve fitting by polynomials in one variable. *In* (J. G. Hayes, Ed.) "Numerical Approximation to Functions and Data", pp. 43–64. Athlone Press, London.

Jerome, J. W. (1973). On uniform approximation by certain generalized spline functions. *J. Approx. Theory* **7**, 143–154.

Peters, G. and Wilkinson, J. H. (1970). The least squares problem and pseudo-inverses. *Comput. J.* **13**, 309–316.

Powell, M. J. D. (1970). Curve fitting by splines in one variable. *In* (J. G. Hayes, Ed.) "Numerical Approximation to Functions and Data", pp. 65–83. Athlone Press, London.

Rice, J. R. (1971). The challenge of mathematical software. *In* (J. R. Rice, Ed.) "Mathematical Software". pp. 27–41. Academic Press, London and New York.

Schoenberg, I. J. and Whitney, A. (1953). On Pólya frequency functions. *Trans. Amer. Math. Soc.* **74**, 246–259.

Scowen, R. S. (1965). Algorithm 271. Quickersort. *Comm. Assoc. Comput. Mach.* **8**, 669–670.

Wichmann, B. A. (1973). "Estimating the Execution Speed of an ALGOL Program." Report NAC 38. National Physical Laboratory, Teddington, Middlesex.

14. Piecewise Quadratic Surface Fitting for Contour Plotting

M. J. D. POWELL

Theoretical Physics Division, U.K.A.E.A. Research Group,
Atomic Energy Research Establishment,
Harwell, Didcot, Berkshire, England.

1. Introduction

We consider the problem of plotting contours of a function of two variables, given function values at the grid points of a regular rectangular mesh. Specifically we let $f(x, y)$ be the function, we let the function values be the quantities

$$f(x_p, y_q) = f(pd_x, qd_y), \qquad 1 \leqslant p \leqslant n_x, \qquad 1 \leqslant q \leqslant n_y, \qquad (1.1)$$

and we let the required contour line be defined by the equation

$$f(x, y) = h. \qquad (1.2)$$

Here d_x and d_y are the spacings between grid lines in the x and y directions respectively, n_x and n_y are the number of grid lines in the x and y directions respectively, and h is a constant, namely the contour height.

A common method for contour plotting is "threading". In this method the points of intersection of the contour line with the grid lines are estimated by interpolation, and then a curve is threaded through these points, for instance by McConalogue's (1971) algorithm. However it is not suitable for the shapes of contours that occur near saddle points of smooth functions of two variables, and occasionally contour lines of different heights may cross. Therefore the emphasis of this paper is to seek a function, $\phi(x, y)$ say, that is a good approximation to $f(x, y)$ and whose contours can be plotted quite directly.

We would like $\phi(x, y)$ to have the following five properties:

(P1) $\phi(x, y)$ is equal to $f(x, y)$ at the data points (x_p, y_q) defined by eqn (1.1).

(P2) $\phi(x, y)$ has continuous first derivatives.

(P3) When $f(x, y)$ has bounded third derivatives, the error function

$$e(x, y) = f(x, y) - \phi(x, y) \qquad (1.3)$$

is of third order in the spacing between grid lines.

(P4) Contour lines of $\phi(x, y)$ are easy to plot.

(P5) The definition of $\phi(x, y)$ has good localisation properties, that is a change in a data value $f(x_p, y_q)$ has little effect on $\phi(x, y)$ for points (x, y) that are remote from (x_p, y_q).

We now make some remarks on these properties. Property (P1) implies that we are not trying to smooth the function values in case there are data errors. The cases with and without smoothing are both important. Property (P2) usually ensures that the direction of a contour line of $\phi(x, y)$ is continuous. Property (P3) implies that $\phi(x, y)$ is often a good approximation to $f(x, y)$ for quite large mesh sizes, in particular $\phi(x, y)$ can show the usual behaviour of functions of two variables at saddle points. Property (P4) is essential to the utility of $\phi(x, y)$. Property (P5) is particularly important when $f(x, y)$ includes some isolated peaks. In Section 3 we identify a function $\phi(x, y)$ that has all these properties.

A usual way of satisfying condition (P1) in surface fitting is to let $\phi(x, y)$ be a bicubic spline (see Ahlberg, Nilson and Walsh, 1967, for instance). Then conditions (P2) and (P5) and a condition that is stronger than (P3) are satisfied also. However it is not straightforward to plot contours of bicubic functions, so we require the form of $\phi(x, y)$ to be more simple.

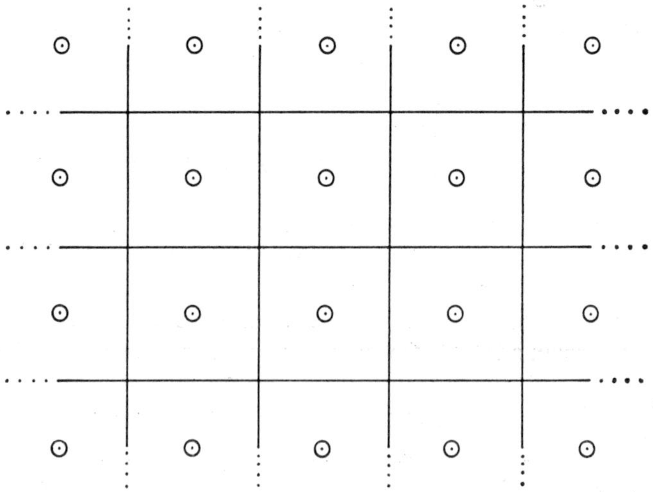

FIG. 1. The mesh lines for a biquadratic spline.

Therefore the use of biquadratic splines seems promising. In this case $\psi(x, y)$ is composed of pieces of the form

$$\phi(x, y) = \sum_{i=0}^{2} \sum_{j=0}^{2} a_{ij} x^i y^j \tag{1.4}$$

and, in order that condition (P5) is satisfied, the pieces of $\phi(x, y)$ meet at lines that are midway between the grid lines of the mesh of given function values. Specifically in Fig. 1 the circles indicate some of the data points (pd_x, qd_y) $(1 \leqslant p \leqslant n_x, 1 \leqslant q \leqslant n_y)$, and $\phi(x, y)$ has the form (1.4) in each of the small rectangles that are shown. However at the boundaries of the rectangles the second derivative of $\phi(x, y)$ is allowed to be discontinuous. Thus it is possible to satisfy conditions (P1), (P2), (P3) and (P5).

Therefore the use of biquadratic splines gives the problem of drawing the contours of a function of the form (1.4) in each mesh square of Fig. 1. If it were straightforward to draw these contours, then there would be little value in the main purpose of this paper, which is to let $\phi(x, y)$ be a piecewise quadratic function instead of a piecewise biquadratic function. Therefore we note some difficulties that may occur when plotting biquadratic contours. We do not claim that these difficulties rule out the feasibility of using bi-quadratics, rather they provide some good reasons for seeking a more simple form for $\phi(x, y)$.

Some difficulties arise due to the possible forms of the contour lines of a biquadratic. For instance if $\phi(x, y)$ is the function

$$\phi(x, y) = x(x - 1) y(y - 1), \tag{1.5}$$

then the contour line $\phi(x, y) = 0$ is a "noughts and crosses grid". Further if $\phi(x, y) = h$ and $|h|$ is small, then the function (1.5) gives curved contours that together form a pattern that is close to the noughts and crosses grid. Moreover the contour line defined by the equation

$$(x - y)^2 + (xy - 1)^2 = \tfrac{1}{2} \tag{1.6}$$

consists of two closed loops. Because these different forms can occur it is not easy to ensure that all branches of a biquadratic contour line are plotted exactly once.

Sometimes the problem of following a contour line can be made easy by finding a parametric form

$$\left.\begin{array}{l} x = x(t) \\ y = y(t) \end{array}\right\} \quad 0 \leqslant t \leqslant T. \tag{1.7}$$

However another disadvantage of biquadratic functions is that there seems to be no general parametric form that is convenient for numerical computation. Unfortunately the form

$$x(t) = (b_0 + b_1 t + b_2 t^2)/(b_3 + b_4 t + b_5 t^2) \\
y(t) = (b_6 + b_7 t + b_8 t^2)/(b_9 + b_{10} t + b_{11} t^2) \Big\} \tag{1.8}$$

is not quite suitable, although it seems to contain plenty of parameters, and although it always describes a contour of a biquadratic function. Surprisingly there are only seven degrees of freedom in the curve (1.8), because the parameters of $x(t)$ may be scaled by a constant, the parameters of $y(t)$ may be scaled by a different constant, and because the change of variable

$$\tau = (c_0 + c_1 t)/(c_2 + c_3 t) \tag{1.9}$$

does not alter the form of expression (1.8). However there are eight degrees of freedom in contour lines of biquadratic functions.

Therefore this paper shows the feasibility of letting $\phi(x, y)$ be composed of quadratic pieces

$$\phi(x, y) = \sum_{i=0}^{2} \sum_{j=0}^{2-i} a_{ij} x^i y^j. \tag{1.10}$$

In other words we remove the $x^2 y$, xy^2 and $x^2 y^2$ terms from expression (1.4). It follows that the contour lines $\phi(x, y) = h$ are composed of pieces of conic sections, which is very convenient for numerical computation, because, except for the degenerate case of two straight lines, each conic section has a parametric form

$$x(t) = (b_0 + b_1 t + b_2 t^2)/(b_3 + b_4 t + b_5 t^2) \\
y(t) = (b_6 + b_7 t + b_8 t^2)/(b_3 + b_4 t + b_5 t^2) \Big\} . \tag{1.11}$$

At first sight it seems impossible to satisfy conditions (P1)–(P5) by piecewise quadratic functions for the following reason. Let the divisions of $\phi(x, y)$ into quadratic pieces be based on a rectangular grid, and let $\phi_{pq}(x, y)$ be the quadratic function in the (p, q)th rectangle as shown in Fig. 2. Then it may be proved that condition (P2), that $\phi(x, y)$ is to have continuous first derivatives, implies the equation

$$\phi_{pq}(x, y) = \phi_{p-1\,q}(x, y) + \phi_{pq-1}(x, y) - \phi_{p-1\,q-1}(x, y), \qquad p \geqslant 1, q \geqslant 1. \tag{1.12}$$

It follows that if $\phi_{pq}(x, y)$ is known in the left-hand and bottom grid rectangles of Fig. 2, then $\phi_{pq}(x, y)$ is known for all the grid rectangles. Therefore

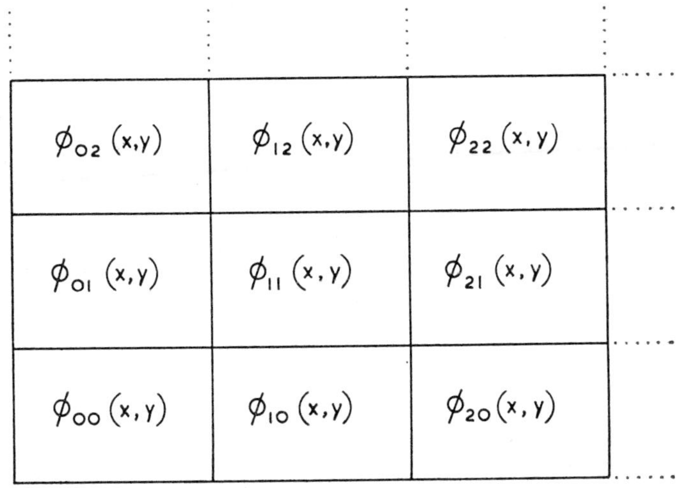

$\phi_{02}(x,y)$	$\phi_{12}(x,y)$	$\phi_{22}(x,y)$
$\phi_{01}(x,y)$	$\phi_{11}(x,y)$	$\phi_{21}(x,y)$
$\phi_{00}(x,y)$	$\phi_{10}(x,y)$	$\phi_{20}(x,y)$

FIG. 2. Piecewise quadratic functions on a rectangular grid.

condition (P5) is not satisfied, and usually condition (P1) cannot be satisfied either.

Therefore it is not feasible to let $\phi(x, y)$ be composed of quadratic pieces, associated with a rectangular grid. Instead we divide the (x, y) region into triangles, and we consider two different triangulation schemes in this paper. In Section 2 we describe a technique that requires about four triangles for each of the given function values (1.1), and in Section 3 we consider a scheme that requires about eight triangles per function value. The method of Section 2 does not satisfy all the conditions (P1)–(P5), but we are able to satisfy either conditions (P1) to (P4) or conditions (P2) to (P5), and in both cases the violation of the unsatisfied condition may be acceptably small. However the scheme that uses more triangles does satisfy all of the conditions very well. Finally, in Section 4, we discuss some properties of our approximation methods.

2. Piecewise Quadratics with Four Triangles per Data Point

The method of this Section is based on the approximation of the biquadratic function (1.4) on a rectangle by a piecewise quadratic function. We now use the notation $\bar{\phi}(x, y)$ for the biquadratic function, and $\phi(x, y)$ for its approximation. We let the rectangle be $ABCD$, and $\phi(x, y)$ is composed of four quadratic pieces, one for each of the four triangles shown in Fig. 3. We choose the quadratic pieces so that $\phi(x, y) = \bar{\phi}(x, y)$ on the perimeter

M. J. D. POWELL

of the rectangle, and so that the first derivative of $\phi(x, y)$ is continuous across the diagonals AC and BD.

To show that there is always a function $\phi(x, y)$ that has these properties, and that they define $\phi(x, y)$ unambiguously, we note that $\phi(x, y) = \bar{\phi}(x, y)$ on the perimeter of $ABCD$ if and only if the two functions match at the points A, B, C, D, P, Q, R and S. Also we note that $\phi(x, y)$ has at least eight degrees of freedom, namely the usual six coefficients of a quadratic function of two variables, and second derivative discontinuities across the diagonals AC and BD. Therefore we just have to demonstrate that if $\phi(x, y)$ is zero at the eight points on the perimeter of the rectangle, then it is identically zero inside the rectangle.

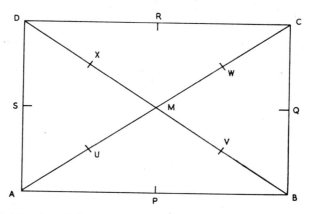

FIG. 3. The triangulation to approximate a biquadratic function on a rectangle

Since the two components of the gradient of $\phi(x, y)$ at A are equal to $(-3\phi_A + 4\phi_P - \phi_B)/l_x$ and $(-3\phi_A + 4\phi_S - \phi_D)/l_y$, where l_x and l_y are the lengths of AB and AD, and where ϕ_A is the value of $\phi(x, y)$ at A etc., it follows that the first derivative of $\phi(x, y)$ at A along the direction AC is zero when the eight perimeter function values are zero. Similarly the first derivative of $\phi(x, y)$ along AC at C is also zero. In this case consider the function $\phi(x, y)$ on the diagonal AC. It is composed of two quadratic pieces, joined at M so that its first derivative is continuous, and its value and first derivative are zero at A and C. Therefore $\phi(x, y)$ is identically zero on AC. Similarly it is identically zero on BD. Thus each quadratic piece of $\phi(x, y)$ is zero on the perimeter of a triangle. Therefore $\phi(x, y)$ is zero throughout the interior of the rectangle $ABCD$, which is the required result.

Because it is sometimes convenient to define a quadratic function on a triangle by its values at the vertices and at the mid-points of the sides, we note that the equations

$$\phi_M = \tfrac{1}{2}(\phi_P + \phi_Q + \phi_R + \phi_S) - \tfrac{1}{4}(\phi_A + \phi_B + \phi_C + \phi_D) \qquad (2.1)$$

and

$$\phi_U = (10\phi_P + 10\phi_S + 2\phi_Q + 2\phi_R - \phi_A - 3\phi_B - \phi_C - 3\phi_D)/16 \qquad (2.2)$$

hold. Similar equations for the function values ϕ_V, ϕ_W and ϕ_X can be deduced from the symmetry of Fig. 3.

We now have a method for approximating a biquadratic function on a rectangle by a piecewise quadratic function, which we may apply on each rectangle of Fig. 1, to replace the biquadratic spline mentioned in Section 1. Thus we obtain a piecewise quadratic function, $\phi(x, y)$ say, whose pieces correspond to the triangles shown in Fig. 4. This construction ensures that $\phi(x, y)$ is continuous everywhere, and that its first derivatives are continuous across the diagonal lines of the mesh. We prove that in fact the first derivatives of $\phi(x, y)$ are continuous across all the lines of the mesh.

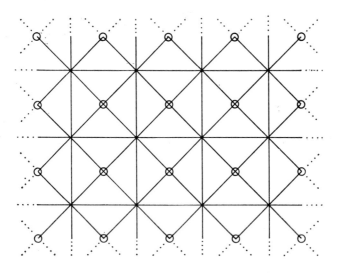

FIG. 4. A grid with four triangles per data point.

Let AB be any horizontal or vertical line segment that separates two quadratic pieces of $\phi(x, y)$. On AB the gradient vectors of the two quadratic pieces are both linear functions of the distance along the line segment. Therefore the gradient of $\phi(x, y)$ is continuous across AB if and only if it is continuous at A and B. Now on both the horizontal and vertical mesh lines through A and B, $\phi(x, y)$ is equal to a biquadratic spline, so its derivative is continuous at A and B. Thus $\phi(x, y)$ satisfies property (P2) of Section 1.

The function $\phi(x, y)$ also satisfies properties (P4) and (P5), but unfortunately it usually does not satisfy the interpolation condition (P1), because $\phi(x, y)$ is equal to the biquadratic spline on the horizontal and vertical mesh lines of Fig. 4, rather than at the data points which are indicated by small circles. Therefore let us consider the difference between $\phi(x, y)$ and $\bar{\phi}(x, y)$ inside the rectangle $ABCD$ of Fig. 3.

We shift coordinates so that the point M of Fig. 3 is the origin $(0, 0)$, and we let the coefficients of the biquadratic function $\bar{\phi}(x, y)$ be given by the right-hand side of eqn (1.4). It follows that ϕ_A and ϕ_P have the values

$$\phi_A = \sum_{i=0}^{2} \sum_{j=0}^{2} a_{ij}(-\tfrac{1}{2}d_x)^i (-\tfrac{1}{2}d_y)^j$$

$$\phi_P = \sum_{j=0}^{2} a_{0j}(-\tfrac{1}{2}d_y)^j \tag{2.3}$$

and that similar expressions define the function values ϕ_B, ϕ_Q, ϕ_C, ϕ_R, ϕ_D and ϕ_S. Thus, in the triangle ABM, $\phi(x, y)$ is the quadratic function

$$\begin{aligned}
\phi(x, y) = & (a_{00} - \tfrac{1}{16} a_{22} d_x^2 d_y^2) + (a_{10} - \tfrac{1}{4} a_{12} d_y^2) x \\
& + (a_{01} - \tfrac{1}{4} a_{21} d_x^2) y + (a_{20} - \tfrac{1}{2} a_{21} d_y + \tfrac{1}{4} a_{22} d_y^2) x^2 \\
& + (a_{11} - a_{12} d_y) xy + (a_{02} - \tfrac{1}{2} a_{21} d_x^2/d_y + \tfrac{1}{4} a_{22} d_x^2) y^2,
\end{aligned} \tag{2.4}$$

so the error in the approximation of $\bar{\phi}(x, y)$ by $\phi(x, y)$ is given by the expression

$$\begin{aligned}
\bar{\phi}(x, y) - \phi(x, y) = & \, a_{12} x(y + \tfrac{1}{2} d_y)^2 \\
& + a_{21}(y + \tfrac{1}{2} d_y) (x^2 + \tfrac{1}{2} d_x^2 y/d_y) \\
& + a_{22}(x^2 - \tfrac{1}{4} d_x^2) (y^2 - \tfrac{1}{4} d_y^2).
\end{aligned} \tag{2.5}$$

Similar expressions are appropriate to each of the triangles BCM, CDM and ADM in Fig. 3.

Therefore, if the mesh sizes d_x and d_y are made to tend to zero, we deduce from eqn (2.5) that the difference between $\bar{\phi}(x, y)$ and $\phi(x, y)$ is of order $d_x d_y(d_x + d_y)$, in the usual case when the coefficients a_{ij} $(i, j = 0, 1, 2)$ remain bounded. Thus property (P3) of Section 1 is preserved when $\bar{\phi}(x, y)$ is approximated by $\phi(x, y)$. However eqn (2.5) shows that in general property (P1) is not obtained, instead the difference between $\phi(x, y)$ and the data values (1.1) is of fourth order in the mesh size.

Frequently this departure from property (P1) is so small that it can be neglected, so the technique that has been described for obtaining a piecewise quadratic approximation to the data (1.1) does yield some useful contouring algorithms. However sometimes one requires the contour line to pass through any data points that have height h, see eqn (1.2). Therefore the remainder of this paper describes some techniques that preserve condition (P1).

The first of these techniques comes from the remark that in the method that has been described already a biquadratic spline is used as an intermediate approximation, and, instead of using a biquadratic spline, we could have tried to satisfy condition (P1) directly. Therefore we now consider the feasibility of calculating a piecewise quadratic approximation, whose mesh lines are given in Fig. 4, to match the function values (1.1), subject to continuity of first derivatives.

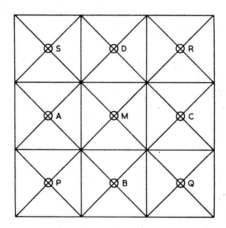

FIG. 5. The mesh lines for a basic element of $\phi(x, y)$.

In calculations of this type it is usually helpful to find a basis of the set of approximating functions, such that each basis function is non-zero over only a small part of $x - y$ space. We obtain suitable basis functions in the following way. Figure 5 shows nine grid squares of Fig. 4. Let the vertical and horizontal grid lines of this figure be the lines

$$
\begin{aligned}
x &= x_{p+j} = (p + j)\,d_x \quad (j = -1\tfrac{1}{2}, -\tfrac{1}{2}, \tfrac{1}{2}, 1\tfrac{1}{2}) \\
y &= y_{q+j} = (q + j)\,d_y \quad (j = -1\tfrac{1}{2}, -\tfrac{1}{2}, \tfrac{1}{2}, 1\tfrac{1}{2})
\end{aligned} \right\} . \tag{2.6}
$$

Then the function

$$
\begin{aligned}
\bar{\sigma}_{pq}(x, y) = {} & [\{x - x_{p-1\frac{1}{2}}\}_+^2 - 3\{x - x_{p-\frac{1}{2}}\}_+^2 + 3\{x - x_{p+\frac{1}{2}}\}_+^2 \\
& - \{x - x_{p+1\frac{1}{2}}\}_+^2] \\
* {} & [\{y - y_{q-1\frac{1}{2}}\}_+^2 - 3\{y - y_{q-\frac{1}{2}}\}_+^2 + 3\{y - y_{q+\frac{1}{2}}\}_+^2 \\
& - \{y - y_{q+1\frac{1}{2}}\}_+^2],
\end{aligned}
\tag{2.7}
$$

where the subscript $+$ has the meaning

$$
x_+ = \begin{cases} 0, & x \leqslant 0 \\ x, & x \geqslant 0, \end{cases}
\tag{2.8}
$$

is a biquadratic spline that is non-zero only inside the large square of Fig. 5. We apply the method that has been described already to approximate this biquadratic spline by a piecewise quadratic function, $\sigma_{pq}(x, y)$ say. Thus $\sigma_{pq}(x, y)$ has continuous first derivatives, and is zero everywhere outside the large square of Fig. 5. It can be shown that, if $\sigma_{pq}(A)$ denotes the value of $\sigma_{pq}(x, y)$ at A etc., then the equations

$$
\sigma_{pq}(A) = \sigma_{pq}(B) = \sigma_{pq}(C) = \sigma_{pq}(D) = \tfrac{1}{4} \sigma_{pq}(M)
\tag{2.9}
$$

are satisfied. Further $\sigma_{pq}(P)$, $\sigma_{pq}(Q)$, $\sigma_{pq}(R)$ and $\sigma_{pq}(S)$ are all equal to zero. Therefore if we express the function $\phi(x, y)$ in the form

$$
\phi(x, y) = \sum_{pq} c_{pq} \, \sigma_{pq}(x, y),
\tag{2.10}
$$

then matching the data (1.1) gives a system of linear equations in the unknown coefficients c_{pq}, that is equivalent to the linear equations that arise from the well-known five point Laplace difference operator (see Forsythe and Wasow, 1960, for instance). Therefore many numerical methods are available already for the main part of the calculation of $\phi(x, y)$.

However special techniques are needed to treat the boundary of the plotting area properly. It happens that the mesh lines of Fig. 4 give more parameters than are necessary to match the data (1.1), and the number of parameters exceeds the number of data by $(2n_x + 2n_y - 1)$. We prefer not to discuss this point further, because we see in the next paragraph that this technique for defining $\phi(x, y)$ is rather unsatisfactory anyway, because the local properties of the approximation are poor. In other words property (P5) of Section 1 is not satisfied well.

Let $\phi(x, y)$ be any piecewise quadratic approximation with continuous first derivatives and the mesh lines of Fig. 4. We use the notation of eqns

(1.1) and (2.6). It follows from Fig. 3 and eqn (2.1) that, in the grid square whose centre is the point (x_p, y_q), the equation

$$
\begin{aligned}
\phi(x_p, y_q) = \tfrac{1}{2} \{ & \phi(x_{p-\frac{1}{2}}, y_q) + \phi(x_{p+\frac{1}{2}}, y_q) + \phi(x_p, y_{q-\frac{1}{2}}) \\
& + \phi(x_p, y_{q+\frac{1}{2}}) \} - \tfrac{1}{4} \{ \phi(x_{p-\frac{1}{2}}, y_{q-\frac{1}{2}}) \\
& + \phi(x_{p-\frac{1}{2}}, y_{q+\frac{1}{2}}) + \phi(x_{p+\frac{1}{2}}, y_{q-\frac{1}{2}}) \\
& + \phi(x_{p+\frac{1}{2}}, y_{q+\frac{1}{2}}) \}
\end{aligned}
\tag{2.11}
$$

is satisfied. Therefore, if there are at least $(r+1)$ grid lines between (x_p, y_q) and each edge of the plotting area, we have the equation

$$
\begin{aligned}
\sum_{i=-r}^{r} \sum_{j=-r}^{r} (-1)^{i+j} \phi(x_{p+i}, y_{q+j}) = \tfrac{1}{2} \sum_{j=-r}^{r} (-1)^{r+j} \{ & \phi(x_{p-r-\frac{1}{2}}, y_{q+j}) \\
& + \phi(x_{p+r+\frac{1}{2}}, y_{q+j}) + \phi(x_{p+j}, y_{q-r-\frac{1}{2}}) \\
& + \phi(x_{p+j}, y_{q+r+\frac{1}{2}}) \} - \tfrac{1}{4} \{ \phi(x_{p-r-\frac{1}{2}}, y_{q-r-\frac{1}{2}}) \\
& + \phi(x_{p-r-\frac{1}{2}}, y_{q+r+\frac{1}{2}}) + \phi(x_{p+r+\frac{1}{2}}, y_{q-r-\frac{1}{2}}) \\
& + \phi(x_{p+r+\frac{1}{2}}, y_{q+r+\frac{1}{2}}) \}.
\end{aligned}
\tag{2.12}
$$

Now the question of local dependence is really the question of the change in $\phi(x, y)$ that is caused by altering a single data function value, say $f(x_p, y_q)$, by one unit, leaving the other data function values unchanged. In this case the right-hand side of eqn (2.12) must also alter by one unit. Therefore at least one of the function values that occurs on the right-hand side changes by not less than $1/(4r + 3)$ units. It follows that the contribution from $f(x_p, y_q)$ to $\phi(x, y)$ decays no faster than the reciprocal of the number of mesh lines between (x, y) and (x_p, y_q). Because this rate is far too slow for many practical problems, we do not recommend the technique of satisfying condition (P1) by a piecewise quadratic function whose mesh lines are given in Fig. 4.

3. Piecewise Quadratics with Eight Triangles per Data Point

In order to be able to satisfy conditions (P1)–(P5) of Section 1 by a piece-wise quadratic function, we have to use a mesh that is finer than the one shown in Fig. 4. Therefore now we study the mesh of Fig. 6, which has about eight triangles per data point. It provides an approximating function $\phi(x, y)$ that is very satisfactory for contour plotting. Since the idea of having far more parameters than data is rather unusual, we introduce the advantages of this idea by showing first how it can help the problem of interpolating equally spaced values of a function of one variable.

We consider the problem of interpolating the data

$$f(x_i) = f(id), \qquad i = 1, 2, ..., n, \tag{3.1}$$

by a quadratic spline, $s(x)$ say. We suppose that we wish to improve on the excellent local properties that occur when the knots of the spline are placed mid-way between the data points. Then it is necessary to use more knots than data points. Therefore we let $s(x)$ have knots at the $(2n - 1)$ points $x = \frac{1}{2} jd$ $(j = 2, 3, ..., 2n)$, that is at all the data points and also midway between the data points.

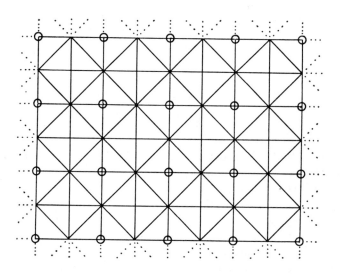

FIG. 6. A grid with eight triangles per data point.

In this case we note that the spline $\hat{\sigma}_i(x)$, defined by the equation

$$\tfrac{1}{2} d^2 \hat{\sigma}_i(x) = (x - x_{i-1})_+^2 - 2(x - x_{i-\frac{1}{2}})_+^2 + 2(x - x_{i+\frac{1}{2}})_+^2 - (x - x_{i+1})_+^2, \tag{3.2}$$

is zero at all the data points except x_i, where it has the value one. Further $\hat{\sigma}_i(x)$ is non-zero only when x is in the interval (x_{i-1}, x_{i+1}). It follows that the spline

$$s(x) = \sum_i f(x_i) \hat{\sigma}_i(x) \tag{3.3}$$

interpolates the data, and that its local properties are perfect, for $f(x_i)$ makes no contribution to $s(x)$ when x is outside the range (x_{i-1}, x_{i+1}).

However the spline (3.3) has the disadvantage that its first derivative is zero at every data point. Therefore we replace $\hat{\sigma}_i(x)$ by another cardinal spline, $\sigma_i(x)$ say, that satisfies the derivative conditions

$$\begin{aligned} \sigma_i'(x_{i-1}) &= 1/(2d) \\ \sigma_i'(x_{i+1}) &= -1/(2d) \end{aligned} \Bigg\}, \tag{3.4}$$

and that is zero outside the range (x_{i-2}, x_{i+2}). Specifically $\sigma_i(x)$ is given by the equation

$$\begin{aligned} d^2\,\sigma_i(x) = &-\tfrac{1}{4}(x - x_{i-2})_+^2 + (x - x_{i-1\frac{1}{2}})_+^2 \\ &+ \tfrac{1}{2}(x - x_{i-1})_+^2 - 3(x - x_{i-\frac{1}{2}})_+^2 \\ &+ 3(x - x_{i+\frac{1}{2}})_+^2 - \tfrac{1}{2}(x - x_{i+1})_+^2 \\ &- (x - x_{i+1\frac{1}{2}})_+^2 + \tfrac{1}{4}(x - x_{i+2})_+^2. \end{aligned} \tag{3.5}$$

It follows that if we let $s(x)$ be the spline

$$s(x) = \sum_i f(x_i)\,\sigma_i(x), \tag{3.6}$$

then again the interpolation conditions are satisfied, and again $s(x)$ has very good local properties. However now the derivative of $s(x)$ at the data point x_i has the value

$$\begin{aligned} s'(x_i) &= f(x_{i-1})\,\sigma_{i-1}'(x_i) + f(x_{i+1})\,\sigma_{i+1}'(x_i) \\ &= \{f(x_{i+1}) - f(x_{i-1})\}/2d. \end{aligned} \tag{3.7}$$

Therefore the right-hand sides of expression (3.4) have been chosen so that $s'(x_i)$ is equal to the estimate of the first derivative of $f(x)$ given by the central difference formula, so the error in approximating $f(x)$ by $s(x)$ is of order d^3.

Thus, by using more knots than data points, we have found a good quadratic spline approximation to $f(x)$, such that each function value $f(x_i)$ makes a contribution to $s(x)$ only when $|x - x_i| \leq 2d$. We now apply this idea to the problem of interpolating the data (1.1) by a piecewise quadratic function of two variables with continuous first derivatives.

Therefore first we seek a piecewise quadratic function on the mesh of Fig. 6 with continuous first derivatives, that has the value one at the data point (x_p, y_q), that is zero at all the other data points, and that is zero except on a small part of the grid whose centre is (x_p, y_q). In fact the function called $\sigma_{pq}(x, y)$ in Section 2, that we obtained by approximating the biquadratic spline (2.7), is almost suitable. We recall that this function is zero outside the large square of Fig. 5.

To use this function, imagine that Fig. 5 is rotated anti-clockwise through 45 degrees, so that the point M coincides with the mesh point (x_p, y_q) of Fig. 6, and so that the points P, Q, R and S coincide with the data points (x_p, y_{q-1}), (x_{p+1}, y_q), (x_p, y_{q+1}) and (x_{p-1}, y_q) respectively. Then the mesh lines of Fig. 5 correspond to mesh lines in Fig. 6, but the points A, B, C and D of Fig. 5 do not become data points in Fig. 6, due to the extra fineness of the grid. Thus, corresponding to $\sigma_{pq}(x, y)$, it follows from eqn (2.9) that for the grid of Fig. 6 there is a function, $\hat{s}_{pq}(x, y)$ say, that satisfies the conditions

$$\left.\begin{array}{l} \hat{s}_{pq}(x_p, y_q) = 1 \\ \hat{s}_{pq}(x_{p\pm\frac{1}{2}}, y_{q\pm\frac{1}{2}}) = \frac{1}{4} \end{array}\right\}. \tag{3.8}$$

Also the remark following eqn (2.9) and the construction of $\sigma_{pq}(x, y)$ imply that $\hat{s}_{pq}(x, y)$ is identically zero unless $|x - x_p| < d_x$ and $|y - y_q| < d_y$. Therefore $\hat{s}_{pq}(x, y)$ has the properties that we require.

However if we let $\hat{\phi}(x, y)$ be the function

$$\hat{\phi}(x, y) = \sum_{pq} \hat{s}_{pq}(x, y) f(x_p, y_q), \tag{3.9}$$

then we have the situation that occurred for the approximation (3.3), namely that the first derivatives of $\hat{\phi}(x, y)$ are zero at all the data points. Therefore we require a device that is equivalent to the replacement of $\hat{\sigma}_i(x)$ by $\sigma_i(x)$ at the beginning of this section.

For this purpose we find a piecewise quadratic function with continuous first derivatives, that is based on the mesh of Fig. 6, that is zero at all the data points, that is identically zero except for a small part of (x, y) space, but that has non-zero first derivatives at a few data points. Let this function be $\tau_{pq}(x, y)$. Then we make the definitions

$$\left.\begin{array}{l} s_{pq}(x, y) = \hat{s}_{pq}(x, y) + \lambda \tau_{pq}(x, y) \\ \phi(x, y) = \sum_{pq} s_{pq}(x, y) f(x_p, y_q) \end{array}\right\}, \tag{3.10}$$

where λ is chosen so that the gradient of $\phi(x, y)$ at (x_p, y_q) is equal to an expression that is analogous to eqn (3.7).

To construct $\tau_{pq}(x, y)$, we note that the mesh of Fig. 6 permits the functions $\hat{s}_{p\pm\frac{1}{2} \, q\pm\frac{1}{2}}(x, y)$. Therefore we define $\tau_{pq}(x, y)$ by the equation

$$\begin{aligned} \tau_{pq}(x, y) = \hat{s}_{pq}(x, y) &- \{\hat{s}_{p-\frac{1}{2} \, q-\frac{1}{2}}(x, y) + \hat{s}_{p-\frac{1}{2} \, q+\frac{1}{2}}(x, y) \\ &+ \hat{s}_{p+\frac{1}{2} \, q-\frac{1}{2}}(x, y) + \hat{s}_{p+\frac{1}{2} \, q+\frac{1}{2}}(x, y)\} + \tfrac{1}{2}\{\hat{s}_{pq-1}(x, y) + \hat{s}_{p+1q}(x, y) \\ &+ \hat{s}_{pq+1}(x, y) + \hat{s}_{p-1q}(x, y)\} + \tfrac{1}{4}\{\hat{s}_{p-1 \, q-1}(x, y) + \hat{s}_{p-1 \, q+1}(x, y) \\ &+ \hat{s}_{p+1 \, q-1}(x, y) + \hat{s}_{p+1 \, q+1}(x, y)\}, \end{aligned} \tag{3.11}$$

because it follows from eqn (3.8) that $\tau_{pq}(x, y)$ is zero at all the data points. In this case expression (3.10) and some algebra give the equation

$$[d\phi(x, y)/dx]_{(x_p, y_q)} = \lambda\{f(x_{p-1}, y_{q-1}) + 2f(x_{p-1}, y_q) + f(x_{p-1}, y_{q+1})$$
$$- f(x_{p+1}, y_{q-1}) - 2f(x_{p+1}, y_q) - f(x_{p+1}, y_{q+1})\}/d_x,$$
$$(3.12)$$

so we let $\lambda = -1/8$.

Thus the cardinal function $s_{pq}(x, y)$ is defined, centred on the data point (x_p, y_q). We note that it is identically zero if $|x - x_p| \geqslant 2d_x$ or $|y - y_q| \geqslant 2d_y$.

FIG. 7. Values of the cardinal function $s_{pq}(x, y)$ multiplied by 128.

To show its form in the region where it is non-zero, Fig. 7 gives the values of $s_{pq}(x, y)$ multiplied by 128 at the intersections of the grid lines of Fig. 6 for the square $|x - x_p| \leqslant 2d_x$, $|y - y_q| \leqslant 2d_y$. We see that the values are zero at the data points $(x_{p\pm1}, y_q)$, $(x_p, y_{q\pm1})$ and $(x_{p\pm1}, y_{q\pm1})$.

It is clear that the piecewise quadratic function $\phi(x, y)$ defined by the second line of eqn (3.10) satisfies conditions (P1), (P2), (P4), and (P5) of Section 1. Now we show that it satisfies condition (P3) also. Because of the strong local properties of our method for construction $\phi(x, y)$, it is sufficient to show that the error function (1.3) is identically zero when $f(x, y)$ is any quadratic function.

Therefore let $f(x, y)$ be a quadratic function. The definition of $\phi(x, y)$ satisfies the condition

$$e(x_p, y_q) = 0, \qquad 1 \leqslant p \leqslant n_x, \qquad 1 \leqslant q \leqslant n_y. \tag{3.13}$$

Moreover the choice of λ and eqn (3.12) give the derivative values

$$[de(x, y)/dx]_{(x_p, y_q)} = 0, \tag{3.14}$$

so we deduce that $e(x, y)$ is identically zero on the grid lines $y = y_q$. By symmetry the error function is also zero on the grid lines $x = x_p$. Therefore Fig. 6 implies that if we can establish the equations

$$[de(x, y)/dy]_{(x_{p+\frac{1}{2}}, y_q)} = 0$$
$$[de(x, y)/dx]_{(x_p, y_{q+\frac{1}{2}})} = 0, \tag{3.15}$$

then property (P3) is proved. Now we can use the definitions (3.10) to obtain the value

$$[d\phi(x, y)/dx]_{(x_{p+\frac{1}{2}}, y_q)} = 2\lambda\{f(x_p, y_{q-1}) + f(x_{p+1}, y_{q-1})$$
$$- f(x_p, y_{q+1}) - f(x_{p+1}, y_{q+1})\}/d_y, \tag{3.16}$$

so, because $\lambda = -1/8$, the first line of expression (3.15) is true when $f(x, y)$ is a quadratic function. By symmetry the second line is also true. Therefore our function $\phi(x, y)$ satisfies the properties (P1)–(P5) of Section 1.

So far we have ignored completely the problem of constructing the function $\phi(x, y)$ near the boundary of the plotting area. The following method works quite well. Imagine that the regularly spaced function values, given as data, extend outside the plotting area $d_x \leqslant x \leqslant n_x d_x$, $d_y \leqslant y \leqslant n_y d_y$. If true values are available then we will use them. Otherwise we may apply the quadratic extrapolation formulae

$$\left.\begin{aligned}
f(x_0, y_q) &= 3f(x_1, y_q) - 3f(x_2, y_q) + f(x_3, y_q) \\
f(x_{n+1}, y_q) &= 3f(x_n, y_q) - 3f(x_{n-1}, y_q) + f(x_{n-2}, y_q) \\
f(x_p, y_0) &= 3f(x_p, y_1) - 3f(x_p, y_2) + f(x_p, y_3) \\
f(x_p, y_{n+1}) &= 3f(x_p, y_n) - 3f(x_p, y_{n-1}) + f(x_p, y_{n-2})
\end{aligned}\right\} \tag{3.17}$$

for $q = 1, 2, ..., n_y$ and $p = 0, 1, ..., n_x + 1$. Then $\phi(x, y)$ is constructed in the usual way, even close to the boundary of the plotting area. This technique preserves properties (P1)–(P5) of Section 1.

The description of the piecewise quadratic function that we recommend for interpolating the data (1.1) is now complete.

4. Discussion

Probably the most important question that arises from the piecewise quadratic approximation methods of this paper is the amount of computation that is needed to apply them. It may seem that when there are four or eight triangles per data point then the work is excessive, but my rather limited experience so far with numerical examples is encouraging. Unfortunately the whole process has not yet been programmed, so the present remarks are not firm.

First let us consider the work in defining $\phi(x, y)$. If we proceed as recommended in Section 2, calculating the biquadratic spline $\bar{\phi}(x, y)$ as an intermediate approximation, then to obtain $\bar{\phi}(x, y)$ requires a small multiple of $n_x n_y$ multiplications, and to calculate $\phi(x, y)$ from $\bar{\phi}(x, y)$ requires a small fixed amount of work per grid triangle. Usually this work need not be carried out for all the grid triangles, because often the function values indicate that many of the triangles are well away from the required contour line. Thus, this calculation is quite moderate. However the method mentioned at the end of Section 2 requires more calculation, because we have noted already that condition (P1) gives equations that are similar to the equations from the five point Laplace difference operator. Further the poor localization properties make this second method unsatisfactory.

For the method of Section 3, the calculation of $\phi(x, y)$ is easier than for the other two methods, because of the absolute local properties. Indeed, by using the cardinal function of Fig. 7, there are no equations to solve. It follows that if originally there are a large number of data values, then if it is convenient we may treat small regions of the plotting area separately, without affecting the contour line at all. Thus computer storage for data values need never be a problem due to a large number of data. Moreover we may include the technique, mentioned in the last paragraph, of excluding grid triangles from consideration when the function values indicate that they are well away from the contour line.

Next we consider the work of drawing the contour lines through the grid triangles. Here it is encouraging to note that the number of important grid triangles depends mainly on the length of the contour line, so it is proportional to the square root of the total number of grid triangles. To treat an important grid triangle, we have to find a parametric form for the contour line, and then we generate a suitable sequence of points on this line, in order that the contour can be plotted as a piecewise linear function. Thus the extra work required by using eight grid triangles per data point, instead of four, is that the number of parametric forms increases by about the factor $\sqrt{2}$. However in this case the calculation of $\phi(x, y)$ may be faster, and the other operations take about the same time. Thus any percentage increase in the total amount of work is small, especially if one takes into account the processing and the plotting of the line segments that represent the contour line. For example, in the graphs given by Marlow and Powell (1972) for drawing a curve through a sequence of points by McConalogue's method, the time spent in processing the line segments is greater than the total time spent in calculating them. Therefore the method of Section 3 seems to be the most useful of the techniques that are described in this paper.

However all three techniques have a property that is sometimes unrealistic. The deficiency occurs when the data (1.1) are values of a non-negative function, and when some of the data are zero. In this case the approximating function $\phi(x, y)$ is liable to be negative for some (x, y) values near to the points where $f(x, y)$ is zero. It is unavoidable if the definition of $\phi(x, y)$ depends linearly on the data, and if property (P3) of Section 1 is satisfied. Therefore we must accept that many good algorithms will possess the deficiency, and we should be concerned only about the magnitude of any negative values of $\phi(x, y)$.

From this point of view the method of Section 3 is quite satisfactory, because the negative values of the cardinal function of Fig. 7 are small. Specifically, if the cardinal function is normalized in the usual way, so that its maximum value $s_{pq}(x_p, y_p)$ is equal to one, then the least value of $s_{pq}(x, y)$ is $-\frac{1}{24}$. Another advantage of this small value is that it implies that any errors from the extrapolation formulae (3.17) are not damaging, because at most one twenty fourth of each of the function values (3.17) is added into $\phi(x, y)$.

Fortran subroutines for contour plotting based on the methods of this paper will be available from the author soon.

Acknowledgement

I am indebted to Mr. M. Sabin and to Professors A. R. Mitchell and G. Strang for much helpful advice and encouragement. Also I wish to acknowledge my gratitude to Dr. J. K. Reid for many helpful comments on drafts of this paper.

References

Ahlberg, J. H., Nilson, E. N. and Walsh, J. L. (1967). "The Theory of Splines and Their Applications". Academic Press, New York and London.

Forsythe, G. E. and Wasow, W. R. (1960). "Finite-difference Methods for Partial Differential Equations". John Wiley and Sons, New York.

McConalogue, D. J. (1971). An automatic French-curve procedure for use with an incremental plotter. *Comput. J.* **14**, 207–209.

Marlow, S. M. and Powell, M. J. D. (1972). "A FORTRAN Subroutine for Drawing a Curve Through a Given Sequence of Data Points". Report No. R 7092, A.E.R.E., Harwell.

Discussion: Curve and Surface Fitting

Mr. Albasiny Are there any practical difficulties in determining rank-deficiency?

Mr. Hayes. In a general situation, of course, the determination of the rank of a matrix can be tricky, but in data fitting, where the data is often only accurate to two or three decimal places, there doesn't seem to be any difficulty in practice. Certainly this was the experience, for example, in the extensive testing of our bicubic spline algorithm carried out by Halliday and his colleagues at B.A.C. Of course, one must use a reasonable set of basis functions: it wouldn't be difficult to think of a set, say powers of x when the values run from 10^3 to $10^3 + 1$, which would give trouble. But with a good basis there isn't usually any difficulty: and, if there is, the choice made is unlikely to make an appreciable difference to the accuracy of fit.

As regards the general context, Dr. Wilkinson could give a more authorative answer.

Dr. Wilkinson. The only fully reliable way of recognising rank deficiency is via the singular-value decomposition, though even here there are difficult decisions when A is 'badly' scaled. In practice though, even Gaussian elimination with complete pivoting is quite reliable and QR decompositions with column interchanges are even less fallible.

Prof. S. Cabay (*University of Alberta, Canada*). The basis functions, discussed by Mr. Powell, being of compact support are therefore of the kind used in finite element methods. There are many papers which discuss the approximation of functions by finite-element methods. One introductory reference on finite-element regression is a chapter in "Spline Analysis", M. H. Schultz, Prentice–Hall, 1973.

Mr. Powell. Here I should acknowledge my gratitude to Professor A. R. Mitchell and to Professor G. Strang for advising me of results in the finite element literature. It seems that my method for using piecewise quadratic functions with continuous first derivatives is original, and clearly it is very appropriate to contour plotting. However, in finite element calculations it is not awkward to use higher order polynomials, so the elaboration of my triangulation scheme is unnecessary. Therefore the emphasis of my work is different from usual, nevertheless I hope it will be of value to work with finite elements.

Dr. Liddell. What method would you recommend for curve fitting to functions which are sums of exponential functions?

Mr. Hayes. Fitting with a sum of exponentials, i.e. with

$$f(x) = \sum_{i=1}^{n} a_i \exp(-b_i x),$$

where the b_i as well as the a_i are free parameters, is a notoriously nasty problem, and indeed, in the L_2 norm, is often used to provide a severe test when developing algorithms for general unconstrained optimization (see for example Gill, Murray and Pitfield 1972, NPL Report NAC11). I don't think I've seen any satisfactory result with $n > 4$. The sort of trouble that can arise is that one of the terms by chance becomes negligible in the early iterations, and then its coefficient and exponent can vary wildly without appreciably affecting the value of $f(x)$. The problem also has the unsatisfactory feature of possessing local minima. It is a particular instance of the remark in my paper that, because one is unlikely to get physically meaningful values for the parameters, it is usually better to fit with some linear function. One such possibility is to fix the b_i at values which span a physically reasonable range (since the implication is that the precise values are not critical), and so be left with the very much simpler problem of determining only the a_i.

MR. POWELL. I would like to draw attention to a method that was developed at Harwell recently by Dr. M. D. Hebden. It minimizes the sum of squares of residuals by an extension of Marquardt's method, using first and second derivatives that are calculated from the analytic formula. Thus, if one allows for the inherent instability of exponential fitting, the method provides good reliability and accuracy.

MISS JUDITH DANIELS (*U.C. Computing Centre, London*). In view of the fact that users of data fitting routines tend to be particularly inexperienced, does the panel feel there is a case for including a spline routine with automatic knot selection in his package. In my experience, if there is a choice between two routines, the user will almost always choose the routine which does not require him to specify the knot points.

MR. HAYES. Certainly, the user should try Mr. Powell's program. My view of this program is that it is particularly suited to complicated curves with lots of data and similar behaviour throughout the range. In cases where the behaviour differs widely in one part of the range from another, the utility of the algorithm is limited by the restriction it places on the rate at which the knot-spacing can vary across the range. In such cases, it can produce unwanted fluctuations by putting too many knots in regions where the underlying function is changing only slowly.

15. Rational Approximations for Special Functions

C. W. Clenshaw

*Department of Mathematics, Cartmel College,
Bailrigg, Lancaster, Lancashire, England.*

1. Introduction

A discussion of special functions should start with a clarification of the meaning of the term. In the present context a "special function" is simply a function which may be evaluated to arbitrary precision at any point in its domain of definition (that is to say, there is no dependence on physical constants) and which is of common occurrence in physical problems.

For convenience we may consider two classes of special functions. The first consists of those which are so widely encountered that their properties have been deeply explored and their values comprehensively tabulated. They include, for example, the trigonometric and exponential functions, the gamma function, the Bessel functions and so on. Software for their efficient computation exists (see Chapter 16, this volume) though the subject cannot be regarded as closed. These functions are computed so frequently that further research could be justified if it resulted in even a relatively small improvement.

In the second class we place those unnamed functions of less widespread importance which nevertheless arise frequently enough for us to seek effective methods for their calculation. Here it is less vital that we should pursue the utmost economy in each individual case; rather we seek a general approach which will enable us to deal with a wide variety of functions with a fair degree of efficiency. It is this latter problem which we treat here: we limit the discussion to the case of a real function on a finite interval of a single real variable.

The classical method of tackling this problem is the use of the orthodox table of function values together with some interpolating procedure such as Everett's formula. Before investigating the suitability of this approach, however, we should note that in mentioning the mathematical table we make the tacit assumption that interpolation by polynomials is indeed permissible. This implies that any intrusive singularities have been dealt with. Moreover if any *near*-singular behaviour has also been treated, the subsequent interpolation task is greatly eased.

There is an inescapable vagueness about this most vital first step in the approximation process, the treatment of singularities. Sometimes the singular part should be removed by subtraction or division; sometimes it may reasonably be ignored; sometimes an intermediate course of action (such as removal of a simple factor which *resembles* the singularity) is preferable. Only human experience and intelligence can tackle this problem at present. The following example illustrates the way in which we might proceed in particular cases.

We suppose that the exponential integral, defined as

$$E_1(x) = \int_x^\infty \frac{e^{-t}}{t} \, dt,$$

is to be tabulated for the semi-infinite interval $[0, \infty)$. First we split the interval into two parts, and deal with $[0, X]$ and $[X, \infty)$ separately. (Here X is some number chosen for convenience.) In the first of these, there is just a singularity at the origin to be examined. It is easy to see (by considering

$$\int_x^X \frac{e^{-t} - 1}{t} \, dt)$$

that $f(x) = E_1(x) + \ln x$ is nonsingular on $[0, X]$, and this is therefore the function to be tabulated.

To deal with the interval $[X, \infty)$, we first find (by successive integration by parts) that $E_1(x)$ has an asymptotic expansion of the form

$$E_1(x) \sim x^{-1} e^{-x} \left(1 - \frac{1}{x} - \frac{2!}{x^2} + \dots \right).$$

This suggests removal of a factor $x^{-1} e^{-x}$ (or, perhaps, just e^{-x}) followed by use of x^{-1} as a new independent variable. That is to say, we actually tabulate values of $f(x) = E_1(x) + \ln x$ on $0 \leqslant x \leqslant X$, and values of $g(t) = t^{-1} e^{t^{-1}} E_1(t^{-1})$ on $0 \leqslant t \leqslant X^{-1}$. The tabulation might be expected to be reasonably smooth. When values of $E_1(x)$ are required, they will be recovered from

$$E_1(x) = f(x) - \ln x \qquad \text{if} \quad 0 \leqslant x \leqslant X,$$

and

$$E_1(x) = x^{-1} e^{-x} g(x^{-1}) \quad \text{if} \quad X \leqslant x < \infty.$$

(Of course, this procedure presupposes the existence of adequate tables of the fundamental special functions $\ln x$ and e^x.)

It would appear that in considering the programming of computer software for approximating special functions, just as in the construction of a table, we must assume that singular behaviour has been investigated and accorded the appropriate treatment. Thus our remaining problem, that for which we seek to devise computer software, is the approximation of a special function which is free from singularity. (For instance, in the above example we should approximate the auxiliary functions $f(x)$ and $g(t)$.) We now confine our attention to this problem.

2. Approximating Functions

Perhaps the first decisions to be taken are

(i) the choice of approximating function, and

(ii) the choice of the norm, which determines our method of measuring the "distance" between the function and its approximation.

We need say little about (ii), because experience suggests that the choice of norm is largely a matter of computational convenience. The choice of approximating function is, however, of fundamental importance.

The mathematical table together with its interpolating formula (that is, a piecewise polynomial) is an approximating function which may still be useful on occasion, expecially in its modern guise of the spline function, with continuity of low-order derivatives at the tabular points. However, we usually look elsewhere for an approximating function which will give an effective compromise between fast, simple evaluation and compact storage.

The most popular solution to date has been the simple polynomial. If the singularity removal is carried out very thoroughly, the task of polynomial approximation is not difficult. There are nevertheless many occasions on which a more powerful approximating function may be sought. There may be nearby singularities whose removal may be difficult to carry through, by virtue of the analytical complication of the function definition, or perhaps because they are so numerous that direct numerical attack is preferred. In these circumstances we might revert to a cubic spline function (Hayes 1970, Chapter 4). If we still wish to economize on storage, however, we might well prefer to consider approximation by the ratio of two polynomials.

One immediate argument in favour of this step is that the rational function is the most general form that can be evaluated on a computer using the ordinary arithmetic processes. The extra flexibility that the form provides, compared with the simple polynomial, may be of inestimable value in approximating functions which, while nonsingular, nevertheless have some near-singular features. On the other hand, rational approximation often presents numerical difficulties which do not arise in polynomial approximation; these will be mentioned in the next section.

3. Minimax Rational Approximation

We suppose here that our problem is the approximation of f, continuous on $[-1, 1]$ by a rational function $R_{m,n}$ (a polynomial of degree not exceeding m, divided by a polynomial of degree not exceeding n). We make the problem clear-cut by asking for the L_∞ norm of the approximation to be a minimum: that is, we choose the coefficients of the rational function so that

$$\max_{[-1,1]} |f - R_{m,n}|$$

is as small as possible. (We could incorporate a weight function w in the definition of our norm, of course, and this is frequently useful in rational approximation. Since it is a simple matter to insert it when desired, however, we omit it here in the interest of clarity.)

There is a unique solution, as long as we regard two rational functions as being the same if they are equal when reduced to their lowest terms. Let this minimax solution be expressed in its lowest terms as

$$R_{m,n} = \frac{P}{Q}$$

where P and Q are polynomials, with ∂P denoting the actual degree of P, etc. (i.e. P is a polynomial of degree ∂P, but is not a polynomial of degree $\partial P - 1$). Then the *defect* of $R_{m,n}$ is $d_{m,n}(R) = \min(m - \partial P, n - \partial Q)$, and when this is positive we say that $R_{m,n}$ is *degenerate*. It is degeneracy, or near degeneracy, which is responsible for many of the numerical snags in rational approximation. (Near degeneracy can arise if, for example, P has a factor which is very close to a factor of Q.) The phenomenon has been discussed by several workers in the field, including Cody (1970), Ralston (1973) and Rice (1964). It is to be noted that degeneracy with its attendant difficulties does not occur in polynomial approximation.

Apart from these matters, however, there is the sheer labour of computation to be considered. In the polynomial case, we can use fast and stable direct methods to compute the coefficients a_r in the Chebyshev series expansion

$$f = \sum_{r=0}^{\infty} {}' a_r T_r. \tag{1}$$

This topic is discussed in detail in Hayes 1970 (Chapter 3). The basic result is that the truncation

$$f_n = \sum_{r=0}^{n}{}' a_r T_r$$

is close to the minimax polynomial approximation of degree n, for all sufficiently large n. Thus, the calculation of the leading coefficients in the expansion (1) virtually solves the problem of polynomial approximation. Unfortunately however, no corresponding expansion appears to exist for rational approximation. (It is true that in some special cases a continued-fraction expansion may be readily available, but this cannot be expected generally; nor is there any guarantee that the truncation of such an expansion will be near-minimax in character.) Minimax rational approximation, sought numerically through the use of an iterative technique such as a Remes algorithm, may run into the snags that we have already mentioned. Moreover, it seems unlikely that the situation can be significantly eased by a simple modification of the norm. Replacement of the continuous L_∞ norm by the discrete L_2 norm (with an appropriate selection of point set) has the desired effect in the polynomial situation, but no corresponding device appears likely to succeed with rational functions.

4. Algorithmic Considerations

We now attempt to examine the approximation problem strictly from the viewpoint of practical implementation. That is to say, given f, continuous in $[-1, 1]$, we wish to apply a standard algorithm which will give us an economical approximation with some specified degree of precision. Since a polynomial approximation will often be effective, the first natural step in this algorithm will be the production of the coefficients in the formal Chebyshev series (1). If the series so obtained converges with sufficient rapidity (it certainly converges uniformly if f is of bounded variation) then our task is virtually complete. It may often happen, however, that the series converges so slowly that a polynomial approximation of desired accuracy would be of unacceptably high degree. Then our algorithm should proceed to its next step, of finding rational approximations. It would appear natural, therefore, to attempt to derive rational approximations to f using the information that has been gained already in finding the coefficients a_r in (1). This is the motivation for the present approach.

We may observe that the new situation, finding rational functions which resemble a given Chebyshev series, has much apparent similarity with Padé approximation, in which we find rational functions which resemble a given Taylor series.

Padé Approximation

We start with f, a function of the complex variable z, defined in a neighbourhood of the origin by the power series

$$f(z) = \sum_{r=0}^{\infty} c_r z^r. \tag{2}$$

Let $R_{m,n}$ be a rational function (with exact degrees m and n) whose Taylor series expansion is given by

$$R_{m,n}(z) = \sum_{r=0}^{\infty} C_r z^r. \tag{3}$$

(For simplicity we here assume that $R_{m,n}$ is bounded near the origin, and that its numerator and denominator have no common factors.)

Then $R_{m,n}$ is a Padé approximant to f if $c_r = C_r$ for $r = 0,1, 2, \ldots, m+n$, and the (m, n) array of such approximants is called the Padé table of f.

Padé approximation has been well covered in the literature; Handscomb 1966 contains a useful discussion for the numerical analyst. For our present purposes we need merely note that if

$$R_{m,n} = \frac{P}{Q} \quad \text{where} \quad P(z) = \sum_{r=0}^{m} p_r z^r, \quad Q(z) = \sum_{r=0}^{n} q_r z^r, \tag{4}$$

then the coefficients q_r $(r = 1, 2, \ldots, n)$ may be found by solving the linear system

$$\sum_{s=0}^{n} q_s c_{r-s} = 0, \qquad r = m+1, m+2, \ldots, m+n, \tag{5}$$

where $q_0 = 1$ and where $c_{-k} = 0$ for $k > 0$. The calculation of p_r $(r = 0, 1, 2, \ldots, m)$ then follows directly from

$$p_r = \sum_{s=0}^{n} q_s c_{r-s}, \qquad r = 0, 1, 2, \ldots, m. \tag{6}$$

5. Generalizations

When faced with our present problem, that of deriving a rational approximation from a series other than a simple power series, it is natural that we should consider extending the idea of Padé approximation. Generally, suppose that we start with f, defined by a formal series expansion

$$f = \sum c_r \phi_r,$$

and seek to approximate it by the rational function P/Q, where

$$P = \sum_{r=0}^{m} p_r \phi_r, \qquad Q = \sum_{r=0}^{n} q_r \phi_r$$

with $q_0 = 1$. Here ϕ_r is a polynomial of degree r. In order to preserve the Padé analogy as closely as possible, we should then determine $\{p_r\}$ and $\{q_r\}$ from the set of equations obtained by annihilating the leading terms in the expansion of

$$f - \frac{P}{Q}. \tag{7}$$

Unfortunately however, these equations are nonlinear in character, except in special cases. It is usual, therefore, to adopt the alternative procedure of annihilating the leading terms in the expansion of

$$Qf - P, \tag{8}$$

which yields a set of *linear* equations. This is described by Cheney (1966), for example, as "generalized Padé approximation."

It transpires, however, that the two approaches may be regarded as equivalent in two important special cases; that is to say, in those cases we can obtain the close Padé analogy (expressed by the vanishing of the leading terms in (7)) by solving a *linear* system. Those cases are those in which

(i) ϕ_r satisfies a homogeneous first-order difference equation. (That is, $\phi_{r+1} - x\phi_r = 0$, the familiar Padé case.)

(ii) ϕ_r satisfies a symmetric homogeneous second-order difference equation. (That is, $\phi_{r+1} - 2x\phi_r + \phi_{r-1} = 0$, which we might call the Chebyshev–Padé case.)

At least one *nonlinear* case has been treated in some detail. If f is defined by an expansion in Legendre polynomials, then the close Padé analogy can be preserved only by solving a nonlinear system. This case has been discussed by Fleischer (1972).

We now examine the second of the two special cases in which a linear system is available. This has been treated, from somewhat different viewpoints, by Hornecker (1960), and by Frankel and Gragg (1972). Our aim remains that of constructing the foundations upon which reliable and widely applicable computer programs may be built.

6. Chebyshev-Padé Approximation

Details of the process in this case are given by Clenshaw and Lord (1973), and again we merely sketch the main features.

We write

$$f = \sum' a_r T_r,$$

and suppose this series to be uniformly convergent on $[-1, 1]$. Let a rational approximation be

$$R = \frac{P}{Q} = \sum' A_r T_r, \quad \text{where} \quad P = \sum_{r=0}^{m}{}' p_r T_r, \quad Q = \sum_{r=0}^{n}{}' q_r T_r,$$

with $q_0 = 2$ (which is a permissible normalization if R is nonsingular on $[-1, 1]$). For simplicity we here assume R to be nondegenerate. Multiplication by Q, and subsequent comparison of coefficients of T_r for $r > m$, gives

$$\sum_{s=0}^{n}{}' q_s(A_{r+s} + A_{r-s}) = 0, \quad r = m + 1, m + 2, \ldots \tag{9}$$

where we understand that A_{-k} $(k > 0)$ is to be replaced by A_k. The simple replacement of A_r by a_r for $r = 0, 1, 2, \ldots, m + n$ will *not* now enable us to solve the first n of the eqns (9) for q_s, because these equations involve A_r for values of r as large as $m + 2n$. However, the symmetry of the eqn (9) (which stems from the symmetry of the relation $T_{r+1} - 2xT_r + T_{r-1} = 0$) enables us to reduce its order from $2n$ to n. The knowledge that $A_r \to 0$ as $r \to \infty$ permits the assertion that the symmetric difference equation of order $2n$ (given in (9)) may be replaced by an unsymmetric difference equation of order n; suppose this is

$$\sum_{s=0}^{n} \gamma_s A_{r-s} = 0, \quad r = m + 1, m + 2, \ldots. \tag{10}$$

Comparison of (9) and (10) readily yields the relation

$$q_s = 2 \sum_{i=0}^{n-s} \gamma_i \gamma_{s+i} \Big/ \sum_{i=0}^{n} \gamma_i^2, \quad s = 0, 1, \ldots, n. \tag{11}$$

A direct solution of the linear problem is now available. Replacement of A_r by a_r for $r = 0, 1, 2, \ldots, m + n$ gives the system

$$\sum_{s=0}^{n} \gamma_s a_{|r-s|} = 0, \quad r = m + 1, m + 2, \ldots, m + n, \tag{12}$$

which can be solved for γ_s $(s = 1, 2, \ldots, n)$, taking $\gamma_0 = 1$. Equation (11) then gives the coefficients q_s $(s = 0, 1, \ldots, n)$ directly and we may finally compute the coefficients p_r from

$$p_r = \tfrac{1}{2} \sum_{s=0}^{n}{}' q_s(a_{r+s} + a_{|r-s|}), \quad r = 0, 1, \ldots, m. \tag{13}$$

In constructing the array of Chebyshev–Padé approximants, we can take advantage of the strong similarity of the linear systems which determine neighbouring elements. If, for a specified m and n, the eqns (12) are

$$\sum_{s=0}^{n} \gamma_s^{(m,n)} a_{|r-s|} = 0, \qquad r = m+1, m+2, \ldots, m+n,$$

we find relations like

$$\gamma_s^{(m+1,n+1)} = \gamma_s^{(m+1,n)} + \sigma^{(m,n)} \gamma_{s-1}^{(m,n)},$$

where $\sigma^{(m,n)}$ is given by

$$0 = \sum_{s=0}^{n} \gamma_s^{(m+1,n)} a_{|m+n+2-s|} + \sigma^{(m,n)} \sum_{s=0}^{n} \gamma_s^{(m,n)} a_{|m+n+1-s|}.$$

In each of a number of cases which have been investigated numerically, the Chebyshev–Padé table bears a striking resemblance to the Walsh array of minimax rational approximations. Corresponding elements have similar errors, and degeneracy or near-degeneracy in one array reflect similar phenomena in the other. In particular, the nonexistence of an element of the Chebyshev–Padé table (i.e. the divergence of the formal Chebyshev series expansion of the element, implying a pole on $[-1, 1]$) indicates the near-degeneracy of the corresponding element of the Walsh array.

The near-minimax quality of the Chebyshev–Padé approximation can be argued from the nature of its error curve $(f - P/Q)$, which of course has an expansion of the form

$$\sum_{r=m+n+1}^{\infty} (a_r - A_r) T_r,$$

and so has at least $(m + n + 1)$ sign changes on $[-1, 1]$ (see Clenshaw and Lord, 1973). Thus a Chebyshev–Padé approximant furnishes an effective starting point for a Remes algorithm, if a minimax rational approximation should be required.

Conclusion

An array of rational functions of near-minimax character can be constructed numerically by direct methods from the coefficients in a Chebyshev series expansion. It is suggested that examination of the errors of the elements of this array will indicate which element will best serve a particular approximation purpose. Moreover, the array provides immediate information about the nature of the Walsh array.

Standard computer software for special functions frequently includes an algorithm for evaluating the coefficients in a Chebyshev series expansion. Such an algorithm might well be accompanied by another which will generate a Chebyshev–Padé table.

References

Cheney, E. W. (1966). "Introduction to Approximation Theory". McGraw-Hill, New York.
Clenshaw, C. W. and Lord, K. (1973). *In* "Studies in Numerical Analysis", B. K. P. Scaife (Ed.). Academic Press, London and New York.
Cody, W. J. (1970). *SIAM Review* **12,** 400–423.
Fleisher, J. (1973). *J. Math. Phys.* **14,** 246–248.
Frankel, A. P. and Gragg, W. B. (1972). (Private communication).
Handscomb, D. C. (Ed.) (1966). "Methods of Numerical Approximation". Pergamon Press, Oxford.
Hayes, J. G. (Ed.) (1970). "Numerical Approximation of Functions and Data". Athlone Press, London.
Hornecker, G. (1960). *Chiffres* **3,** 193–228.
Ralston, A. (1973). *J. Inst. Maths Applics* **11,** 157–170.
Rice, J. R. (1964). *Math. Comput.* **18,** 617–626.

16. Special Functions in the NAG Library

J. L. SCHONFELDER

Computer Centre,
University of Birmingham,
Birmingham, England.

The Problem

The problem we are faced with is to provide a set of library routines to give approximations for the commonly used special functions. These routines must be callable from either FORTRAN or ALGOL 60 on a wide range of different machines. (Owing to the incompatibilities in the output of compilers on some machines, notably the ICL 1906A on which NAG was originally developed, mixed language programming is difficult so all routines are coded separately in each language).

The commonly used functions may be taken to be those covered in the "Handbook of Mathematical Functions" by Abramowitz and Stegan and comprises a list of roughly fifty separate functions. (We are only considering at the moment functions of a single real variable; functions of more than one variable or sets of related functions, like a set of Legendre polynomials, are not included in this paper although they are included or will be included in the library.)

A problem of this magnitude cannot sensibly be tackled in a haphazard way but must be treated systematically with a large number of decisions taken and conventions defined in advance. It is a description of these choices and conventions which are the main subject of this paper.

Requirements of Routine

The properties which routines in such a library must possess may be summarised as follows:

1. *Full Machine Accuracy*

Where possible a routine should give an approximation which is accurate to full machine precision whatever that is for the machine in question. Furthermore this should be relative accuracy if that is at all feasible. In general the distinction between relative and absolute accuracy is one that requires attention only near zeros of the function.

It should be noted here that we are not going to be worried about extracting the last "bit" of machine accuracy but rather we shall want, on a machine such as a 1906A which works to slightly less than 11D accuracy, to produce routines that give at least 10D correctly and have errors in the eleventh figure produced by the arithmetic of the machine. At the moment the NAG library is being implemented on machines with precisions of 6D and 14D as well as the original 11D and there are possibilities of other precisions up to 20D which must be allowed for.

2. *Robustness*

Routines should detect their own failures. For instance should a routine be called with an argument such that it cannot satisfy properly this should be detected and some appropriate action taken.

3. *Ease of Use*

The user should not have to become involved in any special procedure to enable him to call a routine. Ideally they should be available on a similar basis to the compiler provided functions.

4. *Ease of Implementation*

This property is one of considerable import and it will have considerable effect on the choices to be described later. We must design our methods of producing routines and testing them in such a way that implementing them on any machine range at any precision is as straight forward as possible.

5. *Language Compatibility*

We want the user interface to be as similar as possible in both languages. The argument lists should be the same and the numerical behaviour should be the same.

6. *Efficiency*

Last but not least we want our routines to be as efficient as possible consistent with our other requirements.

Certain of the most basic functions are available as compiler provided. Unfortunately the set in ALGOL 60 is not as extensive as it might be compared to FORTRAN. So we take the minimal set the functions ln, exp, sin, cos, artan and sqrt. These do not then have to be provided in our library. Thus we can state the constraints that are placed on us by machines and compilers simply. We are limited in that the only functions we can evaluate directly are polynomials, ratios of polynomials (rational functions) and combinations of these involving the above set of functions.

Considering this summary of the nature of the problem and the constraints that apply the decisions we must take and the conventions we must define fall broadly into three areas:

(i).   Choice of approximating technique and norm to measure accuracy.

(ii).   Coding conventions to be followed.

(iii).   Testing procedures to be followed.

Choice of Approximating Technique

The first choice of approximating technique is obviously the most efficient. Therefore we should use the rational form with the parameters of the rational function chosen to satisfy the minimax or Chebyshev norm condition. That is, we use an approximating form which is the ratio of two polynomials, the coefficients of which are chosen to minimise the maximum error. It is well known that such approximations provide us with most efficient and flexible approximating technique. However for our purposes this technique has a number of major disadvantages:

1. For a given maximum error, E (machine precision) the finding of the parameters, c, of the rational function is a far from trivial problem, particularly finding the set of smallest number, N, and hence the most efficient approximation.

2. Any change in E requires a complete regeneration of the set c with a different value of N.

3. There are many different methods of evaluating a rational function and unfortunately the stability of these methods is somewhat dependent on the actual values of c, N and possibly x, the argument of the function. This could result in different methods of evaluation being needed for implementations on different machines.

Obviously eventually we would hope to implement approximations of this form but at the development stage, as we are now, of a multimachine library we must look for an approximating technique which although less efficient is still reasonable but which does not suffer from these problems. The minimax polynomial is the next thought but this too suffers from the above disadvantages, albeit to a lesser degree. However, if we are prepared to retreat from the minimax norm we can turn to the now well tried Chebyshev expansion to find polynomial approximations which if suitably chosen are not significantly worse than the true minimax polynomials and which have a large number of telling advantages.

Chebyshev Expansions

Provided that $f(x)$ is absolutely integrable on the interval $x \in [-1, +1]$, there exists a convergent expansion of the form.

$$f(x) = \sum_{r=0}^{\infty}{}' a_r T_r(x) \tag{1}$$

where $T_r(x)$ is the rth degree Chebyshev polynomial.

$$T_r(x) = \cos r\theta, \qquad \theta = \arccos x. \tag{2}$$

$T_r(x)$ is a polynomial of degree r which oscillates between $+1$ and -1 and it reaches its extreme values $r + 1$ times in the interval $[-1, +1]$. Hence provided that $|a_r| \to 0$ sufficiently rapidly, the error made in using a truncated expansion is given approximately by the magnitude of the first neglected term, i.e. if we truncate at $r = n$, say, then

$$E \doteqdot |a_{n+1}| \tag{3}$$

and the difference, $\varepsilon(x)$ between our function and the approximating polynomial so produced, is given by

$$\varepsilon(x) \doteqdot a_{n+1} T_{n+1}(x). \tag{4}$$

Thus we approximately satisfy the well known condition for a minimax solution. We have an approximation which oscillates between $+E$ and $-E$ and takes its extreme values $N + 1$ times $(n + 2)$ in the approximation interval, where N is the number of parameters in the approximating form.

The difference between a truncated Chebyshev expansion and the true minimax polynomial of the same order is seldom sufficiently great to justify the use of the true minimax polynomial. It is unfortunate that there is no simple analogue of the Chebyshev expansion for rational approximations.

To summarise, the advantages of the Chebyshev form for our purposes are:

1. The coefficients a_r are easy to generate and need only be done once (if done to sufficient accuracy 20D, say).

2. Changes in accuracy may be produced by simple truncation.

3. A good estimate of the error is available by inspection.

4. Evaluation can always be performed in the same stable manner.

These advantages must be balanced against the loss of efficiency inherent in use of a polynomial approximation compared to a rational form. However, because of the greater implementation simplicity, it is a price worth paying at least at this stage in development of the library. Another very telling argument in favour of the Chebyshev expansion technique is the considerable number of expansions already known and in the literature.

In general, we shall be working with approximations of the form:

$$f(x) = g(x) \sum_{r=0}^{n}{}' a_r \, T_r(t), \qquad X \in [a, b] \tag{5}$$

where $g(x)$ is some suitable auxiliary function which extracts singularities and/or asymptotes of the function and $t(x)$ is a function which maps the general region $[a, b]$ onto the required $[-1, +1]$. The most suitable method for summing such a series is using backward recursion, i.e. defining:

$$b_{n+1} = 0, \qquad b_n = a_n$$
$$b_j = 2tb_{j+1} - b_{j+2} + a_j \tag{6}$$

it can easily be shown that:

$$\sum_{r=0}^{n}{}' a_r \, T_r(t) = (b_0 - b_2)/2 \tag{7}$$

Coding Conventions

Since we are talking of a library of some fifty odd routines, it is not only desirable but essential that some systematic conventions be defined covering the way in which routines are to be coded.

Any routine which works by evaluating expressions of the form (5) has 5 basic tasks to perform:

1. It must set up an array containing the appropriate number of coefficients.

2. Must deal with any special values of the argument and/or failure conditions.

3. Evaluate the argument, $t(x)$ of the expansion.

4. Sum the series.

5. Evaluate the auxiliary function, $g(x)$ and hence the required function.

As we have noted before all routines of this type should have the same argument list viz:

(X,IFAIL)

where

X—is the argument of the function (transfer by value) unchanged by the routine

IFAIL—is a variable which is used to indicate failures in the routine

>On entry IFAIL selects the mode of failure

>>= 0   for hard fail (terminate execution after printing a message)

>>= 1   for soft fail (set IFAIL to failure number and return)

>On exit IFAIL = 0 for a successful call

>>= 1, 2, 3...etc. depending on the failure detected

At this point the two language versions part company owing to the very different constraints imposed by the language definitions.

Fortran Coding

To set up the array of constants the obvious device in FORTRAN is the DATA statement which fills the array at load time. Thus, each routine will contain the following conventional code:

DIMENSION C($\langle N \rangle$)

DATA NCF/$\langle N \rangle$/, $\langle$other machine dependent constants$\rangle$/

A, C(1), C(2), C(3)......C($\langle N \rangle$)

B/$\langle a_0 \rangle$, $\langle a_1 \rangle$, $\langle a_2 \rangle$......$\langle a_n \rangle$/

The quantities in angular brackets will be replaced by the actual constants for each particular case.

This structure has the elegant feature of grouping all precision dependent features of the routine in one block at the start of the routine. The series can be summed by the conventional code

BJP2 = 0.0

BJP1 = C(NCF)

J = NCF − 1

```
1 BJ = T2 * BJP1 − BJP2 + C(J)
  IF (J.EQ.1) GO TO 2
  BJP2 = BJP1
  BJP1 = BJ
  J = J − 1
  GO TO 1
2 SUM = 0.5*(BJ − BJP2)
```

where T2 holds twice the argument of the expansion.

The following is a listing of the actual code for the 1900 version of the routine S10ABF, sinh (x) based on the algorithm.

$$\sinh (x) = x \sum_{r=0}^{n}{}' C_r \, T_r(t), \qquad t = 2x^2 - 1, \qquad |x| \leqslant 1$$

$$\sinh (x) = 0{\cdot}5 \, (e^x - e^{-x}) \, R \geqslant |x| > 1$$

for $|x| > R$ the routine fails IFAIL$=1$ due to danger of setting overflow.

Listing 1. 1900 (11D) version of S10ABF (Sinh(x))

```
ROUTNS10ABF

      FUNCTION S10ABF(X, IFAIL)
C     MARK 4 RELEASE NAG COPYRIGHT 1973
C     SINH(X)
      INTEGER P01AAF
C
      DIMENSION C(5)                                           111
      DATA NCF/5/, XUP/150.0/                                  111
     A, C(1), C(2), C(3), C(4), C(5)                           111
     A/2.1730421940, 8.75942219E−2, 1.0794778E−3, 6.3748E−6, 2.20E−8/  111
C
      DATA ERR/6HS10ABF/
      XA=ABS(X)
      IF(XA.LT.1.0) GO TO 20
      X2=EXP(SIGN(AMIN1(XA, XUP), X))
      S10ABF=0.5*(X2−1.0/X2)
      IF(XA.GT.XUP) GO TO 10
      IFAIL=0
      RETURN
   10 IFAIL=P01AAF(IFAIL, 1, ERR)
      RETURN
C
C     SMALL X
   20 X2=2.0*(2.0*X*X−1.0)
C     SUMMATION BEGIN
      BJP2=0.0
      BJP1=C(NCF)
      J=NCF−1
```

```
   30 BJ=X2*BJP1-BJP2+C(J)
      IF(J.EQ.1) GO TO 40
      BJP2=BJP1
      BJP1=BJ
      J=J-1
      GO TO 30
   40 S10ABF=X*0.5*(BJ-BJP2)
      IFAIL=0
      RETURN
      END
```

A point to note about this code is the presence in the sequence field of the characters "111" on cards containing machine dependent code. These characters are two numbers—"1" and "11". The "1" is an edit code and "11" is the machine precision to which these cards apply. These quantities can be used to produce a general version of the routine by duplicating the machine dependent statements for each precision that is required. The corresponding general version of S10ABF is:

Listing 2. General version of S10ABF

LSGENS10ABF

```
      FUNCTION S10ABF(X, IFAIL)
C     MARK 4 RELEASE NAG COPYRIGHT 1973
C     SINH(X)
      INTEGER P01AAF
C
      DIMENSION C(5)                                                111
      DATA NCF/5/, XUP/150.0/                                       111
      A, C(1), C(2), C(3), C(4), C(5)                              111
      A/2.1730421940, 8.75942219E-2, 1.0794778E-3, 6.3748E-6, 2.20E-8/   111
      DIMENSION C(4)                                                1 6
      DATA NCF/4/, XUP/70.0/                                        1 6
      A, C(1), C(2), C(3), C(4),                                   1 6
      A/2.17304, 8.759E-2, 1.08E-3, 1.E-5/                         1 6
      DIMENSION C(7)                                                114
      DATA NCF/7/, XUP/200.0/                                       114
      A, C(1), C(2), C(3), C(4), C(5), C(6), C(7)                  114
      A/2.1730421940472, 8.75942219228E-2, 1.0794777746E-3, 6.374849E-6   114
      A, 2.20237E-8, 4.99E-11, 1.E-13/                             114
C
      DATA ERR/6HS10ABF/
      XA=ABS(X)
      IF(XA.LT.1.0) GO TO 20
      X2=EXP(SIGN(AMIN1(XA, XUP), X))
      S10ABF=0.5*(X2-1.0/X2)
      IF(XA.GT.XUP) GO TO 10
      IFAIL=0
      RETURN
   10 IFAIL=P01AAF(IFAIL, 1, ERR)
      RETURN
C
```

```
C      SMALL X
20  X2=2.0*(2.0*X*X-1.0)
C      SUMMATION BEGIN
       BJP=0.0
       BJP1=C(NCF)
       J=NCF-1
30  BJ=X2*BJP1-BJP2+C(J)
       IF(J.EQ.1) GO TO 40
       BJP2=BJP1
       BJP1=BJ
       J=J-1
       GO TO 30
40  S10ABF=X*0.5*(BJ-BJP2)
       IFAIL=0
       RETURN
       END
```

A runnable version of the routine can be simply produced for a 6D, 11D or 14D implementation simply by editing out those statements not needed.

Algol Coding

It is unfortunate that mixed language programming is not possible since for coding this type of algorithm ALGOL is a considerably less suitable language than FORTRAN. In ALGOL we have no analogue of the DATA statement for initializing the array of coefficients. The most suitable mechanism for setting up the array is by assignment which must be performed at execution time. In order that those assignments should be executed only when necessary the array is filled and the summation is performed by an inner block of code.

```
begin read BJP2, BJP1, BJ; integer J;
        array C[1:⟨N−1⟩];
        C[1]:= ⟨a₀⟩: C[2]:= ⟨a₁⟩;...... C[⟨N − 1⟩]:= ⟨aₙ₋₁⟩;
        BJ: = ⟨aₙ⟩;
        BJP1:=0.0;
        for J:= ⟨N−1⟩
        step −1 until 1 do
        begin
             BJP2:=BJP1;BJP1:=BJ;
             BJ:=T2*BJP1−BJP2+C[J];
        end;
        SUM:=0.5*(BJ−BJP2);
    end;
```

SUM and T2 are declared in an outer block.

The following is the listing of the general version of S10ABA

Listing 3. General version of S10ABA

```
'REAL' 'PROCEDURE' S10ABA(X, IFAIL);
'VALUE' X;'REAL' X;'INTEGER' IFAIL;
'COMMENT' MARK 4 RELEASE NAG COPYRIGHT 1973
SINH(X);
'BEGIN'
        'REAL' XA, X2;
        XA:=ABS(X);
        'IF 'XA 'GE' 1.0 'THEN'
        'BEGIN'
                'REAL' XUP, MIN;                                        0111
                XUP:=150.0;                                             0111
                XUP:=70.0;                                              0106
                XUP:=200.0;                                             0114
                'IF' XA<XUP' THEN' MIN:=XA 'ELSE' MIN:=XUP;
                X2:=SIGN(X)*MIN;X2:=EXP(X2);
                S10ABA:=(X2-1.0/X2)*0.5;
                'IF' XA>XUP 'THEN'
                'BEGIN'

                        'INTEGER' 'PROCEDURE' P01AAA(IFAIL, N, STRING);
                        'VALUE' IFAIL, N; 'INTEGER' IFAIL, N; 'STRING' STRING;
                        'ALGOL'
                        IFAIL:=P01AAA(IFAIL, 1, '('S10ABA')');
                'END'
                'ELSE' IFAIL:=0;
        'END'
        'ELSE'
        'BEGIN'
                'REAL' BJP1, BJP2, BJ, X2, 'INTEGER' J;
                'ARRAY' C[1:4];
                'ARRAY' C[1:4];                                         0111
                C[1]:=2.1730421940; C[2]:=8.75942219&-2;                0111
                C[3]:=1.0794778&-3; C[4]:=6.3748&-6; BJ:=2.2&-8;        0111
                'ARRAY' C[1:3];                                         0106
                C[1]:=2.17304; C[2]:=8.759&-2; C[3]:=1.08&-3; BJ:=1.0&-5;   0106
                'ARRAY' C[1:6];                                         0114
                C[1]:=2.1730421940472; C[2]:=8.75942219228&-2;          0114
                C[3]:=1.0794777746&-3; C[4]:=6.3748493&-6;              0114
                C[5]:=2.20237&-8; C[6]:=4.99&-11; BJ:=1.0&-13;          0114
                BJP1:=0.0;
                X2:=2.0*(2.0*X*X-1.0);
                'FOR' J:=4                                              0111
                'FOR' J:=3                                              0106
                'FOR' J:=6                                              0114
                'STEP' -1 'UNTIL' 1 'DO'
                'BEGIN'
                        BJP2:=BJP1; BJP1:=BJ;
                        BJ:=C[J]+X2*BJP1-BJP2;
                'END'
                S10ABA:=X*(BJ-BJP2)*0.5;
        'END'
'END';
```

The point to note is that the machine dependent records are not now grouped at the top of the routine but are scattered through it. However since the editing is to be done by machine using the sequence field information this is not really a problem, just an inelegance.

Testing Procedures

NAG requires that all routines be subjected to two levels of testing:

1. Example programs

There are simple programs which illustrate the use of the routine the most elementary way. Example programs as well as being very important first level testing are also reproduced in the documentation along with data and results. Each routine has only one such example program.

2. Stringent Test Programs

Each routine must have one or more stringent test programs. Such programs are meant to give a 'complete' test of all pathways through a routine. The stringent test programs are meant to fully investigate the behaviour of a routine both on problems which it is designed to handle in a stable manner and on problems which lie on or outside its boundary of applicability, including actual misuse of the routine.

As well as maintaining the routine library NAG also keeps the full test program library and no implementation is considered complete until all the test/example programs have been implemented and run, obtaining the same (or equivalent) results as those found by the original contributor or validator. This means that the ease of implementation property is also a major criterion in designing test programs as well as routines.

The special function area is a very convenient one for the design of test/example programs. By convention all routines have the same argument list and hence essentially the same program may be used to test all routines.

By making the test/example program data driven the only thing that requires changing from routine to routine is the actual calling sequence which names the routine and the data.

The following is the example program for S10ABF along with its data and results. The program is driven by a data deck which starts with a caption identifying the routine, subsequent cards each contain two numbers, a value of the entry IFAIL and the argument X at which the function is to be evaluated. These are read one at a time, the function evaluated, the results printed and the loop repeated until a negative value for IFAIL terminates the program.

Listing 4. Simple example program

```
EXMPLS10ABF

C       EXAMPLE PROGRAM FOR SPECIAL FUNCTION ROUTINE WITH
C       ARGUMENT LISTS  (X, IFAIL)
        DIMENSION CAP (80)
        DATA, NIN, NOUT /5, 6/
        READ(NIN, 1001)  CAP
        WRITE(NOUT, 2001)  CAP
      1 READ(NIN, 1002)  IFAIL, X
        IF(IFAIL.LT.0) STOP
        WRITE(NOUT, 2002)  IFAIL, X
C
        Y=S10ABF(X, IFAIL)
C
        WRITE(NOUT, 2003)  Y, IFAIL
        GO TO 1
   1001 FORMAT(80A1)
   1002 FORMAT(I5, F40, 20)
   2001 FORMAT(1H0, 80A1//6H ENTRY, 31X, 4HEXIT/6H IFAIL, 8X, 13X, 1HY
        A7X, 5HIFAIL)
   2002 FORMAT(4X, I2, 2X, 1PE12.3)                                        0111
   2003 FORMAT(1H+, 21X, 1PE12.3, 5X, I2)                                  0111
        END
```

DATA

```
DATAES10ABF

EXAMPLE USE OF  --S10ABF--  SOFT AND HARD FAILURE OPTIONS
        1                -10.0
        1                 -0.5
        1                  0.0
        1                 25.0
        1                200.0
        0               -200.0
       -1
```

RESULTS

```
RSLTES10ABF
```

EXAMPLE USE OF --S10ABF-- SOFT AND HARD FAILURE OPTIONS

ENTRY			EXIT
IFAIL	X	Y	IFAIL
1	-1.000E 01	-1.101E 04	0
1	-5.000E-01	-5.211E-01	0
1	0.000E-01	0.000E-01	0
1	2.500E 01	5.211E-01	0
1	2.500E 01	3.600E 10	0
1	2.000E 02	6.969E 64	1
0	-2.000E 02		

LIBRARY FAILS IN ROUTINE S10ABF WITH ERROR 1

Since a large amount of testing in this area is checking against published tables, the basic test program has a very similar structure, except that to allow for the possible use of auxiliary functions and/or arguments in the tables the calling sequence may have to be more complex. To this end, a copy of the actual calling sequence is included in the data as a second caption. A further difference is that stringent test programs must print results to full accuracy, whereas example programs only require a fixed low accuracy print out (4 figures). Hence, of necessity, test programs contain more machine dependent features. The corresponding test program for S10ABF is as follows:

Listing 5. Simple test against table program

```
TESTOS10ABF

C       GENERAL TEST PROGRAM FOR NAG SPECIAL FUNCTION ROUTINES WITH
C       ARGUMENT LISTS (X, IFAIL)
        DIMENSION CAP(80)
        DATA NIN, NOUT/5, 6/
        READ(NIN, 1001) CAP
        WRITE(NOUT, 2001) CAP
        READ(NIN, 1001) CAP
        WRITE(NOUT, 2002) CAP
     1  READ(NIN, 1002) IFAIL, X
        IF(IFAIL.LT.0) STOP
        WRITE(NOUT, 2003) IFAIL, X
C
        Y=S10ABF(X*3.1415926536, IFAIL)
C
        WRITE(NOUT, 2004) Y, IFAIL
        GO TO 1
 1001   FORMAT(80A1)
 1002   FORMAT(I5, F40, 20)
 2001   FORMAT(1H0, 80A1/  37H0 FUNCTION TABULATED Y(X) IS GIVEN BY)
 2002   FORMAT(10X, 80A1//6H ENTRY, 49X, 4HEXIT/6H IFAIL, 14X, 1HX, 22X, 1HY,
       A10X, 5HIFAIL)
 2003   FORMAT(5X, I1, 1X, 1PE21.10)
 2004   FORMAT(1H*, 29X, 1PE21.10, 7X, I1)
        END
```

```
        DATAOS10ABF

 TEST OF  --S10ABF-- AGAINST TABLE A.&.S.  4.16 PAGE(219)
           Y=S10ABF(X*3.1415926536, IFAIL)
     1             -0.75
     1             -0.25
     1              0.0
     1              0.25
     1              0.5
     1              0.75
     1              1.0
    -1
```

```
RSLTOS10ABF
```

TEST OF --S10ABF-- AGAINST TABLE A.& S. 4.16 PAGE(219)

FUNCTION TABULATED Y(X) IS GIVEN BY
Y=S10ABF(X*3.1415926536, IFAIL)

ENTRY IFAIL	X	Y	EXIT IFAIL
1	-7.5000000000E-01	-5.2279719249E 00	0
1	-2.5000000000E-01	-8.6867096142E-01	0
1	0.0000000000E-01	0.0000000000E-01	0
1	2.5000000000E-01	8.6867096142E-01	0
1	5.0000000000E-01	2.3012989023E 00	0
1	7.5000000000E-01	5.2279719248E 00	0
1	1.0000000000E 00	1.1548739358E 01	0

As with routines we can produce general versions of these programs, examples of which are shown below. A new edit code now appears, "2". This code is used to flag the necessity of editing in the routine name or calling sequence depending on the second number in the sequence field. "2 9" means that the dummy name must be replaced by the actual routine name starting at column 9 of the card. The absence of a second parameter means the whole calling record is to be replaced with the card from the appropriate data deck.

Listing 6. General forms of example and test programs

```
      LSGENEXMPAF

C     EXAMPLE PROGRAM FOR SPECIAL FUNCTION ROUTINE WITH
C     ARGUMENT LISTS  (X, IFAIL)
      DIMENSION CAP(80)
      DATA NIN, NOUT/5, 6/
      READ(NIN, 1001) CAP
      WRITE(NOUT, 2001) CAP
    1 READ(NIN, 1002) IFAIL, X
      IF(IFAIL.LT.0) STOP
      WRITE(NOUT, 2002) IFAIL, X
C
      Y=DUMNAM(X, IFAIL)                                      02 9
C
      WRITE(NOUT, 2003) Y, IFAIL
      GO TO 1
 1001 FORMAT(80A1)
 1002 FORMAT(I5, F40, 20)
 2001 FORMAT(1H0, 80A1//6H ENTRY, 31X, 4HEXIT/6H IFAIL, 8X, 1HX, 13X, 1HY,
     A7X, 5HIFAIL)
 2002 FORMAT(4X, I2, 2X, 1PE12.3)                             0111
 2003 FORMAT(1H+, 21X, 1PE12.3, 5X, I2)                       0111
      END
```

```
      LSGENTSNAF
C     GENERAL TEST PROGRAM FOR NAG SPECIAL FUNCTION ROUTINES WITH
C     ARGUMENT LISTS (X, IFAIL)
      DIMENSION CAP(80)
      DATA NIN, NOUT/5, 6/
      READ(NIN, 1001) CAP
      WRITE(NOUT, 2001) CAP
      READ(NIN, 1001) CAP
      WRITE(NOUT, 2002) CAP
    1 READ(NIN, 1002) IFAIL, X
      IF(IFAIL.LT.0) STOP
      WRITE(NOUT, 2003) IFAIL, X
C
      DUMMY—CALLING SEQUENCE WILL BE PROVIDED BY EDITNAG—        02
C
      WRITE(NOUT, 2004) Y, IFAIL
      GO TO 1
 1001 FORMAT(80A1)
 1002 FORMAT(I5, F40, 20)
 2001 FORMAT(1H0, 80A1/  37H0 FUNCTION TABULATED Y(X) IS GIVEN BY)
 2002 FORMAT(10X, 80A1//6H ENTRY, 49X, 4HEXIT/6H IFAIL, 14X, 1HX, 22X, 1HY,
      A10X, 5HIFAIL)
 2003 FORMAT(5X, I1, 1X, 1PE21.10)                                  0111
 2004 FORMAT(1H+, 29X, 1PE21.10, 7X, I1)                            0111
 2003 FORMAT(5X, I1, 1PE23.13)                                      0114
 2004 FORMAT(1H+, 29X, 1PE23.13, 6X, I1)                            0114
 2003 FORMAT(5X, I1, 4X, 1PE15.5)                                   01 6
 2004 FORMAT(1H+, 32X, 1PE15.5, 10X, I1)                            01 6
      END
```

All the development work in this area was done on a 1906A computer using the GEORGE 3 operating system. Except for the generation of some of the Chebyshev expansions not already available which was done on CDC7600 making use of the high precision arithmetic possible with 120 bit double precision arithmetic. The filestore and macro-facilities under GEORGE 3 make the near automation of this sort of testing and editing quite simple. All the NAG contribution work at Birmingham is now done under a pseudo user :BINAG who owns a number of conventionally named files containing source for routines and test/example programs (both 11D and general), data and results. The naming conventions for files is outlined below and also a brief description of the two main MACRO's we use for running and editing our NAG work.

:BINAG files

Runnable files:—

EXMPL ⟨routine name⟩   TEST ⟨digit⟩ ⟨routinename⟩

ROUTN ⟨routine name⟩

DATAE ⟨routine name⟩   DATA ⟨digit⟩ ⟨routinename⟩

RSLTE ⟨routine name⟩   RSLT ⟨digit⟩ ⟨routinename⟩

A Macro RUNNAG ⟨routine name⟩, ⟨optional parameters⟩ merges the appropriate source files, runs the program using the appropriate data file and causes the results to be listed and, depending on the optional parameters, retains the new results in the results file for later reference.

General Files:

LSGENEXMPA {A/F}   LSEGENTESTA {A/F}

LSGEN ⟨routine name⟩

A Macro EDITNAG ⟨routine name⟩, ⟨optional parameters⟩ causes a program to be run which according to information in the optional parameters edits the appropriate general file to produce a runnable source file for the given routine at the specified precision. Communication of work to NAG control office is also simple in that all that has to be done is that a copy of this filestore is sent on magnetic tape along with accompanying documentation.

I have not said anything about the procedure used to actually generate the Chebyshev coefficients used in these routines. Most of the existing routines have been based on the expansions of Clenshaw but some new expansions have been used and I have developed a set of programs to do this based on solving differential equations. This system is still under development and could be the subject of another paper by itself. All new expansions will be produced on the CDC machine in Manchester working in double precision giving sets of coefficients correct to at least 20D accuracy which should be sufficient for almost all foreseeable needs.

I hope what I have said has given some idea of the sort of reasoning behind the special function section of the NAG library and some idea of the sort of procedure at present being followed. This in no way is the final answer. This is merely the present state of the art. In the future I would hope to be able to develop the area to make available more nearly optimal routines but for the present the pressing need to get at least a not unreasonable library available on a wide range of machines has been the main determining criterion.

Acknowledgements

I would like to thank Mr. A. Reed who helped in the writing of the macros and Mr. Z. Mahmood who has assisted in the running of the test programs.

References

Fox, L. and Parker, I. B. (1968). "Chebyshev Polynomial in Numerical Analysis". Oxford University Press.
Clenshaw, C. W. (1962). "Mathematical Tables" Vol. 5. National Physical Laboratory. H.M.S.O.
Hart, J. F., et al. (1968). "Computer Approximations". John Wiley & Son, New York.
Luke, Y. L. (1968). "Special Functions and Their Approximations". Mathematics in Science and Engineering Series. Academic Press, New York and London.
Clenshaw, C. W., Miller, G. F. and Woodger, M. (1963). *Num. Math.* **4**, 403–419.

Discussion: Special Functions

Dr. J. D. Pryce (*University of Aberdeen*). The only way of putting lists of data constants into an ALGOL 60 program seems to be by a *for* list. For instance to evaluate a 5th degree polynomial one can write a backward recursion loop as

$$y := c_5;$$
$$\text{for } c := c_4, c_3, c_2, c_1, c_0 \text{ do } y := c + x + y;$$

J. D. Beasley (*Rothamsted Experimental Station*). With respect to Dr. Pryce's point, in the few ALGOL compilers I have known the efficiency of any "*for*" statement other than the simple "*step ... until*" is terrible: typically they make the "*for*" body into a subroutine and call it once for each element.

Dr. Tingleff. Concerning the lack of data statements in ALGOL: In many ALGOL compilers, you can introduce constants as arithmetic expressions with integers, for instance $a := 2/3 + 5 \& 3;$. The idea is, that "constant expressions" like this are calculated before the execution and do not take up computing time and that you get full precision independent of the machine.

Dr. Schonfelder. I would suspect that this is not a general feature of all compilers and integer expressions to compute real numbers accurate to potentially 20D could be rather long and thus result in great inefficiency on a compiler which did not evaluate them at compile time.

Dr. J. A. Grant (*University of Bradford*). In your approach to Chebyshev coefficients, do you use the exact coefficients, or do you use those calculated numerically by the summation process?

Prof. Clenshaw. The formal presentation certainly implies that the a_r are the true coefficients in the infinite expansion. In numerical practice however, we shall use the values calculated by the summation process. The fact that these differ slightly from the true values is unimportant, because the procedure is well-conditioned; that is, small changes in the a_r will give rise to only small changes in the rational approximations.

17. Application of On-Line Techniques to the Numerical Solution of Partial Differential Equations

A. SYKES

Theory Division, Culham Laboratory,
UKAEA Research Group,
Abingdon, Berkshire, England.

1. Introduction

This is an account of some work carried out recently at UKAEA Culham Laboratory. As such there are three areas of interest: (a) the physical origin of the problems; (b) the numerical analysis; (c) the computing techniques used to find and exhibit the solution.

The problems described arise in the study of anomalous resistivity and toroidal stability, subjects of current interest in plasma physics. The relevant numerical analysis involves the solution of parabolic and hyperbolic equations in two space dimensions, and it will be emphasised how physical insight can aid the numerical treatment.

The computing techniques involve extensive use of interactive computing and graphics. As this area is probably the one of main general interest, we start by discussing the computer facilities and techniques in use at Culham, and use the problem solutions as examples.

2. Computing Facilities and Techniques

The configuration consists of an ICL 4–70 main computer, operating under the MULTIJOB System. This supports about 30 teletypes, 5 storage tube terminals and a refresh display. The usual supervisor provides two Roll-In-Roll-Out (RIRO) streams, one used for compilation purposes, the other available for interactive programs. Normal batch programs use a large fixed stream.

The distinction between batch and interactive (on-line) computing is now well-known. The advantages claimed for interactive computing include:

simpler programming (since decisions—e.g. timestep, or iteration control—can be made by the user); saving of computer time by immediate rejection of irrelevant or incorrect runs; and, most important, better understanding of the problem under study obtained by the ability to see immediately the effects of parameter variations.

When interactively solving time-dependent partial differential equations in two space dimensions, it is obviously impracticable to print out at the teletype all the meshpoint values, as these typically number 1000 at each step. Some form of "instant" graphics is essential for full understanding. At Culham this is available on a refresh display, or on storage tubes. We now discuss the software required for this type of work.

3. Software for Interactive Computing

The main requirements are that the program should be easy to write and develop; capable of either on-line or off-line operation; and, if possible, be simple enough to be used by other than professional programmers.

To avoid the necessity of learning an additional language, we use FORTRAN, the main computing language at Culham. Secondly, the same program may be run either in interactive or batch mode merely by reading in different input/output channel numbers. Finally, by using prompts and keywords, the physicist or engineer user can communicate with the program in the language of his own subject.

These points are illustrated by the following sample section of program:

```
    ----
    DT = 0.1                                 }  define all default values
    CALL MAP (0.0, 1.0, 0.0, 1.0)
    ----

999  WRITE (NWRITE, 10)
 10  FORMAT ('TYPE KEYWORD, VALUES')
     READ (NREAD, 100) WORD, VAL1, VAL2, VAL3, VAL4
100  FORMAT (A8, 60Y, 4F1.0 ) (free format)

     IF(WORD.EQ.'DT        ')DT = VAL1
     IF(WORD.EQ.'NWRITE')NWRITE = VAL1
     IF(WORD.EQ.'MAP       ')CALL MAP(VAL1, VAL2, VAL3, VAL4)
     IF(WORD.EQ.'START    ')GO TO 1
     -----
     GO TO 999
     -----
```

Note the use made of free format input. This should allow any spacing between data items; should repeat the prompt if invalid characters are met; and should have the ability to satisfy any unmentioned data with zero values. Thus for example, to set DT = 0.2, the prompt and response are:

TYPE KEYWORD, VALUES?DT   0.2

so WORD = 'DT   '; VAL1 = 0.2; and VAL2, VAL3, VAL4 are given zero values by the 4F1.0 part of the free format.

Besides giving a good user image, the use of keywords gives partially self-documenting code, plus meaningful records of work done whether on teletype or in data file.

Although the ability to transfer reading and writing to different channels is widely available, the corresponding ability for graphics is not; all too often a program needs to be re-written if a different graphics device is used. At Culham the 'GHOST' graphics system (Prior, 1971) pre-processes all graphics (except for cine-film, which goes directly to magnetic tape) into an intermediate form (GRID file) from which it may be processed onto any device.

Note that the graphics discussed so far does not require any graphical *input* of information, and so it is not quite the 'interactive' graphics used in computer aided design applications, such as architecture or circuit layout. Interactive graphics is used at Culham, and an example will be given later. But we first describe some partial differential equation problems which have benefited from interactive study.

4. Quasi-Linear Theory of Anomalous Resistivity

A plasma consists of a very hot ionised gas, which must be contained by electromagnetic fields for sufficient times so that energy may be released by the fusion processes. Theoretically, when an electric current is passed through such a plasma, very little resistance should be met. In practice, however, an anomalously high resistance occurs. This produces further heating of the plasma—which is useful—but also considerable turbulence, which may allow the plasma to diffuse away. Figure 1 shows turbulence in phase space (velocity against space) produced during a computer simulation. By using experimental evidence—which is difficult to obtain, due to the short time and high temperatures involved—and direct computer simulation, analytical theories can be developed.

The electron distribution function in velocity space is $f = f(r, \theta, t)$. Initially it is usually a Maxwellian (Gaussian) displaced from the ion distribution which is at the origin (Fig. 3a); physically, this represents an electron beam streaming through the relatively motionless ions.

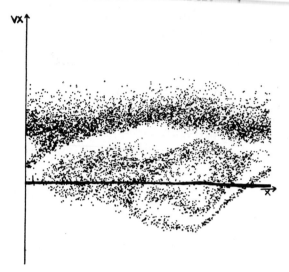

FIGURE 1

The evolution of f is given by

$$
\begin{cases}
\dfrac{\partial f}{\partial t} = c\,\dfrac{1}{r^3}\,\dfrac{\partial}{\partial \theta}\left(W(\theta)\,\dfrac{\partial f}{\partial \theta}\right) + E(t)\left(\sin\theta\,\dfrac{1}{r}\,\dfrac{\partial f}{\partial \theta} + \cos\theta\,\dfrac{\partial f}{\partial r}\right) \\[2ex]
\dfrac{dW(\theta)}{dt} = 2\gamma(\theta)\,W(\theta) \\[2ex]
\gamma(\theta) = \displaystyle\int_l \dfrac{1}{r}\,\dfrac{\partial f}{\partial \theta}\,dr \\[2ex]
+\ \text{feedback equations to determine } E(t)
\end{cases}
$$

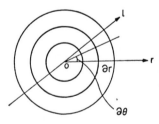

FIGURE 2

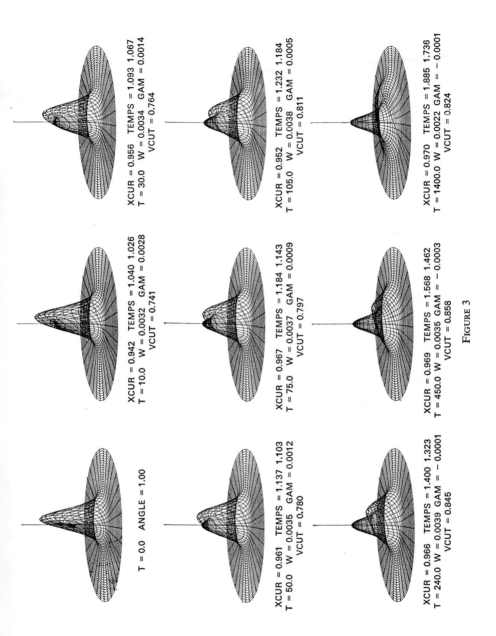

FIGURE 3

Solution of this parabolic equation (and auxiliaries) will give not only the resulting electron distribution but the turbulence $W(\theta, t)$ and growth rates $\gamma(\theta, t)$.

The polar coordinate mesh has been chosen because the physics indicates that although rapid diffusion will occur in θ, only very slow diffusion should occur radially. This knowledge greatly eases the numerical calculation, reducing it in effect to a one-dimensional computation.

Numerical analysis

If the simple equation $u_t = c u_{xx}$ is solved by the explicit scheme

$$\frac{u_i^{n+1} - u_i^n}{\delta t} = c \frac{u_{i+1}^n - 2u_i^n + u_{i-1}^n}{\delta x^2},$$

a Fourier analysis gives the stability condition

$$\frac{c\delta t}{\delta x^2} \leqslant \frac{1}{2}.$$

Thus if $c = 1$ and $\delta x = 0 \cdot 1$, $\delta t \leqslant 0 \cdot 005$ for stability. For our equations, we find $\delta t \leqslant 10^{-5}$ for stability although the physics evolves in times of order 1000.

An implicit scheme is therefore essential. We solve implicitly around each circle of constant r in turn, treating the r-derivatives explicitly. This produces (cyclic) tridiagonal matrix equations which are easily solved. The actual timesteps used are typically 5 or 10 units, and the evolution of f is shown in Fig. 3.

If a rectangular mesh had been used, the resulting implicit equations could have been solved by ADI (Alternating Direction Implicit) or LOD (Locally One Dimensional) methods, i.e. by successively sweeping in x and y directions.

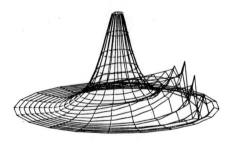

FIGURE 4

Advantages of interactive study

Although useful for the immediate detection of any coding errors or numerical instabilities (Fig. 4), the main advantage of the interactive approach is in the study of the significance of the many physical parameters in the problem.

5. Stability of Plasma in a Torus

The hot plasma is held away from the torus walls by electromagnetic fields. Equilibrium configurations of the plasma can be computed for certain fields by the solution of elliptic partial differential equations, but the stability of these equilibria is not known.

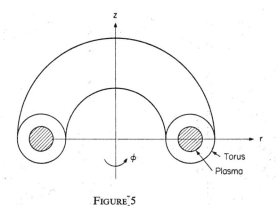

FIGURE 5

We here follow an initial perturbation of the equilibrium. If this dies away or oscillates boundedly, the equilibrium is stable; if the perturbation grows, we need to find the dominant mode and its growth rate, so that its importance may be assessed. For example, a mild instability may be acceptable if the bulk of the plasma is confined for sufficient time for the fusion processes to occur.

The linearised perturbation equations are given below. $p_0(r, z)$ and $B_0(r, z)$ are the given equilibrium configurations of pressure and magnetic fields; $\xi = (\xi_r, \xi_\phi, \xi_z)$ is the displacement.

$$\rho_0 \frac{\partial^2 \xi}{\partial t^2} = -\nabla p' + (\mathbf{j}_0 \times \mathbf{B}') + (\mathbf{j}' \times \mathbf{B}_0)$$

$$p' = -\gamma p_0 \nabla \cdot \xi - \xi \cdot \nabla p_0$$

$$\mathbf{j}' = \nabla \times \mathbf{B}'$$

$$\mathbf{B}' = \nabla \times (\xi \times \mathbf{B}_0).$$

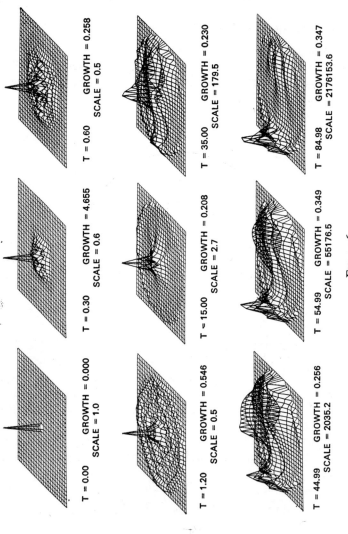

FIGURE 6

Numerical Analysis

This is difficult. To obtain sufficient accuracy and stability, we have used a variationally derived difference scheme (cf. Forsythe and Wasow, 1960) starting from the corresponding energy integral. This method, with a suitable choice of mesh basis, provides spatially averaged differences which have good numerical stability properties.

Further difficulty is met at the boundaries, where the only boundary condition is $\xi \cdot \mathbf{n} = 0$, that is, no displacement across the boundary. Attempts at producing energy conserving boundary schemes have proved unsatisfactory, and we use the technique of extrapolating values from as large an area as possible, then averaging.

Results

The time development of a delta function perturbation is shown in Fig. 6. Each plot shows $|\xi_r^2 + \xi_\phi^2 + \xi_z^2|$, normalised by the factor SCALE. The circular region shown is a minor cross-section of the torus, as in Fig. 5. In this example the axis of the torus is to the left, and the equilibrium magnetic field $B(r)$ varies very rapidly; this produces the very localised modes shown at later times.

Figure 6 shows that the growth times of interest are much larger than the wave oscillation period, which explicit schemes must follow. To combat this, we have used some implicit schemes due to McKee (1972, 1973), suitably modified to be unconditionally stable for variable coefficient problems whilst also supplying our special space-averaged difference replacements. Usually however, we need to revert to the explicit code because of difficulties with using non-rectangular regions.

Advantages of interactive study

This stability problem is difficult, in that we need to distinguish between genuine physical instabilities, spurious numerical instabilities, boundary errors, etc.

Unlike diffusion problems (such as the Anomalous Resistivity example) in which small numerical errors are harmlessly smeared out, in this hyperbolic system any errors are liable to propagate indefinitely. If we knew that the physical modes sought were long wavelength, we could remove shorter effects and greatly ease the computation, but we do not have this knowledge for the general case.

Interactive study provides a measure of confidence in the computation; we find it of great value also in testing new difference techniques, introducing new physical terms, altering boundary conditions, and so on.

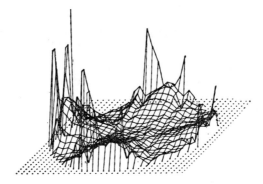

FIGURE 7

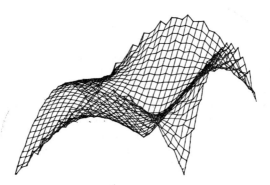

FIGURE 8

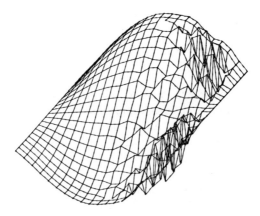

FIGURE 9

Figures 7, 8 and 9 show numerical instabilities arising from boundary errors; use of unsuitable spatial differencing; and violation of the numerical stability condition.

6. An Application of Interactive Graphics

The problem of obtaining suitable mesh triangulations prior to using the finite element method is well known. The triangulation is very tedious by hand, but it is very difficult to guarantee 100% success for all cases by automatic computation. Interactive graphics can play a useful role, as follows. A simple code performs the initial triangulation, getting say 98% of it correct, and projects its attempt on the display. Figure 10 shows a simple hole-in-plate example, which has been well triangulated by the simple program. The engineer/physicist can now 'touch up' any defects by moving corners with the light pen, using the 'menu' keywords ZOOM (zooms in on a specified part of the picture); MOVE (moves an indicated node to an indicated position), and UNZOOM (returns to normal view). To refine the mesh is equally simple; the keyword REFINE is given, and a triangle interior indicated. This triangle is then subdivided by the program into three triangles.

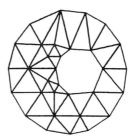

FIGURE 10   FIGURE 11

The final result of a single node adjustment, plus some additional refinements, is shown in Fig. 11. The mesh is now ready for presentation to the numerical part of the program to obtain the desired field or stress solution.

Acknowledgements

The physical examples are based on work undertaken with Dr. John Wesson. The numerical analysis has benefited from many discussions with Professor K. W. Morton, and the computing techniques have been developed in conjunction with T. J. Martin.

References

Prior, W. A. J. (1971). "The GHOST Graphical Output System User Manual". CLM PDN 8/71 (revised: Issue 2).

Forsythe, G. E. and Wasow, W. R. (1960). "Finite Difference Methods for Partial Differential Equations". John Wiley and Sons, New York.

McKee, S. (1972). *J. Inst. Maths Applics* **9**, 350.

McKee, S. (1973). *J. Inst. Maths Applics* **11**, 105.

18. POTENT—A Package for the Numerical Solution of Potential Problems in General Two-Dimensional Regions

C. Ll. Thomas

Theory Division, Culham Laboratory,
UKAEA Research Group,
Abingdon, Berkshire, England.

1. Introduction

At Culham Laboratory considerable effort is employed on the design and analysis of electrostatic and magnetostatic fields.

The electrostatic fields are produced by voltages applied to conductors of general shape. The region enclosed by the conductors may be a vacuum which could be occupied by electric charge, or the region could be made up of several different insulators. Frequently this region may not be closed, but we can close it by a fictitious boundary sufficiently far away from the conductors so that the field is uniform on this boundary.

In general the problem is to solve

$$\mathbf{\nabla} . \varepsilon \mathbf{\nabla} \phi = -\rho \tag{1}$$

inside a given region with either the voltage ϕ, or the outward normal component of the field $(\partial \phi / \partial n)$ specified on the boundary. Here

ϕ is the electrostatic potential where $\mathbf{E} = -\mathbf{\nabla}\phi$ and $\mathbf{D} = \varepsilon \mathbf{E}$,

$\mathbf{E}$ is the electric field,

$\mathbf{D}$ is the electric flux density,

ε is the local absolute permittivity of the medium,

ρ is the local charge density.

The magnetostatic fields are produced by steady currents flowing in conductors. Most problems can be solved using approximations to the Biot–Savart law. However, when iron cores or infinite regions or distributed

315

currents are involved we must resort to solving the differential equation. Again, when the region is infinite in some direction, it must be closed by a fictitious boundary where an appropriate boundary condition is imposed.

In general, the problem is to solve

$$\nabla \times (1/\mu) \nabla \times \mathbf{A} = \mathbf{j} \tag{2}$$

inside a given region with $\mathbf{A}$ given on the boundary. Here $\mathbf{A}$ is the vector potential where $\mathbf{B} = \nabla \times \mathbf{A}$ and $\mathbf{B} = \mu \mathbf{H}$

$\mathbf{H}$ is the magnetic field

$\mathbf{B}$ is the magnetic flux density

μ is the local absolute permeability of the medium

$\mathbf{j}$ is the local current density.

For all these problems there is in general no closed form of the solution, so we have to resort to numerical methods. We use a finite difference method with an iterative solution of the difference equations.

Most problems encountered so far have either exhibited a high degree of cylindrical symmetry or have been much more complicated in two dimensions than in three dimensions. Hence R–Z and X–Y coordinates respectively are used, so a rectangular grid is appropriate. The need for two-dimensional calculations only is fortunate because of storage limitations and also eqn (2) reduces to a single scalar equation in this situation. The shapes and gaps between conductors can vary considerably in any problem so we allow the rectangular grid to be nonuniform. This means that mesh points can be concentrated in regions where the solution is rapidly changing and can be spread out where the solution is slowly changing.

Equations (1) and (2) give rise to eight different differential equations since each can be in (X, Y) or (R, Z) coordinates with zero or non-zero right-hand side. Each of these equations occurs frequently.

All these problems are produced by engineers and physicists who in general regard programming as a chore and would like a program to be a "black box". With a minimum amount of work on their behalf, they want answers which are accurate to say 10%. Such a black box has been produced. The user has to write a FORTRAN subroutine which defines the boundary of the problem, the boundary conditions, the initial approximation of the solution, the permittivities (permeabilities) and the charge (current) densities. He also has to provide a certain amount of numerical data, e.g. the finite difference grid.

The package is written in FORTRAN. Five-point finite difference equations are set up on the variable rectangular mesh. The system of equations is solved by one of three iterative methods—ADI, SOR or SLOR. Field and flux density components are computed by differencing the potential. Graphical output consists of contours of the potential, the orthonormal contours to the potential contours, i.e. the field lines in the electrostatic case and the scalar potentials in the magnetic case (provided $\mathbf{j} \equiv \mathbf{0}$) and contours of the field components and magnitude.

2. The User Image of POTENT

To specify the boundary of his region to the package, the user must provide a function $F(X, Y)$ such that $F(X, Y) > 0$ if the point (X, Y) lies inside the region, $F(X, Y) = 0$ if (X, Y) is on the boundary and $F(X, Y) < 0$ if (X, Y) lies outside the region. Furthermore $F(X, Y)$ must give the distance of (X, Y) from the boundary—this property is particularly useful when setting up the difference equations.

If the boundary can be defined by an analytic curve, the form of the function $F(X, Y)$ is easily obtained. For example, if the region is the interior of a circle centre (X_0, Y_0) radius R then

$$F(X, Y) \equiv R - \sqrt{(X - X_0)^2 + (Y - Y_0)^2}.$$

For more complicated boundaries we make use of some basic principles and in particular the FORTRAN functions AMIN1 and AMAX1, which take respectively the minimum and maximum values of the values in their argument lists.

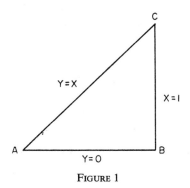

FIGURE 1

As an example, suppose we wish to define the region inside the triangle ABC in Fig. 1. A point (X, Y) is inside ABC if it is

(1) above the line $Y = 0$ i.e. $Y > 0$,

and (2) to the left of the line $X = 1$ i.e. $1 - X > 0$,

and (3) to the right of the line $Y = X$ i.e. $(1/\sqrt{2}) (X - Y) > 0$.

Thus (X, Y) is inside the triangle if all the expressions on the left-hand sides of the above inequalities are positive, and in particular if the minimum of these expressions is positive. Also the distance of (X, Y) from the boundary is the minimum of the three values. Hence the region ABC is defined by

$$F = \text{AMIN } 1(Y, 1 - X, (X - Y)/\text{SQRT}(2.0)).$$

This region is the intersection of the three half planes $Y \geqslant 0$, $1 - X \geqslant 0$ and $(X - Y)/\text{SQRT}(2.0) \geqslant 0$.

Hence in general taking the *minimum* of a set of functions gives the *intersection* of the set of regions which the functions define i.e. the logical *AND* of the regions. Similarly taking the *maximum* of a set of functions gives the *union* of the set of regions which the functions define, i.e. the logical *OR* of the regions.

The package contains three basic building blocks in the form of functions:

BLINE $(X, Y, X1, Y1, X2, Y2)$

This function is positive if (X, Y) is to the right of the line joining $(X1, Y1)$ to $(X2, Y2)$ in the direction from $(X1, Y1)$ to $(X2, Y2)$. The function is negative on the other side.

CIRC (X, Y, A, B, R)

This function is positive if (X, Y) is inside the circle centre (A, B) radius R and negative on the outside.

RECT $(X, Y, XMIN, XMAX, YMIN, YMAX)$

This function is positive if (X, Y) is inside the rectangle defined by the four lines $X = XMIN$, $X = XMAX$, $Y = YMIN$ and $Y = YMAX$, and negative if (X, Y) is outside this rectangle.

These three functions together with horizontal and vertical lines $A \pm X$, $B \pm Y$, have been found to be sufficient for users to construct the regions of their problems.

A subroutine which plots the user's boundary is provided to enable the boundary to be checked before execution. This is imperative where complicated boundaries are involved since frequently more than 20 FORTRAN statements are required. The boundary conditions must also be provided through a subroutine. The user can define "boundary values" over the whole region and then use them as the initial approximation for the iterative solution of the difference equations. For a pure Dirichlet problem, this initial approximation will be exact on the boundaries.

The user must also provide the permittivities/permeabilities of the material of his region. If the material is uniform, the permittivity may be scaled out of the differential equation, but its value is still required for the calculation of the flux density. If the problem has a non-zero right-hand side, the charge/current densities must be provided.

All these functions and values are written into one subroutine as in the example. This is the only piece of code that the user has to write. An example of this subroutine is given in Appendix 1.

For the data input, keywords and default options have been adopted. There are two reasons for this choice:

(1) The inexperienced user need only specify a small amount of data in order to obtain a solution to his problem, although this solution may not be the best he could get with more care over the data.

(2) The user may easily interpret his data by looking at his input file.

Default options have only been given to those data items which do not affect the specification of the problem. For example, the data which specifies the equation to be solved does not have a default option. Failure to read in any mandatory data will cause the run to terminate. An example of the data file is given in Appendix 2.

Note the question and answer appearance of the data. This makes it easy to have interactive data input using a separate program which sets up a data file and then checks its validity.

3. The Derivation of the Difference Equations

Since the difference equations are automatically set up, it is useful to formulate them in a manner which facilitates this process. To derive the finite difference replacement for either of the differential equations, we examine the integral forms of these equations.

Equation (1) is derived from Gauss' Law

$$\int_S \mathbf{D} \cdot \mathbf{n} \, dS = \int_V \rho \, dV$$

where S is a three-dimensional closed surface with volume V and unit outward normal $\mathbf{n}$. This equation can be written

$$\int_S \varepsilon \frac{\partial \phi}{\partial n} \, dS = - \int_V \rho \, dV. \tag{3}$$

We consider the rectangular cartesian case.

Consider a grid point P with all its six neighbours inside the region. Construct a rectangular parallelepiped made up of the perpendicular bisecting planes of the mesh lines joining P to these six neighbours, as in Fig. 2.

We approximate (3) on this shape. The grid lines divide the "cube" into eight parts and we assume that ε is constant in each "eighth" of the figure. This effectively replaces any interface by a step interface coinciding with the grid lines.

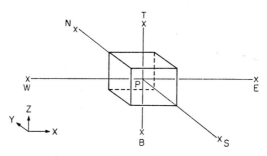

The contributions from the top and bottom faces are zero since the problem is two-dimensional. $(\partial\phi/\partial n)$ is taken as constant over each face and is approximated by a central difference. $\int_S \varepsilon \, dS$ is evaluated exactly.

The contribution from the eastern face is

$$\frac{\phi_E - \phi_P}{H_E} (\tfrac{1}{4}H_S H_B \varepsilon_{SBE} + \tfrac{1}{4}H_N H_B \varepsilon_{NBE} + \tfrac{1}{4}H_N H_T \varepsilon_{NTE} + \tfrac{1}{4}H_S H_T \varepsilon_{STE}).$$

The contributions from the western, northern and southern faces are respectively

$$\frac{\phi_W - \phi_P}{H_W} (\tfrac{1}{4}H_S H_B \varepsilon_{SBW} + \tfrac{1}{4}H_N H_B \varepsilon_{NBW} + \tfrac{1}{4}H_N H_T \varepsilon_{NTW} + \tfrac{1}{4}H_S H_T \varepsilon_{STW}),$$

$$\frac{\phi_N - \phi_P}{H_N} (\tfrac{1}{4}H_W H_B \varepsilon_{WBN} + \tfrac{1}{4}H_E H_B \varepsilon_{EBN} + \tfrac{1}{4}H_E H_T \varepsilon_{ETN} + \tfrac{1}{4}H_W H_T \varepsilon_{WTN})$$

and

$$\frac{\phi_S - \phi_P}{H_S} (\tfrac{1}{4}H_W H_B \varepsilon_{WBS} + \tfrac{1}{4}H_E H_B \varepsilon_{EBS} + \tfrac{1}{4}H_E H_T \varepsilon_{ETS} + \tfrac{1}{4}H_W H_T \varepsilon_{WTS}),$$

where

$$\varepsilon_{SBE} = \varepsilon(X_p + \tfrac{1}{2}H_E, \; Y_p - \tfrac{1}{2}H_s, \; Z_p - \tfrac{1}{2}H_B), \text{ etc.}$$

The contribution from the right-hand side is

$$-\rho_p \tfrac{1}{8}(H_N + H_s)(H_E + H_W)(H_B + H_T).$$

After some manipulation we arrive at the difference equation

$$\frac{\phi_E - \phi_P}{H_E} \tfrac{1}{2}(H_S \varepsilon_{SE} + H_N \varepsilon_{NE}) + \frac{\phi_W - \phi_P}{H_W} \tfrac{1}{2}(H_S \varepsilon_{SW} + H_N \varepsilon_{NW})$$

$$+ \frac{\phi_N - \phi_P}{H_N} \tfrac{1}{2}(H_W \varepsilon_{NW} + H_E \varepsilon_{NE}) + \frac{\phi_S - \phi_P}{H_S} \tfrac{1}{2}(H_W \varepsilon_{SW} + H_E \varepsilon_{SE})$$

$$= -\rho_P \tfrac{1}{4}(H_N + H_S)(H_E + H_W) \tag{4}$$

with the notation of Fig. 3.

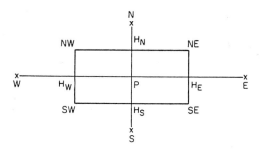

FIGURE 3

We could have derived (4) by reducing (3) to two dimensions, but we have retained the three-dimensional nature of the problem since this is necessary for (3) in cylindrical polars (see Varga, 1962).

Equation (2) is derived from Ampère's Law

$$\int_S \nabla \times \mathbf{H} \cdot \mathbf{n} \, dS = \int_S \mathbf{j} \cdot \mathbf{n} \, dS$$

where S is a two-dimensional surface with unit outward normal n, bounded by a curve C with target vector l. We can reduce this equation to

$$\int_C \frac{1}{\mu} \nabla \times A \cdot dl = \int_S \mathbf{j} \cdot \mathbf{n} \, dS. \tag{5}$$

Equation (5) is a vector equation but certain problems reduce to a single scalar equation. In rectangular cartesians we require $\mathbf{A}$ and $\mathbf{j}$ to have the forms $\mathbf{A} = (0, 0, \phi(X, Y))$ and $\mathbf{j} = (0, 0, j_z(X, Y))$ and in cylindrical polars, the forms $\mathbf{A} = (0, A_\theta(R, Z), 0)$ and $\mathbf{j} = (0, j_\theta(R, Z), 0)$. Then in each case (5) reduces to an equation similar to (3), which we can approximate in a similar manner.

This approach to deriving difference equations is similar to that of Wachspress (1966). He shows that the appropriate interface conditions are satisfied and that the truncation error of the difference equation is $O(h)$ for a non uniform mesh and $O(h^2)$ for a uniform mesh.

When the point P has one or more neighbours outside the region, we must modify the difference equation by eliminating the exterior point(s).

We consider the electrostatic (X, Y) case with ε a constant, since the devices employed are common to all eight equations and the extension to the case of ε variable is then obvious.

Case (1)   Dirichlet boundary condition

The point B in Fig. 4 is the boundary point on the grid line EP. We are given the solution ϕ_B at B. Hence we can eliminate ϕ_E from the difference equation by extrapolating a value at E using either the values at P and B, or the values at P, B and W (or the appropriate boundary value if W is outside the region). In the former case the equation becomes

$$\frac{\phi_N - \phi_P}{H_N}\tfrac{1}{2}(H_E + H_W) + \frac{\phi_S - \phi_P}{H_S}\tfrac{1}{2}(H_E + H_W) + \frac{\phi_B - \phi_P}{H_B}\tfrac{1}{2}(H_N + H_S)$$

$$+ \frac{\phi_W - \phi_P}{H_W}\tfrac{1}{2}(H_N + H_S) = -\rho_P\tfrac{1}{4}(H_N + H_S)(H_E + H_W)$$

and in the latter case

$$\frac{\phi_N - \phi_P}{H_N}\tfrac{1}{2}(H_B + H_W) + \frac{\phi_S - \phi_P}{H_S}\tfrac{1}{2}(H_B + H_W) + \frac{\phi_B - \phi_P}{H_B}\tfrac{1}{2}(H_N + H_S)$$

$$+ \frac{\phi_W - \phi_P}{H_W}\tfrac{1}{2}(H_N + H_S) = -\rho_P\tfrac{1}{4}(H_N + H_S)(H_B + H_W).$$

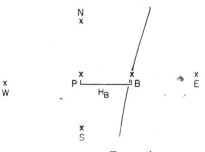

FIGURE 4

Diagrammatically, we are evaluating (3) on the flux-boxes shown in Figs 5 and 6. The term "flux-box" is used since the left hand side of the difference equation is the total flux out of the box.

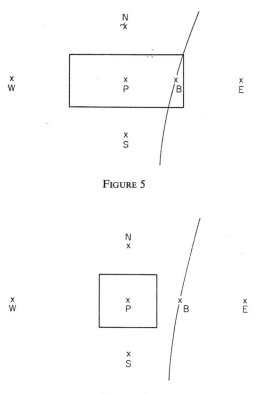

FIGURE 5

FIGURE 6

In the first case the flux box is the same as if P and its four neighbours were inside, but the term $(\phi_E - \phi_p)/H_E$ is replaced by $(\phi_B - \phi_p)/H_B$.

In the second case the flux box is adjusted so that the eastern side is the perpendicular bisector of the line PB.

In the first case there is flux conservation across all sides of flux boxes which are shared by adjacent boxes. Hence the matrix of difference equations is symmetric. In the second case any curvature of the boundary will destroy flux conservation across for example, the northern side of the flux box in Fig. 6. The matrix of difference equations will only be "almost symmetric" but the local truncation error will be at least $O(h)$ at all interior grid points. (We have used this formulation in POTENT).

Case (2)   Neumann boundary condition

Now, we only know the outward normal derivative of the solution at the point B, $(\partial\phi_B/\partial n)$. We deform the flux box so that it is made up of the same northern, western and southern boundaries and some approximation to the tangent at B. We approximate the slope of the tangent by evaluating the boundary intersections of the lines NE and SE in Fig. 7. Evaluating (3) on this flux-box the difference equation is

$$\frac{\phi_N - \phi_P}{H_N} L_N + \frac{\partial\phi_B}{\partial n} L_B + \frac{\phi_S - \phi_P}{H_S} L_S + \frac{\phi_W - \phi_P}{H_W} L_W = -\rho_p A$$

where L_N, L_B, L_S and L_W are the lengths of the sides of the flux box, corresponding to the points N, B, S and W respectively, and A is the area of the flux box.

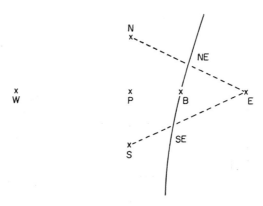

FIGURE 7

Case (3)   Radiative boundary condition

In this case we know a linear relation between the solution and the outward normal derivative at B i.e. $(\partial\phi_B/\partial n) = f_B - \sigma_B \phi_B$. Writing the boundary condition in this form we can treat it as a Neumann condition if we can obtain a value for ϕ_B. This we do by extrapolating from ϕ_p and ϕ_W. The difference equation becomes

$$\frac{\phi_W - \phi_P}{H_W} L_W + \frac{\phi_N - \phi_P}{H_N} L_N + \frac{\phi_S - \phi_P}{H_S} L_S$$

$$+ \left[f_B - \sigma_B \phi_p + \sigma_B \frac{\phi_W - \phi_P}{H_W} H_B \right] L_B = -\rho_p A.$$

We now have the procedure for setting up the difference equation.

If the point P is a distance greater than $\sqrt{2} \times$ maximum mesh length, then all its 4 neighbours are inside the boundary and the difference equation is given by (4).

If P is nearer the boundary, then some of its neighbours may be outside. Each neighbour is examined in turn. If a neighbour is outside, the intervening boundary intersection is computed, together with its boundary condition. If an exterior neighbour corresponds to a derivative boundary condition then the slope of the tangent is computed. Interior and exterior (Dirichlet) neighbours give horizontal or vertical sides to the flux box. If all exterior neighbours correspond to Dirichlet boundary conditions, the difference equation is given by (4) with adjusted mesh lengths. Otherwise we compute the flux out of the flux box.

The matrix of difference coefficients is of the usual five diagonal form. It is symmetric if all boundaries are parallel to the grid lines, with Dirichlet or Neumann boundary conditions but not if there is a radiative boundary condition. If we have a pure Dirichlet problem with curved boundaries we can make the matrix symmetric as shown above. However, Neumann boundary conditions on a curved boundary give a non-symmetric matrix.

In all cases, the matrix is strictly diagonally dominant with non-negative, off-diagonal, elements and negative diagonal elements. Convergence of the point Jacobi and Gauss–Seidel methods for this type of equation has been proved, see Varga (1962). For curved boundaries, the matrix is "almost symmetric". Theoretical work on matrices of this type has been done by Ostrowski (1954), Stein (1951) and Brenner and de Pillis (1972).

We solve the set of equations by one of three iterative methods; alternating Direction Implicit (ADI), Successive Overrelaxation (SOR) or Successive Line Overrelaxation (SLOR). SLOR is the default. We choose iterative methods because

(1) They are easy to program, e.g. SOR is one FORTRAN statement inside a double *DO* loop.

(2) The matrix of coefficients can be stored as five vectors.

(3) Advantage can be taken of solutions to previous similar problems by using them as initial approximations to the iteration.

For SOR and SLOR the user can provide a value for ω, the overrelaxation parameter, or use the default. The default is the value for the Dirichlet problem in a rectangle with the same number of x and y grid spacings. We do not dynamically compute ω since (1) the time taken to solve the equations is a relatively small part of a typical run ($\sim\frac{1}{4}$) and (2) the matrix may not be symmetric, in which case dynamic computation could be quite involved. A value of 1·9 for a 50×50 problem using a crude initial approximation gives acceptable convergence in less than 200 iterations in most cases.

Similarly, the user has a default value for the ADI parameters. We compute the minimum and maximum eigenvalues of the matrices H and V for the same model problem. H and V are the contributions to the matrix from the horizontal and vertical derivatives respectively. A sequence of iteration parameters is computed using Wachspress' algorithm when the number of parameters is a power of 2. The user can specify the length of sequence.

In our experience, one of these three methods is always suitable for a given problem. SOR and SLOR always perform satisfactorily. ADI is rather inconsistent in that it either converges rapidly in less than 50 iterations or does not converge at all.

4. The Computation of the Field Vector

As such, the potential matrix is not particularly useful to the engineer. He wants to know the field (E or H) and the flux density (D or B) in his configuration.

The method of setting up the difference equations gives a method for computing the field at points inside the boundary. Taking a weighted mean of the divided differences evaluated on opposite sides of the flux box we have

$$\frac{\partial \phi}{\partial X} = \frac{H_W\left(\dfrac{\phi_E - \phi_P}{H_E}\right) + H_E\left(\dfrac{\phi_P - \phi_W}{H_W}\right)}{H_E + H_W}$$

$$\frac{\partial \phi}{\partial Y} = \frac{H_S\left(\dfrac{\phi_N - \phi_P}{H_N}\right) + H_N\left(\dfrac{\phi_P - \phi_S}{H_S}\right)}{H_N + H_S} \cdot$$

However, on the boundary the point at which we are evaluating derivatives does not have four neighbours.

Several courses of action are open.

(1) Take two-sided derivatives wherever possible and one-sided derivatives otherwise.

(2) Take two-sided derivatives wherever possible and fit a one-sided quadratic otherwise. In Fig. 8 a two-sided quadratic would be fitted at point 2 and a one-sided quadratic at point 3. This is described by Scott et al. (1972).

(3) Fit harmonic polynomials over the grid. Winslow (1967) does this on a triangular grid.

(4) Take two-sided derivatives wherever possible and at grid points the boundary use extra boundary information and the differential equation to give two-sided derivatives.

FIGURE 8

We outline the fourth approach.

Case (1) *Grid point on boundary with Dirichlet boundary condition and one exterior neighbour* (*Fig.* 9)

Applying the differenced form of the differential equation at the boundary point gives a value at the exterior point in terms of the values at the four other interior points. We then use two-sided differences for both derivatives.

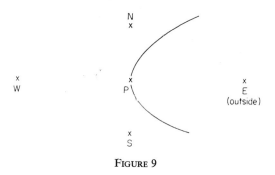

FIGURE 9

Case (2) *Grid point on boundary with Dirichlet boundary condition and two exterior neighbours* (*Fig.* 10)

Applying the difference equation at the boundary point introduces two un-known values. However, a second equation is given by evaluating the tan-gential derivative at the boundary point using the boundary values at the points *NE* and *SW* in Fig. 10. We then have two equations in two unknowns.

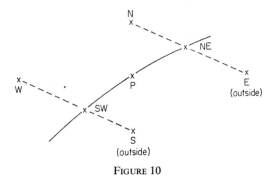

FIGURE 10

Case (3)   *Grid point on boundary with Dirichlet boundary condition and three exterior neighbours (Fig. 11)*

This case only rarely occurs, e.g. a horizontal grid line passing through the centre of a circle, meeting a vertical line tangential to the circle. Here we have resorted to known properties of the solution in order to compute the field. If the boundary is a conductor, all the tangential derivatives of the potential are zero at the boundary. Hence in Fig. 11, the vertical derivative is zero and the horizontal derivative can be evaluated as in Case (1).

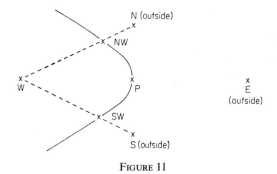

FIGURE 11

If the boundary is not a conductor, we evaluate the tangential derivative by introducing the boundary points *NW* and *SW* in Fig. 11. We then evaluate the horizontal derivative as in Case (1). Similar approaches are used to evaluate the field when Neumann boundary conditions occur.

5. Portability of POTENT

Although POTENT is aimed at electric and magnetic field problems, it can be easily adapted to solve other problems. Since we have included the radiative boundary condition the steady heat conduction equation is an obvious candidate. We merely need to redefine the permittivity of free space ε_0, and then treat the problem as electrostatic.

The package is written in modular form so equations further removed from electric and magnetic can be solved if a routine which calculates the difference equation is provided.

The Culham version of POTENT runs on an ICL 4–70 under the Multijob Operating System. With a 50×50 grid, the program is segmented and requires $150k$ bytes of core store. A typical run, computing the potential and flux density on a 50×50 grid and producing contours of the potential and flux density takes five minutes. The graphical output routines are a subset of the Culham graphical output system GHOST, (Prior, 1971). The output is produced on a CI120 microfilm recorder. Again, the modularity of the package allows these graphical routines to be substituted on other systems.

6. Experience with a Sample Problem

We give examples of the effect of variable permittivity, variable mesh, shape of boundary and value of boundary condition on the performance of the three iterative methods as implemented in POTENT.

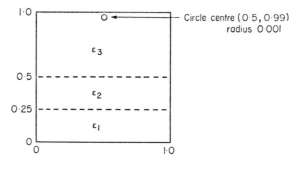

FIGURE 12

We solve (1) inside the region in Fig. 12 with various choices of permittivity, grid and boundary value. The charge density ρ is set equal to zero.

Test 1 A square 50×50 grid is used with $\varepsilon_1 = \varepsilon_2 = \varepsilon_3 = 1$. The boundary values are set equal to zero. Hence the solution is identically zero. The initial approximation is set equal to 1 everywhere.

None of the grid lines intersect the circle, so the algorithm for setting up the difference equations does not detect the circle. Hence this is the model problem. The results are shown in Table 1.

In each case the iteration is stopped when the maximum residual is less than 10^{-4}. The maximum error in the solution is always less than 10^{-6}. Since this is the model problem, the package chooses the optimum iteration parameter(s) for each method. The overrelaxation parameter ω is 1·88.

TABLE 1.

Method	No. of iterations	Maximum initial residual (IR)	Maximum final residual (FR)	Time (secs)	Efficiency = LN(IR/FR)/time
ADI	20	$6·0 \times 10^2$	$3·6 \times 10^{-7}$	31	0·685
SOR	150	$6·0 \times 10^2$	$7·5 \times 10^{-5}$	61	0·261
SLOR	145	$6·0 \times 10^2$	$9·9 \times 10^{-5}$	100	0·156

Test 2 This is the same as Test 1 except that $\varepsilon_1 = 1$, $\varepsilon_2 = 2$ and $\varepsilon_3 = 4$. The results are shown in Table 2. The iterations are stopped at the same point as before and the error is of the same order. The model problem parameters are again chosen. It is seen that whereas ADI is considerably effected by the variable permittivity, SOR and SLOR perform almost exactly the same as for Test 1.

TABLE 2.

Method	No. of iterations	Maximum initial residual (IR)	Maximum final residual (FR)	Time (sec)	Efficiency = LN(IR/FR)/time
ADI	60	$6·0 \times 10^2$	$3·6 \times 10^{-5}$	94	0·177
SOR	150	$6·0 \times 10^2$	$9·5 \times 10^{-5}$	64	0·245
SLOR	145	$6·0 \times 10^2$	$7·3 \times 10^{-5}$	100	0·159

Test 3 We take advantage of the variable mesh to concentrate mesh points around the circle. We make grid lines intersect the circle so the difference equation setting-up algorithm detects the circle. Otherwise this is the same as Test 2. The results are given in Table 3. Stopping criteria and maximum error are as before. Using the model problem parameters ADI and SLOR converge in a tolerable number of iterations but SOR still has not converged to the required residual after 1000 iterations. SOR would however achieve satisfactory convergence if run sufficiently long. Rerunning SOR with optimum $\omega (= 1·95)$, the efficiency becomes better than that of ADI.

Test 4 We go a step further than Test 3 and set the boundary value on the circle equal to 1. Hence it is imperative to concentrate mesh points in the narrow region since there is now a non-zero field between the circle and the rectangle. A smooth initial approximation is used. The results are given in Table 4. Guided by our experience with Test 3 we use $\omega = 1.88$ with SLOR and $\omega = 1.95$ with SOR. The residual will not reduce below the figures shown. ADI reduces the residual rapidly to 4·6 but the residual oscillates about this value thereafter. This has been our experience with all problems where ADI would not converge.

TABLE 3.

Method	No. of iterations	Maximum initial residual (IR)	Maximum final residual (FR)	Time (sec)	Efficiency = LN(IR/FR)/time
ADI	185	7.4×10^4	8.0×10^{-5}	277	0·075
SOR ($\omega = 1.88$)	1000	7.4×10^4	1.6×10^{-2}	388	0·012
SOR ($\omega = 1.95$)	555	7.4×10^4	8.8×10^{-5}	215	0·096
SLOR ($\omega = 1.88$)	160	7.4×10^4	5.3×10^{-5}	105	0·201

TABLE 4.

Method	No. of iterations	Maximum initial residual (IR)	Maximum final residual (FR)	Time (sec)	Efficiency = LN(IR/FR)/time
SLOR ($\omega = 1.88$)	90	3.2×10^3	8.9×10^{-2}	60	0·175
SOR ($\omega = 1.95$)	270	3.2×10^3	8.7×10^{-2}	105	0·100
SLOR ($\omega = 1.95$)	240	3.2×10^3	9.9×10^{-2}	158	0·066

The variable mesh used in Tests 3 and 4 is:

Along X-axis

14×0.03, 2×0.02, 1×0.014, 1×0.01, 1×0.008, 1×0.004, 1×0.002, 1×0.001, 4×0.0005, 1×0.001, 1×0.002, 1×0.004, 1×0.008, 1×0.01, 1×0.014, 2×0.02 and 14×0.03.

Along Y-axis

38×0.025, 1×0.02, 1×0.01, 1×0.005, 1×0.003 and 6×0.002.

These four tests indicate the wide range of performance of the three methods. They show that we can rely on at least one of the methods working even in the pathological tests 3 and 4.

In general, users have found that SLOR works most satisfactory and hence this is the method most frequently used. As we see above ADI either works extremely well or not at all. It is included in the package primarily for numerical interest, but several users have obtained acceptable results with the method.

Conclusion

A powerful aid to the design and analysis of two-dimensional electric and magnetic fields has been produced. Fields can be computed in a general region in an acceptable amount of computer time, with comparatively little effort on the user's behalf. Iterative methods of solution of the difference equations are quite suitable and at least one of ADI, SOR and SLOR converges satisfactorily for most problems. The package is easily adapted to solve other equations.

Acknowledgements

The author would like to acknowledge the work of B. Allen who devised the first version of the package, in a rather different form on KDF9, and also the work of H. Salwan and J. Phillpott who made improvements to that version. The author would also like to thank his colleagues of the Computing and Applied Mathematics Group of Culham Laboratory for their help and encouragement during this project.

References

Varga, R. S. (1962). "Matrix Iterative Analysis". Prentice-Hall, Englewood Cliffs, New Jersey.

Wachspress, E. L. (1966). "Iterative Solution of Elliptic Difference Equations". Prentice–Hall, Englewood Cliffs, New Jersey.

Ostrowski, A. M. (1954). On the linear iteration procedures for symmetric matrices. *Rend. Mat. e. Appl.* **14,** 140–163.

Stein, P. (1951). The convergence of Seidel iterants of nearly symmetric matrices. *MTAC* **5,** 237–240.

Brenner, J. L. and de Pillis, J. (1972). Partitioned matrices and Seidel convergence. *Num. Math.* **19,** 76–80.

Winslow, A. M. (1967). Numerical solution of the quasi-linear Poisson equation in a non-uniform triangle mesh. *J. Comp. P.* **2,** 149–172

Scott, M. F., *et al.* (1972). Computation of electric fields. Recent developments and practical applications. *In* "Proceedings of the International Symposium on High Voltage Technology, " Technical University Munich, pp 52–58.

Prior, W. A. J. (1971). "The GHOST Graphical Output System User Manual" Culham Laboratory Report CLM PDN 8/71.

Appendix 1. Example of Subroutine FUNC

```
      SUBROUTINE FUNC(I, X, Y, F)

C
C                     THE COMMON BLOCK CONTAINS ALL THE DATA
C                     FOR THE ROUTINE
      COMMON/DATA/VALUE(10), ITYPE(10), PERM(10), RHS(10),
     1    SURF(10), PARAM(100), NV, NT, NP, NR, NS, NM
C
C                     THE COMPUTED GOTO DETERMINES WHICH
C                     FUNCTION IS EVALUATED
C
      GO TO  (1, 2, 3, 3, 6, 4, 6), I
C
C                     THE DOMAIN OF THE PROBLEM IS A
C                     RECTANGLE WHICH WILL NOT BE CHANGED
C                     IN FURTHER RUNS. THE PARAMETERS
C                     DEFINING THE REGION HAVE BEEN SET
C                     CONSTANT
    1    F=RECT(X, Y, 0.0, 10.0, 0.0, 10.0)
      GO TO 3
C     - - - - -
C

C
C                     THE PROBLEM IS DIRICHLET WITH A
C                     BOUNDARY VALUE TO BE READ IN
    2 N=ITYPE(1)
      F=VALUE(1)
      GO TO 3
C
C     - - - - -
C                     THE MATERIAL INTERFACE IS A FIXED
C                     RECTANGLE
    4 RECT4=RECT(X, Y, 2.0, 8.0, 2.0, 3.0)
      IF(I-7)43, 7, 43
C
C                     THE RELATIVE PERMEABILITIES ARE
C                     PERM(1) OUTSIDE RECT4 AND PERM(2)
C                     INSIDE
   43 IF(RECT4) 41, 42, 42
   41    F=PERM(1)
         GO TO 3
C     - - - - - -
   42    F=PERM(2)
      GO TO 3
      - - - - - -
C
C                     WHEN I=7 F HAS THE VALUE OF THE
C                     REGION WITH RELATIVE PERMEABILITY
C                     NOT EQUAL TO 1. THIS ENABLES THE
C                     INTERFACE TO BE DRAWN ON THE
C                     GRAPHICAL OUTPUT
    7    F=RECT4
      GO TO 3
```

Appendix 1—*continued*

```
C       - - - - -
C
C                         THE REGIONS WITH NON-ZERO CURRENT
C                         DENSITY ARE FIXED RECTANGLES
C
    6      RECT2=RECT(X, Y, 4.0, 6.0, 7.0, 9.0)
           RECT3=RECT(X, Y, 3.0, 7.0, 4.0, 6.0)
         IF(I-8)65, 8, 65
C
C                         THE CURRENT DENSITIES ARE RHS(2)
C                         INSIDE RECT2, RHS(3) INSIDE RECT3
C                         AND RHS(1) ELSEWHERE
   65 IF(RECT2)61, 62, 62,
   62      F=RHS(2)
         GO TO 3
C       - - - - - -
   61 IF(RECT3)63, 64, 64,
           F=RHS(3)
         GO TO 3
C       - - - - -
   63      F=RHS(1)
         GO TO 3
C       - - - - - -
C
C                         WHEN I=8 HAS THE VALUE OF THE REGION
C                         WITH NON-ZERO CURRENT DENSITY
C
C
    8      F=AMAX1(RECT2, RECT3)
    3 RETURN
      END
```

Appendix 2. Example of Input File

```
MAJORRAD
5.0
ZMIN
0.0
ZMAX
10.0
RMIN
0.0
NRSPACES
49
RSPACES
0.6 0.5 0.5 0.3 0.1 0.1 0.1 0.1 0.1 0.1 0.1 0.1 0.1 0.1 0.1 0.1
0.2 0.4 0.2 0.2 0.2 0.2 0.2 0.2 0.2 0.2 0.2 0.2 0.2 0.2
0.2 0.4 0.2 0.2 0.2 0.2 0.2 0.2 0.2 0.2 0.2 0.2
0.2 0.3 0.4
PROBLEM
MAGNETIC
EQUATION
```

Appendix 2—*continued.*

```
POISSON
SYMMETRY
NONE
INAPPROX
FUNCTION
2
NVALUES
1
BVALUES
0.0
NTYPES
1
BVTYPES
1
NPERMS
2
PERMS
1.0 1000.0
NBPARAMS
0
NRSIDES
3
RHSIDES
0.0 200000.0 300000.0
GRAPHICS
END
```

This data file inputs the following information to the program.

(1) The equation to be solved is the magnetic case of Poisson's equation in (r, z) coordinates, where r is measured from a point five units along the r axis.

(2) The grid in the z direction consists of the default number of points, 50, equi-spaced between $z = 0$ and $z = 10$.

(3) The grid in the r direction starts at $r = 0$ and consists of the 49 spaces indicated after 'RSPACES'.

(4) There are no symmetry conditions.

(5) The initial approximation is taken from the user's routine FUNC with $I = 2$.

(6) There is only one boundary value i.e. the Dirichlet condition $\phi = 0$.

(7) There are two relative permeabilities—1000 in the iron and 1 elsewhere.

(8) There is no adjustable boundary data i.e. this is a one off job as far as the shape of the region is concerned, or the user is prepared to recompile FUNC and recompose the program if he wants a different shape region.

(9) There are three current densities in the region.

(10) The user wants the default for graphical output i.e. 21 contours of the solution, equispaced between the minimum and the maximum values of the solution.

Other default options are: the iterative method is SLOR, a maximum of 200 iterations, a maximum absolute value of the residual of 10^{-4}, the over-relaxation factor of the model problem with the same number of grid points in the mesh rectangle.

19. A New Scheme for Interactive Numerical Computation

D. HUTCHINSON AND P. JESTY†

Centre for Computer Studies,
University of Leeds, Leeds, England.

1. Introduction

A review of the developments of computing facilities over the last fifteen years suggests that the user with large numerical computations is particularly well favoured, both in the scale of problem possible and speed of solution: the developments clearly involve both hardware and software. Facilities for performing short computations have also improved, especially for the non-programmer, notably by the provision of on-line terminal systems with associated interactive language schemes. Many such schemes are little used because of their relative inconvenience or poor response, but this type of computer use must grow with the increasing popularity of terminal systems.

The design of a language may proceed in one of two ways, either by careful formulation of the objectives, bearing in mind both the performance criteria and the typical user, or by meeting immediate requirements and allowing the language to grow in response to later demands. These approaches may be exemplified by ALGOL 60 and FORTRAN, respectively, though the objectives are not too precise in either case. Since detailed design criteria are seldom discussed it is necessary to devote some time to them in this paper, and to show how the design of STEFAN follows from them. A passing look is taken at a number of existing languages which evidently have the same or similar design objectives.

Before considering the particular design features of any language for solving numerical problems it is as well to recognize that a user's objective may be primarily:

   (i) to obtain numerical results,
   (ii) to obtain a tested numerical algorithm,
   (iii) to perform numerical analysis, or
   (iv) a combination of these.

† Formerly Leeds Polytechnic, Leeds.

Systems have been produced for numerical analysis, such as NAPSS due to Symes and Roman (1969), but will not be discussed further here. The former common objectives may also be qualified by associating with them the problem characteristics. For example, the numerical results required may be new, verifiable, or already available, and we may range from a one-off calculation with few results to repeated calculations with extensive tabulated results: again, a required algorithm may be new, a modification of an existing one, or be already published, and the algorithm may be special or general purpose, intended for either local or universal use. This classification is only outlined here but is easily refined. The design objectives should be given an order of priority since compromise is usually involved.

2. Remarks on On-Line Terminal Systems

2.1. *Language/System Objectives*

It is convenient to distinguish between

   (i) on-line calculating,
   (ii) on-line program development,
   (iii) batch processing,

and it is our intention to identify the desirable features of a language/system designed for each of the first two categories. STEFAN is designed to facilitate both these modes of operation, though only the most noteworthy features of STEFAN are mentioned. Nearly every language/system can be employed at each of the three levels, though with varying degrees of efficiency: the on-line calculating systems have normally been expanded to provide greater sophistication, whereas batch processing systems have been extended at the simpler, calculator level. The design priorities for STEFAN are to provide firstly an efficient calculator facility, secondly efficient program development, and finally an efficient batch processing mode. If a user's objective is an algorithm he will be primarily interested in program development; if his objective is numerical results then, depending on the scale of the problem he will be interested in the calculator facility or batch processing (probably with program development).

2.2. *Interactive and Conversational Language/Systems*

The terms *interactive* and *conversational* are adjectives commonly applied to on-line languages or systems, but it is difficult to separate facilities in a language from the system itself. Hence the use of either word is highly subjective, and a strict general definition of interactive, say, is virtually impossible. A satisfactory definition should certainly include and exclude those systems about which there is no ambiguity: it is pertinent therefore to list a number of features:

necessary   (i) program initiated interrupts
                (ii) run-time text modification
                (iii) immediate execution of non-storable statements

desirable   (i) rapid response
              (ii) error messages
              (iii) easy language
              (iv) file storage and handling.

But if we consider just one feature, say rapid response, a delay of one minute to invert a matrix of order 1000 may be acceptable but if the order is only 3 the user may take a different view; moreover, the user's attitude will vary with the power of the system. In considering STEFAN we shall be concerned primarily with the language, but comments on other languages will frequently refer to a specific system implementation.

3. Design Objectives and Associated Characteristics of a Language

3.1. *On-Line Calculating*

We may assume the existence of a suitable computer system, though this may range from a mini-computer with a typewriter input/output to a sophisticated terminal system with associated software. In designing the syntax and semantics of a language for on-line calculating (direct arithmetic operations) the following general features are desirable:

    (i) very easy language with natural presentation of arithmetic expressions,
    (ii) simple, brief documentation,
    (iii) immediate computation of small units, e.g. one expression or one line,
    (iv) minimum input (key depressions), minimum obligatory output,
    (v) fast system response,
    (vi) good testing facilities, preferably immediate and transient,
    (vii) easy correction, including aborting of current characters, expressions and lines,
    (viii) emergency exit to environmental system, on normal input and during execution.

These requirements may be most easily met by designing the language to have a short formal definition, and providing an interpreter mode of operation with associated syntax analysis which functions on single expressions, statements or lines. Efficient input/output will be of particular interest to occasional, "non-programmer" users.

3.2. On-Line Program Development

Every high level language is claimed to be designed for easy program development (i.e. the production of valid and relevant algebraic statements) though normally through batch working. Again, without exhaustive discussion we may list desirable features of a language for which this is the main objective:

    (i) clear, well defined language,
    (ii) program storage facility, in small and large units, e.g. expressions, lines, blocks,
    (iii) immediate syntax analysis of recognized units, including small units contained in larger ones, e.g. expressions within loops,
    (iv) good testing facilities, preferably immediate and transient,
    (v) good diagnostics on syntax analysis and execution,
    (vi) text modification and a file storage system,
    (vii) a modular language with proper subsets excluding the more sophisticated language facilities.

These design features are assumed to be quite familiar and point to the advantages of a formal language definition with a nested modular structure. The latter permits the progressive learning of the language through proper inclusive subsets or modules with progressive documentation; the program developer may operate at his own level of sophistication. Interpretive mode is again desirable, and the immediate testing facility is easily met by the provision of a calculator facility in the innermost module.

3.3. Batch Processing

Little need be said here except that good diagnostics and efficient computation are often provided by a compromise between the compile and execution times. The diagnostics should be particularly related to run-time errors. Good batch processing systems normally include a wide range of extra or library facilities for such operations as double length working, matrix manipulation or file editing. If rapid program development is also a design objective we have a compromise with the conclusions in the previous section.

3.4. Summary

We can limit design objectives to any one of the three categories above, though concentrating on an efficient compiler for batch processing would be in the knowledge that a distinct program developing system exists or that adequate programs are already developed. Again, the user of a calculator may frequently wish for a smooth transition from spontaneous to prepared and routine calculations performed by a standard program. This is best provided by a single modular interpretive-type system.

Factors such as key depressions in assessing the convenience and efficiency of a calculator facility appear trivial but experience has shown that they do influence the novice who is no expert typist. A formal language is a considerable advantage in simplifying documentation and providing a readily comprehensible modular system.

4. A Consideration of Existing Languages

4.1. *Introduction*

There is no attempt here to present an exhaustive list of languages with a definitive classification, though a more detailed study is given elsewhere (Hutchinson and Jesty, 1973). We distinguish broadly between those languages designed primarily for on-line calculating (usually extended into conventional high level languages) and those for on-line program development (often extended to give a calculator facility).

Any language which includes arithmetic operators, ranging from machine code to the highest level, can be implemented to give a calculator facility; even at the upper end it simply requires an interpreter or fast load-and-go mode, such as the Waterloo University WATFOR load-and-go FORTRAN, or ICL 1900 series conversational FORTRAN.

All languages have some form of stored program mode and text modification, though of varying efficiency; at one extreme we have on-line text editing and at the other the correcting of a program in binary on paper tape. However, we shall reserve the description "stored program mode" for systems permitting the internal storage of more than one line of text. Thus efficient program development may be equally possible on a conversational system or on a fast load-and-go system: the conversational language is the important feature of the former and the computer system the important feature of the latter.

4.2. *Languages Designed Essentially for Efficient On-Line Arithmetic*

There are few languages which fall clearly into this category, and the design is heavily influenced by the system environment. The language WORKSHOP developed by M. H. Beilby at the University of Birmingham operates on the small ICL 1900 series machines, normally on the single on-line terminal. Honeywell's ABACUS, the University of Leeds' FRED, and the language CALC developed by Rolls Royce at the Bristol Engine Division all assume the existence of a terminal system—the latter two use distinct systems on ICL KDF9 computer installations.

All these languages exhibit the majority of the desirable features quoted in Section 3.1; nevertheless it is interesting to consider a number of differences. CALC meets the specific design objective of providing the facility of a straightforward desk calculator, and apart from the provision of twenty-one storage registers (already labelled) does *not* provide a stored program mode—nor is there a direct loop command say for the production of numerical tables. ABACUS and WORKSHOP do provide a stored program mode of simple form, but FRED extends to an ALGOL-like language, which includes such facilities as Booleans, procedures, and file handling; loops are readily achieved in these three languages. In each case the basic unit for direct evaluation is the expression, but only CALC provides a formal definition. Similar care is taken in CALC (and in FRED) over detailing number range and precision in arithmetic operations, and providing for appropriate output. The result is good documentation. Documentation on ABACUS is too brief, with many questions unanswered; WORKSHOP and FRED suffer mainly from the embellishment of extended languages such as FORTRAN, and documentation is a mixture of definition and illustration.

Time spent on input and output is most important, especially where other users are affected—waiting for access to the computer in the case of WORK-SHOP!. WORKSHOP uses a command word syntax for arithmetic which increases the necessary input. Immediate evaluation of expressions in all but WORKSHOP is initiated by a single character, but WORKSHOP requires the command RUN (and the expression is preceded by PRINT). Diagnostics are relatively verbose in WORKSHOP, e.g. LNE TOO LNG is the mnemonic for too many characters on a line, whereas CALC prints ? and rejects the line. FRED would print, say, F5 and ABACUS prints INPUT ERROR with ↑ pointing to the approximate location of the error.

```
>  £AAA001  cr.lf.
>  CALCULATE  G=2*7  -  4*6
>  WHERE  A  =  2
>  WHERE  B  =  4
>  WHERE  C  =  5
>  WHERE  D  =  6
>  PRINT  (C*7  -  B*8)/G
>  RUN
- .300000000000
>  PRINT  (A*8  -  C*D)/G
>  RUN
1 .40000000000
>
```

FIG. 1. Illustration of WORKSHOP.

```
**!
CALLF←
2.3 * SIN(PI/3) + 5←
        6.991858
43 - 6.7₁₀2/56 $>A ←
        23.89*A←
        741.443214
!PROCEDURE P:
A*B + 1$>C; SQRT(C↑3)$>X;
!EXIT←
3$>A; 4$>B; !DO P←
X←
        46.872167
2$>A;  !DO P; X←
        27.000000
!←
```

FIG. 2. Illustration of FRED.

In general, diagnostics are related to stored program mode, only FRED distinguishing carefully between input mode and execution. Facilities for altering characters and lines on input are also variable, but potentially important to the novice.

Of the many restrictions and idiosyncrasies, the most useful are:

(i) the use of $ and > to insert into, or extract numbers from, the nesting store in FRED;

(ii) the use of pre-named registers in CALC with a similar effect.

In contrast, variables in ABACUS are restricted to a maximum of three characters and they must not form command words in ABACUS or the language BASIC! WORKSHOP produces a paper tape record of a calculation as well as the over-detailed teletype record.

Finally, the quality of documentation must influence the judgement of a language as an effective tool; nevertheless FRED has clear advantages over the other three.

4.3. *Languages Designed Essentially for Prepared Calculations and Efficient On-Line Program Development*

If we accept that prepared calculations may require—or benefit from—more powerful language facilities than spontaneous calculations, then we can appropriately relegate languages such as the ICL 1900 series JEAN, or the Four PI Corporations CALCTRAN to the present section, even though their "calculator" facility is usually emphasised. The user will now be prepared to learn a more sophisticated language, and anticipate that conventional program development may be necessary; he will therefore appreciate conversational mode. The Rand Corporation's JOSS is similar to JEAN, and we may also include in this section the very powerful POP 2 developed at Edinburgh University. At the other end of the scale is the less well known FOCAL developed by J. W. Elder and co-workers at Cambridge University for their TSS/8 computer. These languages are all thoroughly documented but only POP 2 is expressed with the conciseness and intelligibility that seems to come from a formally defined grammar. The others have a command structure; for example in JEAN a command has the form:

	Verb	Predicate	Modifying Clause
e.g.	TYPE	X, SQRT(X)	IN FORM 3 FOR X = 1(1) 10

The command-type language is easy to extend by introducing new categories of command word whereas the formally defined language can have a modular development or simply have an associated library. The actual design objectives and necessary compromises are spelt out most clearly in the case of POP 2: the claims that the other languages were aimed primarily at a calculator facility is not accepted here.

These languages all meet a majority of the requirements for on-line program development, existing as, or within, conversational systems. It is not appropriate to discuss in detail their many differences, but one or two comments are in order. CALCTRAN has indeed a concise calculator facility, but the user is overburdened with options (languages in the previous section include about a dozen standard functions; CALCTRAN provides twenty-five trigonometric functions alone, and they are defined for complex arguments).

```
←  *THIS LINE IS IGNORED
←  TYPE 5+7, 2*10, [7.1+COS(PI/3)*2]
         5+7 = 12
         2*10= 20
         [7.1+COS(PI/3)*2]  = 8.1
←  SET  A = 2
←  SET  B = 8
←  SET  C = 19*A+B
←  TYPE C+12
         C+12  = 58
←  LET F(X)  = SIN(X)/COS(X)
←  TYPE F(1.27)
         F(1.27)  = 3.22363319
←  *NOTE THAT LET ESTABLISHES A FORMULA
```

FIG. 3. Illustration of JEAN.

```
11.0 + 5₁o3 ⇒
** 5011.0
VARS X1 X2;
5 → X1;  10 → X2;
X1↑2 + X2↑2 ⇒
**125
2+4, 5*6, SQRT(9) ⇒
**6, 30, 3
FUNCTION ROOTS A B C;
VARS P Q;
-B/(2*A)→P;
(SQRT(B↑2 - 4*A*C))/(2*A) →Q;
P+Q, P-Q
END;
ROOTS(1 -2 1) ⇒
** 1,1
```

FIG. 4. Illustration of POP2.

The calculator facilities of JEAN and to a lesser degree FOCAL have the verbosity of WORKSHOP: expressions preceded by TYPE in JEAN are copied out again as text followed in each case by their value after an equals sign; in both languages assignment statements are preceded by SET. However, FOCAL was actually designed to introduce numerically oriented users to the computer at an elementary level, and is certainly suitable for this purpose; CALCTRAN and JEAN successfully meet this particularly objective also. POP 2, like FRED, is a procedural language and embodies more difficult concepts; nevertheless, despite the consequent power of these two languages they are designed for easy introduction through simple modules or subsets and could plausibly be included in every section (4.2, 4.3, 4.4).

4.4. *Languages Designed for Standard Usage and Batch Processing*

As remarked earlier, the design objectives are seldom quoted, and would involve many compromises. Recent languages such as SNOBOL and ALGOL 68 can provide "efficient" source programs but not necessarily efficient object programs. POP 2 has the merit of balancing powerful language facilities against easily learned modules or subsets.

Efficient batch processing, therefore, may be best achieved by compilation followed by an "optimiser" rather than through language facilities. But the occasional or untrained programmer may still prefer a language like BASIC or FORTRAN (so long as he can achieve his purpose), knowing that the efficiency of the object program is not highly dependent on his command of the language.

"Standard usage" (for numerical computation) and "efficient batch processing" are rather contradictory design objectives, though often quoted as synonymous. It is salutary to recall that opinions differ markedly as to the respective efficiencies of COBOL, BASIC and PL/I for data processing work!

```
 10 READ A,B,D,E
 20 LET G = A*E - B*D
 30 IF G = 0 THEN 90
 40 READ C,F
 50 LET X = (C*E - B*F)/G
 60 LET Y = (A*F - C*D)/G
 70 PRINT X,Y
 80 GOTO 999
 90 PRINT "NOT UNIQUE"
100 DATA 2,4,6,7
110 DATA 5,8
999 END
```

FIG. 5. A conventional program in BASIC.

5. Stefan

5.1. *Basic Philosophy*

The language/system STEFAN is designed principally as an on-line calculator and program developer. The main features for each of these have been stated in the earlier Sections of this paper, and are incorporated in the "objective function" for this design. It must, however, be remembered that once a program has been developed the user will normally wish to run it as a whole. This requires system characteristics in opposition to the above requirements, in particular suggests a compiler rather than an interpreter, and so another compromise has to be made at some later stage.

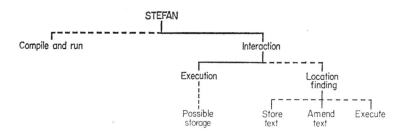

FIG. 6. Main structure of STEFAN.

STEFAN is designed on a modular basis so that, as far as the user is concerned, Mark N is a subset of Mark N +1. The documentation follows each implementation on the same modular basis, i.e. rather than make alterations to the previous text, sections on the new features are added. This enables the user to build up his knowledge of the language in modular fashion. Modularity has two additional advantages for the language designer:

(i) STEFAN can be available on general issue at an early stage, enabling feedback to occur at a time when action can be easily taken;

(ii) As a result of users' experience new ideas can be tried and implemented without too much delay.

The language STEFAN also has a formal grammar which makes it machine independent, self consistent and aesthetically pleasing. In effect each Mark has its own grammar, with that of a lower Mark being a proper subset of a higher one.

5.2. Structure

The main structure of STEFAN is shown in Fig. 6. The solid line shows the path taken when STEFAN is being used as a calculator. This is the main or default option, and for program development other paths are followed as indicated by an appropriate Command Word. The program under development is held in a file and there are two main ways by which it may be developed:

(i) as a sequel to the execution of a line of text in the calculator mode—it can be added to the file if required—and by this means the program can be checked as it is built up;

(ii) by use of the Location Finding facility, which allows amendments to be made to the stored text. In the second case a given line, identified by its first few characters, can be printed out on the terminal. At this stage the following actions can be initiated:

(i) changes to individual characters or groups of characters,
(ii) insertion or deletion of program text,
(iii) by using this line as a reference point a following line can be found,
(iv) execution from the beginning of a statement in the line.

Finally, there is the "Compile" mode when the whole of the text stored so far can be executed.

5.3. Implementation

It can be seen from the above that the dividing line between any on-line system and its associated language is very indistinct. STEFAN is no exception, and by design the particular Command Words are considered part of the language but with special meanings.

So far the basic Calculator part of STEFAN, STEFAN Mk. 1, has been implemented on an ELLIOTT 903, which has no backing store; but the next stage of development will be on the ICL KDF 9 at Leeds University, which has the powerful Eldon terminal system. STEFAN will therefore be available to students from various disciplines.

Any implementation of a language should aid the user by providing a comprehensive set of error messages. In STEFAN these take the form of a FAIL reference number, rather than a complete message. There are two reasons for this:

(i) the terminal printing speed is slow and so time is saved (cf WORK-SHOP),

(ii) a complete set of error messages requires considerable storage, and in the 903 implementation storage is at a premium. However, it is also desirable to keep the storage requirements of STEFAN down on the KDF9 as only a small amount of core should be tied permanently to the system, and changing overlays impares the response time.

The Failure Messages are an essential part of the documentation; it is also policy at Leeds to hold reference files on KDF9 which contain the failure messages for *all* languages available. Hence, it is not considered that this decision will impose difficulties on the user, particularly as experience with other languages shows that after a very short time, most errors are recognized, without reference to the actual message, as soon as they are indicated.

So far the discussion has been on syntactic errors. In the calculator mode the failure refers to the line just entered, and if a syntactic error is found during "Compilation" the whole of the line with the error will be printed.

Run time errors are more complex as they are usually embedded within the logic of the program. In this case the precise location of the error is of secondary importance to identifying the section of the program with the incorrect logic. Add to this the fact that code generated to provide the precise location of any errors that occur is long both in terms of number of instructions and execution time. The compromise that was chosen was to simply print out the FAIL reference number; but the user has two additional aids:

(i) The "arrow output"—provided mainly for printing the values of statements in the calculator mode, but which can also be used here for giving the value of any statement required.

(ii) A trace facility whereby the name of every label is printed during execution on each pass.

These diagnostics should produce just enough information to locate the section in error.

The syntax analyser and code generator is strictly neither an Interpreter nor a Compiler, but a compromise. It is capable of processing both single statements and the stored text of many statements; however in both cases the whole code is generated before execution. This type of implementation has produced a very rapid response time and, of course, makes the execution of loops more efficient than when using a normal interpreter.

5.4. *The Language*

Limitations of space do not allow a complete description of STEFAN which is given in Hutchinson and Jesty (1973); however certain features are worth mentioning and are used in Fig. 7 which shows how a simple program is developed.

(i) Immediate Assignment—this unusual feature is an aid to program development and takes the form:

$$\langle \text{variable} \rangle \, (= \langle \text{expression} \rangle).$$

This has the effect of assigning the value of the expression (normally a single number) to the variable before that variable is used in its own expression; in addition, as soon as the assignment has taken place the text inside the brackets is lost so that on storage only the main expression remains. This allows the user to evaluate a complex expression with easy numbers and check the result before the expression is added to the program.

(ii) A frustrating feature of some "desk-calculator languages" (e.g. FRED) is that after evaluating an expression the user may realise that assignment to a variable is necessary for future use, and thus has to re-input the complete expression. This is not necessary in STEFAN as the identifier $ contains the value of the preceding statement at all times, and we may simply use $ = variable, say.

(iii) When a numerical analyst is stating an algorithm on paper the rules of mathematics do not specify which side of the equals sign he has to put a variable. Most programming languages however impose the restraint of right to left assignments only (TNP developed by D. Krall, Universidad de Chile, has left to right assignments only). STEFAN imposes no restrictions, permitting either left to right or right to left assignments as the user's thoughts progress. (This does mean that $X = Y$ is undefined in the context of assignment; but the statements X; $ = Y; will have the desired effect).

```
-B(=4)←
-4.00000₁₀+00
STORE
$=Q
STORE
B↑2-4*A(=1)*C(=3)←
4.00000₁₀+00
STORE
SQRT(4
```

The variables A, B and C are set by the immediate assignments to suitable values for checking. The arrow output is used when required, and if the results are satisfactory the lines are then stored

After an error this line has been deleted.

```
SQRT($)←
2.00000₁₀+00
STORE
P=$
STORE
R1=(Q+P)/(2*A)←
-100000₁₀+00
STORE
(Q-P)/(2*A)=R2←
-3.00000₁₀+00
STORE
OUT(R1, R2)
-1.00000₁₀+00
-3.00000₁₀+00
STORE
```

OUT is only used for the roots of the quadratic.

```
RUN
-4.00000₁₀+00
4.00000₁₀+00
2.00000₁₀+00
-1.00000₁₀+00
-3.00000₁₀+00
-1.00000₁₀+00
-3.00000₁₀+00
CANCEL ←
RUN
-1.00000₁₀+00
-3.00000₁₀+00
```

Once the program has been built up it is RUN, but, in this case, as well as obtaining the solutions R1 and R2, all the arrows have been executed. CANCEL← suppresses them and in the following RUN's only the solutions are printed.

```
A=2; B=5; C=2
RUN
-5.00000₁₀-01
-2.00000₁₀+00
```

A line can consist of more than one statement separated by semicolons.

Fig. 7. Solving a quadratic using STEFAN.

(iv) STEFAN has two types of output instruction.

(a) The arrow output is used during program development or testing. The value of any statement may be printed by placing $a \leftarrow$ at the end. The effect of the arrow may be suppressed or reset by the Command Words CANCEL← or SET← respectively.

(b) Normal output is obtained by using the procedure

OUT (⟨expression⟩, ⟨expression⟩, ..., ⟨expression⟩)

which is always obeyed.

Although the facilities of the language are being implemented in modules the main aims of the language (Calculation, Program Development and Batch Processing) are all in the single structure of STEFAN. This does mean that there is a completely smooth transition between calculation and program development, say, and that the user of STEFAN has all he requires to progress from his initial idea to completion in one language.

6. Future Marks and Conclusions

Future Marks of STEFAN will include a number of additional facilities including subscripting, subroutines, operator declaration, complex and interval arithmetic, list processing and extensions to the Input/Output. The main aim has always been to provide the user with an efficient easy language with as many basic building blocks as possible, without creating a white elephant full of non-standard functions and operators that the casual user never requires. They can easily be created in STEFAN by those few users who do require them.

We are thus designing an on-line interactive language which we hope will serve the user of terminal systems in the way that he wants. The principal requirements for both performing simple calculations and developing programs have been identified and STEFAN is being designed to meet them. Nevertheless, user feedback should throw more light on the relation between particular design objectives and the corresponding language.

Note. It has subsequently proved desirable to pursue the development of STEFAN on the ICL 1906A rather than KDF9 at Leeds.

References

Beilby, M. H. (1970). "Manual of Workshop System". University of Birmingham/ Marconi-Elliott Computer Systems Limited.

Burstall, R. N., Collins, J. S. and Popplestone, R. J. (1971). "Programming in POP2". Edinburgh University Press.

Cuttle, G. and Robinson, P. B. (1970). "Executive Programs and Operating Systems". Macdonald Computer Monographs.

Dewar, R. B. K. and Rosen, B. J. (1969). "CALCTRAN, A Conversational Desk Calculator Programming Language". Technical Report, Four PI Corporation.

Elder, J. W. (1969). "Manual for a Course on Numerical Methods". Department of Applied Mathematics and Theoretical Physics, University of Cambridge.

Hutchinson, D. and Jesty, P. H. (1973). "Users' Manual for STEFAN—A Language for On-Line Calculating and for Program Development". Technical Report No. 25, Centre for Computer Studies, University of Leeds.

Hutchinson, D. and Jesty, P. H. (1973). "The Design of Languages for On-Line Calculating and for Program Development". Technical Report No. 20, Centre for Computer Studies, University of Leeds.

Jesty, P. H. (1973). "Users' Manual for an Interactive Language Implemented on KDF9—FRED". Technical Report No. 17, Centre for Computer Studies, University of Leeds.

Shaw, J. C. (1964). "JOSS: A designer's view of an experimental on-line computing system," AFIPS 26, 1964 Fall.

Symes, L. R. and Roman, R. V. (1969). "The Syntactic and Semantic Description of the Numerical Analysis Programming Language (NAPSS)". Computer Sciences Department, Purdue University.

Symes, L. R. and Roman, R. V. (1968). "Structure of a Language for a Numerical Analysis Problem Solving System (Interactive Systems for Experimental Applied Mathematics". M. Klerer and J. Reinfelds, Eds.)

I.C.L. (1968). "JEAN". Technical Publication 4153.

I.C.L. (1970). "Introduction to MOP". Student edition.

Rolls Royce Limited (1970). "CALC". AMOS Module 6.0 Issue 3, Bristol Engine. Division.

Honeywell (1972). "ABACUS". Customer Bulletin 42; System Supplement 17.

Bibliography

Bull, G. M. (1972). "Dynamic debugging in BASIC." *Comput. J.* **15** (1).

Iverson, K. E. (1962). "A Programming Language". John Wiley and Sons, New York.

Klerer, M. and Reinfelds, J. (1968). "Interactive Systems for Experimental Applied Mathematics". Academic Press, London and New York.

Discussion: On-Line Techniques

PROF. EVANS. (a) Could Mr. Sykes comment on the accuracy of the results obtained from the LOD method as compared say to those obtained from the ADI and SOR methods? (b) In solving the cyclic tridiagonal schemes on the torus calculations, do you use any pivoting strategies in the elimination algorithm?

MR. SYKES. (a) I have insufficient experience of the LOD method, but it is generally supposed that its accuracy is inferior to the other methods. (b) The matrix is diagonally dominant, so no pivoting is necessary.

PROF. EVANS. Could Mr. Thomas comment on the following points concerning his POTENT package for the numerical solution of potential problems. (1) How much core does the program take up? (2) Can the program cope with refined meshes, irregularly spaced grids, singularities, re-entrant corners, mixed and free boundaries conditions? (3) I would have expected a much greater convergence rate from the SLOR method as compared with the SOR method as shown in your Table 1. Could you give a reason for this? (4) Do you plan to adopt the package for on-line usage. If so, what difficulties are you likely to encounter?

MR. THOMAS. (1) The segmented program takes up $150k$ bytes of core, of which $60k$ bytes is data. (2) The solution may be written to a file at the end of a run. The user may then refine his grid in a subregion, and impose boundary conditions around a rectangle surrounding the subregion. The boundary conditions are interpolated from the solution over the full grid. This facility is in frequent use at Culham.

As I mentioned in the talk, the program can cope with irregularly spaced grids since the user is allowed to place grid lines through any horizontal or vertical coordinates.

Since the user provides his initial approximation as a function of space, he could in principle insert his asymptotic expansion around the singularity by including it in the user subroutine. The program is not designed to specifically treat singularities, although the user can have a re-entrant corner in his region. Mixed boundary conditions are treated by the "flux-box" method in the same way as pure Dirichlet or pure Newmann condition. The program will not treat free boundary conditions.

(3) As the residuals decrease, the convergence rate of SLOR in Test 1 is increasing compared with SOR, so I would expect that had I run the iteration further, the ratio of the two convergence rates would approach $\sqrt{2}$. (4) I have some plans to introduce a certain amount of user interaction, but this would only be in the data preparation program. This is referred to in the paper.

Since the program is so large it is not very amenable to on-line usage. On the ICL 4-70 at Culham, interactive programs are limited to $100k$ bytes.

Personally I see no need to make the solution phase of the program interactive. We could conceivably have a separate program to produce the graphical output. The user could interact with the program by typing in the data regarding graphical output, e.g. size of frame, contour heights.

Since we have instant graphical output at Culham on the Tektronix 4010 graphics terminal, users seem quite satisfied with the present facilities of the program.

DR. L. H. SEITELMAN (*Pratt & Whitney Aircraft, Connecticut, U.S.A.*). I should like to take this opportunity to underscore the importance of the data verification function of interactive graphics, which was mentioned briefly by Mr. Sykes. More generally, it should be said that the interactive environment is (or should be) a powerful medium for user convenience.

The plain fact is simply this: for the (numerically) unsophisticated user who is relatively uninformed about computers, (and this includes the vast majority of users in industry, I suspect), if a program is not relatively easy to use, it will not be used.

An important problem which arises in large-scale analyses (e.g., finite element problems), or in the design of systems to combine several related analyses, is the necessity of providing a mechanism for generating and manipulating engineering data for input to the program/system and for reviewing these data for accuracy before embarking on a lengthy (= expensive) computer run. It is in this area that interactive graphics has a tremendous impact.

For example, in practical finite element work, nodal co-ordinate data must either be input or generated from boundary co-ordinate data. For the case where data is supplied by the user, a simple visual display of a breakup is generally quite adequate to detect simple keypunch errors. Anyone who has prepared card input for such a program will appreciate the unlikelihood of detecting typographical errors by a straightforward (human) search.

Indeed, the importance of preprocessor development to large-scale analysis should also be mentioned. Although almost all test problems of academic interest are associated with regular geometrical shapes, almost all "applied" problems are associated with very inhospitable geometries. A finite element preprocessor that can accept boundary data and generate a reasonable breakup for such an irregular region is a necessary practical link to program usage.

In short, the watchword is convenience even more than sophistication. In an interactive environment, the effective use of engineering judgment and intuition can probably be used to reduce both total cost and elapsed time required for computing at least as much as can the most efficient fully automatic solution procedure.

MR. SYKES. I am in full agreement with Dr. Seitelman's comments.

MR. D. J. MULLINGS (*Sheffield University*). What is the block structure of the language you describe?

MR. JESTY. The block structure of a language such as ALGOL 60 is not suitable for an interactive language, as it requires a knowledge of the program as a whole, which is not possible with on-line program development. Thus the basic structure, in particular the scope of the variables, is global.

MR. MULLINGS. In that case how do you handle a modular program?

Mr. Jesty. Independent subroutines will be available, which can be called from a small controlling main program.

Mr. Mullings. How are identifiers declared?

Mr. Jesty. It is considered that the user requiring quick calculations should not be burdened with having to remember to declare identifiers before they are used. Since *real* variables are mainly used in this type of work, these are implicitly declared when they appear in the 'program'. All other types of variables, such as *integers, complex,* etc. will have to be declared explicitly. Labels are the only exception to this rule as they are mainly declared implicitly, but may be stated explicitly as in ALGOL 60.

Mr. Mullings. What special modes of operation is it intended to have to handle the more complex applications such as List Processing?

Mr. Jesty. There is only one mode of operation for STEFAN. The later marks will include the code necessary for complex and interval arithmetic, and the basic subroutines for List Processing will be included in the "Standard" subroutines.

Dr. Zoltan Csendes (*McGill University, Quebec, Canada*). During the past five years several general purpose programs have been developed to solve potential problems using the finite element method. I would like to ask Mr. Thomas how his "potent package" compares with these established programs in terms of accuracy, computing speed and ease of usage.

Mr. Thomas. I have not compared POTENT with any of the established finite element programs, but about two years ago we compared an earlier version of POTENT with a prototype finite element code developed at Culham. The finite element code used linear shape functions on triangular elements.

We did our tests on triangular regions, so that they were biased towards the finite element program. We found that the accuracies of the methods were very comparable.

However this prototype used a complicated list structure to keep track of the mesh points and consequently was rather slow.

Dr. P. K. W. Vinsome (*Shell Labs, Rijswijk, Netherlands*). Why not use one of the more recent methods such as SIP (strongly implicit method) instead of ADI (alternating direction implicit method), SOR or SLOR (successive line over-relaxation method).

Dr. Thomas. I think three methods in one package is sufficient but I have followed Wachspress's experience in not adopting the strongly implicit method as a standard. He says that although the SIP method is iteratively six times faster than SOR it requires six times as many arithmetic operations and so takes the same amount of computer time. Since SIP uses much more store and "red tape" than SOR, it has no advantage over SOR.

Prof. Evans. It is quite common for general purpose programs such as POTENT to use SOR or SLOR methods rather than the more recent research methods such as SIP or LOD. The philosophy behind this is that the program has to cope with so many parameters in setting up the procedure correctly that the user is quite content to have a method which is likely to converge under all conditions rather than a newer method which may give trouble. Also, of course, the time taken by the program in setting up the problem is usually far longer than the actual solution process even by the SOR method.

20. The Organisation of Numerical Algorithms Libraries

B. FORD AND S. J. HAGUE

*Numerical Algorithms Group, Oxford University
Computing Laboratory, Oxford, England.**

1. Introduction

This paper falls into four distinct parts:

(1) Why numerical algorithms libraries are needed.
(2) The organisation of a library.
(3) The NAG Library—a case study.
(4) The extension of the aims of a library.

Much of the material in this conference has been a discussion of the algorithms that are available for use to solve problems requiring numerical computation. Throughout, the emphasis has been on the development of improved algorithms in each of the many numerical areas discussed. The mathematical software librarian is the link man between the algorithms and their developers on the one hand, and the computer users and their problems on the other.

1.1. *Distinction between numerical analyst and mathematical software librarian.*
The distinction between the software librarian and the numerical analyst is an important one. The interests of a numerical analyst are well understood. Whilst perhaps aware of the needs of computer users, the motivating force for the analyst is a personal one. A better algorithm or clearer mathematical insight is his total *raison d'être*. His role is as an academic (in the best sense of the word).

The work, motivation and interests of the mathematical software librarian are the topic of this paper. We hope it will become clear that the creation and organisation of numerical algorithms libraries, which forms a large part of such work at the present time, is quite different from the work

* Formerly the Nottingham Algorithms Group, Cripps Computing Centre, University of Nottingham.

of a numerical analyst. Obviously the two are related. This is why there has been such confusion between the two activities. There are many individuals who serve both functions. Increasingly, however, software librarians are being seen as a separate group.

Their role is one of support to other workers, and their *raison d'être* is a successful numerical service for computer users. They are not, nor do they generally seek to be, numerical analysts. Whilst it is essential that they are fluently numerate, equally important is a ready command of high level languages, an appreciation of computing hardware and operating systems, a facility to write clear documentation, some organisational ability, sensitivity to the needs of computer users, and a desire to sell their product.

1.2. *Why have a library*

There are advantages for users, software librarians, and numerical analysts in having a library.

For a defined group of users an algorithms library can be developed which optimises their use of computing resources and its existence saves them valuable research time. Further, the job of choosing, coding, testing, documenting, maintaining and updating mathematical software is someone else's responsibility.

For the mathematical software librarian, the availability to users of the tested semi-compiled version of the library on the machine, and of supporting documentation, means that 95% of user queries are answered immediately. He has ready control of library software for updating, its integrity cannot be impaired by user "improvements", and he has a firm foundation for handling programming errors.

The numerical analyst knows that his work in algorithms is reaching its intended audience, who will give it a far more thorough testing than he could ever envisage. The library activity will generate statistics, queries and problems which suggest areas for further research.

1.3. *What is an algorithms library?*

The concept of an algorithms library has developed considerably over the last ten years. Initially, it was seen as a collection of unrelated algorithms taken from *Numerische Mathematik, C.A.C.M.* etc., with little supporting user documentation, and virtually no local testing. The library was carried as source text in a file, or files, of the computing system for incorporation into user programs. Gradually, the importance of user documentation and local testing of software was appreciated. The library was also increasingly carried as machine compiled code in a file of the computing system. The present state of the art is a selection of tailored software with full validation of contents and documentation. The semi-compiled version of the library is tested in detail prior to release as the central feature of a library service. The development of such a service has been discussed by Ford (1972).

1.4. *What distinguishes a library from an arbitrary set of routines?*

In the development of algorithms software for a library, five distinct steps can be discerned, each of which carries the software one step further from simply being an arbitrary set of routines.

(i) The chapter subjects are chosen.

(ii) Naming, error-flagging and parameter-ordering conventions and input/output standards, (if any) are agreed, and machine and environmental constants are collected into a library.

(iii) Individual algorithms to solve "probable" user problems are selected, chapter by chapter, with cross calling of material where relevant.

(iv) Algorithms are coded into routines, or collected algorithms modified to conform to agreed naming, programming and languages standards. At this stage similar variables are given similar names etc.

These four elements are referred to as tailoring library software.

(v) A machine code library is created, and thoroughly tested prior to release for inclusion in the computing service.

TABLE 1. Summary of access to the NAG Library Mark 2 (ALGOL and FORTRAN) on the Nottingham University ICL 1906A via the UNIQUE operating system.

Accounting period: 16 weeks from December 1972 to March 1973.

Grand cumulative total	=	10,763 calls*†
Grand cumulative ALGOL total	=	5,914 calls (54·9%)
Grand cumulative FORTRAN total	=	4,849 calls (45·1%)
Grand weekly total	=	823 calls (16th week)
Grand weekly ALGOL total	=	459 calls (55·8%)
Grand weekly FORTRAN total	=	364 calls (44·2%)
Cumulative number of routines used	=	173 (52·5%)
Weekly number of routines	=	108 (29·7%)
Weekly number of routines unused	=	256 (70·3%)
Number of new routines used	=	6 (1·6%)

* A "call" is defined as the consolidation of a NAG routine (excluding auxiliaries) into the user program under the standard system.

† Total includes 1,745 calls to the NAG error trapping routines P01AAA/F.

TABLE 2. Chapter analysis for 16 week period in Table 1.

Chapter	Name	No. of routines in chapter	Total calls	% total	Total calls/No. of routines (approx).
A02	Complex arithmetic	3	263	2·4%	88
C02	Roots of polynomials	3	15	0·1%	5
C05	Zeros of one or more transcendental equations	5	19	0·2%	4
C06	Fast Fourier transforms	3	54	0·5%	18
D01	Quadrature	2	100	0·9%	50
D02	Ordinary differential equations	4	336	3·1%	84
E01	Interpolation	3	33	0·3%	11
E02	Curve and surface fitting	3	146	1·3%	48
E04	Minimisation	11	187	1·7%	17
F01	Matrix operations including inversion	33	2309	21·4%	69
F02	Eigenvalues and eigenvectors	20	485	4·5%	24
F03	Determinants	8	1004	9·3%	126
F04	Simultaneous linear equations	13	1428	13·3%	109
G02	Correlation and regression analysis	3	291	2·7%	97
G04	Analysis of variance	3	0	0%	0
G05	Random number generators	24	2130	19·7%	89
H	Operational research	5	7	0·1%	1
M01	Sorting	16	145	1·3%	9
S	Special functions	20	66	0·6%	3

1.5. *How user attitudes to libraries have developed*

During the last ten years education of the user community has brought us from undocumented packs of cards "which worked on another machine", through "I got this program from a friend so I don't understand it", to use of particular algorithms for particular problems, then to the use of the local algorithms library. An obvious progression for the user is for the same algorithms library to be available on *all* the machines he is likely to use.

We would suggest that these changing attitudes can be related to three factors:

(i) The rapid improvement in algorithms over the last ten years.

(ii) The greater awareness and improved technical competence within certain sections of the user communities.

(iii) The development within computing centres of the concept of a "computing service."

The need for the computing service, and the pre-selection of library contents is in part due to other new groups of users of the machine, who have little interest in programming and no interest in numerical techniques.

A summary of user access to the NAG Mark 2 Library (ALGOL and FORTRAN) on the ICL 1906A at Nottingham University via the UNIQUE operating system shows the local demand for an algorithms library.

During an accounting period of 16 weeks from December 1972 to March 1973, statistics summarised in Tables 1 and 2 were collected.

The inter-relation of the contents of various chapters of the library causes a distorted picture to be created of the apparent demand for individual chapters, (for example the F03 chapter contains secondary routines required for the solution of simultaneous linear equations, and this explains the considerable use of the contents of that chapter). The overall impressions from the statistics are nevertheless useful.

As the distribution of demand is anticipated to vary from centre to centre it is hoped to acquire similar statistics in some 30 other university computing centres.

1.6. *How broad can your audience be?*

When creating a library for a body of users, there are limitations on the diversity of interests and motivations that can be covered if you are to mount a successful library service.

Three conflicting bodies of interest are:

(i) *Between research and teaching.*

A teaching library requires traditional methods to be included (e.g. Jacobi → Givens → QL for the real symmetric eigenvalue problem) whilst a general purpose research library only requires the currently accepted "best" algorithm in a given area. For teaching purposes you also need poor methods for comparison with good ones.

(ii) *Between a general research library and specialist research library.*

Specialist research groups, because of their penetration into particular numerical areas, require a far more thorough coverage in those areas than a general library can reasonably afford.

(iii) *Between general users and numerical analysts.*

Numerical analysts will wish to change the contents, codings and documentation of the library software virtually daily. The general user wishes the software and documentation to stay the same virtually for ever.

If common aims cannot be achieved, the development of sublibraries for the different groups is essential for the organisation of a successful library service.

1.7. *Why we cannot develop a perfect algorithms library*

All mathematical software librarians would like to create a perfect library. Unfortunately, all library activities start at a given point in time, and must base their work on "the present state of the art". Further, all are limited by factors of manpower, computing time, mortality and finance. Each of us works to different timescales.

We cannot define a perfect algorithm. One hopes that with the development of performance profiles for algorithms (Cody, 1972), a scientific basis for algorithm selection will eventually be defined.

We cannot restrict our library to contain only software which is mathematically and algorithmically proven. If we do not provide software in "risky" areas, the users will acquire or write their own! Hopefully, our work will reflect the latest algorithmic findings, and will be regularly updated.

We must do a professional job and attempt a full, general library service— "warts and all".

2. The Organisation of a Library

These are two distinct approaches to discussion of the principles behind the creation of an algorithms library. The first is to start with the individual algorithms and discuss the processes through which they pass (plus their associated materials) until they finally emerge as a library.

The second approach which we have chosen to follow, is to start with the idea of a library, and to work down through the implications and ramifications of library development in a number of distinct areas.

2.1. *Aims*

These should be drawn from answers to the following questions: To what group of computer users is the library directed? What are their software, information and advisory service requirements? Are there any professional standards that should be included?

The answers to these questions will yield the long term aims of the library. To them may be added short term aims which will assist long term realisation. It is essential that long (and short) term aims are agreed before project design commences.

2.2. *Selection criteria*

A development policy for library contents is required. Criteria are required for the choice of individual algorithms, within a framework of chapters (chosen according to subject or...). The basis of these three distinct selection processes may need modification to allow for development in the light of new aims.

2.3. *Library characteristics*

Perhaps the fundamental consideration of any library project is how the chosen algorithms, which are the basic units in the library, are tailored to form a library. This is due to the importance to the user of simple naming policies for routines, consistent parameter ordering in calling sequences, common error trapping, etc. Equally, specifications and standards should be agreed for supporting software, for documentation and of advisory (and other support) services. The languages of implementation should also be decided.

2.4. *Software and documentation development*

Library routines can now be developed, or culled from the literature and tailored to agreed conventions. Specially designed software, which is required for testing library contents is simultaneously produced. User and software support documentation has to be written.

2.5. *Validation*

All software should be tested and documentation scrutinised in a validation activity which is preferably totally independent of the initial contributor.

2.6. *Library support services*

(i) There is a need for a numerical methods advisory service.

(ii) The creation and testing of the semi-compiled version of the library requires fail-safe, machine-based, techniques for servicing considerable volumes of software and automatic checking of results.

(iii) Errors inevitably occur in software and documentation. It is essential that the nature of a mistake is clearly understood and quickly rectified. In the interim, users should be notified of their existence.

(iv) Master files of software and documentation must be maintained.

(v) Documentation has to be prepared, printed and distributed.

(vi) There is the day-to-day maintenance associated with the library.

2.7. *Plan of development*

All of the above have to be processed. Hence a plan of development is required. This proceeds under four heads:

    2.7.1   Organisation.

    2.7.2   Ideology.

    2.7.3   Constraints.

    2.7.4   Review mechanisms.

A regular review is required of the decisions made and actions taken, as described under headings 2.1 to 2.7.3. Vital factors in such reviews are the feed-back from users via the advisory services and user advisory committees; the results of regular market research which contacts individual users directly; expert opinion regarding technical or managerial aspects of the library; and unprovoked directives regarding changed resources or company policy.

2.8. *Further observations*

The stability of library contents and documentation formats are fundamental to any library activity. A fixed mode of access to the library within the computing service, and the ready availability of documentation are essential if the library is to be widely and confidently used.

Once the activity has commenced, changes should never be made simply for their own sake. They can be justified only in terms of greatly increased "value to user" effectiveness, which is preferably immediate rather than eventual.

If a change appears necessary, particularly in the aims, its implications under the other headings must be consciously thought through. If the change is then agreed, these implications must be accepted and vigorously acted upon. The integrity of the library and its supporting software and documentation is exposed to its greatest risk during such periods of uncertainty.

3. The NAG Library—A Case Study

3.1. *Aims*

The NAG Library was developed for general users of a university computing service. In particular, our aims were:

    (i) To develop a balanced, general purpose numerical subroutine library, in ALGOL 60 and ANSI FORTRAN, initially for the ICL 1906A.

(ii) To support such a library with detailed user documentation.

(iii) To ensure the accuracy of the contents of the subroutine library by the maintenance of a test program library.

3.2. *Selection criteria*

It was intended that the library and documentation would fulfil an educational role in numerical computation. We wished to avoid the need to mount the manufacturer's subroutine package.

(i) It was decided that a numerical library, even on a medium sized machine should be a selection of the best material available in the various areas of numerical analysis rather than a collection of all known routines.

The selection of library contents was on the basis of algorithms, within a chapter structure based on subject areas of numerical analysis.

(ii) Subject areas were chosen which were believed to be necessary in any generally useful numerical library. Unfortunately, no quantitative grounds could be established since no relevant statistics had been acquired or were known. Further, other generally available libraries appeared to have no known development policy for library contents. Hence the separate experiences of members of the contents committee with their numerical libraries on previous machines were the qualitative basis upon which library contents were chosen. We have reviewed at regular intervals the algorithms available for the solution of partial differential equations, and decided that no sufficiently general purpose software can be developed, at the present time, to warrant their inclusion.

(iii) Since no rigorous standards are available for the selection criteria for individual algorithms their choice is, of necessity, subjective to some degree.

The criteria we choose, in order of importance, are their

(a) usefulness,

(b) robustness,

(c) numerical stability,

(d) accuracy,

(e) speed.

Where many algorithms are available, only the most satisfactory one is included.

The temptation to include material for the sake of completeness must be avoided. Equally, a single routine which includes as auxiliaries many subsidiary algorithms, each slightly different, can be a result of indecision during algorithm selection. Each subsidiary algorithm should undergo a more rigorous performance evaluation than the primary algorithms. Otherwise, the library may lose that integrity discussed under the next heading which is one of its essential characteristics.

3.3. *Library characteristics*

Library characteristics are chosen to make the library as easy as possible for a programmer to use. This user orientation of software is of vital importance.

(i) It is important that the FORTRAN and ALGOL codings of an algorithm can be immediately related. As the name of a FORTRAN subroutine or function is permitted only six characters, it was decided for consistency that the name of an ALGOL procedure should be similarly limited.

It was found to be impossible to give mnemonics in six characters for all routines in the NAG Library and an ordered naming policy was therefore developed. The six character name falls into three parts. Let us consider an example, G05AEA.

G05—The Modified Share Classification Index entry for Random Number Generation.

AE —The routine following AD (I and O are excluded).

A   —To be called from an ALGOL 60 program.

The comparable call from a FORTRAN program would be G05AEF.

This naming scheme, although it initially met considerable scepticism, is now readily accepted by the users.

(ii) A general ordering of parameters for input, input-output, output, work space and control, in routine calling sequences is observed throughout the library. Within individual chapters care is taken to maintain common calling formats and similar variables for similar functions.

(iii) There is no input or output within any numerical routine of the library.

(iv) However, an integer parameter is included in the calling sequence of most routines, which may be set to signify that a given mathematical condition has or has not been met.

(v) Where intermediate output is necessary (e.g. optimisation) a procedure for output, to be written by the user, is included in the calling sequence.

(iv) The documentation of an individual routine bears the same name as the routine it describes.

There are detailed characteristics for test program software, for documentation and of advisory services. Shirley Lill has described the NAG documentation in some detail elsewhere in this volume.

3.4. *Software and documentation development*

For each routine in the library there are two test programs. The first is a simple example program. This serves two purposes. It is included as an example in the user documentation of the routine and demonstrates the calling sequence, input and output. It is also used to test a newly created semi-compiled version of the routine. The second is a stringent test program. This is a rigorous examination, mathematically and computationally, of the routine. These test programs are an integral part of the library software.

How does one test the effectiveness of user documentation other than perhaps asking individual guinea pigs for their comments? Full specifications have been agreed for the structure, format and style of all documentation.

3.5. *Validation*

All software is tested, and documentation scrutinised in a centre other than that in which it was developed. The importance of this thorough evaluation of library material by carefully selected individuals, independent of the contributing centre, cannot be overemphasised.

3.6. *Library support services*

(i) Numerical advisers to assist users in the formulation and solution of their numerical problems are regarded as a prerequisite of the successful support of the NAG Library, and of efficient use of local computing resources. The documentation is invaluable as a first line of advice.

(ii) The central office of the project is responsible for the creation and testing of the semi-compiled version of the library. It cannot be stressed too often that this is the definitive library as far as the users are concerned. FORTRAN library routines and test programs are first compiled in a strict ANSI standard compiler (developed by Ellison, Collins and Rohl (1971)) to ensure that necessary language standards have been met. After successfully passing this test, the semi-compiled library is created from the routines, and all example and stringent test programs run. The results from this are checked automatically with those obtained previously. Software failing this test, is reported by the program to the library programmer, with general guidance as to the reason for failure. Modifications are made, and the cycle repeated for these routines until the tests are successfully completed. A library tape for the new mark of the library is then created containing

(a) the source text of the individual routines in the library,

(b) source text, data and results files for each of the example and stringent test programs in the Test Program Library,

(c) the semi-compiled version of the new library.

The automatic servicing of large volumes of software, under conditions of restricted file and backing store and requiring secure, fail-safe manipulation, is vital to any library project. (The Mark 3 routine and test program libraries tapes contain over 2,500 files).

(iii) An efficient error handling mechanism has been developed. This has been described elsewhere by Ford (1972).

3.7. *Plan of development*

3.7.1. *Organisation*

(i) The structure of the project is

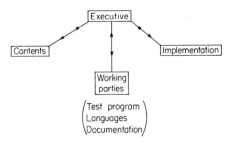

(ii) Within the library contents committee each contributor accepts responsibility for a chapter, or chapters of the library. The implications of this have been discussed elsewhere by Ford (1972).

(iii) Library releases of software and documentation are at approximately nine months intervals. Each mark contains three elements, the last mark, corrections and modifications to the last mark and new material. Each mark is a major distribution unit within the project. It is supported by a new mark of the library manual, and of the test program library.

(iv) Contributed software and documentation is sent to, and the NAG Library distributed from, the NAG central office. Master files of software and documentation are kept at the office. Hence, all software corrections and modifications are sent to the office as amendments to these files rather than as complete new versions. There are agreed assembly and release dates for each mark of the library.

(v) The Chairman and co-ordinator of the project have day-to-day responsibility for managerial and technical matters within the project between meetings of the NAG Executive.

(iv) A constant flow of information to all members of the project is essential, particularly as the membership is geographically widespread. The importance of good communications cannot be exaggerated.

3.7.2. *Ideology*

(i) Co-operation between members of universities and now also government laboratories is the basis on which work on both the library contents and library implementation committees has processed.

(ii) We have encouraged the numerical analysis community to take an interest in the library, and have been delighted by the wholehearted response in the form of advice and software that we have received. A series of seminars on the contents of individual chapters have been a particular help in this regard. Perhaps it is appropriate to mention especially members of the Division of Numerical Analysis and Computing at NPL and of the Applied Mathematics Division, Harwell.

(iii) There is active co-operation with our colleagues in the NATS project whose activities are described elsewhere in this volume.

(iv) In developing a numerical algorithms library for use in universities it is an act of faith that slowly determined "significant" answers are infinitely more valuable than quickly calculated "meaningless" ones.

(v) Standards for documentation and software are first agreed by members of the project, and thereafter rigorously enforced.

3.7.3. *Constraints*

(i) Co-operation is a considerable constraint. Fortunately, it has been a most effective one in decision making to date.

(ii) The first meeting of the project was in May 1970. It was decided at that meeting to co-operate in developing a library. The Oxford service on their new ICL 1906A was due to commence in October 1971.

(iii) We have attempted to avoid all the pitfalls described so succinctly in the recent book by Hamming (1971).

(iv) An upper bound of 400 algorithms has been suggested for the contents of the NAG Library.

(v) Due to inconsistencies in the tracing mechanisms of the ALGOL and FORTRAN compilers on the 1900 series, mixed languages programming is very difficult on these machines.

4. Extended Aims

We now consider the provision of the NAG Library on several different machine ranges, ICL 1900, IBM, CDC, ICL System 4, ICL 4100, ICL KDF9, PDP10. Our aim is to provide for the users of these various computers an "equivalent" numerical algorithms library. Although the precise definition of "equivalence" is elusive, we can look at some of the organisational implications of achieving the desired aim.

4.1. *Numerical considerations*

We must now add the notion of "portability" to the criteria by which we choose algorithms, the degree of portability being the extent to which the behaviour of a routine on a particular computer is attributable to the algorithm which the routine implements, rather than the arithmetic properties of the machine itself. These properties involve the computer's word length, the mantissa and exponent size, and the rounding operation of the arithmetic unit. There are other factors which can affect the performance of a routine, e.g. whether certain qualities should be stored and/or accumulated to greater than normal working precision. If so, what are the storage and timing overheads? Does the computer have hardware or software extended precision? Is there a restricted core size? Is the machine paged, and if so, what is its paging algorithm? The overriding consideration, particularly for the numerical analyst, is still the usefulness and robustness of a routine, and the accuracy of the answers it produces. Nevertheless, the contributor of algorithms to a library must bear in mind those aspects which limit portability.

The question of testing, both at the algorithm selection stage and in monitoring performance across machine ranges, is a major topic which deserves discussion on its own. We have mentioned here only some of the additional requirements of software selection and implementation which testing software must reflect.

Often one difficulty in developing portable numerical software is gaining regular and sustained access to the machines in mind. It is therefore worthwhile to consider simulating the arithmetic characteristics of any computer on the machine, to which the contributor has access. This simulation, the "software machine" enables the numerical analyst to vary the size of the mantissa, the exponent and other arithmetic factors. It can prove a useful experimental device in giving some insight into those algorithms which may require modification to become portable.

4.2. *Programming and language considerations*

The structure of software, both routines and test programs, in a portable library must allow for the easy adjustment of explicit machine dependencies, and for the ready alteration of the less obvious dependencies which may not emerge initially. The commonly occuring machine constants such as "macheps" present little problem. They can be supplied:

(i) by the user through the parameter list,

(ii) in the first statements of the routine,

(iii) by a supplementary set of standard functions.

A combination of the approaches in (ii), and (iii) above, seems the most attractive. For the less obvious changes, e.g. the conversion of certain variables to hold double precision numbers, several valuable suggestions have been made for "semi-automation".

There are two main points to make on programming structure:

(i) The external and internal consistency. The "tailoring" within the library must be maintained as far as possible across the machine ranges.

(ii) When changes are necessary for a particular implementation, they should disrupt the logical structure as little as possible. Adherence to language standards, in so far as they exist, is of crucial importance in multi-machine software.

4.3. *New language versions of the library*

Versions of the library in a new language should not be encouraged unless the language offers substantially more scope for algorithmic expression and commands sufficient support from users. A pilot project has been initiated to estimate the viability of an implementation of the NAG Library in a subset of ALGOL 68. Assembly code routines should only appear when necessary and, given a satisfactory algorithmic language and powerful hardware to match, hopefully not at all except to perform a basic utility role.

4.4. *The master library*

We have described some of the computational implications for a multi-machine library project. By careful planning and discussion, many of these implications can be foreseen at the design stage. There is not much experience, however, of the systemmatic implementation of numerical software on this scale. A primary organisational function must be to absorb and to disseminate the experience which will accumulate as the library develops. The NAG project involves many people, who despite having common aims, may work in different areas, in both a technical and a geographical sense. The problems of communication within such a dispersed project are acute.

Because of the volume of software involved, it is essential that there is some mechanism for assisting in the prevention of divergence between the different implementations of the library. The NAG master source file scheme, is the proposed mechanism. The general philosophy of a master source file is described by D. B. Taylor, and the specific NAG implementation by J. A. Prentice, elsewhere in this volume.

References

Cody, W. J. (1972). "The Evaluation of Mathematical Software". (To appear).

Ellison, H. D., Collins, R. C. and Rohl, G. S. (1971). "Standard FORTRAN Compiler Users' Manual". University of Manchester Regional Computing Centre.

Ford, B. (1972). Developing a numerical algorithms library. *I.M.A. Bulletin* **8**, 332–336.

Hamming, R. W. (1971). "Introduction to Applied Numerical Analysis". McGraw-Hill, New York.

21. Management Practices in the Development and Distribution of Mathematical Software With Emphasis on Computational Aids in a Multi-Machine Environment

D. B. TAYLOR

*Edinburgh Regional Computing Centre, Edinburgh University
Edinburgh, Scotland.*

B. FORD AND S. J. HAGUE

*Numerical Algorithms Group,
Oxford University Computing Laboratory,
Oxford, England.*

1. Introduction

The development and distribution of mathematical software for use on a single range of machines or family of machines has been achieved more or less successfully by a number of organizations.

Software management practices have evolved to promote the controlled distribution of substantially correct code and associated documentation. The roles of advisory and educational services have been recognised. The aim has been to establish the user's confidence in the software and in the men behind it.

When mathematical software is required to run on different machines and operating systems, the cost in human resources of maintaining the user's confidence may be high. It is natural for the computer professional to turn to the file handling and text editing capabilities of the computer to assist in the management, development and maintenance of a large body of software.

An attempt will be made to define the characteristics of a machine-readable management document, known as a Master Source document, from which variant texts may be derived by text selection on a computing machine. A syntax for text selection is proposed. The problem of updating the master source document without hazarding its integrity is also discussed.

2. Growth Patterns in Library Software

Subroutine libraries, program packages and associated documentation are subject, during their realm of relevance, to continual modification and enhancement. In the early stages of development of Library Software, modifications and enhancements typically involve technical matters—correction of algorithms faults and the provision of new manipulative facilities. In the middle period of growth, system related features also play a significant part. If the software is popular, then resources are found to optimise the operation in a specific system environment and to move the software to other environments. In a terminal period, loss of influential users to competitive software leads to a curtailment of the resources needed to maintain the software in a changing system environment. Technical enhancement of the software ceases. Eventually, resources even for maintenance are insufficient.

It is not the object of this paper to delineate in detail those working practices which are essential to the writer of application subroutine

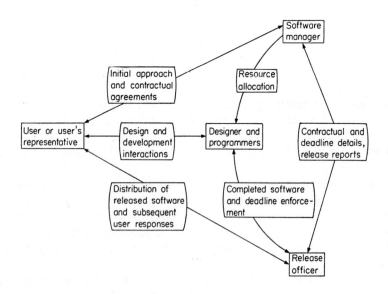

FIG. 1. An organizational structure for developing software for a single machine.

libraries and packages. It is clearly his aim to produce software which will remain in the middle period of growth for a long period of time. It is sufficient to recognize certain desirable structural relationships within any organization intending to create and distribute reliable software. A separation of roles which has been found advantageous when creating software for a single machine is exemplified diagrammatically in Fig. 1.

Most important is the separation of design and development activities from release and distribution activities.

With this separation, the management of the organization can insist on certain standards being met before software and its associated documentation are released. The processes of design enhancement and correction of errors can be passed on to the user in a systematic way. The software can be constrained to pass through a sequence of identified states variantly known as "Versions", "Releases" or "Marks". Documentation, software updates and alerts must relate to these defined states.

3. Software Development in a Multi-machine Environment

Software may be written and released on one machine and subsequently moved to other machines or it may be constructed from parts independently developed on different machines. In both cases two activities are identified: writing software for one machine and implementing existing software on another machine. These tasks require equally high ability of both the writer and implementor if integrity of the software is to be achieved.

The development process may well lead to a plethora of variant texts and it may no longer be possible to identify a single sequence of state through which the software passes as it develops. A single sequence can still, of course, be identified for each implementation.

In practice the distribution of software for a machine other than that for which it was originally developed may be delegated by the originators to another organization but this necessarily involves a loss of control over the integrity of the software. To maintain such control the originating organization must maintain and update within their own organization all the variant texts.

The relationships between the texts must be maintained in such a manner that enhancement to the original implementation can be passed on to derived implementations. Furthermore, if erroneous code is found in one implementation, the possible repercussions in other implementations must be identifiable.

An organizational interpretation of this approach can be envisaged by adding to the diagram (Fig. 1) a third dimension in which designer–

programmer groups and release officers are appointed to deal with difficult machine ranges. The difficulties are compounded if the various groups are physically distant from one another. The possibility of achieving an efficiently coordinated release mechanism becomes remote. The need for a number of design and implementation teams at distant sites is largely unavoidable due to the geographic distribution of computing machines of various types. The release activity however can be centralized provided a means of regimenting variant texts can be found.

To this end, a Master Source document is envisaged which contains a complete record of the identified states, releases, through which the software passes, and which also contains all the variant texts needed for implementations on different systems. It is also desirable that it should contain management information dates of completion, names of personnel, etc. The most all-embracing master source document would involve not only the software source code but also the documentation which describes it. The master source document must be machine-readable. It would then be possible to recover source code and related documentation for a specific implementation and release using the computer.

An added advantage of the master source concept for software arises once the master document has been developed to embrace several computing systems. Areas of machine dependence become clearly divided and the task of implementing the software on a new system becomes less arduous, if not trivial.

4. The Structure of a Master Source Document

Individual text variants may be recovered from a master source document containing several variants in a number of ways. If each text record in the master source document has a unique sequence number then a list of those sequence numbers relevant to a specific variant may be created and subsequently used to recreate the variant. This method has the disadvantage that the text selection cannot be performed easily by eye from a listing of the master source document.

This objection can be met by adding, to each record of the master, a list of those variant texts for which the record is required. Lists of sequence numbers for each variant may be dispensed with. In a fixed record length environment the need to allow space for long lists on a small number of records could well lead to considerable wasted space. The system can be made fairly compact if the lists are coded but readability is then lost.

This method of selection, however, does have the advantage of simplicity in processing particularly when editing of the master source document is considered.

A third approach will be described which minimizes the amount of space used to add selection criteria to the master document. This involves inserting into the master source document records containing selection commands which apply to all further text records until another selection command is encountered. The selection commands contain lists which identify the variant texts for which the following text is required.

The variant program texts which arise in the management of software can be identified by the name of a computer or computing system and by the name of a release of software on that computer.†

Identification can be viewed as picking out a point in a selection space spanned by two orthogonal lists. Since some of the named releases will not apply to some of the implementations some points in this space will not correspond to a selectable text.

To avoid repetition of text common to several variants it is important that the selection commands be able to specify a number of points in the selection space. If the number of points is large, it may be economical to specify all the points and to specify points which are not required. (See ⟨ALL_⟩ .. ⟨BAR_⟩ in Section 5). A smaller subset may be obtained by specifying all computing systems except certain named ones and giving explicit release specifications. (See ⟨ALL_⟩⟨REL_⟩ ... ⟨BAR_⟩ in Section 5).

The sequential nature of releases can be used to further simplify the selection commands. When code is first written it is assumed to be correct and it is desirable to be able to select it for a specific release and for all following releases in an as yet undefined sequence. At a later date if the code is no longer required this specification should be readily modifiable to specify a subsequence of defined releases. (See ⟨_ON_⟩ and ⟨_TO_⟩ in Section 5).

If an attempt has been made to write source code to a widely accepted standard, e.g. ANSI FORTRAN, then text variations for different implementations are largely the result of hardware differences. The syntax for the selection of computing machines can be reduced by recognizing that machine hardware variations can often be grouped in an inverted tree structure. Machines with eight bit bytes can be related by the structure shown in Fig. 2.

If special names corresponding to the nodes of the tree are recognized

---

† This very general specification may be undesirable from the management point of view when the ancillary requirement for documentation, associated with every release, is considered. A reasonable management requirement would be that derived implementations have release states which in terms of facilities offered lie between the release states of the original implementation. In this way a single sequence of releases can be constructed. The selection syntax which is proposed does not, however, embody this restriction.

in the selection commands then commonly recurring lists of computing system names can be dispensed with, e.g. BYTES might be used in place of a list of names specifying IBM 360, IBM 370, ICL SYSTEM 4, RCA SPECTRA 70. This technique has the advantage that it identifies the hardware feature which makes a given textual variant necessary.

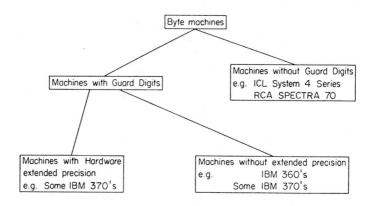

FIG. 2. The inverted tree relationship between byte machines.

5. A Syntax for Text Selection

The master source document which has been discussed contains two distinct types of text: text which directs selection and the text which may or may not be selected. The statements used to select text will be referred to as Selection Commands.

A version of a document relating to a specific system and release can be obtained from the master source document using a computer program which will be referred to as the SELECT preprocessor which analyses each selection command and applies it to the text which follows until a further selection command is encountered. The document so selected will not contain selection commands. A more sophisticated preprocessor could select a master source for a subset of computing systems.

The syntax which is suggested here satisfies the irksome requirement that it be processed with reasonable efficiency by a FORTRAN program. All keywords consist of 4 or 8 characters. Readability is improved if the last of these is a space. Selection commands are punched with keywords beginning on column 1, 5, 9, etc.

The syntax is as follows:

SYNTAX OF SELECT (REVERSE–BNF: TERMINALS IN ANGLE-
    BRACKETS):
COMMAND :: = ⟨EXIT⟩/⟨FOR NONE⟩/⟨FOR⟩ LIST/⟨FOR⟩
                  LIST ⟨BAR⟩ LIST
LIST   :: = ⟨ALL⟩/⟨ALL⟩ FORMLIST/SPECLIST/⟨ALL⟩
                  FORMLIST SPECLIST
SPECLIST :: = NAMELIST/SPECLIST FORMLIST/SPECLIST
                  SPECLIST
NAMELIST :: = NAME/NAMELIST NAME
FORMLIST :: = FORM/FORMLIST FORM
FORM   :: = ⟨REF⟩ MARK/⟨REF⟩ MARK ⟨ON⟩/⟨REF⟩ MARK
                  ⟨TO⟩ MARK
NAME   :: = WORD WORD (NOT INCLUDING A SYMBOL)
MARK   :: = WORD
SYMBOL   :: = ⟨ ⟩/⟨EXIT⟩/⟨FOR⟩/⟨AND⟩/⟨REF⟩⟨NONE⟩/
                  ⟨ALL⟩/⟨BAR⟩/⟨ON⟩/⟨TO⟩
WORD   :: = CHAR CHAR CHAR CHAR
(NOTES: CHAR MEANS ANY CHARACTER FROM THE
CHARACTER-SET. ⟨AND⟩/⟨FOR⟩/⟨EXIT⟩ MUST BE THE FIRST
WORD OF A COMMAND-LINE. YOU MAY INSERT ⟨ ⟩
BETWEEN ANY 2 WORDS TO IMPROVE LEGIBILITY. IF A
COMMAND-LINE IS MORE THAN 18 WORDS LONG, IT CON-
TINUES ONTO THE NEXT LINE WHICH MUST START WITH
⟨AND⟩).

The use of the above syntax will be made clear by examples.

FOR_NONE

Following text will not be selected until a further command is executed.

FOR_ALL_

Following text will always be selected.

FOR_ALL_REF_MK1_TO_MK4_

Following text will be selected for all computing systems, for all releases
in a defined sequence of release names from MK1 to MK4.

FOR_ALL_BAR_ICL 1900_REF_MK4_

Following text will be selected for all machines and releases except for Release MK4 on the ICL 1900.

FOR_IBM-360_REF_MK2_IBM-370_REF_MK4_TO_MK7

Following text will be selected for IBM-360 Release MK2, IBM-370 Release MK4, MK5, MK6 and MK7.

FOR_ALL REF_MK1_ON_BAR_IBM-360_AND_IBM-370_

Following text will be selected for all machines for all defined marks except for IBM-360 and IBM-370.

EXIT

This marks the physical end of the master source document.

6. Editing a Master Source Document

The security of the text and selection commands in a master source document is of paramount importance. Since a number of designers and implementors may wish to update the master and to borrow text from one another, an editing system which strictly controls the areas of code which a given individual may change must be developed. The master source document must be given a reference system so that text within it may be referenced and variant text in different implementations be related.

In a sequential file to sequential file editing environment the difficulties arising from the general syntax which has been described are considerable and a technique using extended records provides a possible solution.† In a multiaccess paged environment in which system facilities provide effective random-access to text files, the problems are considerably reduced. Before considering a reference technique for such an approach, the traditional role which sequence numbers on text records play in the editing and security of files will be examined.

Sequence numbers arose as a natural adjunct of punched card technology. Sequence numbers in arithmetic progression on the cards of a deck provide security against loss of cards, except possibly at the beginning or end, and a means of recovery if the deck is dropped. This last feature requires only that

---

† A further paper is being presented to deal with this case.

the sequence numbers be a monotonic sequence. Monotonically increasing sequences have become the standard means of identifying records in sequential files both on cards and magnetic devices. If sequence numbers are initially assigned using an arithmetic progression then unassigned values can be used to sequence inserted cards in subsequent editing of the file. It is accepted that at some stage re-sequencing of the file may be necessary. The continuity of relationship of text records and their sequence numbers over several years and many edits for a given piece of software is a by-product of the status of the sequence number as part of the text record. It is not essential to the editing process which requires only that each editable record in an identified text be associated with a unique numerical identifier. A line or record number would be sufficient. In any card deck derived from an editor which always re-sequences records, these numbers would provide deck security superior to that provided by monotonic sequence numbers. The only extra requirement of such an editing procedure would be that it should, on request, list the text with both old and new sequence numbers so that a visual check of the success of an edit can be made.

Turning now to the problem of editing a master source document, since all insertions of text involve either insertion of a selection command or the modification of an existing command, it would appear that the basic textual unit in the master source document is not an individual record but rather a set of records beginning with a selection command and terminating just before the next selection command. This unit will be called a paragraph. It is natural to assign monotonic numerical identifiers to paragraphs rather than to individual records. Line numbers within paragraphs can provide unique references for records. As a master source document grows, paragraphs may be sub-divided but they will not expand. A paragraph and line reference used before sub-division can still be used to identify a record after the paragraph has been split up provided the selection criteria associated with the original paragraph are known. This will certainly be the usual case. Any previous state of the master document can in fact be re-created.

An editing procedure is envisaged which will allow read only access to the master document and allow the user to create a related edit file which he can privately integrate with the master file to produce a new selected text. He may then test the correctness of this by proof reading or if it is a source program by running test examples and hence re-edit the pseudo-file consisting of the read only unedited master and his own related edit file. The system must be managed by a release officer who from time to time collects the edit files produced by designers and implementors and concatenates them into the master document.

A considerable degree of sophistication is possible in the concatenation procedure for edit files so that the master document does not contain an excessive repetition of similar records. When a new master is created, the designers and implementors are free to list and to absorb the benefits of each other's work.

7. Conclusions

The need for master source documents when distributing code to several different computing systems has been made clear. A syntax for text selection has been presented. Such a syntax has been implemented in the Program Library Unit, Edinburgh Regional Computing Centre. The problems of editing a master source document have been briefly discussed and a method of reference within the document has been proposed. An editor for master source documents embodying text protection and paragraph referencing is currently under development in the Program Library Unit.

22. The Development and Maintenance of Multi-Machine Software in the NAG Project

J. A. PRENTICE

Computing Centre, Loughborough University of Technology,
Loughborough, Leicestershire, England.

1. Introduction

The NAG project was initiated as a co-operative venture by Universities and the Atlas Computer Laboratory to provide libraries of numerical routines for the ICL 1906A computer. After the release of Mark 1 of the library 18 months ago there were many requests for the library to be made available on other machine ranges. NAG accordingly broadened its aims to include the provision of the library on all British University machines. In parallel with this activity, contributions were being received for subsequent marks of the 1906A version of the library, Mark 3 of which has just been issued.

Thus, the characteristic of the project is a large number of people both contributors and implementors all geographically remote from each other either working directly, or via a co-ordinator with the NAG Central Office. The contributors are members of the Library Contents Committee. The implementors are grouped according to machine range into Implementation Groups each of which is responsible to the Implementation Committee for their implementation. The Library Contents and Implementation Committees are sub-committees of the NAG Executive whose day to day business is conducted by the Central Office.

This method of working has many advantages especially the large amount of manpower it allows to be tapped but it introduces problems in co-ordinating the updating and error reporting of the documentation and software. A system to handle the updating of the source text of the routines of the library is described in this paper.

383

2. The Master Library

The heart of the solution to the problems described above is a machine readable file with the source of all implementations of all the routines of the library. The term implementation means a distinct mark of the library for a particular machine range.

The file is structured so that records within it that are common to all implementations (common lines) only appear once and the records that are implementation dependent are each identified so that they can be selected.

The file can be processed to select one implementation for compilation or several implementations for comparison. Software is provided as part of the master library system to handle the amendment of common lines, replacement of common lines by implementation dependent lines and the conversion of the master file to tapes containing one or more implementations for issue to the implementation groups. There are two distinct processes— the updating of the master and selection from it.

3. Justification of the Master Library

It is evidently necessary to justify the effort that is required to set up the master library, to write the associated software and especially the discipline that it will impose on contributors and implementors. There are four major reasons why a master library is required:

(a) To avoid divergence between implementations of the library.

(b) To provide a consolidated record of the changes that have occurred from mark to mark in all the machine ranges and the master and to allow extrapolation of experience to any new machine ranges for which the library is required.

(c) To be a framework for secure updating of routines by contributors.

(d) To avoid the need for implementors to re-implement routines with the release of each mark of the contributed library.

One of the great strengths of the library will be its wide availability. With the growing use of regional and shared computing facilities there will be a large number of users who have to switch between machines or use several machines at one time. The availability of a standard library is of funda- mental importance to such users. Divergence between implementations is probably one of the biggest dangers to the project.

Each implementation group provides the alterations to the master to generate their implementation. These will be replacements or additions to common lines. The Central Office will incorporate these amendments in the Master File which is then used to produce a file from which the given implementation can be compiled. This gives a strong incentive not to "cut corners" and only implement "the routines our user wants". This practical aspect reinforces the obligations placed on implementors by NAG policy decisions.

In a long term project, with some changes in membership inevitable, it is desirable to have a record of the developments that have occurred. This allows retrospective checking of enhancements and is a valuable guide to anyone taking over a routine from a person that has left the project. The collation of the differences between implementations will prove of great value when an implementation for a new machine is required as analogies with previous similar implementations can easily be drawn.

It is difficult for people working on parts of the library to realise the enormity of the task of maintaining the whole library. The source of the Mark 3 version of the 1906A library is 20,000 records in 450 routines. This shows the vast volume of information involved. The existence of the master library will be a framework which will support the standards set for submission of amendments and enhancements and so greatly reduce the effort required at the Central Office.

The imposition of a standard and systematic updating procedure will allow implementors to be reliably informed of changes made to routines by the contributors. This will avoid the need to re-implement the whole library for each new mark.

It is considered that these points fully justify a master library; in fact it is generally felt that without one, multi-machine implementations of the library are not practicable.

4. Technical and Social Requirements of the Master Library

Before discussing the form of the master library used, it is instructive to study some of the requirements underlying its design.

It is perhaps a truism to say that there can only be one copy of a master file that is definitive. This will be held and updated by the Central Office. Updates will come from contributors who alter common lines and from implementors who alter lines belonging to their implementation or replace common lines by implementation dependent lines. These groups of people work quite independently of each other and in practice, one implementor will have no idea of what alterations another implementor is making.

Thus, there must be a method of specifying amendments to the master that is independent of any changes that may be made by other implementors. There is also a possibility of conflict with changes made by contributors. Either such changes are made by amending lines in an existing mark of the master, in which case the incorporation of these changes must be notified, to all implementations, or they alter a new and unreleased mark, in which case they will not effect implementors. Furthermore, it is vital that simple errors in amendment decks cannot cause alterations to unexpected parts of the library. For example, one implementation must not be able to alter the code of another. Some manual checks by the Central Office will be necessary but these should be kept to a minimum.

Within the framework of these requirements the system must be as simple as possible. The objectives of the project are the writing and distributing of numerical software not devising elaborate systems programs. Many implementations may be on machines without comprehensive operating systems or utility software. An ideal would be a system that could be used on a large machine with a file store or by hand with decks of cards with equal ease.

In addition to the need to specify changes to the master it is necessary to select from it to distribute to the implementors. There are many different requirements here. The simplest is a tape with one implementation on it that can be compiled. This is termed an Implementor's Release Tape (IRT). Other structures that may be required are combinations of implementations for comparative study. This aspect is further discussed in Section 8.

Implementors tapes will have to be in a format suitable for reading on the implementor's machine. Thus the master library system provides programs for transforming the master file to implementation sub-sets which are in a form which can readily be processed on the implementor's machine.

The use of this technique rather than attempting to design a master format that is acceptable to all implementations is one of the fundamental aspects of the system. It allows the master to be structured to maximise ease of updating and permits experience to dictate the best form for the output for human study during implementation.

5. The Format of the Master File

The library consists of a series of routines grouped into chapters. The master library is physically divided into subfiles for each routine and each subfile is considered as a unit. Thus it is only necessary to consider the format of the records of one routine. Each record of a routine has the following components:

(a) a sequence number stem,

(b) an implementor's sequence field,

(c) a machine selection field,

(d) the first mark the record is included in,

(e) the last mark the record is included in,

(f) the mark of the master record that an implementation dependent line was derived from,

(g) the source text of the line in the routine.

For example a record might be

$$0170030, \text{ KDF9, MK3, MK4C, MK1, } X = 1.03751.$$

As the master file is essentially for machine processing these fields would be coded in some way. This coding does not affect the principles and the uncoded form will be used for examples.

6. The Selection of Records for IRTs

Consider the process of selecting the records for a specified machine and mark of the library, i.e. the production of an IRT.

The program preforming this selection is given the machine, the mark number and the mark number of the master on which the implementation is based. A scan of the records of the master will be made checking for ones to be included in the IRT.

The machine selection will be either

(i) The name of a specific machine, or

(ii) Common—possibly excluding certain machines.

In the first case, if the name is the same as the machine for which the IRT is being produced the record is a candidate for inclusion. In the second case if the machine is not excluded the record is a candidate.

If the record is a common record a check is made to see if the mark number of the master from which the implementation is derived is between the first and last marks of the candidate. If it is, the fields (a), (b) and (g) of the record are output to the IRT. If the record is a machine dependent record the same mark number checks are performed with the mark number of the implementation being selected. Thus the records on a IRT will contain the text of the record and a sequence number made up from the sequence stem and the implementor's sequence field. These records can be standard 80 column card images.

For example in constructing Mark 3 of the 1900* implementation, which is derived from Mark 2 of the master, the following records would be accepted

0010060, 1900*, MK1, MK99Z, MK2,.....................

0023000, COMMON-EXCEPT KDF9, MK1, MK4, MK1,.....

while the following would not

0220073, 4100, MK2, MK3, MK1,.........................

0121000, COMMON-EXCEPT 1900*, MK1, MK6, MK1,....

0024000, COMMON, MK3, MK6, MK3,...................

It can be seen that a record is never deleted from the master file. When it is no longer required the last mark in which the record is included is set. Thus it will always be possible to generate any mark of the library for each implementation.

7. Updating the Master file

The updating operation is based on the fact that each record in the master file is uniquely identified by items (a) to (e) and each record on an IRT is uniquely identified by (a) and (b). The identification is used to perform updating.

Records may be replaced or their selection criteria altered by reference to the sequence number. New records can be inserted between two existing records by use of suitable intermediate numbers. If the editor program is given the machine and mark that is being edited these alterations can be provided on 80 column cards in a form suitable for amending both IRTs and the master file.

If a common record is altered by an implementation then the common record must be excluded from the implementation and an implementation dependent record added, e.g. if

$$Y = 1.0376$$

is to be replaced by

$$Y = 1.0381$$

for all KDF9 marks

0180000, COMMON, MK1, MK99Z, MK1, Y = 1.0376

would be transformed by the master editor to

0180000, COMMON-EXCEPTKDF9, MK1, MK99Z, MK1, Y = 1.0376

0180000, KDF9, MK1, MK99Z, MK1, Y = 1.0381

If a contributor alters a common record then a report must be sent to all implementations, not excluded from that record, to inform them of the change which may have included machine dependencies. This report will be generated automatically by the master library system.

The sequence number is in two fields. The stem is used by contributors for master lines for which the implementors' sequence field will be zero. Implementors use this field and can replace one common line by several implementation dependent lines

It can be seen that with this updating system there is no risk of one implementation altering the code of any other and it does not matter in which order amendments are inserted.

8. The Selection of Composite Sub-Masters

As mentioned earlier it will frequently be convenient to have a file with some combination of marks and machines. This file might be printable in some form that is easy for humans to understand, and cannot have records of more than 80 characters without being in danger of machine dependence. A further disadvantage of the format of the master file is that all the different implementors' versions of one record are grouped together whereas for study all records for one implementation should be grouped together. One format for such a legible file is to have the blocks of records delimited by records defining the selection criteria.
e.g.

```
    FOR 1900*, MK1 ON
       ⋮
       ⋮
    records
       ⋮
       ⋮
    FOR IBM360, MK2 TO MK3A
       ⋮
       ⋮
    FOR ALL
       ⋮
       ⋮
```

It is evident that this transformation and grouping of adjacent records for each implementation is a simple process and results in an easily readable listing.

There may be other forms of output that experience will show to be useful, e.g. the text of one mark with the lines different from it for another mark printed beside it. These can all be easily produced from the master file.

9. Contributors, Implementors and the Generation of Amendments

It has been shown how a set of amendments to a routine can be applied to an IRT and the master file with equivalent effect. For security it is evidently desirable that the amendments submitted for the master file should have been tested on an IRT. Contributors amendments should also be checked mechanically before incorporation in the master. There are two ways of doing this. Implementors could be issued with a version of the editor that would enable them to edit the IRTs on their machine. The production of such editors even in a high level language would be a major job. Alternatively, if an editing system on the implementor's or contributor's machine range is used to produce an updated copy of the rouutine then, provided it is sequenced in order, it can be anti-edited at the Central Office to produce the changes to be made to the master. Such a local editing system might be hand amendment of a deck of cards.

10. Some Problems

A problem yet to be faced by the project is that all current routines have been developed for the 1906A. Thus the common source is the 1906A version of the library. In time different machines will be used to develop different routines. This need not affect the structure of the master library but it is bound to complicate the task of the implementor.

It is probable that the alterations made by several distinct sets of implementors will be sufficiently similar to make the sharing of lines of implementation dependent code attractive. The master library permits this by allowing several machines for one line.

e.g.

0010060, 1900* + 1906A, MK1, MK3, MK1,..........

but it is not proposed to use this as there are serious problems with the responsibility for updating of such records. The only solution to this would be for the implementation groups concerned to amalgamate.

11. Conclusions

In this paper we believe we have described a solution to the problem of many people maintaining a large amount of developing software for many machines and created a system providing self documentation of developments and if necessary, capable of reverting to any previous state.

The NAG library is supported by a set of test programs. It is intended that the master library system should be extended to cover these.

The acceptibility of the practical implementation of the scheme to people connected with the NAG project remains to be discovered.

23. The NATS Approach to Quality Software†

BRIAN T. SMITH, J. M. BOYLE AND W. J. CODY

Applied Mathematics Division,
Argonne National Laboratory,
Argonne, Illinois, U.S.A.

Introduction

The NATS project was conceived in early 1970 and funded in early 1971 as a pilot project to explore the problems of testing, certifying, disseminating and maintaining quality mathematical software. Intrinsic to the study was the creation of two software packages. The first of these is EISPACK, a package of matrix eigensystem programs which became available to the public in May, 1972, and which has now been distributed to over 150 computer installations. The second is the embryo FUNPACK package of subroutines for special functions of mathematical physics, the first elements of which are now ready for release to the public.

Various aspects of the project and its products have been discussed in the literature. For example, the fundamental paper (Boyle *et al.*, 1972) contains discussions of the NATS concept of certified mathematical software and the organizational procedures involved in its production, while a general progress report and a brief description of the events leading to EISPACK and FUNPACK are found in Smith (1972). Future publications will treat the special purpose information processing aids designed for the project (Boyle and Smith, 1974) and the EISPAC control program (Boyle and Grau, 1973).

This paper concerns the NATS ideas on the key concept of quality in software and how to achieve it. We first discuss the desirable attributes of subroutines and the techniques NATS used to obtain them. The idea of systematized collections of subroutines is next introduced and discussed. Finally, we consider production and user benefits derived from our approach.

† Work performed under the auspices of the National Science Foundation and the United States Atomic Energy Commission.

Quality of Subroutines

NATS subroutines are organized into systematized collections, the characteristics of which are discussed in the next section. Since the quality of collections is predicated upon the quality of the individual elements, we consider quality in subroutines first. NATS subroutines have five attributes which we feel contribute to their quality, namely: reliability, robustness, structure, usability, and validity. As we shall see in the next section these same attributes apply to the organization of software into systematized collections, suggesting that they are somehow basic to software quality in general.

The first attribute is reliability, the ability of a subroutine to perform a well-defined calculation accurately and efficiently. Reliability begins with the proper choice of underlying algorithms. Subroutines implementing poor algorithms or algorithms based on incomplete analytic investigation will probably not be reliable. This does not imply the converse, that all implementations of good algorithms backed by complete analysis will necessarily lead to reliable software, only that the probability of producing a reliable subroutine can be increased.

It is important at this point to realize the distinction we are drawing between an algorithm and an item of software. A mathematical algorithm is an abstract idea, perhaps presented in mathematical language or published in an algebraic computer language in a refereed journal, whereas an item of mathematical software consists of a working computer program together with its documentation. The same basic algorithm can be imbedded in computer programs which differ widely in details of performance and organization, hence in all of the attributes we discuss.

The point we are trying to make is that reliability in software starts with quality in analysis but quality in analysis can be transformed into reliability in software only with care in implementation. Detailed analysis helps define the problem set over which an algorithm can be used, and describes the computational error to be associated with correct usage, but only careful implementation assures that the software is faithful to the original algorithm and that the accuracy realized is close to the theoretical prediction. A detailed knowledge of the computer environment is the important new ingredient in the successful implementation of an algorithm. Programming language and machine considerations may dictate use of subtle constructions which greatly improve software performance.

Robustness is closely related to reliability, but distinctly different. By robustness we mean the ability of a computer program to detect and gracefully recover from abnormal situations without involuntarily terminating the computer run. Robust software contains error monitoring facilities which filter out improper arguments and which predict computational trouble such as underflow or overflow before it occurs. Such software resorts to an error recovery only when precise computational results cannot be achieved, and then it provides appropriate default numerical results and precise diagnostic information. If possible, it does not just examine the data until it finds the first inconsistency and then return a diagnostic, but it continues to examine data after detecting an error and returns diagnostic information on all subsequent errors as well.

The existence of complete analytic information about an algorithm, clearly defining the classes of problems for which it will and will not work, is an enormous aid to the creation of robust software. But again, robustness is an attribute of the software and not of the underlying algorithm. Together with reliability, it determines how well the software will perform. The basic concern of the software designer is to produce a computer program that is reliable, robust and useful while still remaining faithful to the algorithm being implemented.

We illustrate these ideas with an example. The EISPACK package of eigensystem subroutines is based upon the algorithms published in ALGOL by Wilkinson and his colleagues (Wilkinson and Reinsch, 1971). These algorithms are well documented with extensive analysis and hence offer all the essential background ingredients for quality. One subroutine in this group, called RATQR, determines the algebraically smallest eigenvalues of a symmetric tridiagonal matrix using the rational QR method with Newton corrections. The ALGOL version of this subroutine requires an input parameter which specifies whether or not the input matrix is known to be positive definite, and the procedure selects a shorter computational path when it is. The procedure malfunctions if the input specification is wrong, but there are no error handling facilities in the ALGOL version at all. The EISPACK version of this program has been restructured to avoid underflows which occur frequently in the ALGOL version on certain machines. Moreover, it checks when a user claims his input matrix is positive definite to be certain that it really is, returning a diagnostic if it is not. Thus even when properly used, the ALGOL procedure may give disturbing system-generated underflow messages even though returning correct numerical results. And even worse, an incorrect claim that an input matrix is positive definite may result in reasonable appearing yet erroneous results with no indication that anything is wrong. In our terms, the EISPACK program is more robust than the ALGOL procedure.

The third attribute of quality software is good structure. While the principles of structured programming, *per se*, were not followed in the preparation of NATS software, the programs have many of the features of structured programs, later programs more so than earlier ones. The logical flow within a program tends to be from top to bottom with few reverses of direction. Variable names are chosen to default to type real or integer in FORTRAN; even so, all variables are explicitly declared.

Furthermore, we have attempted to format the programs to display their structure. FORTRAN statements conform closely to the ACM conventions for the publication of FORTRAN algorithms, with additional judicious but systematic use of blanks within a statement to improve readability. Loops are set off by comment cards and indentation, and major logical flow is commented as are unusual constructions designed to improve numerical performance. A comment card at the end of the program, containing its name, facilitates separation of programs in continuous listings.

The fourth attribute, usability, refers to the ease with which a user can choose a program and apply it to his problem. There are two facets to usability—the ease with which a program interfaces with the user and the ease with which it interfaces with other software. These facets manifest themselves in documentation and calling sequences.

Good documentation should be complete, succinct, unambiguous, well-organized and well-formatted. What constitutes completeness is debatable, of course. In NATS we feel that complete documentation includes first, information on how to use the subroutine, and then additional information on the underlying algorithm and the performance of the subroutine. This organization places most frequently needed information early in the document, and less used or more detailed information at the end. The more vital information for the use of a subroutine, such as statement of purpose, the role of each parameter, output parameter values in case of abnormal termination, causes of abnormal termination, other subroutines required, and so on, is also inserted in comments at the beginning of the source program.

Within NATS we found that the preparation of good programs and good documentation complement one another. The study necessary to build robustness into the software provides information for discussions of the problem domain of the program, the causes of abnormal termination and the remedial action taken. If a program is well structured, the source listing obviates the need for a flow chart—indeed, it may even contain more information than the normal flow chart. Furthermore, the existence of extensive commenting in the subroutines enables extraction and augmentation of the comments to form machine readable documents, greatly simplifying the preparation of documentation. On the other hand, efforts to document the causes and consequences of abnormal termination frequently lead to program changes that improve reliability and robustness.

The second facet of usability relates to the calling sequences. We generally strove to keep calling sequences simple, and free of parameters whose roles are confusing. In particular, unsophisticated users find it difficult to specify machine dependent parameters, such as those relating to word length and exponent range of the machine arithmetic. Improper specification of these can lead to unpredictable malfunctions. Therefore, both usability and reliability of a program are improved when such parameters are defined within the program.

The final attribute of quality software, validity, refers to the existence of evidence that the software has performed well in a particular computer environment, and to the testing aids necessary to demonstrate that the present installation of the software is performing well. Validity of NATS software is a by-product of our certification process. As described in (Boyle et al., 1972), NATS software is exercised by field test sites, viz., computing centers representing a variety of computers and operating systems, prior to its general release. To expedite these field tests, demonstration programs which apply the software to non-trivial problems are prepared with almost the same care as the subroutines themselves. These programs are largely input-free. Output includes a statement of each problem solved, the numerical solution, and an evaluation of how well the software has performed. These demonstration programs, as well as the field test results, are available to users upon request.

Systematized Collections

Subroutine libraries frequently contain several subroutines overlapping in intent and purpose, yet do not contain sufficient subroutines to cover a particular problem area completely. Where a choice between similar subroutines exists, there may be little documentation to help a prospective user in his choice. Frequently such subroutines have entirely different calling sequences, making substitution of one for another more than just a trivial task. Where several subroutines must be used in succession, the calling sequences frequently are not conducive to the smooth flow of information. These characteristics are independent of the quality of the individual subroutines in a library; they are considerations relating to a subset of the library considered as an entity in itself and have to do with the interaction between library elements.

Despite the obvious care that went into the original preparation of the ALGOL procedures representing the eigensystem algorithms, and the care with which these were individually translated, these antecedents of EISPACK suffered from most of the deficiencies just outlined. The realization that a package of subroutines should possess the same attributes as the individual subroutines themselves was a major turning point for NATS. Thus was born the concept of a *systematized collection*. We emphasize that such a collection is a set of subroutines which collectively solve a wide spectrum of problems and which individually reflect all of the attributes of quality software previously defined. Systematization imposes these same attributes on the set as a collection. In practice, the process of systematization frequently proceeds simultaneously with the previously described work of restructuring the individual programs.

One interesting result of the NATS project is that systematization may suggest, and benefit from, the creation of additional pieces of software. An obvious instance of this occurs when systematization exposes a problem area within the spectrum of the collection for which no routine applies. It is then necessary to find, or to write, a program to fill this gap. In EISPACK, the transformation programs for real tridiagonal and complex Hermitian matrices were added in response to such a stimulus. Less obvious, and perhaps more important, instances are the creation of additional software to enhance the robustness or usability of the collection. The desirability of such additional software may become apparent during systematization of a package, while its creation may provide important feedback to the systematization process, particularly for decisions about structure. Examples of such software in the NATS project are the error monitoring subroutines in FUNPACK and the control program for EISPACK.

In discussing the specific attributes of a systematized collection we start with good structure, for this attribute is not only the most apparent, but it is also instrumental in achieving some of the others. From a package viewpoint, good structure requires first that the calling sequences and use of parameters be as uniform as possible throughout the package, and that similar computations in different elements of the package be carried out in a similar manner. To illustrate this point, consider again the ALGOL antecedents of EISPACK, and in particular the problem of balancing (Wilkinson and Reinsch, 1971, p.315) a matrix and passing the balancing parameters on to subsequent subroutines. The ALGOL programs for balancing a matrix and for the back-transformation of eigenvectors of the balanced matrix use two parameters called LOW and HI, whereas these same parameters are variously called K and L, or LOW and UPP in other programs. Even worse, HI refers to the imaginary portion of a Hessenberg matrix in still other programs. Two programs which calculate both eigenvalues and eigenvectors recognize eigenvalues isolated by the balancing routines, whereas the corresponding programs which calculate only the eigenvalues do not. Thus these latter programs differ in programming detail from the functionally similar portions of the former programs. In systematizing the EISPACK collection, the parameters related to balancing were renamed LOW and IGH in all programs to make them uniform, unique, and integers in FORTRAN by default. In addition, the eigenvalue programs were restructured to make them almost proper subsets of the eigenvalue–eigenvector programs.

Such "massaging" of a package to ensure that a particular parameter has a unique name throughout helps give a family appearance to the package, but it is only a part of the structuring process. Decisions on ancillary considerations, which may have been made on a local *ad hoc* basis for individual subroutines, must now be reviewed on a global package basis. For example, it is necessary to examine subroutines which could possibly be chained together to be sure that the output from any subroutine meshes with the input requirements of the later ones. It is essential, for example, that information about pivoting generated in one program be stored and saved properly for the programs where it is needed even when other programs intervene. This is particularly critical when advantage is taken of the fortuitous availability of released storage to preserve this information.

A second structural consideration relates to the method of returning error diagnostics. The uniformity of a package suffers when some elements print diagnostic messages while others return error flags. The EISPACK elements uniformly return error flags, hence are I/O free. This is not a viable alternative for the elements of FUNPACK, where calls to the functions may be implicitly imbedded in larger algebraic expressions. Therefore, a sophisticated error processing routine was created for FUNPACK, eliminating unnecessary duplication of program segments, assuring package-wide uniformity of error monitoring, and localizing dependence upon I/O and other system conventions.

The reliability and robustness of a package result from the reliability and robustness of the individual elements and from the care with which the package is structured. The problem area encompassed by the package is defined as the union of problems which the individual elements can handle reliably. When several package elements must be called in succession to solve a problem, reliability involves the internal structuring of the package as well. Unless additional software is provided as part of systematization, the robustness of a properly structured package is simply the direct sum of the robustness of the individual elements. On the other hand, additional software may provide error detection facilities that cannot be incorporated in individual programs, such as the detection of errors related to chaining of subroutines.

The usability of a package again refers to the interface of the package with the user and with other software. But this interface is now at a higher level. Systematization has insured, for example, that the elements of the package interface properly with one another. Now one of the chief contributions to usability, assuming adequate documentation of the individual subroutines, is the documentation describing the use of the package as a whole. We apply the generic term *user's guide* to this higher level documentation. The user's guide delineates the problem set that the package will handle. From a description of the problem, it directs the user to the appropriate subset of the package most likely to solve the problem. Where more than one subset can be used, the advantages and disadvantages of each are spelled out. The user's guide thus provides what Fletcher (1972) calls a decision tree. In addition, the user's guide may contain package-oriented performance information not contained in the documentation of the individual elements. For example, EISPACK has been implemented for a variety of different computer environments, and the user's guide for EISPACK (Smith *et al*, 1974) contains timing information for many of these.

For some packages the creation of overall package control programs can also enhance usability. Such control programs automate the selection of routines from the package according to the decision tree, and load and execute the selected routines. This may contribute significantly to usability when the package structure dictates that a sequence of several routines is needed to solve a problem, as is the case in EISPACK. Furthermore, a control program can contribute to the robustness of a package by helping to avoid errors in selecting routines and composing paths, and by providing a central location for checking argument validity and handling error indications. The control program for EISPACK, and the ways in which it contributes to EISPACK usability and robustness, are discussed in detail in Boyle and Grau (1973).

The attribute of validity for a package is an obvious extension of validity for the individual elements. Indeed, many of the demonstration programs written for individual elements of a package actually invoke a sequence of elements, hence are demonstration programs for subsets of the package. The provision of additional demonstration programs to insure that the entire package is exercised in the manner in which it is intended to be used is, of course, necessary.

Production Benefits

The benefits to be derived from systematization of software packages, as we have described it, are enormous for both those producing the software and those using it. From the producer's viewpoint, there are two things that stand out: the ease with which portability is achieved and the semi-automation of maintenance.

The remarkable thing about portability is that it originally worried the NATS group a great deal. Recently we realized that we had not thought consciously about portability problems for some time. Portability seems to be almost free in the approach followed.

True portability of quality software is a myth, of course. Such software reflects the design of the hardware and software system on which it is to be compiled and used. Machine dependent parameters related to convergence of iterations are one obvious example of things that must change from machine to machine if high quality is to be maintained. Less obvious are changes in source programs dictated by the various dialects of a language, in our case FORTRAN, as implemented by the manufacturers. Compiler requirements differ not only from one manufacturer to another, but also from one compiler to another within a given company line and even on a given machine. What is necessary for one compiler may not even be allowed on another. For example, WATFIV requires that certain of the standard Fortran library and intrinsic functions used be named in type declarations, while other compilers object to such declarations. Our experience has shown that it is possible to structure programs so that they are written largely in ANSI Fortran, and so that machine dependent sections of a program are isolated and pinpointed. Programs written in this way are "portable" in the sense that they are *transportable with minimum change*.

The initial effort to structure programs was done manually using text editing facilities available in RESCUE, an Argonne-developed time-sharing system. As the work progressed, certain patterns in the process began to emerge, suggesting the possibility of developing special-purpose information processing aids for maintenance. This became a necessity as the number of subroutines grew and as versions of the packages for different machines were added. Information processors seemed to be the only way to insure that design changes were made uniformly and reliably throughout the software, and that no unintended changes were made.

The processors finally implemented are best described in terms of the EISPACK package where the software is less machine dependent than in FUNPACK. The original Fortran programs are IBM long precision programs for which source statements are maintained in data sets on-line to our computer and time-sharing system. A program called GENERALIZER was written to convert the IBM programs to composites which contain the alternate source statements necessary for ANSI single precision versions of the programs. The composite thus contains the original source statements interspersed with alternate source statements and appropriate control statements. Variable declaration statements exist in tandem, for example, with control statements indicating which declaration is to be used for the IBM long precision version and which for the ANSI single precision version. Major portions of the composite source (indicated by appropriate control statements) are used in both versions.

A second program called SELECTOR was written to extract from the composite source the appropriate version for a particular machine. In addition, this program modifies certain statements to implant machine dependent constants related to word length, thus producing final source designed for that machine. With these machine aids it is now possible to make a manual modification once to the original source program and to propagate the change automatically and correctly to all versions of the program.

The use of these aids for FUNPACK is more restricted, since the initial elements of the package are highly machine dependent with only short sequences of source statements common to all versions of a program. GENERALIZER is bypassed in favour of concatenation of separate source decks into a composite, merely separating them in their entirety with appropriate control statements. This merged source is a convenience for storage purposes only. SELECTOR is still used to extract the desired version. GENERALIZER will be used to maintain certain future elements of FUN-PACK which will be less machine dependent.

The text editing facilities in RESCUE and the relatively simple information processing programs just described have greatly aided the NATS project and have convinced all of us of the soundness of this approach to software production. However, these information processors depend for their successful operation on the careful formatting of the NATS programs, rather than on their underlying structure. Thus, they will not work on a less-well-formatted set of programs regardless of how well structured they are. Furthermore, the formatting task itself is a thankless one, and we would like to automate it insofar as possible.

To create a more generally applicable system we intend to produce a new set of information processing programs which can be used in conjunction with time-sharing text editing facilities in the following way. We want to be able to start with a more or less arbitrary FORTRAN text which is the working version of a piece of software on some computer. This text would be processed, partially by hand but largely by program, to produce an intermediate *abstract form* in which the underlying structure of the program would explicitly and from which details of specific dialects of FORTRAN would be excluded. Once the program in this form, a number of systematization processes could be carried out on it again either by hand or by program. Finally, when the program has been thoroughly systematized (or at any earlier time, for testing purposes), the abstract form could be processed automatically to produce a carefully formatted, well-structured text in the dialect of FORTRAN required for a particular machine.

This method of operation, employing an intermediate abstract form, should provide some important benefits. Most of the details by which a dialect of FORTRAN for a particular machine differs from those for other machines will be shed in the process of converting a program to abstract form. When the abstract form is automatically processed to produce a working program for a (possibly different) machine, only the essential differences between dialects, particularly those involving syntax, will be reconstructed.

Thus the abstract version of a program will be "clean" and relatively free of trivial machine dependencies. Indeed, most of the systematization processes we wish to automate properly depend upon the structure of a program, not upon its particular format. Thus these processes should be easier to automate when they apply to the abstract form.

The composite storage for programs which is so valuable now can be introduced at any stage of this process. Since the differences between dialects will be handled automatically, composite storage will be used primarily to preserve significant semantic differences between the versions of a program. Such differences, for example those required because the UNIVAC compiler treats the construction $(.5 - x) + .5$ (required in one of the FUNPACK programs) as if it were $(1. - x)$, will probably still have to be introduced into a program by hand. But once these constructions have been introduced, they will be propagated automatically to the final version of that program for the appropriate machines. A forthcoming paper (Boyle and Smith, 1974) provides some further description of these planned information processors, as well as discussing the existing NATS processors in detail.

User Benefits

We feel that the attributes of NATS software discussed above all contribute to potential user acceptance of, and confidence in, the software. Perhaps confidence is the real benefit from the user's viewpoint. Ideally, the user should be relieved of any concern over the software package he is using, and should be able to concentrate his attention on his own program.

A user's initial contact with software is generally with the documentation or listings. Favorable first impressions being important, the appearance of the software is probably second only to performance in establishing user confidence. Structuring, formatting, and systematization all contribute to the pleasing appearance of software. This impression is enhanced by well-formatted careful documentation. The care apparent in detailed programming and documentation suggests care in the development of the programs, which in turn suggests reliability and builds confidence.

Software based on algorithms accepted and respected in the literature acquires an initial reputation by association. But the software must perform well to retain that reputation and build upon it. Reliability and robustness are the components of that performance. Demonstration programs and testing aids provided with the software are an obvious means of attracting users. These aids also help users to determine when the software has been successfully installed on their computer systems, and they augment the documentation by providing examples of correct usage.

Last, but not least, because of the extensive testing that has been done, the NATS group knows from actual experience that the software will perform correctly in all computer environments for which it is advertised. This makes possible a statement of certification and pledge of support which is prominently attached to each program. The statement declares that the programs have been thoroughly tested on specified hardware and software configurations, and that they will be supported for those configurations in the sense that the developers are committed to examine malfunctions and to maintain the software.

In summary, we feel that the intangible image of pride and competence which a software package projects about its developers manifests itself in user acceptance of the software. In the NATS project we have believed this from the beginning and have developed the philosophy, procedures, and information processing aids described here to help insure that our software has these attributes.

Acknowledgments

The NATS project is the result of the combined efforts of many people. W. R. Cowell (Argonne), as coordinator and principal investigator of the NATS project, under advisement from co-principal investigators W. J. Cody (Argonne), Y. Ikebe (The University of Texas at Austin), and C. B. Moler (The University of New Mexico), organized the project into its present form. Other Argonne participants were J. M. Boyle, B. S. Garbow, V. C. Klema, and B. T. Smith.

We have been greatly assisted by the careful testing and cooperation of our test representatives. They are T. J. Aird at Purdue University, A. K. Cline at the National Center for Atmospheric Research. S. C. Eisenstat at Yale University, I. Farkas at The University of Toronto, B. Ford of the Numerical Algorithms Group, F. N. Fritsch at Lawrence Livermore Laboratory, R. E. Funderlic at Oak Ridge National Laboratory, L. Harding at the University of Michigan, R. G. Hetherington at The University of Kansas, L. Kaufman at Stanford University, R. J. Lambert at Ames Laboratory, D. Raden and the late H. Kuki at The University of Chicago, J. Stein at Northwestern University, and P. Wolfe, H. Hull and W. Wallace at The University of Wisconsin.

References

Boyle, J. M. and Grau, A. A. (1973). Modular design of a user-oriented control program for EISPACK. Applied Mathematics Division Technical Memorandum No. 242, Argonne National Laboratory, Illinois.

Boyle, J. M. and Smith, B. T. (1974). Information processing aids for software development: a case history (in preparation).

Boyle, J. M., Cody, W. J., Cowell, W. R., Garbow, B. S., Ikebe, Y., Moler, C. B., and Smith, B. T., (1972). NATS, a collaborative effort to certify and disseminate mathematical software. *In* "Proceedings 1972 National ACM Conference," Vol. II, Association for Computing Machinery, New York, 630–635.

Fletcher, R. (1972). Methods for the solution of optimization problems, *Comp. Phys. Comm.* **3**, 159–172.

Smith, B. T., The NATS project, a national activity to test software, *SHARE SSD* 228, October 1972, item C-5732, 35–42.

Smith, B. T., Boyle, J. M., Garbow, B. S., Ikebe, Y, Klema, V. C., and Moler, C. B. (1974). "Matrix Eigensystem Routines–EISPACK Guide", Lecture Note Series in Computer Science, Vol. 6, Springer–Verlag.

Wilkinson, J. H. and Reinsch, C. (1971). "Handbook for Automatic Computation", Volume II, Linear Algebra," Part 2, Springer-Verlag, New York, Heidelberg, Berlin.

Discussion: Organisation and Portability of Program Libraries

MR. POWELL. How long does the collection to the distribution of material by NAG take?

MR. FORD. As I described in the paper we have divided the areas of numerical analysis into the chapters of the Modified Share Classification Index. Each contributor to the Library is responsible to the Contents Committee for the choice of algorithms in his or her particular chapter. As the contributor would generally be in touch with a NAG consultant who would be an authority on the given subject. we would hope to be aware of the algorithm prior to its publication. Assuming the algorithm satisfied the necessary criteria for possible selection, it would then be exhaustively compared with competing algorithms from the same numerical area. The selected algorithms in each chapter for inclusion in the next Mark of the Library would then be discussed by the Library Contents Committee, and the new contents agreed. The algorithm would by now have been coded into an ALGOL 60 procedure and ANSI FORTRAN subroutine. Example and stringent test programs would be developed in each language and user documentation written. Finally, the software and documentation would be sent to the Validator for comments, and when any corrections or alterations had been completed, the material despatched to the NAG Central Office for inclusion in the next Mark of the Library. As collection and release dates for each Mark of the Library are agreed well in advance (usually of the order of a year) the timetable suggested for these activities are well known. However, this timetable acts only as a guide to both contributors and validators, as it is more important that software and documentation is correct than actually distributed in a given Mark.

Hence the time from receipt of an algorithm to its inclusion in the Library may be a year. The time from receipt of software and documentation for a given Mark to the distribution of a tested semi-compiled library, test program library and supporting documentation is usually three months.

DR. GOURLAY. Could you please indicate your process for handling "errors" communicated by users, and the possible response time for same?

MR. FORD. In the original ICL 1906A project, the error handling process is relatively straightforward. If a fault is found, users are encouraged to notify their local advisory service of the mistake. The advisory service report the error to the 1906A co-ordinator who takes the following actions:

(i) Records the receipt of the error.

(ii) Acknowledges its receipt.

(iii) Sends details of the fault to the relevant contributor who in turn studies it, and replies to the co-ordinator.

(iv) Sends to the centres which mount the library, a description of the error, of its effect, and the likely correction period.

(v) Incorporates the contributor's correction to the fault. The updated software or documentation is included in the next release (a new Mark or intermediate updated).

So far new Marks, have been issued between 6–9 month periods. A minor update if required, probably takes place in intervals of about two months. The situation in a multi-machine library project is slightly more complex, and one must take active steps to prevent error reporting and correction procedures being "drowned by bureaucracy". The library co-ordinator for a machine range now receives error reports from centres within that group. He decides whether these errors are of consequence only to his implementation or to other versions of the library. In the former case, he initiates the correction procedures; in the latter, the report is sent to the NAG Central Office. Here the reports from the various implementations are sorted and collated, and the appropriate expert contacted to provide or check a solution to the error. The master library source file or documentation is then updated (immediately) and in general this correction is available to all implementations of the library for their next release.

The same interim error notification scheme as for the 1906A group operates within the other groups.

In furnishing a correction to a serious error, any response time greater than zero is unsatisfactory. We anticipate that a response time of normally about two months (i.e. the time taken to test, prepare and distribute minor updates in a suitable form) is still feasible but it does require an adequate level of resources and support. Given these, we believe that we can give an acceptable response time for error correction, and avoid at the same time jeopardising the integrity of the library which might result from instantaneous "user-applied" remedies.

PROF. EVANS. If a good algorithm appeared in a journal tomorrow, by what procedure and how long will it take to appear in the Library?

MR. FORD. As I mentioned earlier this tends to be variable but the usual period is upwards to a year or so.

PROFESSOR ANDREW YOUNG (*New University of Ulster*). Is any step being taken to make your system "biodegradable"?

MR. PRENTICE. By this, I take you to mean, do we have mechanisms for the removal of outdated techniques? The answer is yes. We do however, have an overlap period to allow users to convert their programs. This is the old problem of standardisation versus progress.

DR. JAMES C. T. POOL (*Argonne National Laboratory, U.S.A.*). The monitoring of the usage of mathematical software is important to determine future allocation of resources in developing, refining and implementing algorithms. Are other NAG Computer Centres besides Nottingham also monitoring usage? The resulting statistics will be extremely important for guiding future work.

MR. FORD. Discussions are taking place regarding the monitoring of Library usage on other ICL 1906A's, ICL 1900's, System 4, PDP10, CDC 7000/6000 and IBM machines. We hope to be able to collect statistics for a minimum peroid of one month on approximately twenty-five university machines.

MR. J. E. CARRINGTON (*City of Leicester Polytechnic*). Is the NAG Library going to be available to Polytechnics in the future?

MR. FORD. We hope so. The majority of Polytechnics have ICL 1900 machines. Following an initative by the Polytechnics members of the 1900 University Users group an ad hoc working party of representatives from these centres has been formed to develop a framework in which the Library can be made available to Polytechnics.

MISS JUDITH DANIELS (*University College Computing Centre, London*). I was very impressed by the description of the coding standards, structure and commenting of the programs in the NATS project outlined by Dr. Smith. What plans does NAG have to improve the standardization of their coding and how and when are they going to implement any plans for inserting comments, improving structure etc.?

MR. FORD. The NAG Languages working party, of which I believe the questionner is a member, is discussing these and related matters at the present time.

DR. TAYLOR. The NAG Library is a collaborative project depending for its numerical integrity on the good-will of a large number of people. It is difficult to maintain coding standards in such an environment. An early NAG policy of not distributing source code—a policy which has since been modified—has in fact encouraged laziness in inserting comments. Various working practices are being evolved by implementation groups which will in the course of time lead to more standardization and structuring of the material. The implementation of the master source concept will allow an ad hoc cross fertilization of these practices. The NAG Central Office will have an opportunity to coordinate this process.

MR. R. W. MCINTYRE. (*Rolls-Royce Ltd.*) How do NATS and NAG compare on the extent to which the libraries have been made available to and have been used by industry.

DR. SMITH. NATS is a research project and no charge can be made for provision of a service which has come from a project supported from public funds. This applies to users inside and outside the United States. No charge can be made even for the copying of the library onto the tapes (which the users supply). Of 150 NATS users in the United States 60 are from industry.

MR. FORD. NAG was developed initially with the universities in mind. General release of the software would not be right until the NAG Library reaches a maintenance phase in about 18 months time. At the present time, although it is hoped that all chapters are sound, not all are good and the contents of some are sparse. Already industry has shown interest in NAG, but enquiries have been directed toward specific routines rather than the complete system. It has been possible to supply specific routines to several firms.

DR. POOL. EISPACK has been distributed to 150 centres. Approximately 60 of these are governmental or industrial research laboratories. The policy of the USAEC and NSF allows this distribution when the material is published, i.e. when it is in the public domain. Currently, EISPACK is available, without charge by contacting the address indicated in Dr. Smith's lecture.

MR. FORD. The EISPACK User's Guide will be published with listings of the code. However, you are advised not to punch up decks from these listings.

DR. J. A. ENDERBY (*UKAEA Risley*). Are programs that use backing store excluded from the NAG and NATS projects? In addition, are programs having physical content, such as the algorithmic version of the International Steam Tables, to be allowed in the projects? Linear equations (real, symmetric, sparse) and sorting are areas in which backing store routines are already very widely used.

MR. FORD. As was mentioned in the talk, industry would probably require a somewhat different library to that developed for use in universities. This would certainly include backing store algorithms in a number of areas, most notably linear algebra and sorting. Certainly specific routines, such a one for the determination of elements of the International Steam Tables, could be included.

MR. J. S. ROBINSON (*British Steel Corporation*). What extensions are foreseen for the implementation of NAG library in ALGOL 68, in view of the flexible data type available?

MR. PRENTICE. There is currently a pilot project implementing a sub-set of the library in ALGOL 68. The aim of this is to translate not transliterate the routines and this will ensure exploitation of ALGOL 68 for these algorithms.

A more difficult problem is whether there are algorithms that are valuable but only writable in ALGOL 68 and whether the optimality of choice of an algorithm is in fact a function of the language in which it is expressed. We hope the pilot project will give some feel for this.

MR. J. E. PHYTHIAN (*Open University*). What difficulties would you envisage in an attempt to implement the NAG Library on a BASIC system using terminals? Would the global nature of all BASIC parameters make this implementation difficult?

MR. PRENTICE. This depends on what you mean by BASIC. The subroutine structure and parameter mechanism of most implementations are not really adequate to support a subroutine library and there would be problems caused by the size of the library and the effort to document a version in a new and not well standardised language.

DR. REID. It may be of interest to report that there is just one subroutine in the Harwell library that has backing storage. This is for solving band symmetric and positive-definite systems of linear equations, where large cases can be handled almost as fast as if all storage were in core.

MR. POWELL. Establishments with many computer users will probably wish to supplement the NAG library with other library subroutines that are important to their work. Would the Panel please say how they think establishments should combine the NAG library with their private libraries.

MR. FORD. In a number of university computing centres the NAG Library is already available in conjunction with a local library, which contains routines that for one reason or another have not been included by NAG at the present time. The local computing system permits contents from either or both of the libraries to be included in a user program.

MRS. DIXON. It seems to me that NAG is in a good position to carry out comparative testing of algorithms. Certainly where several routines (or methods) are available to do the same job and since NAG space is limited some comparative testing must be done to decide which one to implement. Do you intend to exploit this at all by publishing the results of comparative studies?

MR. FORD. We would hope eventually to publish the results of our comparative studies.

DR. GOURLAY. The aims for the construction of large program libraries seem to be set for a head-on clash with manufacturers who sell these packages. What strategy are you going to use?

MR. FORD. Certainly NAG anticipates no head-on collision with hardware manufacturers who sell such packages. Increasingly the British manufacturers are finding the development of such software far too expensive for the return they achieve, and so are encouraging the project to continue their work in the hope that the Library will be made more generally available.

24. Setting up a Numerical Advisory Service

R. FLETCHER AND M. D. HEBDEN

Theoretical Physics Division, U.K.A.E.A. Research Group,
Atomic Energy Research Establishment, Harwell, England.

1. Introduction

Numerical analysts can be divided into two groups: those who regard the subject as a branch of pure mathematics, and those who consider the prime motivation to be towards the solution of practical problems. Most of the latter group would agree that interaction between numerical analysts and people with problems is to the benefit of both parties. We believe it to be essential to keep injecting new problems to prevent numerical analysis from becoming sterile and introspective. We shall describe our experiences at A.E.R.E. Harwell in trying to achieve such interaction, and some of the lessons which we have learned.

Harwell has a professional staff of around one thousand, and they are organized into divisions, representing major scientific and engineering disciplines which are associated with the design of nuclear reactors. The computing service for these divisions is centralized and each has a divisional representative to maintain their interest in the service. Provision of numerical methods has always been considered as a necessary part of this service. However, because of the limited manpower, priority in the past has been given to the development and administration of a subroutine library containing a wide ranging set of high quality numerical routines.

Recent increases in staff have resulted in the formation of a Numerical Analysis Group, both to carry out research and to further assist users in numerical problems. The group consists of five people with a strong research interest in numerical analysis, and two with expertise in both numerical analysis and software who carry out the housekeeping associated with maintaining a subroutine library. The setting up of a numerical analysis advisory service was thought to be good a way of helping to disseminate the advantages being obtained through the continuing research in the subject. This has been done in another important way by giving several courses annually in various aspects of numerical methods, each course consisting of about twelve lectures and practical classes, spread over three successive days.

This paper is concerned mainly with the problems involved in setting up a numerical advisory service. It was felt that the service should be manned by a 'coordinator' or front man, through whom all (or most) queries should be channelled. Details of the way in which the service operates are given in Section 3. However much more important problems must be tackled on the best way of approaching users so that the service becomes well used, and that the advice given is appropriate. Such matters are discussed in Section 2. In Section 4 we present a number of examples, drawn from our practical experience in operating the service, which illustrate these points and the benefits which ensue to the user. Finally, in Section 5 we attempt to extract some conclusions that may be valid for other organizations who are considering setting up such a service.

2. Communicating With Users

Initially it was difficult to decide how to set about the task of establishing contacts with users. It seemed clear however that users who were consuming a lot of computer time might be given help to make their programs more efficient, and those getting incorrect answers helped to get correct ones. It also seemed likely that any deficiencies in the subroutine library would be exposed and could be rectified. In an attempt to gain information about users' attitudes, we discussed the projected service with about ten of the representatives of divisions involved in substantial computing, and with a number of major users. The topics which were discussed included:

 (i) The nature of the problems solved.

 (ii) Which routines in the library were used; and with what failure rate.

(iii) What routines might be added, or improved.

(iv) Whether any problems had been shelved for lack of a known numerical method.

 (v) Whether they anticipated our being able to help, either now, or at some future date.

The results of this survey were quite encouraging in that they suggested that to a large extent users were satisfied with the scope of the library. The most useful effect was to inform users of the projected service and to start the process of creating links between the service and users. However, although a number of instances were given of past occasions on which help would have been appreciated, there was little immediate demand for assistance.

We discussed the outcome of these interviews amongst ourselves, and have come to two conclusions. One is that in the short term we have not realised our original expectation of helping users to speed up their programs. In fact users are not unreasonably averse to spending such effort because of the consequent loss in their time to pursue other research. The user will not spend such effort unless absolutely necessary. More surprisingly, users do not seem to be interested in solving problems which they have shelved in the past through lack of a numerical method. It seems that, in one way or another, users have come to terms with the situation and are now involved in other things. It may well be however that this observation will not apply in a university, where the pressure to solve each problem as it arises and then pass on to the next, is less acute.

The implication is that users only seek advice under the following conditions:

(a) When their program is so long or so large that they can no longer finance its running.

(b) When their program gives what are known to be incorrect answers.

Bearing in mind the users' reluctance to waste undue effort, it seems most worthwhile to encourage users to seek advice not only in (a) and (b) above, but also when the problem is in the formulative stage. One step in doing this was to send out a circular to all users informing them of the existence and aims of the service, and in particular stressing the value of a discussion at the formulative stage. However although this met with some response it proved by no means sufficient. The difficulty was and is to establish an atmosphere in which users are prepared to spend time doing this. It is therefore important to consider why such an atmosphere does not exist *a priori*, and how it can be fostered.

One major cause is that numerical analysts often do not encourage users to approach them with problems, largely because to do so makes demands on their time, and prevents them from doing other apparently more interesting or fruitful research. Some numerical analysts take the unfortunate view that although such contacts may be intrinsically valuable, they themselves do not want any part of it. A user may appreciate this and be loth to impose his problem, unless absolutely necessary. The advantage of formal arrangement such as is described here, is that users no longer feel diffident on this score in making an approach. Furthermore the demands on a numerical analyst's time can be more readily quantified and budgeted for.

However even if the two groups can be brought together, all may not be well. There still remains the real problem of communicating with someone from a totally different scientific background. A language barrier exists between mathematicians and other scientists and engineers and this causes difficulties in understanding each others concepts. It is very important that the scientist is not made to feel stupid merely because he cannot understand some unfamiliar mathematical point. The scientist is mainly interested in solving his problem, to which end he sets up a model which hopefully can be solved. The numerical analyst on the other hand is principally interested in the solution of the model, and its origin is of small concern. One might say that the scientist works in 'problem space' and the numerical analyst works in 'model space'. This also gives rise to a number of difficulties. For instance the scientist may have performed what to the analyst are undesirable transformations on the model before presenting it for solution. Alternatively the method proposed by the analyst might lead to a solution violating certain physical principles not made explicit in the model. Yet again the scientist may be suspicious of the method of solution of the model because it does not have an obvious interpretation in terms of the problem.

As an alternative to consulting a numerical analyst, a user may seek advice from a member of his own department who has experience in solving similar problems, and with whom he can converse readily. Although this takes some of the load off the numerical analyst, it has its undesirable features, one of which is that the user might not get the most up-to-date advice. Another undesirable situation may occur when a knowledgeable user has developed a program to carry out some task, and the program is used by less experienced users. These latter users are not in a position to incorporate new subroutines into the program, and if an error develops they cannot rectify it. Furthermore there may be restrictions on the scope of the program which the originator has not made explicit. Often the situation is not serious unless the original author is no longer concerned with the running of the program in which case there is nobody who knows what is going on.

As may have become apparent, our way of solving such problems has been to attempt to build up a good atmosphere between numerical analysts and users, so that after receiving advice when stuck ((a) and (b) above), users return at the formulative stage of a later problem if the choice of method is not clear. This effect has been very noticeable. Furthermore we find that users encourage their colleagues to use the service if they themselves have had a good experience with it.

Finally in this section we would point out another useful means by which contact has been established with users. This has been through the numerical methods courses mentioned in the introduction. Users often attend such lectures in the hope of learning about techniques which may be applicable to their problems. Discussion of such a problem often takes place during the course, and indicates that the choice of a suitable numerical method may not be obvious, and that there are advantages in consulting a numerical analyst. Furthermore students who have discussed problems with the lecturer on such a course, often return to him or the advisory service at a later date.

3. Operating the Service

Although a formal advisory service has been set up at Harwell, in fact it operates with a fair degree of flexibility and the details to be given here are considered as guidelines rather than hard and fast rules. In the first instance, users are expected to contact the co-ordinator to establish the best procedure. This may involve the co-ordinator recommending a method of solution, possibly after studying the problem to a greater or lesser extent. On the other hand the co-ordinator may suggest that the user sees one of the specialists in the Numerical Analysis Group who back up the service. Alternatively, the co-ordinator may discuss the problem with one or more specialists and then report back to the user. It may be however that the user has received advice from a specialist on a previous occasion in which case he is likely to contact the specialist in the first instance on a later project. In the interests of maintaining good relations, such an arrangement is not ruled out. For most problems a satisfactory line of attack can be decided on fairly readily, and although a number of visits may be necessary to iron out snags or misunderstandings, the total demand on the co-ordinators' time is no more than a day or two. Of course, the user is expected to do the majority of the programming and testing himself, although possibly the advisor might suggest the form that such a program should take.

Less trivial problems involving development and testing of new numerical methods require more organisation. The co-ordinator's salary is buried in the costs of running the computing service and it is not acceptable that a large amount of his time should be made available to individual users on this basis. At Harwell there is the provision for contract work to be carried out, so the user can hire a specialist (subject to availability) to develop a suitable algorithm, should there be funds available. However such arrangements are best regarded as being beyond the scope of an advisory service.

Another question arises as to who should deal with queries about programming (what does this error message mean?—why didn't my job compile? —etc.). It is felt that answering such queries is not the function of the numerical analysis advisory service. In fact at Harwell such questions are handled in the main by one of the two people responsible for the day to day running of the subroutine library. Many university computer installations seem to provide a query answering service of this nature: this is satisfactory and leaves the numerical analyst free to give the advice for which he is most qualified. Nevertheless such queries do arise from time to time, and the advisor has to strike a balance between becoming increasingly bogged down by answering too many such queries on the one hand, or by risking his good relationship with users by answering none on the other.

It had been expected that the operation of the advisory service would lead to feedback on the deficiencies of routines in the subroutine library and the need for new routines. This has in fact happened, and the library has largely met these needs, through the efforts of members of the Numerical Analysis Group. However the prime function of this group is to pursue research into numerical analysis, with the consequence that it has occasionally not been possible to introduce a subroutine for which there has been a request. Perhaps in these circumstances there is a case for contracting out work to research workers in universities, given that money is made available for developing the subroutine library, or for closer liason with other libraries such as the NAG library.

4. Some Technical Problems

In this section we illustrate a number of points that have arisen in the operation of the service. They are chosen to show some of the reasons why users do not use the best available algorithm. Some of them indicate the value that a short discussion with a numerical analyst can have even when the problem appears straightforward, and indeed a few users have been saved a great deal of fruitless work when defects in the model have been noticed.

The first example arises because the library does not contain a subroutine for solving the problem in its most natural formulation. It is necessary to transform the problem to one for which a suitable subroutine does exist and the user, ignorant of a standard numerical technique, applies a transformation that is inappropriate, for instance one which might introduce instability into the problem. Consider the eigenvalue problem

$$A\mathbf{x} = \lambda B\mathbf{x}$$

with A and B symmetric and B positive definite matrices. The most obvious approach which the user might choose is to solve the equivalent problem

$$B^{-1}A\mathbf{x} = \lambda\mathbf{x},$$

but $B^{-1}A$ is no longer symmetric and its eigenvalues may be ill-conditioned If, instead, we form the factorization

$$B = LL^T$$

the problem can be rewritten with a symmetric matrix as

$$(L^{-1}AL^{-T})\mathbf{y} = \lambda\mathbf{y}, \qquad \mathbf{x} = L^{-T}\mathbf{y}.$$

This transformation is well conditioned and reduces the problem to one for which a satisfactory subroutine exists. A note is made of the deficiency in the library so that, resources permitting, a more suitable routine can be added to the library.

The next example is chosen to illustrate the way in which users work with familiar concepts, and lack the perception necessary to distinguish the numerically stable approach. The problem is that of finding the only positive value of t such that

$$a = \sum_{i=1}^{n} \frac{x_i}{y_i + t}$$

for given a, n, x_i, y_i. The user was in little doubt that t could be found satisfactorily by rewriting the expression as

$$P_n(t) = 0$$

where $P_n(t)$ is the appropriate polynomial of degree n in t, followed by using a routine for finding the roots of a polynomial. This method is, however, liable to be unstable, and it would be better to regard the problem as a single non-linear equation in t. A short discussion revealed that x_i and y_i were all positive, and that $\Sigma(x_i/y_i) > a$ so that bisection could be used with the initial interval $(0, a/\Sigma x_i)$.

Occasionally, however, the user has made an unsatisfactory transformation to the problem which cannot easily be overcome. An example of this occurs when wishing to constrain a variable x_i to be positive in the minimisation of a function whose derivatives are not available. One possible transformation is to minimise with respect to a variable $y_i = \sqrt{x_i}$, which is satisfactory except when the constraint is binding at the minimum. As the numerical analysts have provided no better method the user has no choice but to use a method like the above. This problem illustrates the advantage of the advisory service to the numerical analyst, in pointing out directions in which new research ought to be directed.

Another example shows a longer term project. The problem was: given a histogram with bars of unequal width, and with a height accurate to between five and ten per cent, to find a new histogram based on different unequal widths. The user, again working with a familiar concept, had fitted the cumulative distribution and then had derived the new histogram by taking differences of the fit. When this failed he came to the advisory service for help. After some thought and experiment we devised a method based on determining the function whose definite integrals generate the histogram. This was a case where the correct line of attack was not clear and the collaboration was more in the sense of a small joint research project with the user.

Even when the user has formulated his problem correctly, and is conversant with the methods available, he may have good reason to use what the numerical analyst would consider an inferior algorithm. Two readily accepted reasons for doing so are to reduce the time taken or the storage required. There are, however, a number of other possibilities and two examples will be given. One instance occurred when a routine for non-linear least squares calculations was superceded by a new method. The old subroutine had the facility that the variance–covariance matrix would be passed to the calling program, whereas the new routine lacked such a feature. As a result, some users did not use the superior algorithm. On another occasion lack of portability caused a group to use an inferior algorithm. They were developing programs for use on a wide variety of machines and had contracted to write the programs in standard FORTRAN. As a consequence, any of the Harwell Subroutine Library routines which they required had to be converted to standard FORTRAN, and so instead of using the best possible routine for a problem, they tried to make do with routines that they had already converted.

5. Conclusions

By and large the service at Harwell works well except perhaps that its scope could be extended by making a statistician available to consult with users. Much of the smooth running can be attributed to the provision of a subroutine library that is well documented† and in which high priority is given to the rectification of errors. Indeed without a good library it is unlikely that such a service would be effective (it is undesirable that the coordinator should have to write or modify software to any great extent). As a result the user who is familiar with FORTRAN and is reasonably numerate is well catered for. In addition we provide courses that cover the spectrum of Numerical Methods so that other users can acquire some expertise.

Less sophisticated users do not fare so well. Because of their lack of knowledge of numerical analysis they are often using subroutines for methods which they do not understand, so they are liable to use a routine when it should not be applied. This would not be too bad if they utilised all the error checks that are available. However their lack of numeracy causes them to fail to spot indications of trouble, and they often take the attitude that results are correct unless they are known to be wrong. To counteract this we feel that it is important that library subroutines print out an error message when an unreliable answer has been produced. Another way by which numerical analysts can help such users is to alleviate the need for them to develop programs. Clearly it is not practicable for a computer centre to provide all

† M. J. Hopper (1971) "Harwell Subroutine Library, A Catalogue of Subroutines", U.K.A.E.A. Research Group Report A.E.R.E. 6912; and Supplement 1 and Supplement 2 (1972).

users with the program that they want but there are a number of areas where program packages could be provided. A prime area is in the field of non-linear data fitting and others are differential equations and linear programming. An example of what can be achieved is the package FATAL† developed by two users in the Health Physics division at Harwell. This package allows the user to fit data, supplied in any form that is convenient, by any approximating function. The only requirement is that the user can write the necessary FORTRAN statements to evaluate his approximating function. An additional refinement is that by using the remote terminal system the user avoids the need for a knowledge of Job Control Language. This user package is exceptional in that is it well documented and the authors are still concerned with its maintenacne. Indeed they incorporated into the package a new non-linear least squares routine shortly after its introduction into the library. However the standard for other such packages is often much lower, and unfortunately users do not have the discrimination to decide whether a package will prove to be reliable. Packages may prove to be poor not only from an inferior numerical method, but from inadequate facilities, poor maintenance, possibly caused by inadequate or nonexistent documentation, or poor error indications. The only sure way to avoid this misuse of the package is to have it supervised along with the subroutine library to the same high degree of attention.

Given a good library we have found that one person, spending about half his time in an advisory capacity, can cope with almost all of the problems that arise. Occasionally a discussion with a colleague or colleagues is necessary, but the fact that this is possible within a group such as ours at Harwell, we regard as a bonus rather than a necessity. More difficult to handle are jobs that require a large amount of a numerical analyst's time (a few months for example), and exactly how these are handled will depend on the installation. Again these jobs are relatively few. Almost every university has a set-up similar to that at Harwell, in as much as there are specialists who teach Numerical Analysis and users from many disciplines on the campus. It should therefore be possible for them to provide a similar service. There is also no reason why our experience cannot be repeated in any environment with a single numerical analyst who has occasional consultation with experts.

Finally it should be said that co-ordinating a service such as we have described brings the numerical analyst into contact with a wide variety of problems. It is therefore an excellent way for him to apply his training as a numerical analyst, and is particularly stimulating if his background is of a more theoretical nature.

† L. Salmon and D. V. Booker, U.K.A.E.A. Research Group Report A.E.R.E. R7128 (1972).

25. User Documentation for a General Numerical Library: The NAG Approach

SHIRLEY A. LILL

Computer Laboratory, University of Liverpool,
Liverpool, England.

1. Introduction

Documentation plays a dominant role in determining the success of any numerical library that is to be used as part of a general computing service. It is obviously important that a library is well-balanced and contains good, tested routines, but unless it is well-documented it will be virtually useless, and the effort spent on the routines wasted. Documentation is especially important in a wide-spread project such as NAG (Ford; 1972, 1973), where the average user is unlikely to ever have contact with the contributor of a routine, and where even his local computing centre may not have been involved in the project. It provides the interface between the user and the routine, where all the experience gained by the contributor and the implementor in developing or testing the routine can be passed on to the user.

The format of the documentation for the NAG Library was initially designed by the members of the NAG committee. It developed as the Library was being developed, so that by the time the first set of routines was released a standard format had been agreed. Slight inconsistencies in content and layout were tidied up at subsequent releases, but the documentation still retains its original structure. A working party is currently considering restructuring the documentation to make it more appropriate to the multi-machine Library which it now describes. This paper therefore represents the work of all the members of NAG who have contributed towards its documentation.

2. Aims

The overall aim of the Committee was to design a manual which maximized the general usefulness of the Library. The design of documentation involves considering three main aspects:

Volume. The physical size of the manual.

Content. The depth of the information.

Indexing. The means of accessing the information.

For each of these aspects there are restrictions and conflicting needs that must be satisfied. Achieving the overall aim therefore depended upon resolving compromises between the following issues.

(i) The manual should be comprehensive and yet easy to handle. It should be readily available.

(ii) It should contain sufficient detail to be useful to an expert and yet not overwhelming for a beginner.

(iii) It should be indexed to give either access to a particular routine, or advice leading to the solution of a particular problem.

From the favourable response that NAG documentation has received, it is hoped that it does go some way to satisfying these objectives.

3. Structure of Documentation

Comprehensive documentation for a numerical library is of such a size that careful consideration must be given to its structure if 2(i) is to be satisfied. For ease of distribution and updating it was decided that the smallest re-placeable unit of the NAG Library Manual should be a document (i.e. not a page) with one document per routine. However, to avoid the Manual turning into a collection of routine documents some division was needed. In the event, a structure occurred quite naturally with the routines being classified according to the Share Classification Index; i.e. they are grouped into *subject* areas. Each area has its own introduction, which, together with the routine documents, forms a chapter in the manual. In addition, the Manual has an Introduction, a Contents List and an Index, making five documents in all:

(i) *Introduction.* Explains the naming of routines and gives general in-formation on the Library.

(ii) *Contents.* Lists the chapters.

(iii) *Chapter Introduction.* Lists the routines in the chapter and gives general advice on the choice and use of routines.

(iv) *Routine Document.* Explains the use of the routines.

(v) *Index*. Lists the names of the routines and key words in alphabetical order.

Documents (i), (ii) and (v) are written at the Central Office when the Library is assembled. Chapter Introductions and Routine Documents, (iii) and (iv), are prepared by the contributors, so that the person responsible for an area of software is also responsible for all the documentation in that area.

4. Standards

In order to satisfy 2(i) and 2(ii), documentation must be uniform in its appearance and content. However, NAG contributors all work independently and at different Computer Centres, so that detailed standards are absolutely necessary to ensure such uniformity between contributions.

Topics and formats for each of the documents described in Section 2 were set out by the Committee, using other documentation, or lack of it, as a guide. However, although these standards were apparently followed, at the first release of the Library there were several minor differences, especially in lay-out, as each contributor interpreted the standards to suit his own style. In view of the time scale, and the amount of material produced it is perhaps surprising that there were not any more serious deviations!

Before the second release of material, explicit definitions were prepared as part of a "NAG Reference Manual", and more thorough checking procedures were incorporated into the production of the Manual (see Section 5). Thus, the majority of inconsistencies have subsequently been removed.

Brief descriptions of the documents supplied by contributors are given below. For details of the remaining documents the reader is referred to the NAG Reference Manual. Since these are all single documents, written at Central Office, there is no problem with the consistency in content, although layout is important.

4.1. *Chapter Introduction*

The Chapter Introductions are named according to the Share Classification Index. For example, the document describing ordinary differential equations is named $D02$.

In most centres the Library will be backed up by an advisory service, but this is not always so, and in any case a user should ideally be able to work independently of one. In some problem areas, such as sorting, the choice of routine is straight forward, but in others, such as optimisation, where the classification of problems is more difficult, the user may need guidance. Thus the role of the Chapter Introduction is educational, to supply practical information on the choice and use of routines. It also provides a means for the contributor and implementor to pass on useful experience that has been gained in developing routines.

The sections of the Chapter Introduction are:

(1) *Contents*. Lists the routines available in the chapter.

(2) *Background*. Gives practical information on the use of routines, it may contain:

  (i) a brief summary of the state of the art,

  (ii) advice on setting up problems,

  (iii) the range of soluble problems,

  (iv) advice on assessment of results.

(3) *Recommendations*. Gives advice on choosing routines, it may contain:

  (i) prose, describing overall considerations,

  (ii) a decision tree giving explicit recommendations,

  (iii) an alphabetical index giving explicit recommendations.

4.2. *Routine Documents*

A routine document describes the use of a particular routine and has the the same name as the routine. Although the contents of such documents might seem the easiest to determine, they do, in fact, require the most detailed definition. Firstly, there is a wide variety of people contributing material, all of whom have different ideas as to what constitutes an adequate description. Secondly, if a user is to become familiar with the format of the documents it is important that they appear as similar as possible, even between chapters.

A distinct set of headings under which to classify information was agreed initially, and this has led to a standardisation of the contents of the documents. Instructions on notation and layout have also been described in detail in the NAG Reference Manual. Examples of routine documents are given in the appendix.

5. Production Details

All the documentation is collected at Central Office for typing, printing and collation. This allows for a further check for uniformity of layout and notation, and simplifies subsequent distribution. The documentation is printed, double-sided, using off-set Lithographic equipment on A4 paper.

The organization of production is briefly:

(i) Each document is written by a contributor.

(ii) A draft is typed and proof-read.

(iii) It is sent to a validator, at a centre other than that involved in contributing the material, for comments and checking, and returned to (i), (ii) or (iv) as necessary.

(iv) Documentation is typed at Central Office, using the same type face throughout.

(v) It is proof read twice (once by the contributor if possible).

(vi) Documentation is printed, and collated into Manuals.

6. Distribution

The basic requirement of distribution is that every programmer should be able to refer to a manual; many would like their own copy, even though the majority will only use certain routines or certain areas. A further requirement is that the documentation must be acceptable to the information systems of the centres implementing the Library.

The first Library Manual was distributed from the Central Office in full. However, due to its size, it proved too expensive for centres to distribute it widely to users. Therefore, at subsequent releases, a Mini-Manual, consisting of all documents other than routine documents, was assembled. This is compact enough to be made available to all users. It contains all the background and material necessary for a user to be able to choose a suitable routine. Copies of individual routine documents can be obtained from a centrally held full Manual, so that a user can assemble a Manual to suit his own needs from the Mini-Manual and selected routine documents.

7. The Compromises Chosen

The following points explain how the documentation satisfies the objectives of Section 2.

7.1. *Volume*

The Manual should be:

Comprehensive. The Chapter Introduction gives sufficient background information for most users, and the standards on Routine Documents ensure that every possible topic is covered.

Easy To Handle. The document based structure ensures that information is easy to locate, and the uniform layout leads to familiarity.

Readily Available. The Mini-Manual can be distributed to all users. Single Routine Documents are copied from the full manual.

7.2. *Contents*

These must be acceptable to the:—

Expert. There is considerable scope for including useful information. Specific information is included in the Routine Documents, general information in the Chapter Introductions.

Beginner. After referring to the Chapter Introduction, the example and the explanation of the parameters in the Routine Document are all that are needed to attempt to use a routine.

7.3. *Index*

This must give access to a particular:—

Method. The key word index and the contents lists of the Chapter Introductions index and the routines by their name and method.

Problem Solver. The recommendations in the Chapter Introduction index and the routines by their function.

8. Error Reporting

In spite of thorough checking in the production stages, some errors in documentation are bound to persist, and one of the major difficulties in a project the size of NAG can be the notification and removal of such errors. The notification depends upon all users reporting errors, the existence of a system for relaying them to the appropriate person and the willingness of all contributors and implementors to correct errors. The scheme that has developed in NAG for relaying errors is:

Records of minor errors are retained at Central Office for correction in subsequent releases of the Library. Major errors (i.e. those that would cause misuse of a routine) are relayed immediately to all centres implementing the Library.

9. Future Developments

Now that the Library is being implemented on machines other than the ICL 1906A, there is a need for a more flexible documentation system to cater for the machine differences and the differing rates of implementation. As an interim measure, the documentation for each range is based on that designed for the 1906A. The Routine Documents are used as they stand, and any inappropriate or misleading information contained in them is explained, on a chapter by chapter basis, in an extra section that may be added to the Chapter Introduction. This qualifying information, together with an introduction, a Contents document, the Chapter Introductions and an Index forms an "implementation" Mini-Manual.

Although this scheme has the advantage that it requires little extra printing it has the considerable disadvantage that users can read a Routine Document, which may be incorrect for their machine, without knowing that it is qualified by information in the Mini-Manual.

In the near future a new documentation scheme will be introduced when it is hoped to make as many documents as possible machine independent although it is inevitable that some specific comments will be necessary. For the Routine Documents this means that certain sections of the current documents will not be entirely appropriate. For example, in the section on storage, the storage cade of a routine machine is dependent, but the fact that the method uses, say, $4N^2$ real work array elements, is not. Such machine dependent comments will be collected together to form "implementation" documents, perhaps one for each chapter.

The main disadvantage in this approach is that it will necessitate writing the example programs in a standard language and in publication form. Thus, the printed programs may never actually run on a user's machine. However, this could be offset by centres providing hard copies of the NAG Example Program Library for users to test, rather than punching their own versions from the documentation.

It may be possible to allow some simple machine dependent information in Routine Documents by describing the action on each machine, or group of machines. However, this would only be satisfactory if all possible machines were known in advance.

In the new scheme, Chapter Introductions will be based on the latest version of the Library and be machine independent, they may also be language independent. They will cover essentially the same material as the present documents, although they may be split into several separate documents on background, selection, etc. It is possible that, due to differing rates of implementation, certain versions of the Library will not contain the full set of software. Any difficulties that this imposes on, say, the selection of routines, will be described in the "implementation" documents.

Such documentation could be assembled into manuals in a similar way to the present system. All the routine documents could be collected together to form a reference manual. This would serve any machine, and would be particularly useful in centres where several machines are available. Individual implementation manuals, consisting of the present Mini-Manual material and the Implementation documents would then describe the contents and general use of the Library on a particular machine, and perhaps in a particular language.

References

Ford, B. (1972). Developing a numerical library, *I.M.A. Bulletin*, **8**, 332–336.
Ford, B and Hague, S. J. (1973). The organisation of numerical algorithms libraries. This volume pp. 357–372.

Appendix

NUMERICAL ALGORITHMS GROUP   A02AAA
ICL 1900 SYSTEM   Document No: 211
N.A.G. LIBRARY MANUAL   1st May 1972
                                     Replaces Document No: None

---

1. *procedure* A02AAA(XR,XI,YR,YI);
   value XR,XI; *real* XR,XI,YR,YI;

2. This procedure evaluates the square root of a complex number.

3. *Language* Algol 60.

4. *Description*

   The method of evaluating the square root depends on the value of XR.

   For XR $\geqslant 0$ YR = SQRT((|XR|+SQRT(XR^2 + XI^2))/2)
                     YR = XI/(2*YR)
   For XR < 0 YI = SIGN(XI)*SQRT((|XR| + SQRT(XR^2 + XI^2))/2)
                     YR = XI/(2*YI)

   Overflow is avoided when squaring XI and XR by calling A02ABA to evaluate SQRT(XR^2 + XI^2)

5. *References*

   MARTIN, R. S. and WILKINSON, J. H. Similarity reduction of a general matrix to Hessenberg form. Num. Math. Band 12, 1968, Appendix pp 367–368.

6. *Parameters*

   XR — a *real* variable called by *value* containing the real part of the complex number whose square root is required.

   XI — a *real* variable called by *value* containing the imaginary part of the complex number whose square root is required.

   YR — a *real* variable, on exit it will contain the real part of the square root.

   YI — a *real* variable, on exit it will contain the imaginary part of the square root.

7. *Error Indicators*   None.

8. *Auxiliary Routines*

   This procedure calls A02ABA.

9. *Timing*

This procedure takes approximately 0.0007 seconds.

10. *Storage*

The compiled procedure and auxiliary procedure require 149 words.

11. *Accuracy*

The results should be accurate to 10 significant figures.

12. *Further Comments*   None.

13 *Example*

```
'BEGIN REAL' XR,XI,YR,YI;
        XR:=READ;  XI:=READ;
        A02AAA(XR,XI,YR,YI);
        PRINT(XR,0,6);   PRINT(XI,0,6);
        PRINT(YR,0,6);   PRINT(YI,0,6);
'END'
```

If the sample data is −1.7; 2.6;
the results will be

−1.700000& 0 2.600000& 0 8.385836& −1 1.550233& 0

14. *Keywords*

Complex square root

NUMERICAL ALGORITHMS GROUP   A02AAF
ICL 1900 SYSTEM   Document No: 212
N.A.G. LIBRARY MANUAL   1st May 1972
                              Replaces Document No: None.

---

1. SUBROUTINE A02AAF(XR,XI,YR,YI)

2. This routine evaluates the square root of a complex number.

3. *Language*   FORTRAN IV.

4. *Description*

The method of evaluating the square root depends on the value of XR.

For $XR \geqslant 0$ $YR = SQRT((|XR| + SQRT(XR^2 + XI^2))/2)$
          $YI = XI/(2*YR)$

For $XR < 0$ $YI = SIGN(XI)*SQRT((|XR| + SQRT(XR^2 + XI^2))/2)$
          $YR = XI/(2*YI)$

Overflow is avoided when squaring XI and XR by calling A02ABF to evaluate $SQRT(XR^2 + XI^2)$.

5. *References*

MARTIN, R. S. and WILKINSON, J. H. Similarity reduction of a general matrix to Hessenberg form. Num. Math. Band 12, 1968, Appendix pp 367–368.

6. *Parameters*

XR — a REAL variable containing the real part of the complex number whose root is required.

XI   — a REAL variable containing the imaginary part of the complex number whose square root is required.

YR   — a REAL variable, on exit it will contain the real part of the square root.

YI   — a REAL variable, on exit it will contain the imaginary part of the square root.

7. *Error Indicators*   None.

8. *Auxiliary Routines*

This routine calls A02ABF.

9. *Timing*

This routine takes approximately 0.0006 seconds.

10. *Storage*

The compiled routine and auxiliary routine require 134 words.

11. *Accuracy*

The results should be accurate to 10 significant figures.

12. *Further Comments*   None.

13. *Example*

```
      MASTER  MAIN
      READ(5,1)  XR,XI
    1 FORMAT(2F4.1)
      CALL  A02AAF(XR,XI,YR,YI)
      WRITE(6,2)  XR,XI,YR,YI
    2 FORMAT(4E15.6)
      STOP
      END
```

If the sample data is
-1.7 2.6
the results will be

-0.170000E 01   0.260000E 01   0.838584E 00   0.155023E 01

14. *Keywords*

Complex Square Root.

Discussion: Documentation

MR. PHYTHIAN. What is the cost and availability of the NAG Mini-Manual?

MR. HAGUE. The ICL 1906A Mark 3 Mini-Manual is available from the NAG Central Office (currently at the Oxford University Computing Laboratory, Oxford University, Oxford) at a cost of 80p. No explicit documentation fund exists within the project, so production costs must be recouped from sales.

DR. HEATHER LIDDELL (*Queen Mary College, London*). I should like to take up a point made by Dr. Hebden concerning the provision of Input/Output within the library subroutines. For many years I have been a user of the Harwell library optimization routines and we have recently acquired the Harwell library tape. Unfortunately, in order to use it on our 1904S about 10,000 I/O statements need alteration. This could be done by means of a Plan Program but this is somewhat inconvenient and one has to find time to do it. The NAG Library is much more easy to use from this point of view.

DRS FLETCHER AND HEBDEN. The Harwell library was developed for users at Harwell and it is true that no significant effort was expended to cater for outside users. Our point, however, was concerned with the printing of error diagnostics. We think that it is insufficient to put warnings of possible failure or inapplicability of a subroutine in the specification sheet, because many users misuse the routines and then quote incorrect results. The situation can only be relieved when the user cannot avoid seeing that his results are wrong.

The NAG Library is a major step forward in that it sets out to coordinate library effort in numerous establishments. Giving priority to portability they do not allow any I/O in subroutines. However, the number of output statements which are error diagnostics are relatively few, and we feel that the benefits from including this type of output outweighs the loss of portability.

MR. A. C. NICHOLLS (*Bristol Polytechnic*). Has any serious attempt been made to standardize the notation throughout the documentation; and if so, with what success?

MRS. LILL. Yes, considerable efforts have, and are being made. All contributors are asked to standardize notation within a Chapter, but some differences between Chapters are inevitable until there is more manpower available at Central Office for editing documentation and advising contributors. Detailed standards on layout and the wording of certain sections of the documentation are given in the NAG Reference Manual, and these points are thoroughly checked when the documentation is typed at Central Office.

MR. COX. Are there any plans to store a copy of the full Manual in a file on the machine? Then the user can go along to his local teletype and request a copy of the routines he requires, after presumably looking at his Mini-Manual.

MRS. LILL. Yes, methods for storing documentation in the machine are being investigated, especially in connection with the updating of documents, although there are difficulties with representing mathematical symbols. The new documentation is being designed with this possibility in mind.

MR. FORD. (a) Do limited machine resources encourage more use of a Numerical Advisory Service? (b) How many packages do you support and what kind of packages are they? XRAY, STATPACK etc.? (c) Does the Numerical Advisory Service adequately cope with these?

DRS. FLETCHER AND HEBDEN. (a) In Section 2 of our paper we note that users are not interested in reducing the size of a program or in speeding it up, unless it is so long that they can no longer finance its running. The basis for this is that to do this would cause a loss in time available for research, whereas the only gain would be to increase the idle time of the computer. If resources are more limited, notably if the computer is running at capacity, the balance changes because improvements to the program may reduce its turn round time. In such cases, the user can get a real gain from improving his program, and so we would exepct more use of an advisory service to be made. (b) None. (c) Yes.

MR. G. N. C. GRANT (*Loughborough University*). Regarding Dr. Fletcher's comment about conducting a survey of Harwell user's needs, what were his findings, i.e. what problem/algorithm areas were regarded as important?

DRS. FLETCHER AND HEBDEN. Many applications have been observed in the following areas i.e., integral equations, optimization, curve fittings and approximation, ordinary differential equations, some partial differential equations, and linear algebra.

MR. GRANT. The NAG Reference Manual is too comprehensive and unavoidably large. Hence the idea of a Mini-Manual for general users is a good one. However, in my view a more judicious sub-set of the manual than that chosen to form the Mini-Manual would have been to omit some of the general and Chapter introductions in favour of the Routine Documents for each algorithm, with parameter lists and definitions. In other words the Mini-Manual should have been orientated more towards the experienced user. Perhaps an earlier suggestion by Cox (NPL) (concerning the placing of the manual on a machine file which could be user retrievable) would help.

MRS. LILL. NAG Library documentation is designed for use in a university teaching or research environment, and as such it has to satisfy all types of user. The Mini-Manual was introduced to help decrease the bulk of material, by providing all the basic information needed to use the Library (contents, selection, indices, etc.), and to help educate users in the use of routines. Since the Library Manual is document based a user can supplement this Mini-Manual by adding particular Routine Documents to build up his personal manual. This will contain *all* the information on the routines that was documented by the contributor and the implementor.

Selecting material for a Mini-Manual to suit experienced users by only including short descriptions of routines and parameter lists would not provide a *mini* manual. Also, there would be the difficulty of deciding which comments to include and which to leave out and put in the full Manual. The majority of users would never bother to consult the full Manual, and so would never receive the full description of a routine. With the present system they do have a copy of all the material considered to be relevant; they can choose whether or not to read it!

Having said that, I agree that having a machine based documentation system could speed up access to Routine Documents. It is also possible that standardization of names for parameters with the same function, and a slight expansion of the routine descriptions in the Chapter Introductions, could provide enough information for a very experienced user to use the routines.

MR. BEASLEY. Over how many dimensions do you receive requests to integrate?

DR. FLETCHER. Problems of up to 4-dimensions occur frequently (for instance, in molecular wave function calculations) and we have known of problems in up to 6 dimensions.

Author Index

The numbers in *italics* refer to the pages where references are listed in full. Absence of this page number indicates a general reference used in the chapter.

A

437

Subject Index